The Chief
Petty Officer's Guide

Titles in the Series

The U.S. Naval Institute Blue & Gold
Professional Library

For more than 100 years, U.S. Navy professionals have counted on specialized books published by the Naval Institute Press to prepare them for their responsibilities as they advance in their careers and to serve as ready references and refreshers when needed. From the days of coal-fired battleships to the era of unmanned aerial vehicles and laser weaponry, such perennials as *The Bluejacket's Manual* and the *Watch Officer's Guide* have guided generations of sailors through the complex challenges of naval service. As these books are updated and new ones are added to the list, they will carry the distinctive mark of the Blue & Gold Professional Library series to remind and reassure their users that they have been prepared by naval professionals and they meet the exacting standards that sailors have long expected from the U.S. Naval Institute.

The Chief
Petty Officer's Guide

John Hagan

Master Chief Petty Officer of the Navy (Ret.)

and

J. F. Leahy

Naval Institute Press
Annapolis, Maryland

Naval Institute Press
291 Wood Road
Annapolis, MD 21402

Library of Congress Cataloging-in-Publication Data

Hagan, John, 1946 May 20–
    The Chief Petty Officer's guide / John Hagan and J. F. Leahy.
        p. cm. — (The U.S. Naval Institute blue & gold professional
library)
    Includes bibliographical references and index.
    ISBN 1-59114-459-0 (alk. paper)
    ISBN 978-1-59114-459-5 (alk. paper)
    1. United States. Navy—Petty officers' handbooks. I. Leahy,
J. F., 1946–II. Title. III. Series.

    V123.H34 2004
    359—dc22

                                                          2004011079

Printed in the United States of America on acid-free paper ∞

17 16 15 14 13   9 8 7 6 5

For Admiral Frank Kelso,
who always trusted the chiefs
and is much loved for it.

John Hagan

For Margaret.

Jack Leahy

Contents

Part Four. Supporting

Foreword

Our Navy has relied on the Chief Petty Officer for more than one hundred years. Throughout history, you and the Chiefs before you have met every challenge, overcome every obstacle, and accomplished the Navy's mission. Every Sailor, from Seaman to Admiral, knows what a Chief represents. To them you personify experience, competence, credibility, and professionalism.

It is up to you and the Chiefs in your mess to set the tone in your command and meet the expectations that every enlisted and officer Sailor has of you. And they have every right to expect more from you as a Chief. That credibility must be earned each day.

The authors of the *Chief Petty Officer's Guide* have set out to compile many of the lessons we've learned through decades in the Chief's mess, capturing the tried and true bits of wisdom that make Chiefs' messes successful. Much like a chart helps a Sailor navigate, this guide can help you grow and develop in your career.

As we look back on our heritage and history with pride, we also look to the future and another century of meeting new challenges. The influence that you will have on our Navy as a whole is truly immeasurable. The training and mentoring that you provide everyday as a Chief Petty Officer to the Sailors you lead is what will ensure our success in the future.

For more than a century, Sailors have heard the phrase, "Ask the Chief." To you I would say, "Don't wait to be asked!"

Terry D. Scott
Master Chief Petty Officer of the Navy

Acknowledgments

Board of Review Members

Command Master Chief (SW/SCW) Ralph Rao, U.S. Navy. CMDCM Rao first served as a boatswain's mate and later as a ship's serviceman aboard USS *Barbey* (DE-1088), USS *Bowen* (FF-1089), USS *Jessie L. Brown* (FF-1089), and USS *Garcia.* (FF-1040). He earned his ESWS in 1981 and qualified as officer of the deck (under way). He later served at RTC, Great Lakes, as a recruit company commander, and with NMCB-62. In 1987, during his second tour at RTC, he advanced to Senior Chief Petty Officer. In May 1990, he graduated with the U.S. Navy Senior Enlisted Academy Class 46, Gold Group. In 1993, while assigned to USS *Holland* (AS-32), he advanced to Master Chief Petty Officer and again qualified as officer of the deck (under way). He earned his bachelor of science degree from Louisiana State University. Master Chief Rao's personal awards include the Meritorious Service Medal (three gold stars); Navy Commendation Medal (silver and three gold stars); Joint Service Achievement Medal; Navy Achievement Medal (four gold stars); and a variety of unit and campaign awards. CMDCM Rao has served as command master chief aboard USNS *Comfort* (TAH-20), USS *Simon Lake* (AS-33), and as command master chief, Naval Hospital, Camp Lejeune.

Command Master Chief (AW/SW) Steve Gielczyk, U.S. Navy. CMDCM Gielczyk entered the Navy in 1974. An electronics technician, his sea duty assignments have included USS *Somers* (DDG-34), USS *Brunswick* (ATS-3), USS *Bristol County* (LST-1198), and USS *Abraham Lincoln* (CVN-72). He also has served at Base Component Telecommunications, Naval Air Station Whidbey Island, Wash., and as an instructor at ET "A" School, and as the ET detailer at the Bureau of Naval Personnel in Washington, D.C. His decorations include two Navy Commendation Medals, four Navy Achievement Medals, and various unit, campaign, and service awards as well as Master Training Specialist designation. He is a graduate of the U.S. Navy Senior Enlisted Academy, Class 53, Khaki Group, and several Navy advanced electronics schools. He received an associate degree in general studies from Central Texas College in 1994 and a bachelor of science degree from the University of the State of New York in 1995. CMDCM Gielczyk served as command master chief of Airborne Early Warning Squadron 115 (VAW-115) and USS *O'Brien* (DD-975), and he is, at the time of this writing, command master chief and director, Senior Enlisted Academy, Newport, R.I.

Command Master Chief (SW) Leonard (Mike) Solinap, U.S. Navy. Born in Manila, Republic of the Philippines, CMDCM Solinap served as an electrician's mate aboard USS *Kitty Hawk* (CV-63), USS *Dixon* (AS-37), USS *Jason* (AR-7), USS *Robert E. Peary* (FF-1073), and ashore as a learning center instructor at Basic Electronics and Electricity School in San Diego and as a senior instructor at Instructor Training School, Naval Submarine Training Center, Pacific, in Hawaii. He is a graduate of the U.S. Navy Senior Enlisted Academy, Class 49, Blue Group, and Class 71, Khaki Group. He is also a graduate of Coastline Community College, Calif., and University of Maryland University College. His personal awards include the Rifle and Pistol Marksmanship Medals, Good Conduct Medal (silver service star), the Navy and Marine Corps Achievement Medal (two gold stars), and the Navy and Marine Corps Commendation Medal (two gold stars). CMDCM Solinap served as command master chief of USS *Crommelin* (FFG-37), command master chief of USS *John S. McCain* (DDG-56), and command master chief at Naval Base Ventura County (CBC Port Hueneme and NAS Point Mugu), in California.

Command Master Chief (SS) Steve Juskiewicz, U.S. Navy. CMDCM Juskiewicz entered the Navy in 1981 and completed Quartermaster Class "A" School and Basic Enlisted Submarine School before reporting to his first submarine, USS *Seawolf* (SSN-575). His subsequent sea assignments include: USS *Parche* (SSN-683); USS *James Madison* (SSBN-627), and USS *Montpelier* (SSN-765). Previous shore assignments include: Navy Recruiting District, Buffalo, N.Y.; staff, Commander-in-Chief, U.S. Naval Forces Europe, London, England; and staff, Commander Submarine Group Two, Groton, Conn. Master Chief Juskiewicz's personal awards include the Meritorious Service Medal, Navy and Marine Corps Commendation Medal (five awards), Navy and Marine Corps Achievement Medal (four awards), and the Good Conduct Medal (five awards). He is a graduate of the U.S. Navy Senior Enlisted Academy, Class 85, and holds a bachelor of science degree in business and management from the University of Maryland. CMDCM Juskiewicz has served as chief of the boat USS *Connecticut* (SSN-22).

Command Master Chief (AW) Clifford E. Yager, U.S. Navy. CMDCM Yager entered the Navy in 1974. Assignments included USS *Iwo Jima* (LPH-2), Naval Air Station Miramar, California; USS *Tripoli* (LPH-10), USS *Independence* (CV-62), Naval Air Technical Training Center, Lakehurst, N.J.; USS *Forrestal* (CV-59), Navy Recruiting District Albany and Buffalo, N.Y.; USS *Nimitz* (CVN-68), and Naval Air Technical Training Center, Pensacola, Fla.; He holds an associate of science degree in administration and management studies and a bachelor of science degree in liberal arts from the State University of New York, and he is a graduate of the U.S. Navy Senior

Enlisted Academy, Class 89, Blue Group. Command Master Chief Yager's personal awards include the Navy's Meritorious Service Medal, Navy and Marine Corps Commendation Medal (two awards), Navy and Marine Corps Achievement Medal (two awards), and the Navy Good Conduct Medal (fifth award). He also wears the Navy Unit Commendation Medal, Coast Guard Commendation Medal, Navy Meritorious Unit Commendation, Battle Efficiency Award (three Es), Navy Expeditionary Medal (three awards), Southwest Asian Service Medal, Sea Service Deployment Ribbon (two silver stars and one bronze star), and the Navy Recruiting Ribbon. He has served as command master chief, VAQ-139, and as a foreign exchange student at the Royal Australian Naval War College in HMAS *Creswell*, Canberra, Australia.

Master Chief Cryptologic Technician (Collection) Robin D. Todd, U.S. Navy. CTRCM Todd enlisted in the Navy in March 1977 and received basic manual Morse cryptologic "A" school instruction at Naval Technical Training Center, Pensacola, Fla. In 1986 she completed instructor training in Groton, Conn., and was awarded the master training specialist designator from both the U.S. Navy and U.S. Army while assigned to Naval Training Detachment, Fort Devens, Mass., in 1988. Advanced to Chief Petty Officer in 1989, she was selected for her first command chief assignment. Master Chief Todd graduated from the U.S. Navy Senior Enlisted Academy, Class 103, in October 2002. Master Chief Todd has nearly twenty years of overseas service. Tours included Naval Security Group Command, Misawa, Japan; Naval Communications Master Station, Wahiawa, Hawaii; U.S.–Canada Personnel Exchange Program (US-CF PEP), Gander, Newfoundland; Rota, Spain; Queen Charlotte Islands and Ottawa, Canada; and London, England. In 1983, she was the first U.S. woman assigned to Canadian Forces Station Alert, Arctic Circle. Her personal awards include the Navy Commendation Medal (five awards), Good Conduct Medal (seven awards), Overseas Service Ribbon (thirteen awards), Arctic Service ribbon,

Canadian Forces Commander Commendation Medal, and various service awards. Master Chief Todd has served as CMC on the staff of Commander-in-Chief, U.S. Navy, Europe, and command master chief at Naval Information Warfare Activity, Washington, D.C.

Command Master Chief (SS) John Self, U.S. Navy. CMDCM Self joined the Navy in 1979. After recruit training and basic electronic schools, he attended Basic Enlisted Submarine School and 688-class Submarine Electronics Surveillance Measures Pipeline Training in Groton, Conn. He served aboard USS *Boston* (SSN-703) and USS *Dallas* (SSN-700), where he was navigation/ operations department Leading Chief Petty Officer, and he served as chief of the boat aboard USS *Archerfish* (SSN-678). He also was command master chief aboard USS *Oak Ridge* (ARDM-1). His shore-duty assignments included Naval Submarine School and Fleet Technical Support Center, Atlantic, Detachment, New London, and the Senior Enlisted Academy. His personal decorations include: the Navy Commendation Medal (four awards), Navy Achievement Medal (two awards), and the Navy Good Conduct Medal (five awards). He holds an associate of arts degree from the University of the State of New York, Regents, and a bachelor of science degree in education, training, and development from Southern Illinois University at Carbondale. He is also a Navy master training specialist.

Command Master Chief (AW) Thomas C. Whitney, U.S. Navy. CMDCM Whitney first enlisted in the Navy in 1980. Upon release from active duty in October 1984, he immediately entered into the Training and Administration of the Reserve (TAR) program and advanced to master chief personnelman in the TAR program. Other assignments included: USS *Forrestal* (CV-59); Personnel Support Detachment, Pensacola, Fla.; Naval and Marine Corps Reserve Center, Plainville, Conn.; Naval Air Station, South Weymouth, Mass.; Naval Reserve Center, New Bedford, Mass.; Naval Air Station,

Joint Reserve Base, New Orleans, La.; Enlisted Personnel Management Center, New Orleans, La.; and Naval Reserve Readiness Command Northeast. He is command MCPO at VP-92 at NAS Brunswick, Maine. Master Chief Whitney's decorations include three Navy and Marine Corps Commendation Medals; seven Navy and Marine Corps Achievement Medals; the Military Outstanding Volunteer Service Medal; and numerous unit commendations and service awards. He is a 1999 graduate of the U.S. Navy Senior Enlisted Academy, Class 85, Green Group.

Senior Chief Aviation Electronics Technician (AW/NAC) Steven L. Pierce, U.S. Navy. ATCS Pierce enlisted in the Navy in 1983, completed avionics school, and reported first to Fleet Air Reconnaissance Squadron One (VQ-1). He has twice served sea tours with VQ-1 and with Fleet Air Reconnaissance Squadron Five, Detachment Five, and Special Projects Patrol Squadron Two (VPU-2). While assigned to VQ-5, he embarked with Carrier Air Wing Five (CVW-5) in USS *Independence* (CV-62) and USS *Kitty Hawk* (CV-63). He has been awarded the Air Medal (one strike flight), the Navy and Marine Corps Commendation Medal (six awards, with combat distinguishing device), and the Navy and Marine Corps Achievement Medal (three Awards). He has earned the master of science degree in public administration from Troy State University.

Board of Review Associate Members

Sergeant Major Merle B. Streagle, U.S. Army. SGM Streagle enlisted in the Army in 1976 and attended basic training at Fort Leonard Wood, Mo., and advanced infantry training at Fort Benning, Ga. His assignments included Sniper Squad, Scout/Recon, Platoon 4/10 Infantry, Fort Davis, Panama Canal Zone; Squad Leader, 2/12 Cav, 1st Cav Div, Fort Hood, Tex; Training NCO, TRADOC, Fort Monroe, Va; Drill sergeant, Fort Dix, N.J.; Air Operations NCO, U.S. Army South, Fort Clayton

Panama; S-3 NCOIC V Corps Frankfurt, Germany; Platoon Sergeant, 1/36 Infantry, Friedburg, Germany; Platoon Sergeant, 3/7 Infantry Fort Stewart, Ga; First Sergeant HHC and Dco 3/12 Infantry Baumholder, Germany; First Sergeant HHC and Cco, 1/30 Infantry Fort Benning, Ga; instructor and chief trainer, United States Army Sergeants Majors Academy, Fort Bliss, Tex. Deployments included 3/7 Inf, 24th Infantry Division, Operation Desert Shield/Desert Storm, Saudi Arabia and Iraq; 3/12 Inf, IFOR Bosnia; and 1/30 Inf Intrinsic Action/Operation Desert Thunder, Kuwait. SGM Streagle has attended numerous army schools and is a graduate of U.S. Army Sergeants Majors Academy, Class 49. He holds an associate degree in business management and a bachelor of science from Regents College, University of New York. His decorations and badges include Bronze Star, Meritorious Service Medal (two awards), Army Commendation Medal (seven awards), Army Achievement Medal (two awards), Combat Infantryman's Badge, Expert Infantryman's Badge, Drill Sergeant Badge, and numerous campaign, unit, and service awards.

Chief Master Sergeant William S. Mounsey, U.S. Air Force. CMSgt. Mounsey entered the Air Force in 1976 and completed basic military training at Lackland Air Force Base, Tex. Following graduation from Law Enforcement Technical School at Lackland, he began a nineteen-year career as a law enforcement specialist. His assignments include Loring Air Force Base, Maine; Travis Air Force Base, Calif.; Incirlik Air Base, Turkey; March Air Force Base, Calif.; Ankara Air Base, Turkey; and Pope Air Force Base, N.C. He has performed duties as an entry controller, patrolman, desk sergeant, investigator, law enforcement superintendent, chief of training and resources, and as a security police manager. In 1995, Chief Master Sergeant Mounsey became a professional military education instructor at the Air Force Senior NCO Academy, Gunter Annex, Ala., and remained in that position until his arrival at the Senior Enlisted Academy. Chief Master Sergeant Mounsey earned a bachelor's degree in human resource management from Faulkner University and two associate's degrees (criminal justice and instructor in military technology) from the Community College of the Air Force. His decorations include the Meritorious Service Medal with four oak leaf clusters, the Air Force Commendation Medal with one oak leaf cluster, and various service, campaign, and unit awards.

The authors also particularly wish to acknowledge the valuable contributions of:

Members of the Chief Petty Officers' Mess, USS *George Washington* (CVN-73)

Members of the Chief Petty Officers' Mess, USS *McFaul* (DDG-74)

Members of the Chief Petty Officers' Mess, USS *Whidbey Island* (LSD-41)

Members of the Chief Petty Officers' Mess, USS *Boise* (SSN-764)

Members of the Chief Petty Officers' Mess, The Brigade of Midshipmen, U.S. Naval Academy, Annapolis, Maryland

The faculty and staff of the Department of Naval Science, U.S. Naval Academy, Annapolis, Maryland

Plankowners of www.goatlocker.org, whose service as Chief Petty Officers spans seven decades, and who provided valuable insight and assistance in helping us understand those who have gone before us

There are no ex-chiefs—just chiefs no longer on active duty. Thanks, shipmates.

Introduction:

"You Are Now the Chief"

My mission as a Chief Petty Officer is to win wars one battle at a time by teaching my Sailors to do their jobs to the best of their abilities, by leading them courageously while in harm's way, by recognizing their efforts, and by bringing them home safely to a grateful nation.

> Master Chief Quartermaster
> Michael Harrison, U.S. Navy
> *Proceedings,* February 2004

This book is for those who aspire to be Chief Petty Officers, for those who aspire to be better Chief Petty Officers, and for those interested in all things Navy. For those who are striving to become members of the chiefs' mess, this handbook will provide invaluable assistance in helping you through changes that will have a dramatic and immediate impact on your lives. More will be expected of you, more will be demanded of you. There's a world of difference between an E-7 and a Chief Petty Officer in the U.S. Navy!

In the past quarter century, the Navy's senior leadership has increasingly relied upon Chief Petty Officers for policy decisions from the command to the headquarters level. This evolving role has caused a healthy introspection, and recently the MCPON panel defined our core competencies: "Chief Petty Officers are enlisted members, in pay grades E-7 through E-9, who lead and manage Sailors. . . . [They are] responsible for, have the authority to accomplish, and are held accountable for:

- Leading Sailors and applying their skills to tasks that enable mission accomplishment for the U.S. Navy.
- Developing enlisted Sailors and junior officers.
- Communicating the core values, standards, and information of our Navy that empower Sailors to be successful in all they attempt.
- Supporting with loyalty the endeavors of the chain of command they serve and those of fellow Chief Petty Officers with whom they serve."

Leading, developing, communicating, supporting. We've always done that, of course, long before the modern concept of "core competencies" was conceived. It is our heritage and a proud one indeed. We've led at sea against the Barbary Pirates, in the icy waters of the North Atlantic in World War II, and in the steaming waters of the Mekong Delta and the Arabian Sea. We've led on the battlefields of Guadalcanal and Guam; at Dong Ha and Danang; at Basrah and Baghdad, too. We've developed young Sailors and junior officers, and watched them grow and mature, and we've proudly saluted those like John F. Kennedy, Jimmy Carter, or George H. W. Bush who, when their turns came, rose to lead us in perilous times. We've communicated our values and made sure that our traditions and standards were passed, whole and unsullied, to future generations. On occasion, we have stepped back and taken stock of the direction we were heading, and we have been humble and strong enough to admit our errors and get back on track. We've supported our nation and our Navy, sometimes neglecting our own families or private interests, because, quite simply, it was the right thing to do. We are Chief Petty Officers in the world's greatest Navy, a Navy whose greatness is due to the sacrifices and excellence of those who have gone before us.

Leading, developing, communicating, supporting. Our core competencies also drive the organization of this handbook. While the focus is on what we do, we also touch on what makes us who we are: honor, courage, and commitment.

The Navy's Core Values

Once, early in my tour as Master Chief Petty Officer of the Navy, I attended a meeting in the Pentagon. In response to serious lapses in conduct, the secretary of the Navy had asked the executive leadership of the Department of the Navy to revitalize and restate our core values, so that we might communicate to all levels those things which we hold most dear and will not compromise.

At that time, the Navy had adopted integrity, professionalism, and tradition as formal core values for Sailors, and the Marine Corps core values were honor, courage, and commitment. We considered a number of alternatives, including combining the two to be used in the "recovery campaign." Gen. Walter Boomer, then assistant commandant of the Marine Corps, spoke out. "Marine Corps values are honor, courage, and commitment," he said. "Marines learn them in boot camp; they identify with them and remember them. We like them; they are working for us, and we are not going to change them." His words, spoken emphatically but without arrogance, inspired an important revelation—almost an epiphany—for the Sailors in the room.

Sadly, most of us knew that the same passion did not then apply to the Navy's chosen watchwords, watchwords that were not even being taught in recruit training. We made a difficult—and awkward—decision that day to adopt honor, courage, and commitment as our core values, but Navy leaders and Sailors rallied to cherish the words and the power behind them. I thought then—as I think now—that no other community cherishes or respects those words more than Chief Petty Officers. Honor, courage, and commitment are the objective of every day's conduct, and they flow from the solemn oath of enlistment with which we so closely identify.

> And I do solemnly swear (or affirm) that I will support and defend the Constitution of the United States against all enemies, foreign and domestic; that I will bear true faith and allegiance to the same; and that I will obey the orders of the president of the United States and the orders of the officers appointed over me, according to regulations and the Uniform Code of Military Justice, so help me God.

Honor. "I will bear true faith and allegiance . . ." Honor means engaging in ethical conduct in all relationships within the CPO mess, with seniors and with subordi-

"And I will obey the orders of the president of the United States and the orders of the officers appointed over me." Each of us swears that oath upon reenlistment, and this Chief Petty Officer is fortunate to have former President George H. W. Bush on board to administer the oath.
U.S. Navy (PH2 H. Dwain Willis)

nates. It means making honest judgments and recommendations and thoughtfully considering those of junior Sailors. It requires us to do the right thing, even when no one is looking or when it is unpopular; and to take responsibility for our actions and to keep our word, twenty-four hours a day.

Chief Petty Officers have died to keep that promise, because honor requires us to take care of our Sailors, even if our own lives are put at risk. In keeping that pledge, Chief Engineman Don McFaul gave his own life to rescue a wounded shipmate in Panama in December 1989. Part of Seal Team Four serving in Operation Just Cause, Chief McFaul saw his team leader unable to rescue a fallen Sailor, and, without regard for his own life, entered the kill zone and pulled the young petty officer to safety. Riddled by gunfire, Chief McFaul's last conscious act was to throw himself across Petty Officer Moreno's body, shielding him from the enemy, surrendering his own life in the process. He was awarded the Silver Star for bravery, and USS *McFaul* (DDG-74), whose CPO mess contributed significantly to the development of this handbook, is named in his honor.

Courage. "I will support and defend . . ." Courage is that value that helps us to meet the demands of our profession and mission during dangerous, demanding, or otherwise difficult times. Courage is the value that gives us the moral and mental strength to do what is right, even in the face of personal or professional adversity. Courage drives us to make hard decisions without regard to personal consequences; and moral courage helps us resist peer pressure and cultural stresses, without ever giving up, regardless of how desperate things may appear.

USS *Falcon*, nominally a minesweeper, was serving as a submarine rescue vessel in May 1939, when USS *Squalus* (SS-192) went down in the waters off the coast of New England. Water filled the forward and aft engine rooms and crew's compartment, for the high induction valve had failed, and *Squalus* was trapped on the bottom. USS *Falcon* raced to the Isle of Shoals, and, through the use of experimental diving equipment never before used, began the rescue of survivors. After the last known survivor had been rescued, the skipper indicated that others may have survived in the aft torpedo compartment, and, without hesitation, a final and much more dangerous descent began.

Chief Machinist's Mate William Badders, as senior member of the rescue chamber crew, made the last, extremely hazardous trip in the rescue chamber to attempt to rescue any possible survivors. He was fully aware of the great danger involved, because if he or his assistant became incapacitated, there was no way in which either could be rescued. His courage contributed to the success of the operation and characterizes conduct far above and beyond the ordinary call of duty. Three Chief Petty Officers that day—Badders, Chief Metalsmith James McDonald, and Chief Boatswain's Mate Orson Crandall, who had served as the master divers throughout the incident—were awarded the Medal of Honor for their courage in rescuing the men of USS *Squalus*.

Great heroism was shown by three Chief Petty Officers responsible for the rescue of survivors of USS *Squalus* in 1939.
U.S. Naval Institute

Commitment. "I will obey the orders . . ." Commitment means valuing mission success above all else. It means fully accepting that the Navy's mission is warfighting, and that force readiness is not just the main thing, but the only thing.

Chief Gunner's Mate Thomas Eadie understood commitment. In December 1927, while participating in the rescue of *Submarine S-4* off Cape Cod, the air hose of his fellow diver, Chief Torpedoman Michaels, became seriously fouled. An exhausted Chief Eadie, under the most adverse diving conditions, responded to the needs of the rescue mission by promptly descending himself. His own suit became ripped and hopelessly tangled. When it became apparent that only one diver could be recovered at a time, he called out to the surface, "Take Michaels first!" After two hours of extremely dangerous and back-breaking work, his cool, calculating, and skillful labors resulted in the successful return of Chief Michaels to the surface. Chief Eadie was the first Chief Petty Officer to be awarded the Medal of Honor in the twentieth century.

Honor. Courage. Commitment. All are virtues we learn and practice daily in the mess. And our commitment is strengthened and renewed with the oath of allegiance which each of us swears again on the day when we accept appointment as Chief Petty Officers in the U.S. Navy.

Code of Conduct

We serve in a dangerous profession, and we live in perilous and uncertain times. Never before has the individual character of the American Sailor, or our character as Chief Petty Officers, counted so heavily in the defense of our nation. For all the wonders of our technology, history teaches us that success in battle depends upon the moral fiber of those called to defend our way of life. Unlike previous conflicts, technology and asymmetrical threat no longer permit us the luxury of awaiting the first battle to determine whether our forces are mentally and emotionally prepared. The pace of conflict will afford us little if any chance to profit from our mistakes.

Democracy is beset by wily enemies. We learned that on 11 September 2001, just as we learned it in the frozen concentration camps of North Korea fifty years earlier. The Korean Conflict—in which cruel psychological manipulation and brainwashing first stained the annals of warfare—caused us to recalibrate the moral compass upon which each of us must rely when faced with extreme duress and anxiety. Sadly, in Korea a very few Americans broke faith with their fellow prisoners of war, either because they did not fully comprehend their responsibilities or because they lacked the moral fiber to withstand the duress of harsh captivity. On 17 August 1955, Pres. Dwight D. Eisenhower signed Executive Order 10631, establishing a code of conduct for all American military personal. Updated in 1977 and revised again in 1999 to reflect gender-neutral language, the code serves as a compass for our behavior in the face of peril or our enemies:

I am an American, fighting in the forces that guard my country and our way of life. I am prepared to give my life in their defense. I will never surrender of my own free will. If in command, I will never surrender the members of my command while they still have the means to resist. If I am captured, I will continue to resist by all means available. I will make every effort to escape and aid others to escape. I will accept neither parole nor special favors from the enemy. If I become a prisoner of war, I will keep faith with my fellow prisoners. I will give no information or take part in any action which might be harmful to my comrades. If I am senior, I will take command. If not, I will obey the lawful orders of those appointed over me and will back them up in every way. Should I become a prisoner of war, I am required to give name, rank, service number, and date of birth. I will evade answering further questions to the utmost of my ability. I will make no oral or written statements disloyal to my country and its allies. I will never forget that

I am an American fighting for freedom, responsible for my actions, and dedicated to the principles which made my country free. I will trust in my God and in the United States of America.

We rely on a continuous stream of young men and women to maintain readiness, and, sadly, some enlist lacking the intrinsic virtues that will preserve us all in adversity. It's our job as Chief Petty Officers to ensure that these values are taught, unaltered and unsullied, to each generation of young Sailors and junior officers in every venue and at every opportunity.

The Sailor's Creed

Fortunately, few of us will have to withstand the rigors of captivity. But each of us must withstand the hardships of life at sea or long deployments away from family and loved ones. More importantly, we must set aside our own prejudices, be they gender, racial, religious, or ethnic, and recognize that we are one Navy, serving one nation, made up of countless individuals from countless backgrounds. As Chief Petty Officers, it's incumbent upon us to lead all Sailors, without fear or favor. A dozen or more years ago, the Navy adopted the Sailor's Creed after a wide-ranging, thoughtful examination of all areas of recruit training by a blue-ribbon panel. Chief of Naval Operations Adm. Frank Kelso personally made final pen-and-ink changes to the draft of the Sailor's Creed—derived in part from the code of conduct and the oath of enlistment—and approved it with enthusiasm in late 1993. Shortly afterward, recruits began memorizing and reciting the Sailor's Creed during their initial training, at the same time they were earning and reflecting on our core values. The words are simple but an incredible depth of meaning is conveyed in these few words:

> I am a United States Sailor. I will support and defend the Constitution of the United States of America, and I will obey the orders of those appointed over me. I represent the fighting spirit

of the Navy and those who have gone before me
to defend freedom and democracy around the
world. I proudly serve my country's Navy combat
team with honor, courage, and commitment. I
am committed to excellence and the fair treatment of all.

"I am a United States Sailor." In those simple words,
we recognize our unadulterated pride in the choice to
enlist and in its consequences stated as succinctly as
possible.

"I represent the fighting spirit of the Navy." We
acknowledge the ultimate purpose of the U.S. Navy: to
fight when necessary and to do so with the ferocity and
valor that brings victory.

"To defend freedom and democracy around the world."
Pride is strengthened at the thought of the evil defeated
and nations freed from oppression.

"Those that have gone before me." Many are entombed
in USS *Arizona*, and in a hundred barnacled hulks from
Guadalcanal to the North Atlantic. Others are interred at
Arlington and in national cemeteries far and wide. Still
others have completed their honorable service and are living with their memories, proudly standing to attention on
shaky legs when the national anthem is played, still
grieving for shipmates who gave their all. They are worthy of our deepest gratitude and our conduct must meet
the high example they have set for us.

"I proudly serve my country's Navy combat team." We
recognize valor and combat sacrifices in sea battles too
fierce to ever forget. We recall combat at sea which trans-
formed a peaceful cove in an idyllic spot in the South
Pacific into "Iron Bottom Sound," after fierce and deadly
night actions. Our heritage of a Sailor's conduct in combat
is a sacred trust that must never be forgotten or sullied.

"I am committed to excellence, and the fair treatment
of all." Fair treatment of men and women with names like
Ajdulovich and Ashby, Blonski and Baker, Valdez and
Vampatella—men and women of every race, creed, and
ethnic background, from large cities and small towns

from all across America and who serve beside us at sea and ashore. Recognize those names? Each from a different ethnic background and each awarded the Navy Cross for bravery during the Vietnam War.

Sailors First

From seaman recruit to admiral, the phrase "Sailors First" has deep meaning for all Sailors. It matters not what other proud identification we earn: boatswain's mates, yeomen, quartermasters, machinist's mates, surface warriors, submariners, aviators, medical officers, nurses, or chaplains—we are first and foremost Sailors. It's a great strength for all members of an organization to answer to the same name. The Army is composed entirely of Soldiers, every member of the Marine Corps is a Marine, and members of the Air Force proudly call themselves Airmen. Before the introduction of the Sailor's Creed, however, you could poll a hundred Sailors with the query, "What are you?" and get fifty different answers. The Sailor's Creed caught on quickly and continues to promote an awareness and appreciation that our proudest title is neither chief nor admiral, boatswain nor engineman, but that our first pride and greatest strength is in being a Sailor.

Shortly after the Sailor's Creed was formally instituted, Secretary of the Navy John Dalton directed that the word Sailor should be capitalized when referring to any uniformed member of the Navy. Traditionally, the words sailor, soldier, and airman had not been capitalized. Sailors and Marines are the only words that can adequately describe the composition of the naval service, and Secretary Dalton's actions ensured that appropriate recognition be shown to the distinctiveness of our Sailors and Marines.

A short creed and a capital "S" sound like small things, not worthy of much attention, but these small things emphasize profoundly important aspects of our Navy as an institution. Over the decade since the Sailor's Creed was adopted, it has increasingly found its way into important ceremonies and events. To others, it may appear a small thing when the Sailor's Creed is recited from memory by a gathering of CPOs at a dining-in or retirement ceremony, but when the pride accompanying that recitation is so intense that it is palpable, it is a very great thing, indeed.

Initiation: A Rite of Passage, a Tradition of Pride

Navy life is immersed in traditions, and Chief Petty Officers are charged with honoring those traditions and passing on their pride to the Sailors they lead. Late in my tour as MCPON, I was privileged to address the assembled Brigade of Midshipmen at the U.S. Naval Academy. I spoke briefly about tradition and how it is the natural and highly valued by-product of our heritage. One midshipman asked: "How do we tell the difference between a good tradition and a bad tradition?"

I answered that there are no bad traditions. By their very nature, naval traditions can only be good—that is why they are preserved and ultimately classified as traditions. The midshipman's question was thoughtful, and one every chief must be prepared to answer with more depth and detail. Even good traditions can be observed incorrectly. The acid test is a simple one: if following the tradition results in behavior that is inconsistent with our core values, it is either not a naval tradition or it is not being practiced correctly. Honoring tradition demands discernment, distinguishing excellence and assessing situations and character with accuracy. Discerning the true intent in observing a tradition requires the keen insight, good judgment, and experience found only in the CPO mess. Some Navy traditions have grown up around initiation, the vitally important passage from petty officer to Chief Petty Officer. First among these is the charge book.

The Charge Book. One of the first tasks assigned to every CPO selectee, development and routing the CPO charge book, is steeped in tradition. Selectees are tasked with presenting the charge book to every Chief Petty Officer in the mess and with soliciting their wisdom and guidance.

The charge book's direct ancestral line stretches back at least sixty years, but its roots predate the establishment of the CPO rating. Informal records indicate that those who aspired to be promoted to chief kept private log books with information passed down to them by experienced chiefs in the mess. These notebooks were a sort of early warfare qualification, for, in addition to rating-specific professional knowledge, they contained much ship-specific information in areas outside the petty officer's rating. This was particularly important during World War II when commanding officers were authorized to locally advance deserving and qualified Sailors to Chief Petty Officer without reference to outside commands nor approval by the Bureau of Personnel.

Under wartime conditions, determination of "deserving and qualified" could be difficult for the commanding officer. The situation also presented challenges to the Sailor who aspired to attain a chief's rating. How best to prepare and to plan and track preparation? How best to display your qualifications? From these dilemmas sprang the original CPO charge books. As time went on, chiefs began to direct first class petty officers to prepare themselves to assume additional responsibilities by recording all the details of those responsibilities. Professional libraries on ships were generally nonexistent or poorly stocked, and much critical and relevant information came from direct conversations with the chiefs themselves. Notes were taken to be studied later.

In addition to the technical aspects of the various ratings and the general shipboard responsibilities of all chiefs, they also talked to the first class aspirants about leadership, accountability, supporting the chain of command, and other professional subject matter, often using personal experiences to illustrate how something should (or should not) be done. In addition to recording professional knowledge, they occasionally recorded personal advice and a shipmate's wishes for success. The collection of notes and study material eventually came to be called by some a charge book, perhaps because the petty officers who kept them were entrusted to their care—their "charges"—or because the entries included charges or instructions to do something.

Today, the charge book is more symbolic but remains a vehicle through which experienced Chief Petty Officers offer advise, inspiration, and guidance to those who will follow.today's CPO charge book is also rooted in the early "memory book," a kind of scrapbook or diary maintained by many Sailors over their entire tour in the Navy. The anxious recruit knew even before he shipped to Boot Camp that a world-class adventure lay ahead, and many kept a scrapbook containing an extensive collection of small souvenirs of their Navy travels. Beginning in the late 1920s, memory books, photo albums, and scrapbooks became more common; some also included descriptions of their experiences to take home and share with families. Inserted in the pages were rail ticket stubs, photos, news clippings, ships' memos and bulletins, orders, and other things.

At a memorable CPO anniversary dining-in, Adm. Stan Arthur, then the Vice Chief of Naval Operations, read excerpts from the memory book of his father, Machinist's Mate Chief Holland Arthur. The first entry included Recruit Arthur's thoughts on the train ride from his Illinois home to Recruit Training Command Great Lakes in the 1920s. He mused about the good food on the train—it was his first train ride—and wondered if Navy chow would be as good. Later entries recorded his first impressions as he checked aboard his first ship and went on his first San Diego liberty. The chiefs in attendance at the dining-in listened with awe and pride. Although it was a simple recitation of some facts and fond memories, it was nonetheless one of the most effective, inspiring, and memorable speeches I have ever heard at any CPO celebration.

During World War II, some CPO hopefuls merged these memory books with their CPO log books, combining the advice collected in preparation for advancement into the chiefs' mess with the souvenirs of their early Navy years.Whatever the actual evolution of the charge books, the tradition was retained in the years after World War II and used as the first "prop" of CPO initiation. Issued to the selectees, the charge book was intended to combine some lighthearted "charges" with serious advice for the rising CPO and to be the centerpiece of the mock trial that took place at most CPO initiations for several decades.

For a time, the contents of a charge book were seldom worth preserving. They were often nothing more than government issue log books, only sporadically carried by selectees, and became the center of much negative activity, some of it egregious and outrageous. By comparison, today's charge book has become a genuine keepsake in the truest sense of the word. Many are crafted with such creativity and skill that many qualify for a new genre of folk art and instantly acquire status as family heirlooms. They display pride in naval service, in entering the CPO mess, and straightforward patriotism. Today's reinvigorated charge books tap the roots of these early traditions of pride in accomplishment and knowledge, providing yet another example of a tradition evolving in strength from the old tradition, as the chiefs' mess directed.

The Initiation Ceremony. One part of our naval heritage has always been separate communities for those of different rank. Social striation has always been a characteristic of the sea services. The basic distinction between officer and enlisted has certainly been stronger than in the other services. First enshrined in the distance between quarterdeck and fo'c'sle—and now portrayed as the distance between wardroom and the deckplates—this level of consciousness eventually evolved to include a strict social separation between Chief Petty Officers and their "blueshirts." For many years, a main vehicle to build cohesion and to signal the transition from blueshirt to khaki has been a very distinct initiation event immediately preceding advancement or frocking. It is the rite of passage that indelibly marks the Sailor as a Chief Petty Officer.

Formal Navy-wide CPO initiation began in the early 1950s, and for several decades took the form of a mock trial that subjected the newly selected Chief Petty Officer to the judgment of a court of his or her peers. Some aspects of these early initiations were clearly influenced by our Shellback and Golden Dragon traditions, but every part of the plot had a symbolic meaning that became apparent when the day was done. At their best, these trials were well-planned, organized, and effective in fulfilling the most important objectives of the CPO rite of passage.

CPO initiation is a great example of an important tradition being established spontaneously and spreading throughout the entire Navy with no central orchestration. Interviews with World War II–era chiefs suggest that no formal initiation ceremony existed then, yet it is certain that today's tradition has its roots in that era. In the difficult deployed routine of the wartime Navy, something as important and non-routine as promotion to Chief Petty Officer would be treated as a special event, celebrated when circumstances permitted. Additionally the wartime expansion of the Navy brought younger Chief Petty Officers with far less experience. "Old salts" in the mess took the time to impress on the young chief that this wasn't just a promotion to another pay grade. Just as often, however, the pace of life and somber circumstances dictated that advancement was accomplished without any fanfare. The newly advanced CPO not uncommonly "donned the hat" and continued to wear the dungaree uniform as he tackled new responsibilities. Fanfare or no, long before the introduction of our CPO Creed, all parties recognized that promotion to CPO was a momentous event and deserved special treatment—an entire way of life was changing.

Although no systematic Navy-wide CPO initiation existed during the war years or during the downsizing that followed, entry into the CPO mess was often commemorated with special CPO-only events. As the Navy discharged thousands of Sailors and decommissioned hundreds of ships, the tradition of a Navy-wide event marking entry into the CPO mess began to evolve. The return to the pace of a more normal advancement process and the peacetime drawdown facilitated the establishment of a uniform initiation process that included the CPO Creed. By the mid-1950s, events occurring in far flung places bore a remarkable similarity to each other, and before the end of the decade, the initiation tradition was firmly established.

In the days prior to the current practice of "frocking," Chief Petty Officers were promoted in monthly increments throughout the year following the publication of the list of selectees. CPO initiation took place at the command/locality level for each promotion date. With no CPO indoctrination courses in existence, the old salts of the CPO mess soon recognized the need for structured guidance and began assigning sponsors to those about to be advanced. Sponsors were sometimes solid, veteran chiefs, but just as often sponsors were the newest CPOs in the mess. The "throw him in, and he will learn to swim" theory of leadership training prevailed at the time. Sponsor duties were generally minimal, extending no farther than ensuring the new Chief showed up on time for the initiation ceremony!

For many years, CPO initiations were rowdy and boisterous—but closely guarded—private events. Only Chief Petty Officers participated, and even the commanding officer required a personal invitation. For the selectee, exactly what lay ahead was a closely held secret (some aspect of that mystery remains—you'll not get any clues from this handbook!). Selectees looked forward to initiation with a mixture of genuine anticipation, anxiety, and dread, while casually maintaining a feigned "bring-it-on" attitude. Several variations of colorful, creative, scripted pageants were produced that provided a memorable entry into the CPO mess.

Over time, some egregious additions to the colorful and creative crept into the CPO initiation process. At the same time, the CPO mess leadership provided insufficient oversight, and the core values test was not being applied to changes to the process. For a brief period the entire initiation tradition appeared headed for extinction. The most regrettable aspect of this period is not how much harm was done, but how many opportunities to do good were lost when conduct occurred that was not consistent with Navy core values.

Fortunately, after wise deliberation at the most senior levels of the CPO community, we developed a more mature and focused concept of the initiation process. We developed some real insight into good naval traditions that had nearly been destroyed by neglect and misuse. A legitimate rite of passage was preserved, and CPO initiation season is now not only above suspicion and criticism but recognized as providing a unique opportunity for sustained reflection and understanding of the Navy's heritage, tradition, and core values.

Today, as before, the goals of CPO initiation include congratulating, welcoming, inspiring, improving, instilling trust, and motivating the CPO selectee while teaching leadership, building esprit de corps, promoting unity, building teamwork, and having some fun in the process. Selectees join group physical fitness routines (moving to CPO Pride/Navy Pride cadence calls), construct charge books, read about our naval heritage, and participate in core values discussions, civic and community projects, and various leadership and teamwork-training efforts. The season ends with a formal advancement ceremony on 16 September each year, although mentoring by assigned sponsors continues throughout the following year.

The new Chief Petty Officer has much to learn, building on core values, the oath of allegiance, the code of conduct, and the Sailor's Creed. Unique to the CPO, however, is the Chief Petty Officer's Creed. For me, it is on the short list of our most important documents and references. Several versions are in use, with minor word changes here and there, but for the most part the great phrases are left untouched even by the most ambitious and insensitive who attempt to edit it. The creed builds to a powerful crescendo, peaking with the simple yet profound phrase: "You are now the Chief."

The Chief Petty Officer's Creed

During the course of this day, you have been caused to humbly accept challenge and face adversity. This you have accomplished with rare good grace. Pointless as some of these challenges may have seemed, there were valid, time-honored reasons behind each pointed barb. It was necessary to meet these hurdles with blind faith in the fellowship of Chief Petty Officers. The goal was to instill in you that trust is inherent with the donning of the uniform of a Chief. It was our intent to impress upon you that challenge is good; a great, and necessary reality which cannot mar you—which, in fact, strengthens you. In your future as a Chief Petty Officer, you will be forced to endure adversity far beyond that imposed upon you today. You must face each challenge and adversity with the same dignity and good grace you demonstrated today. By experience, by performance, and by testing, you have been this day advanced to Chief Petty Officer. In the United States Navy—and only in the United States Navy—the rank of E-7 carries with it unique responsibilities and privileges you are now bound to observe and expected to fulfill. Your entire way of life is now changed. More will be expected of you; more will be demanded of you, not because you are an E7 but because you are now a Chief Petty Officer. You have not merely been promoted one pay grade, you have joined an exclusive fellowship and, as in all fellowships, you have a special responsibility to your comrades, even as they have a special responsibility to you. This is why we in the United States Navy may maintain with pride our feelings of accomplishment once we have attained the position of Chief Petty Officer. Your new responsibilities and privileges do not appear in print. They have no official standing; they cannot be referred to by name, number, or file. They have existed for over one hundred years; Chiefs before you have freely accepted responsibility beyond the call of printed assignment. Their actions and their performance demanded the respect of their seniors as well as their juniors. It is now required that you be the fountain of wisdom, the ambassador of good will, the authority in personal relations as well as in technical applications. "Ask the Chief" is a household phrase in and out of the Navy. You are now the Chief. The exalted position you have now achieved—and the word exalted is used advisedly—exists because of the attitude and performance of the Chiefs before you. It shall exist only as long as you and your fellow Chiefs maintain these standards. It was our intention that you never forget this day. It was our intention to test you, to try you, and to accept you. Your performance has assured us that you will wear "the hat" with the same pride as your comrades in arms before you. We take a deep and sincere pleasure in clasping your hand, and accepting you as a Chief Petty officer in the United States Navy.

Personal Example: CPO Responsibility as a Leader and Role Model

Much can be learned from handbooks like this or from the study of those who served long before us. But it is the wisdom imparted personally, one-on-one, from one generation of Chief Petty Officers to those who have come to "relieve the watch" that is priceless.

Early in every career—be it four years or thirty—Sailors are exposed to Navy role models. For those who were not raised in a Navy family, the first example of Navy professionalism is the recruiter or recruit division commander. Some of the most effective leadership and personal inspiration comes from those leaders we have observed and respected so much that we wanted to be like them—and we attempted to emulate their behavior.

Sailors must not only look to leaders as role models, they must be role models themselves. The seaman apprentice on recruit leave is an example to his civilian peers. The commanding officer and command master chief are recognized by every Sailor in the command, and their conduct sets the tone for the wardroom and CPO mess. The Sailor's charge to set a standard is a solemn trust, and it is non-negotiable.

One sobering reality of serving as a role model is that we can never be completely sure of what impact we may be having on others who look up to us. Adm. Mike Boorda, perhaps the most inspiring of all chiefs of naval operations, was fond of telling the story of a Senior Chief Petty Officer who profoundly influenced his life more than thirty years earlier. Long out of touch with the senior chief, Admiral Boorda's staff located him and invited him to the change of office in Annapolis. The senior chief was utterly amazed and gratified to learn that his influence over then-PN1 Mike Boorda had been powerful and long-lasting. Like Admiral Boorda's old chief, you may never know the impact you have on a young Sailor.

One of the proudest moments in any enlisted Sailor's life is when he or she becomes a Chief Petty Officer. The newly advanced chief may have as little as twelve years of service, or as many as twenty years or more. The new chief may be entering a mess—without knocking!—filled with many experienced chiefs, senior and master chiefs, but on every level even the newest CPO is accepted as an equal. The CPO mess is much like a family with a strong sense of equality among our brothers and sisters.

- No one member is more important than the next.
- Members have a healthy respect for and sensitivity to the needs of other members.
- The success of one is celebrated by all.
- Forgiveness for errors and omissions is a given.
- Genuine concern for the well-being of others is translated into actions when there is a need.

Welcome home.

Part One

Leading

1

The Art and Science
of Leadership

Case Study: The Newly Advanced
Chief Petty Officer

MMC Burgeo sighed as he hung up the telephone. He fingered his collar device thoughtfully and remembered how proud he'd felt, that day last September when his wife pinned the anchors on his brand new khaki shirt. His whole career—thirteen years in the Navy, and most of that at sea—seemed to reach a pinnacle that bright September morning. But now—now, he wasn't so sure.

"We've got a great billet for you," his detailer had said. "I know you've spent most of the last ten years or so on big-deck ships, but here's a chance for you to really show your leadership skills. I've got an immediate opening on USS *Walter McGinn* (DDG-50) out of Norfolk, and I need you over there fast. I don't have to tell you that things have been tough on *McGinn* these last couple months. They've been deployed almost constantly for the last year or so, and, with all the fallout from that Iraq mess a couple years back, we're still not really back on a good rotational schedule just yet. And of course, they had that shaft freeze up on 'em and had to crawl back across the Atlantic at about six knots—no fun in the wintertime, I'd bet. The crew has been pretty hard stressed, I guess, and there are a lot of new E-1s and E-2s reporting aboard directly out of Great Lakes. To make matters worse, Senior Chief Merasheen has to detach early—he's got some medical problems, so I'll need you on board sometime around 15 January. We'll be able to get you detached immediately for a couple weeks leave, though."

"Man," thought Chief Burgeo, "I'll be walking into a real hornet's nest over there, I bet. Long deployments, poor morale, no senior chief to advise me for a while. Well, this is what it's all about, I suppose. But I sure wish I felt more comfortable about being a leader!"

Defining Leadership

If we're honest with ourselves, we've all felt like Chief Burgeo at one time or another. Leadership is what we're all about, but what makes a good leader? There are as many definitions of leadership as there are leaders. *The War Instructions for the Navy* (1944) defined leadership as "the art of inspiring, guiding, and directing bodies of men so that they ardently desire to do what the leader wishes."

The world has changed a lot since 1944, and so has the Navy. The staff at the Naval Academy, writing in *Fundamentals of Naval Leadership*, more recently defines leadership as

> The art, science, or gift by which a person is enabled and privileged to direct the thoughts, plans, and actions of others in such a manner as to obtain and command their obedience, their confidence, their respect, and their loyal cooperation.

Leadership, simply put, is the art of accomplishing the Navy's mission through people. And—to ease the mind of our friend Chief Burgeo—there is nothing magical about it. You don't have to be born with leadership ability, or inherit it from your ancestors, or learn it from deep study of dusty schoolbooks. Leadership is all about people.

Visit any library, anywhere, and you'll find shelves of books about leadership. Some distill the wisdom of the ages; some merely repeat trendy truisms and aren't worth the paper they're printed on. Some say that leadership is an art, others say it's a science. Some say that leaders are born, not made; others hold that leadership can best be learned by following the secret formulas that only they, apparently, are wise enough to see. Trust yourself. As a Chief Petty Officer, you have lived for years in the best leadership laboratory ever devised. Think back to the great chiefs who have led you, inspired you, and, yes, rebuked you. Think of what they have done and what they would do if they were in your shoes. You have seen leaders lead; you've lived with leaders, and you've followed them. If you just try to emulate a few simple qualities that distinguish great chiefs, your Sailors will follow you, too.

Twenty Qualities of Great Leaders

Knowledge

Know Yourself. Your first requirement as a chief is to be knowledgeable: know yourself, your rating, your ship, and your Sailors. Do you really know your own strengths and weaknesses? Are you prepared to play to your strengths and compensate for or correct your weaknesses? Be honest here. None of us are perfect. But the good leaders, the great leaders, know themselves far better than anyone else.

Know Your Rating. Do you really know your rating? You can't maintain the respect of your people if you don't know your stuff. Things change quickly. When you lead a work center or division, you must know the equipment and every current procedure that your Sailors will encounter.

Know Your Mission. You must know your ship or unit. Above all, you must maintain your warfare qualifications.

It's not enough to have earned them once; you must stay current. Like Chief Burgeo, you may have never served on the type of ship to which you're receiving orders, but quickly learning your own command and your responsibilities in it are essential to success in any CPO leadership position. Once you have a strengthened knowledge base, you will be better able to assess any new situation that arises, make a decision, and come up with a plan of action to deal with it.

Know Your Sailors Just as you must know your own strengths and limitations, you must also know the Sailors who work for you, whether they are your division, work center, or repair locker. Take the time to get to know them, to recognize their strengths and weaknesses so that you can better serve the mission and lead your Sailors. Taking care of your people provides immense satisfaction.

Leadership is, first and foremost, taking care of our Sailors.
U.S. Air Force (SSGT Carrie Hinson)

Integrity

Integrity is the cornerstone of everything that Chief Petty Officers do. More than simple honesty, integrity is the result of an active intellectual process resulting in strongly held beliefs that drive your every action. At some time, you will have to sacrifice for your beliefs. Integrity is the first among many equally important attributes that make up strong character and empower effective leadership. Integrity ensures consistency and activism on behalf of beliefs. The courage to lead follows naturally from conscious awareness and acceptance of your belief in duty and mission. Some introspective searching to define your values before you find yourself challenged may help keep you from making choices you may regret. During the Chief Petty Officer initiation season, experienced chiefs helped you think through your values. Those values—your integrity— lie at the heart of your performance as a leader.

Loyalty

Many different kinds of loyalty will be demanded of you. Your paramount loyalty, of course, lies with the oath you have taken to defend the United States and the Constitution, but you also will, and should, feel loyalty to the Navy, to your ship or unit, to your chain of command, to the members of your mess, your Sailors, your shipmates, and, of course, to your family and friends.

Much is expected of you as a Chief Petty Officer. Perhaps the most difficult test of loyalty is the ability to pass on a superior's unpopular order with which you don't agree, and you have to make it appear to your Sailors as if the order originated with you. Equally important as loyalty up the chain of command is loyalty down the chain of command to those Sailors who look to you for leadership. To them, you are the Navy. Look after your people, their interests, their welfare, and their careers. Such loyalty will help your Sailors build their own loyalty to you.

There will be occasions when different loyalties will pull you in opposing directions, occasions when you find that you cannot be loyal to a shipmate, a superior, or a friend without compromising your loyalty to the mess or command or even the Navy. Those are tough cases, but to a well-formed conscience, the choice is eventually clear. Ask yourself "If I had to stand before a court-martial, or read about my actions in the newspaper, how would I feel?" Then do the right thing.

Maturity

More than simply the state of being fully grown, maturity entails a sense of responsibility, of willingness to take ownership of a problem and see things through to completion. An immature individual often believes that a problem will be taken care of by someone else, that somehow mommy or daddy will ride in to the rescue. Immaturity can be poison in an organization in which individuals must rely on each other to take care of problems without being told. Look around you. There is no one else. You are the chief.

Displaying temper, ridiculing, and verbally abusing Sailors are signs of immaturity. Such behavior is never appropriate and will not be tolerated in today's Navy. Treat every person the way you'd want to be treated, and you won't go far wrong.

Will

In wartime, trying to win is not enough because the only alternative to winning a war is losing it. Will means not giving up in the face of overwhelming obstacles, and instead finding a way around them, over them, or through them to achieve your goal. Will means going beyond simply doing your best; will means undertaking a mission focused on success.

Followership

Although books on leadership are plentiful, books on followership are rare. Yet in an organization where everyone feels that he or she is, or ought to be, the leader, no one is the leader. You cannot successfully lead without being a successful follower of your own leaders. Your ability to do this will reinforce the followership skills of your own Sailors.

Self-Discipline

Learn to set realistic goals and hold yourself to them. From your boss's perspective, discipline is probably the most highly prized quality you can have. You cannot impose discipline on Sailors without first imposing it on yourself.

Confidence

In an emergency, Sailors will look to you to be cool and confident. If you seem frightened or indecisive, or if you lack self-confidence or appear not to trust your own judgment, you will put yourself and your people at unnecessary risk. Mental rehearsals, repetition, and drill will help you learn to maintain your composure in stressful situations.

You can't expect to have confidence in your ability to perform as an experienced Chief Petty Officer right away. True confidence comes from knowledge and experience. Hone and practice your skills, and learn from your own mistakes as well as the mistakes of others until you are comfortable with your expertise and have learned to rely on your own judgment.

Flexibility

The need for flexibility is often mistakenly used as an excuse not to make plans, but that is wrong-headed. In order to be flexible you must not only make plans but also make backup plans, and backup plans for your backup plans. Don't become too comfortable with the status quo and be ready to adapt without complaint when the situation changes without notice.

Endurance

You well know that life in the Navy can be hard and is often both physically and mentally stressful. The sometimes-extreme demands of this profession are one reason the Navy places so much emphasis on physical fitness. No one expects you to be Superman or Superwoman, but you can't effectively lead your people if you are exhausted and stressed out.

Decisiveness

Sometimes, especially in the mess, chiefs think that decisiveness means voicing an instant and unchanging opinion on every subject. A better name for this is stupidity. Decisiveness means the ability to commit yourself and your Sailors to a course of action. Once you have announced a decision and set a plan in motion, you risk sabotaging your success every time you have to change your plans. Although you should not hesitate to reverse your decision when necessary, you should bear in mind the costs of making this change and do so only with good reason.

In peacetime you may have the luxury of taking some time to make up your mind on a possible course of action. If the matter is not urgent, and if the situation is sufficiently complex to warrant it, spend time gathering information and consulting with others before you make your final decision. Don't announce your decision until it is necessary for you to do so; permitting you to keep evaluating new information with an open mind.

Initiative

Initiative has several allied qualities: imagination, aggressiveness, and the ability to look and think ahead. Don't wait for your superiors to tell you what needs to be done. Far better to hear "Nice job, Chief. I was going to mention that to you, but I see you have already taken care of it," than "When are you going to square that area away?"

Justice

At all times you must treat Sailors with absolute fairness. Personal prejudice against race, gender, ethnic origin, personal appearance, or other similarly irrelevant factors has no place in a leader's decision making. It's wrong, and if you fall prey to it, you're wrong, too.

Compassion

Although you must insist on loyalty, discipline, performance, and dedication, you must remember that the same things that motivate you may not always motivate the men and women you lead. Make an effort to find out what motivates your Sailors, and keep it in mind in your dealings with them. Be considerate of Sailors' feelings. Remember the adage "Praise in public, criticize in private." Equally important is consideration of the feelings of your superiors and peers.

Forcefulness

The meek may someday inherit the earth, but in the interim they are unlikely to succeed as Chief Petty Officers. To do your job effectively, you will have to learn to stand up to your peers, to recalcitrant Sailors, and, occasionally, to your boss.

Humility

Don't confuse humility with meekness. Humility is strength quietly demonstrated by reliable, conscientious conduct. Talk is cheap, and a job well done is far more effective than brashly calling attention to your every action. By the same token, humility allows us to recognize our own strengths and unique contributions to the command. "I am what I am," said Popeye, and no philosopher has ever caught the spirit of true humility as did that mythical Sailor.

Positive Attitude

Your attitude is incredibly contagious. If you radiate negativity, the people who work for you will radiate negativity as well, and they won't perform at their best. Be enthusiastic and demonstrate your enthusiasm to your people at every opportunity.

Communication Skills

Remember the four core competencies of a Chief Petty Officer: leading, communicating, supporting, and developing. You don't have to be Peter Jennings or Tom Clancy, but you must be reasonably competent in both written and oral communications, or your lack of skill will adversely affect your performance and the performance of your people. Part Two discusses oral and written communications in detail.

Personal Behavior

In addition to being ethical and moral, as a leader and a role model you must also be seen to be ethical and moral. Strive to set an example for your Sailors. Set the highest standard you possibly can because the standard to which you hold yourself will determine the standard you can set for your Sailors.

Courage

Courage comes in two forms, physical and moral. Physical courage means overcoming your fears to carry out your duties in a dangerous situation. Moral courage, sometimes more difficult, means "calling them as you see them," admitting your own mistakes, and speaking up when you feel that a senior is about to make an error. Moral courage also means counseling Sailors honestly on their weaknesses, one of the hardest and most painful tasks of any Chief Petty Officer.

Leadership and Management

It was cold and rainy when Chief Burgeo exited the downtown tunnel, turning right toward the Norfolk Shipyard. "What shape will the ship be in when I get there?" he wondered. "Reporting aboard a ship in the yards is never easy," he thought as he pulled into a parking spot. As he crossed the brow for the first time, hoses, wires, crates, and boxes littered the deck. The quarterdeck watch, huddled in the lee of an overflowing dumpster, didn't notice him at first, but quickly recovered and directed him to the CMC's office. "Pretty sloppy operation," Chief Burgeo thought to himself but said nothing. He knocked three times firmly on the CMC's closed door and entered when invited.

"Good to have you on board," CMDCM Ramea said as he stood to shake hands. "I can't tell you how relieved we are that you're on board with us. Senior Chief Merasheen left about a week ago, and the engineering refit is going pretty badly. We've got yardbirds clambering all over the ship, and GS1 Toslow, your LPO, tells me that she's shorthanded in every area you can think of. There's lots of welding going on, and we're even hard-pressed to mount enough fire watches. We've got enough work to keep us here for six weeks, but we have to be out in three, and, frankly, I'm not sure if you have enough talent in your department to pull things together. It looks like that frozen shaft is going to take much longer than expected, and there have been a number of other casualties that never got attended to when we were deployed. You're going to be a busy guy for a while—the CHENG has been calling up here every five minutes, asking if you've come on board yet."

Chief Burgeo will face two challenges in his first days aboard. From the slack watchkeepers who greeted him when he reported aboard, he sensed that there'd be some leadership issues he'd have to address. More immediately, however, he knew he'd have to deal with some management issues, and, as he descended into the engineering spaces, he wondered if he'd be up to the task.

"Good to meet you, chief!" Lieutenant Paradise, the chief engineer, picked up an overflowing folder from his desk. "To be honest, I don't know what all we have going on; I just got back from emergency leave. Senior Chief Merasheen is gone, and all I have are the files he left behind." As he spoke, work orders, CASREPS, and other documents fell from the folder to the deck. "Mr. Whitbourne, the yard foreman, seems to be the only person who knows what's going on around here, but yesterday, I caught him instructing his crew from a set of work orders that were meant for our sister ship, USS *Moscrip*. There's no telling what he's doing to our power plant. Everyone is walking around here in a daze, it seems to me."

Management Functions

Good leadership must begin with good management. It's a rare chief who is not resource limited—there are never enough people, parts, tools, time, or opportunity to do the job quite the way it should be done. Management is that skill which enables us to attain our organizational goals efficiently and effectively. Chief Burgeo's mission is to get *McGinn* out of the yards on time. Although the purpose of leadership is to establish the unit's mission and the strategy for getting there, the purpose of management is to implement that strategy through four basic functions:

Planning. Planning defines where the unit wants to be in the future and how to get there. A lack of planning, or poor planning, will cripple a work center or division's performance. Chief Burgeo's first priority must be to determine what repair plan is in place, and, if no plan has been developed, quickly act so that appropriate resources are allocated for the tasks at hand.

Organizing. Organizing follows planning and specifies how the work center accomplishes the plan. Organizing involves the assignment of tasks, grouping of tasks into projects or programs, and allocation of resources. Once Chief Burgeo has a plan in place, his next step will be to determine what resources are available and how best they can be used. As an example, Chief Burgeo knew that a number of non-rated personnel had just been ordered aboard. He made a note to himself to talk to his fellow chiefs about "borrowing" the necessary personnel so that welding operations would not be delayed.

Controlling. Controlling means monitoring Sailors' activities, determining if the work center is on target toward its goals, and adjusting as necessary. While recent efforts empowering and trusting Sailors to work on their own have been successful, management-by-walking-around is never out of style. Computers are useful to track performance and task completion, but getting out from behind the screen and hitting the deck plates is still, by far, the best form of managerial control a chief can practice!

Directing. Directing is the use of influence to motivate Sailors to achieve the unit's goals. Good work centers share culture and values; experienced chiefs communicate their goals to Sailors throughout the organization, while motivating these Sailors to perform at a high level. Chief Burgeo knew instinctively that, with the obstacles facing the engineering department, it would take everyone pulling together to make the yard period a success.

Plan the Work, Then Work the Plan

GS1 Toslow stopped Chief Burgeo in the passageway. "Hey Chief, you've got to do something about those masters-at-arms! I've only got three qualified EMs, and they just took two of 'em off to the weapons range to requalify on the Mossberg shotgun. They said they'd be there all day. . . . I can't get anything done around here, and when I complained to the MA1, he said we can only get the range today, and he wanted as many people as he could get over there so that we don't lose our spot. I hope nobody wants these panels energized anytime soon."

Sometimes, we lose sight of some of the basic goals of good management. For an organization to be successful, it must be both efficient and effective.

Efficiency. Efficiency refers to the amount of effort or resources used to produce a specific output. Efficiency asks the question "Are we doing things right?" From the perspective of the MA1, perhaps loading the weapons range with as many people as can be accommodated is the most efficient use of a limited resource. Overall effectiveness may be at risk, however.

Effectiveness. Effectiveness is the degree to which the organization achieves its stated objective. The organization succeeds by completing its mission or the demands placed upon it by the chain of command. In that light, completing the yard period on time outweighs the desire to fully utilize training facilities, and while efficiency might suffer, effectiveness is better served. Effectiveness asks the question "Are we doing the right things?"

One of the best pieces of conventional wisdom passed to any Chief Petty Officer is "Plan the work, then work the plan." Certainly, there are times when other priorities or even other opportunities arise to throw you off. But remember that being efficient is not nearly as important as being effective. Doing the wrong thing well—like having fully-qualified force protection on a ship that can't get out of the yards—benefits neither you nor your command.

The day continued pretty much the way it had started. The HTs complained that there was no electrical power for their arc welders; the machinist mates complained that they couldn't begin reassembling the damaged shaft until the welding was completed, and the yard foreman disappeared after noon chow, not to be seen again. Chief Burgeo felt like he was running in twelve directions at once, and by the end of the day, his head was spinning. "Why didn't somebody ever tell me things would be like this," he muttered to himself as he answered yet another call on his "brick" from the CHENG.

Chief Petty Officers must quickly develop three coping skills in order to manage successfully. While the ratio of these skills might differ by task and assignment, each is critical to your success as a Chief Petty Officer.

Cognition. Cognition involves thinking, information processing, and understanding the command as a whole and the relationship among its parts. Cognition allows you to see the big picture. While this skill may be most important for LCPOs or chiefs with multiple departments, it's never too soon to stop thinking within the confines of your own rate or billet and attempt to see the bigger picture.

Compassion. Compassion recognizes that all work is accomplished through people. Not everyone will see things the way you do. As a chief, you'll work with and through other people and will work effectively as their group leader. True compassion for the feelings of others allows you to motivate, facilitate, coordinate, lead, communicate, and resolve conflicts. Chiefs at all levels must develop and practice this very human skill.

Confidence. Confidence comes from the understanding of, and proficiency in, specific tasks including mastery of the methods, techniques, and equipment involved. Confidence also requires specialized knowledge, analytical ability, and use of tools and techniques specific to your rating or to the ratings you manage. While technical competence is most important at lower organizational levels, you must guard against becoming a mile wide, but only a foot deep, as you assume greater responsibilities as a department or command authority in your field.

As a Chief Petty Officer, you'll often face major problems mixed with trivial events, and usually in no predictable sequence. You'll be responsible for a great deal of work at an unrelenting pace. That's the nature of today's Navy and the nature of your job. Planning the work and trying to stick to the plan as best you can will help everything go lots easier for you—and for the Sailors you lead.

The Chief Petty Officer as a Manager

Perhaps it didn't occur to you, when you received the hat, but you'll really wear many hats as a Chief Petty Officer. Some of your roles are obvious: you're a leader and mentor to young men and women who have chosen naval service. Other roles may be less obvious—but are equally important to your role as a manager and leader.

Good leadership requires that we first understand fully the tasks our Sailors are called upon to perform. You cannot lead if you don't know the job that needs to be done.
U.S. Navy (PHAN Jo Wilbourn)

The Chief Petty Officer as a Manager of Information

Monitor. The monitoring role involves seeking current information from many sources. As an example, our friend Chief Burgeo would do well to consult the other members of his mess at the first opportunity to get both the history and the command's expectations of the situation he inherited when he reported on board.

Disseminator. The disseminator role is the opposite of the monitor role. As a disseminator, you'll transmit current information to others, both inside and outside the organization. Chief Burgeo's job will be a lot easier if, when he gets the straight scoop from the command and his shipmates, he passes that information along to the folks who are actually doing the job.

Link. In your role as a key link in the chain of command, you'll be the spokesperson to your Sailors and to civilians who may work in your organization or provide services to your command. Perhaps the worst situation of all is to have a link in the chain of command who acts as a cutout—someone who receives the word from the top but neglects to transmit it down the chain to those below.

The Chief Petty Officer as a People Manager

Ceremonial. The ceremonial role involves traditional and symbolic activities for the department or organization. Sometimes chiefs forget that the ceremonial symbols—the hat, the uniform, standing in the front of your division or department at quarters—are not the job. The symbols are the rewards for doing the job, which is accomplishing the unit's mission as efficiently and effectively as possible.

Liaison. The liaison role pertains to the development of information sources both inside and outside the organization. No one but Chief Burgeo has quite the same horsepower to collar the yard foreman and straighten out some of the problems that seem to lie in his domain.

Leader. The leader role encompasses relationships with subordinates, including motivation, communication, and influence. Remember that without the ability to manage, there really can be no ability to lead.

The Chief Petty Officer as a Decision Maker

Entrepreneurial. The entrepreneurial role involves initiating change and being proactive. It's summed up in the phrase "If it's to be, it's up to me."

Peacekeeper. The peacekeeper role involves resolving conflicts among subordinates, peers, or departments. Wisdom, level-headedness, and the ability to compromise go a long way toward getting things done in most organizations.

Resource Allocator. The resource allocator allocates people, time, equipment, budget, and other resources to attain desired outcomes. Somewhere there is a ship or station where these items are all available when and where needed. If you find it, contact the authors at the Naval Institute. We'd like a set of orders there.

The Decision-Making Process

Lieutenant Paradise caught up with Chief Burgeo again later that afternoon. "We've got some decisions to make, Chief," he said. "Something has got to give. It's official—we've got to get out of here on day twenty-one—and there are at least five or six weeks of work left to get things back in shape. Consider all the alternatives and put together a plan to at least get us across the river under our own power. Give it to me right after quarters tomorrow, and I'll take it to the captain."

Decisions

A decision is a choice made among two or more alternatives. As a Chief Petty Officer, you make decisions every hour of every day. Sometimes, like Chief Burgeo, you'll have to make a decision quickly. At other times, you'll have the leisure to consider all the different alternatives. Quick decision or not, the decision-making process can be broken into eight discrete steps.

Identifying a Problem. In this case, the problem is apparent. There's not enough time to accomplish everything that needs to be done in the yards, and DDGs don't come equipped with sails. The main propulsion shaft will have to be fixed. Everything else is secondary.

Identifying Decision Criteria. Ask yourself some tough questions. What happens if we win? What happens if we fail? Can the skipper negotiate a longer stay in the yards? What is needed? What is nice? Can we sail with some equipment red-tagged? Who decides?

Allocating Weights to the Criteria. "First things first" is a simple but powerful management skill. When the challenges are stacked up, it is important to get busy and stay busy, but it is even more important to prioritize. Prioritizing action items is an essential skill, and it is the chief's responsibility. Some things have to be done, and some things might be put off until the next availability. The collective wisdom of the CPO mess, the civilian maintenance managers, and even the wardroom can assist Chief Burgeo in making intelligent decisions. Beware, though, of the individual who champions his or her pet project and fails to see the big picture.

Developing Alternatives. "You can have things fast, good, or cheap. Pick two," goes the old adage. Can the ship's problems be solved by throwing additional resources into the fray? What are the resources? People? Dollars? More time?

Analyzing Alternatives. Imperfect solutions are often necessary in an imperfect world. Do the homework, cross your fingers, and then decide.

Selecting an Alternative. The operative word here is select. Seek counsel if you can, but, when the alternatives are laid out, pick the one that makes the most sense. If you're wrong, people may fault your judgment. If you seek to avoid the decision, however, they *will* fault your moral courage and suitability as a leader.

Implementing the Alternative. Do it. John Paul Jones said, "I intend to go into harm's way." He didn't say, "Well, if things go as planned, maybe we'll go into harm's way. Or then again, maybe we won't." Be decisive.

Evaluating Decision Effectiveness. You may just learn something from what you did well and what you did poorly. The next time your ship heads into the yards, you may just have learned enough to avoid some of the rocks and shoals you'll find there.

Making Rational Choices

Chief Burgeo sat in the engineering office until oh-dark-thirty. He poured over every job order, every work request, every casualty report that he found in Senior Chief Merasheen's desk. He knew he was a good machinist's mate, and he was sure that he understood enough about the other ratings involved to develop a workable plan for the CHENG in the morning. It wasn't perfect—no plan ever really is—but it would meet the requirements to get out of the yards on time and fix enough of the problems so that the ship would be mission-capable if it had to sortie quickly. "I'll give this to Lieutenant Paradise first thing in the morning," he thought. "I just wish that I had more solid information, and that I didn't have to make so many assumptions. But that's the way it goes, I suppose."

Only rarely do we have all the information we'd really like to make informed decisions. Like tools, parts, and people, we could always use just a little bit more. The important thing is making a decision.

We've all met Chief Petty Officers who have exhibited wildly differing decision-making styles. Some are problem avoiders who avoid or ignore information that points to a problem. Surely, someone before Chief Burgeo recognized that the yard period was loading ten pounds of sand into the five-pound bag. In this case, however, no one seemed willing to take the steps necessary to plan an adequate response.

Some are problem solvers who attack problems as they arise. Unfortunately as one experienced master chief once commented, "The problem with being a troubleshooter is that I'm always in trouble." Far better, it would seem, to prevent problems, rather than solve them as they arrive. Others are problem seekers who actively investigate problem areas before difficulties arise. As you walk around a work center, look around you. If you see something that can be dangerous or can present problems later on, now's the time to act. The best problem is the one that never arises.

Remember that bad news, and tough decisions, are a lot like dead fish. The longer we try to avoid them, the worse they smell. Gather your information. Consider your alternatives. You are a Chief Petty Officer. Act decisively.

Proven Leadership Techniques

Captain Smallwood approved Chief Burgeo's plan and, slowly, a sense of calm and order began to return to the engineering department. The deck division pitched in with a few non-rated personnel to act as firewatches, and, after a pointed discussion with the yard foreman, crews began working overtime to complete as many jobs as possible in the time remaining. General housekeeping remained a problem—the decks were littered with debris, ship's tools kept turning up missing, and moving from space to space could be a life-threatening experience. Finally, at quarters one morning, Chief Burgeo sounded off. "I don't care if we are in the yards. We need to get this ship squared away. This ship is named after a great Navy chief, BUC Walter McGinn of MCB-1, who gave his life in Vietnam. He'd be humiliated to see how things look around here. Now, I don't want to see another greasy rag shoved into a corner, and the next Sailor who drops oil on the deck had better clean it up immediately. And that's an order!"

Several leadership techniques that can be employed to motivate Sailors have been used by generations of Navy chiefs and identified by faculty members at the Naval Academy. You may wonder which works best in a particular circumstance. Although no guidebook can anticipate every situation you'll experience as a Chief Petty Officer, if you understand these techniques and their underlying principles, you'll likely choose the right technique to fit the circumstances.

Every act of leadership should make subordinates feel that if they are doing their best to follow, they will be secure and their efforts will be appreciated. Just as there are ways to encourage Sailors, there are ways to quash them, too. A Chief Petty Officer who is arbitrary, or who plays favorites, or who relies on draconian threats may get immediate obedience, but the damage done will soon negate his or her authority as a leader. Good chiefs remember what we all learned in boot camp: commands require immediate action and allow no exception; and orders indicate a course of action to be followed, but may or may not permit variation or initiative on the part of the Sailor(s) receiving the order.

Issuing Effective Commands

- A command must be definite.
- A command must be positive.
- A command must be given in a tone of voice that leaves no doubt that it is to be executed.
- The leader should, when possible, look at subordinates when he gives a command.
- A command must be concise; it must not be so long or involved that Sailors cannot remember it.

Unquestioning obedience when commanded is the basis of our professional lives. A command given by a proper authority demands the follower's immediate action to carry out the directions of the leader. The objective of our military training is to indoctrinate the follower with this concept. When a command is issued, there can be no question on the part of the follower as to whether the command is correct or whether there's any option other than to carry it out. We train our Sailors to immediately carry out the instructions contained in the command to the best of their abilities.

Some commands become familiar: left full rudder; sweepers, man your brooms; parade rest. Other, more immediate situations requiring unquestioned obedience often arise. Suppose Chief Burgeo were inspecting the welding activity and discovered a fire behind a bulkhead. He'd immediately issue commands to everyone in the area. One Sailor might be sent to notify the OOD, another might be ordered to fetch an extinguisher from the passageway, others might be sent to the repair locker for Scott packs and other fire-fighting materials. Each Sailor receiving one of these commands has no alternative but to do exactly as told, immediately and without question. Your leadership skill and the ability to issue commands decisively coupled with the training provided to your Sailors will help you overcome any adversity that may occur.

Issuing Effective Orders

Explain What Is to Be Done. Allow some leeway for initiative among your Sailors. You don't have to lay things out in quite the detail that we do in, say, recruit training. Sometimes the situation doesn't permit explanations or answering Sailor's questions but when possible, it is often a good idea to explain why a particular order is necessary. If time and the situation permit, the order will be clearer because your Sailors understand the reasons behind them.

Respect. Don't talk down to your Sailors in giving instructions. Show confidence in their abilities. Avoid being overbearing and leave openings for questions or suggestions for a better way. Show respect for your own leaders, too. Never criticize another chief or organization in front of your Sailors. Never.

Chain of Command. Work through your LPO or senior rating present. You know how offended you'd be if the division or department officer gave orders directly to your Sailors. Your LPOs and senior ratings will feel the same way if you do that to them. And don't use a senior's name to lend weight to your own order. You are the chief. Act like it.

Encourage. Coach your Sailors when they encounter difficulties.

Teamwork. When giving orders, try to communicate the feeling of "let's go" rather than "get going." We're all in this together. Keep your Sailors informed.

Winning Cooperation and Establishing Discipline

Winning cooperation first will pay dividends later. Showing your own pride will stimulate unit or organizational pride. Use the word we instead of I when appropriate and possible. Give full credit to Sailors whose work and ideas have been beneficial. Let your Sailors know that you think that they are good, and maintain high standards through alert supervision. Don't be sarcastic, and never threaten punishment to make an order effective.

Confident, secure Sailors will have fewer discipline problems. As the chief, you should let them know what is expected. Don't make promises you can't keep, but grant deserved favors willingly. Know the morale of your people. Part Three of this handbook provides detail on developing your Sailors.

In establishing discipline standards, you will find the following time-honored suggestions useful:

- Praise in public, censure in private.
- Give Sailors the benefit of the doubt.
- Punish the individual, not the group.
- Consider a person's record.
- Be impartial, consistent, and humane in giving rewards and punishments.
- Teach understanding of discipline rather than fear of it, punish the guilty promptly, and defend the innocent stoutly.

Points to Ponder

Case Study: The Newly Advanced Chief Petty Officer

Have you ever been in a situation similar to Chief Burgeo's? What kind of credibility or acceptance does a newly advanced petty officer or Chief Petty Officer have among his shipmates? How can you best leverage your position to get things done if you're in a situation such as Chief Burgeo?

What did the condition of the ship as he reported aboard communicate to Chief Burgeo? Did it say that things were under control, or did it send a message that things were a bit out of hand? If you reported aboard to a situation such as he faced, what would you do?

How much help did Chief Burgeo get from his department head? What happens when those up the chain of command are themselves "lost at sea"? How can you bring your experience and wisdom to bear on a situation without making your boss look bad? Suppose Chief Burgeo shrugged and said to himself, "Well, they grew it—let them chew it." Would he be faithful to the leadership principles we've outlined here?

Resources are always limited. How do we deal with the individual or organization that always wants a little larger slice of the pie? Suppose Chief Burgeo had to deal with, say, the weapons department, who wanted additional nice-to-have work done in their spaces. How could he keep his relationships on an even keel while still getting the essential tasks done?

2

Moral Leadership, Morale, and Esprit de Corps

Case Study: Doing the Right Thing

UTC Obetz had a problem. Word had spread around MCB-34 that his best friend, EOC Tom Hayden, was romantically involved with EA3 Karen Truro, a young Seabee on her first deployment. Even though Chief Hayden was outside EA3 Truro's chain of command, he knew there was a power differential—it's difficult for a young EA3 to deal as an equal with a long-serving chief. But EA3 Truro had told several confidants that she really loved Chief Hayden and that he had promised to marry her as soon as they were back from overseas and his divorce was final. UTC Obetz knew the regulations about fraternization, and besides, the ongoing rumors and turmoil were beginning to impact morale. But Tom Hayden was his friend—they'd gone through chiefs' initiation at Gulfport together in 1998, and they had often gone hunting and fishing together on leave. "What the heck should I do?" he thought to himself. "Should I go to the command master chief and tell him what I know? Should I talk to Tom and tell him that his little secret is all over the battalion? Or should I just keep my big nose out of it and play dumb? I hate it when a friend puts me on the spot like this. . . ."

You have probably been in a similar situation. Maybe you've noticed a shipmate's pea coat bulging as he crossed the brow to go ashore. Perhaps you've been at dinner at a friend's place on the beach and commented on the excellent quality of the steaks on the grill. In return, you got that knowing smile telling you that not long ago, the steaks may have resided in the reefer back on the ship. As Chief Petty Officers, we often face ethical questions. How we handle ourselves when presented with these sticky situations is a fair test of our leadership, and, indeed, of our character.

Morals, Ethics, and the Chief Petty Officer

Morals are the principles, standards, or habits that determine what conduct is right or wrong. As leaders, we adhere to our core values of honor, courage, and commitment. Just as old-time quartermasters took frequent sightings off Polaris and other fixed heavenly bodies, so we, too, must take frequent moral fixes off those values which we prize as Sailors.

Ethics is the system or code of morals of a particular person, religion, group, or profession. In the Navy, we think of ethics as the principles by which we act and expect others to act. When you stop to think of it, every act we undertake—moral or immoral, ethical or unethical—can be measured against our core values. Our ethical system is founded on the bedrock virtues of honor, courage, and commitment.

Development of Our Personal Ethics

Sailors come in all shapes and sizes. We're male and female, of every ethnic background imaginable, and we come from large cities, small towns, ranches, farms, or even other countries. Each of us brings a particular set of ethics with us, derived from many sources:

- Parental influences
- Social and work group influences
- Ethnic background

- Age or peer group influences
- Gender group influences (male and female)
- Geographic origins and locations
- Media influences
- Religious heritage
- Economic environment

Institutions develop and teach ethical codes that best suit their goals, support their mission, and sustain their viability. These ethics become the organization's conscience. In our country, the people themselves determine our national ethics through laws and public documents, religious values, cultures, and traditions. An organization within the overall society, such as the Navy, establishes a code of ethics within the larger code and the expectations society holds for it. Sometimes military organizations will be more conservative in their ethics than the general society, because part of our task is to "conserve" the values that the society believes important. The code that develops serves as a guide for the conduct of relationships among people in the organization.

Making Ethical Decisions

Sailors, like all people, will encounter situations involving ethical conflicts and conflict among the various roles of a leader. Sometimes the solution is immediately obvious. In other cases just sorting out right from wrong is a significant challenge, and deciding exactly how to react is even more difficult. Some of the following questions can help you as a leader determine the implications of specific conduct.

Does this conduct have an impact on the mission? Is the mission readiness or mission accomplishment of this unit affected? Could it result in decisions made by your superiors that would be based on an inaccurate picture of your unit's actual achievements or capabilities?

Does this conduct abuse the public trust? If this matter became public knowledge, would you be proud of your actions or would they result in potential damage to the public support of and trust in the Navy and its members?

Does this conduct set the example for subordinates? What would be the long-term effects on our Navy and on its ability to defend the United States if every subordinate petty officer and Sailor used your actions in this matter as a guide?

Does this conduct result in selfishness or personal gain? Does this matter involve career advancement or financial aspects that are outside the expected conduct to further your career or to avoid censure for your own shortcomings? Does this matter involve a cover-up of the real or apparent failure of yourself, your unit, or your subordinates to attain prescribed standards of conduct or performance?

Some ethical choices are no-brainers—there's not much to consider when, for example, a shipyard worker comes up to you and offers you twenty dollars for the computer on your desk. Other situations, like the one Chief Obetz faced, can be more complex. Figuratively patting Chief Obetz on the head and telling him to do the right thing begs the question: Do the right thing for whom? For his friend, Chief Hayden, or for the young and naive EA3? For the battalion? For the Navy? We can momentarily ignore the ethical implications of our decisions and actions, but we cannot prevent them from becoming part of us, and we never escape them. There are several questions you can ask yourself, though, to help you determine just what is the right thing to do.

Is it good? We first ask, "Will I be proud of what I've done?" Think of the logical outcome of your action, the bottom line. Before we do anything else, we must decide if this action is consistent with what we want. Is it worthwhile doing it in the first place? Is it something we will be proud of? We must also consider not only the ultimate goal, but also the way we arrive at the goal. Sometimes, even a desirable end doesn't justify the means to get there.

What's Chief Obetz's goal here? Is it to protect the reputation of his friend? Is it to protect EA3 Truro? Is it to protect morale within the battalion?

Is it right? Ethics measures actions against principles. We prohibit certain behavior and interactions between seniors and subordinates in the same command for one reason only—mission readiness. Complying with fraternization regulations is an important responsibility for all hands. Reporting clear violations is required by our ethical principles. If fraternization is ignored, experience has proven that discipline and morale will suffer, trust and integrity are eroded and ultimately destroyed, and the unit's mission effectiveness is compromised. Romance between leaders and subordinates has predictable negative outcomes in a small unit, and unit cohesiveness cannot be sustained when certain behaviors occur. Punishing violators of policies concerning behavior that may not be prohibited in civilian life is particularly difficult for leaders.

Some might ask what's wrong with two adults who feel strongly about each other entering into a mutually satisfactory relationship? The scuttlebutt on the mess decks is that EA3 Truro is happy; she ordered a catalog of wedding dresses and was showing samples to her closest friends. Chief Hayden also seems happy enough. Chief Obetz has enough to worry about installing the utilities on the battalion's latest projects. Should he risk losing a friend and stirring up controversy by taking this issue to the CMC?

Is it appropriate? Is there a link between a decision and a particular set of circumstances? Sometimes a decision can be good and right but not applicable to the situation. A civilian contractor invites you out for dinner. At the end of the meal, he picks up the check. This situation can easily support the first two questions we have examined. There is nothing wrong with having dinner with a civilian contractor and that person paying for the meal. We have all probably done something similar ourselves. Now add one more piece to the puzzle. The contractor happens to be a supplier of equipment that you use in your shop, and you have some control over who supplies the gear. Notice that so far you have done nothing wrong. You have not been influenced. You haven't given him an order for the equipment, but you have put yourself into a position of having your motives suspect. Accepting the invitation wasn't fitting under the given circumstances.

Chief Obetz works in the utilities shop. He's not the chaplain and not a counselor, and EA3 Truro has not approached him for advice or assistance. He's not seen Chief Hayden in a compromising position, nor has the CMC asked him directly if he knew anything about the situation. But he's proud of his battalion and proud of the long tradition and reputation of the Seabees. He'd hate to have that stained by anyone's actions, even those of someone he considers a good friend.

Is it legal? Behavior doesn't have to rise to the level of a felony or rate captain's mast to be illegal. Every unit has policies, and each person who signs on accepts the policies that are in place. Each person within the unit is responsible for both the integrity of the organization and the consequences of his or her actions. Everyone must be held to the same standards when behavior that can impact the organization is involved.

Chief Obetz thought the matter over some more. "I betcha there are at least five or ten different affairs going on in this battalion," he thought to himself. "And it's not just chiefs and lower rated personnel. I've seen the way that Lieutenant Commander Worthington looks at Ensign Linworth in the personnel office, and one of my guys saw her coming out of his tent one night last week. If they get away with it, who am I to drop a dime on my friend, huh? Maybe I'll just tip him off that people are talking and he can be more careful with what he's seen doing."

Is it balanced? Will the action or decision be fair to everyone, or will it heavily favor one party or another in the short or long term? Each decision must be balanced to promote a win-win environment within the organization.

"OK, so I go to the CMC about Chief Hayden. That doesn't stop the other people from messing around, does it? All I've done is lost a friend, probably ruined his career, broken up a relationship, and stirred up trouble. Why bother?"

Why bother, indeed? Asking that question of yourself gets you to the crux of any ethical problem. Why did our POWs hold out against enemy torture and abuse in Vietnam? Why did the crew of USS *Cole* fight to save their ship? They could have abandoned the fight and helo'd over to the ships that were standing by to assist them. Why should Chief Obetz care about what's happening in his battalion, anyway? The last question we ask of ourselves helps us sum it up.

How will it make me feel about myself? Unethical acts will erode our own self-esteem. Even as you try to rationalize the act, your conscience will work overtime in the realization that what you have done, or failed to do, has violated the standards that you set for yourself, the standards that your organization has set for itself, the standards and principles of our Navy, and, yes, even our own core values. Is there honor in concealing what you know to be wrong? Is there courage in hiding behind what-ifs? Is there commitment in allowing morale to suffer if you can take the steps to improve it? Unlike other case studies in this guidebook, we won't tell you what Chief Obetz did. But answer those questions honestly, and the proper course of action should be clear to you.

Conflict and Controversy

Case Study: Facing the Music

EO2 Galloway walked into recreation tent. MCB-34 was deployed as part of Operation Iraqi Stability, but the Seabees, ever resourceful, had rigged a large stereo system for off-duty enjoy-

Conflict can range from disagreement at the mess table to full-scale combat operations. As Chief Petty Officers, we must always be prepared to spring to action to defend the Navy and the nation. *U.S. Navy (PH1 Arlo K. Abrahamson)*

ment. The space appeared empty, and EO2 Galloway removed the CD of rap music and substituted a CD of country favorites.

"Hey, who's messing with my music?" SW2 Alton exclaimed, as he appeared from behind several stacked pallets of soft drinks. "You Alpha Company guys are all alike—you think you run the battalion. I'm putting my CD back on, and you better keep your greasy truck-driving hands off of it, if you know what's good for you!"

At one time or another, we've all have had run-ins with our shipmates. It's part of life, all the more so when Sailors live and work together in confined spaces for long periods of time, as happens when a ship or unit deploys. These two Sailors are involved in a conflict, even if it's just verbal and goes no further.

Conflict. Conflict is a state of disharmony caused by the opposition or simultaneous functioning of mutually exclusive impulses, desires, or tendencies. Conflict often results when incompatible activities occur, and:

- Can be a test of a command's morale.
- Can create lasting resentment, smoldering hostility, and psychological scars.
- Can be a crisis that can weaken or strengthen the unit.
- Can push members away from one another or pull them into closer and more cooperative relationships.
- Can contain the seeds of group destruction or the seeds of a more unified and cooperative unit, depending on how quickly and wisely unit leaders deal with the conflict.
- Can bring aggression or mutual understanding, depending on the maturity of the participants.
- When handled appropriately, can even bring creative insight and closer relationships among Sailors.

Incompatible Activities. Incompatible activities prevent, block, interfere with, injure, or in some way make the second activity less likely or less effective. There's only one stereo in the tent, and it can't play two CDs at once. Incompatible activities may occur with internal questioning, between two or more people, as in the given example, or between two or more groups. Bravo Company and Delta Company, for example, may want to use the weapons range at the same time.

Positive Effects of Conflict. As Chief Petty Officers responsible for good order and discipline in our work centers, we're conditioned to think of conflict as something to be avoided. But conflict often has a positive, although not always enjoyable, impact on organizations.

- Conflict helps reevaluate positions and relationships.
- Conflict encourages personal and group change.
- Conflict allows problems to surface and not fester.
- Conflict increases group members' motivation and energy, encouraging creativity and innovation.

- Conflict among groups can strengthen unit cohesiveness and increase a sense of identity.

Controversy. Unlike conflict, which implies disharmony, controversy can be a discussion, debate, or dispute in which opposing opinions clash. Ideas can be controversial, while conflict requires direct action. The CMC may propose that the recreation tent be open only between 1700 and 1900; that idea may be controversial, but it's not likely to cause direct conflict.

Organizations with sufficient maturity and strength to embrace controversy often find that controversy helps a group make creative and high-quality decisions, sharpens analysis, stimulates interest and curiosity, and increases involvement in and commitment to the group. Controversy also gives Sailors a chance to develop a better understanding of their own contributions by forcing them to think through their positions, present supporting arguments, and listen and respond to others.

CEC Amlin walked by the recreation tent and heard the commotion inside. When he entered, he found Petty Officers Galloway and Alton in a discussion, which, without intervention, would soon escalate to a physical confrontation. "Hey, you two Seabees, cool your jets a minute here," he said. "You see the rules posted over the stereo—keep it low, respect others' tastes, and first come, first served. Now, which one of you was here first, and, anyway, what's this all about? I know both of you—you're good friends, and I see you on liberty together all the time. What's all this shouting about?"

Strategies to Manage Conflict and Controversy

The ability to resolve conflict successfully is an important leadership skill, and one that Chief Petty Officers will exercise often. All of us respond to different types and levels of conflict differently. Suppose Chief Amlin decided to keep walking past the recreation tent? What would the likely outcome be? A fight? Captain's mast? Two good Seabees who, in the heat of the moment, might do damage to their careers?

Chief Amlin first tries to defuse the situation. Defusion is essentially a delaying action, an attempt to cool off the situation, at least temporarily, or to keep the issues so unclear that attempts at confrontation are improbable. Resolving minor points while avoiding or delaying discussion of the major problem, postponing a confrontation until a more auspicious time, and avoiding clarification of the salient issues underlying the conflict are examples of defusion. Again, as with avoidance strategies, such tactics work when delay is possible, but they typically result in feelings of dissatisfaction, anxiety about the future, and concerns about oneself.

Suppose Chief Amlin said, "I don't care who did what to whom. The stereo is now secured. Both of you—head back to your company areas." What impact would Chief Amlin's actions likely have on morale and unit cohesion within MCB-34? Chief Amlin wisely kept the door open for negotiation.

In negotiation, unlike power confrontations, both sides can win. The aim of negotiation is to resolve the conflict with a compromise or a solution that is mutually satisfying to everyone. Negotiation, far from being a sign of weakness, usually provides the most positive and the fewest negative outcomes of all conflict-resolution strategies.

"Listen up, Seabees," said Chief Amlin. "I've seen more fights start at battalion events, or on the beach or wherever over music than any other subject you can think of. We've got rules posted here. Sure, Galloway didn't see you there behind those pallets, Alton, but you don't need to go getting in his face over a simple mistake. Hey, we've been out here in the desert for the last nine months. We're all on edge a little."

Diagnosing the nature of a conflict is the first step in resolution. The most important issue decided upon is whether the conflict is a value (ideological) conflict or a real (tangible) conflict or a combination of both. Consider what might happen if the debate were over a TV set. Suppose Petty Officer Galloway objected to any TV programs because they violated his religious convictions? Now, no one usually debates the value of watching football over the value of watching the news. It's just that most TV sets can't do two things at once. (ETs, of course, would rig picture-in-picture, but that's another story.) Once we diagnose the situation accurately, we've completed an important step toward conflict resolution.

Because negotiation is the most effective of all conflict-resolution strategies, negotiation skills are vital for the Chief Petty Officer. There are pitfalls, however, which should be avoided:

Discounting. Discounting occurs when a group member responds to another member's opinion or idea in such a way as to disregard it or consider it irrelevant. Nothing will debilitate negotiations so much as the practice of saying, in essence, "What you want or think doesn't matter."

Chief Amlin was at a chiefs' call a few days later. When the issue of morale came up, Chief Amlin suggested that one recreation tent really wasn't enough for a seven-hundred-member battalion. Before he could explain his point, CDMCM Hebron piped up: "I've got a real problem with that." Chief Amlin, nobody's fool, knew immediately the idea was a non-starter and dropped the subject.

Killer Phrases. We must be aware of the phrases we use to critically analyze another's ideas. Although it's not wrong to say how you feel about an idea, using phrases or lead-ins such as these can be debilitating to the recipient during group operation:

- Let me tell you where I am on that.
- Let me clear up your confusion on this.

- Well that's very interesting, but . . .
- Do you really believe that?
- Whatever. [grrrrr!]
- That's absurd.
- I don't buy that.
- I happen to know something about this.
- Wrong!
- I hate to insult your intelligence, but . . .
- Be serious, will you?
- There's no way.

Fault Finding. Fault finding is part of human nature. We're tempted to say, "I've been there, done that, and have the ball cap." Having been in the Navy for fifteen/twenty/ thirty years, we feel we have the right to tell people their ideas won't work because we've seen it all in the past. After all, if their idea works, we'll look like losers because we didn't think of it. We nit-pick new ideas or new solutions and think it makes us look powerful and wise. Sadly, nothing could be farther from the truth.

Our moral compass really does have two poles: our ethical posture and the way we react to conflict and controversy. If you haven't developed sound ethical principles, you'll waver in the wind each time you face a conflict or controversial decision. Be firm, be steadfast, but be certain that you are true to those beliefs that you know are right. You will take your beliefs into every aspect of leadership.

Morale and Esprit de Corps

Case Study: Slacking Off

It had been a long and tough deployment, but there was light at the end of the tunnel. MCB-34 had built bridges, repaired airfields, and constructed base facilities for both Navy and Marine units in Iraq. But, as the end of the deployment drew near, discipline and morale began to sag. "We've got to tighten things up around here," CMDCM Hebron announced to the CPO mess. "We're slacking off—understandable, I guess, given what we've been through—but I want to get this unit back on spot before we're relieved by MCB-1. You know how squared away those guys are. They call themselves the "first and the finest," but I want our discipline and morale to be at a high point when those guys arrive in country next month to relieve us. I'd like each of you to report to me those actions that you will take over the next several days to get your own shops ready when MCB-1 relieves us."

Discipline, morale, and esprit de corps are inseparable. A unit without morale cannot have true discipline, and, conversely, without discipline, no organization will have good morale. Discipline and morale are mutually reinforcing. And both are a Chief Petty Officer's responsibility.

Discipline is an individual's willing adherence to the set of rules that regulate conduct. These rules may be laws developed by duly constituted authority and recorded in writing, or they may be conventions, unwritten but sanctioned by custom and usage, known and respected by members of a society or organization. Sailors accept discipline for the good of the whole. Orderliness and discipline are indispensable to a military organization One of your most important tasks as a Chief Petty Officer is the development and maintenance of discipline in your organization.

CMC Brice returned to the vehicle maintenance area after the meeting. He noticed a few Seabees slacking off, listening to a boombox rather than working on the battalion's vehicles. He stopped for a moment and thought. "I could come down on those two Sailors like a ton of bricks, or I could just walk in there and let them know that I know they've been goofing off." Chuckling to himself, he entered the workspace.

Chief Brice, an experienced Chief Petty Officer, knew there are various ways of securing discipline.

Positive Discipline. When Sailors know what doing the right thing entails, and they choose to do it without specific orders, they are exhibiting positive discipline. Sailors with confidence in and respect for their leaders and the Navy will exhibit positive discipline. Sailors must be taught, however, to know their jobs and standards for positive discipline to function effectively.

Negative Discipline. Negative discipline is based strictly on the fear of consequences for violation of rules. A unit is well-disciplined when there's a maximum of efficiency and contentment generated through positive discipline, and a minimum of negative discipline or punishment. In the Navy, we think of discipline as "a prompt, willing responsiveness to commands." The best discipline is self-discipline—the Sailor doing the right thing because he or she wants to do the right thing. Self-discipline gained through building willingness, enthusiasm, and coopera-

We often find ourselves in unexpected and unfamiliar circumstances that test—and strengthen—our ability as leaders.
U.S. Navy (PH1 Shawn Eklund)

tion exists not only while personnel are under the eyes of their superiors, but when they are off duty as well.

Personal Example. Personal example is the manifestation of real integrity. In striving for a high level of discipline, each Chief Petty Officer must remember that Sailors admire a leader who lives in accordance with the code that is enforced. Nothing but resentment can result when a leader demands behavior from followers that is not expected of the boss. If you expect unflinching obedience and cooperation from Sailors, then give the same obedience and cooperation to your seniors. Combine that with ability and a genuine interest in the well-being of your Sailors, and you'll avoid a lot of problems.

Effective Chief Petty Officers:

- Maintain a general attitude of approval of the organization. Distrust your own superiors, and your Sailors will soon distrust you.

- Let Sailors know what is expected of them. This can be done by formal directives and by clear verbal instructions.

- Keep Sailors informed of their mission in any specific job. An individual works better when he fully understands where his or her work fits into the big picture.

- Let Sailors know that you are behind them as long as they perform their duties to the best of their abilities.

- Keep Sailors informed on the progress they are making. This is equally important whether their work is good or bad.

- Keep Sailors informed, within security restrictions, of changes that will affect their futures. If the deployment has been extended, as happened on USS *Abraham Lincoln* at the beginning of the Iraq War, say so. Don't beat around the bush.

- Assure Sailors by your actions that each of them will receive fair and impartial treatment.

- Improve your own professional ability. Sailors know what makes a good leader. Professional competence is still a major characteristic Sailors appreciate in those who lead them.

· Delegate authority, with corresponding responsibility, as far down in the organization as competence exists.

The Role of Punishment

As a Chief Petty Officer, you should never think of discipline and punishment as synonymous. Punishment, in fact, is deliberately dealt with in the next chapter, which also covers legal issues. The training and educational phase of discipline should be kept constantly in mind, even when it becomes necessary to resort to awarding punishment, the ultimate method of attaining discipline. Some individuals are so constituted that they do not respond to ordinary methods of training. In dealing with these individuals, you, as their Chief Petty Officer, should first attempt to influence them by positive methods of discipline. But if the individual fails to respond to these methods, you should not hesitate to utilize punishment or negative discipline as a leadership technique. Punishment is an element of discipline, albeit the final one.

Punishment is not a pleasant thing. Punishment is like dynamite: strong and dangerous, valuable and destructive, effective to a degree when used correctly, alarmingly destructive when used incorrectly, according to *Fundamentals of Naval Leadership*. Sailors, like everyone, are very largely controlled by two motives, the hope of reward and the fear of punishment. If it becomes necessary to suggest punishment for a particular act, consider the following.

Punishment must be prompt. To be effective, punishment must be prompt. This principle is so well-recognized that, with few exceptions such as murder, desertion, and fraud against the United States, the statutes of limitation prohibit prosecution of an accused person after a certain lapse of time if the suspected offender has not placed himself out of reach of justice. If you reprove a Sailor for some minor breach of discipline committed several months ago, the offender might well have forgotten the incident entirely or might rightfully entertain some doubts as to your competence as a leader. If reprimand or punishment is not given reasonably soon after the offense has been committed, the whole thing might best be forgotten.

Punishment must be impersonal and just. Punishment should never be personal, and it must never be vindictive; that is, never inflicted in revenge for misconduct. Punishment cannot right the wrong that has resulted from an act of dereliction. Instead, its value lies in the object lesson it furnishes—that the offense must not be repeated—to the wrongdoer and others. To be just, punishment must also be consistent, and the recipient and others must recognize it as just. Just punishment is punishment that is administered as soon after the offense as possible, that is not of such a nature as to lower a person's self-respect, and that is not so severe as to be out of all proportion to the gravity of the offense.

Punishment must be appropriate. Because people range from extreme sensitivity to great callousness in their reactions to punishment, any set scale of punishments for specific offenses has its limitations. Punishment should fit the crime and should fit the individual, too. Some Sailors are so constituted that a glance or expression of disapproval, a word of reproof, or even a hint that they have failed to measure up to what is expected of them, will be all that is needed to correct their breach of discipline. Others are so accustomed or hardened to the knocks of life that it takes more severe forms of punishment to make any impression.

Punishment is a command function. You are a leader, but you are not the sole authority in your division, department, or unit. Punishment is a command function, and it cannot be delegated. It can legally be awarded only by the accused's commanding officer or by a legally convened court-martial. You are not the prosecutor, judge, or jury, and if you violate these provisions, you do it at your own great peril. You may be tempted to "send them to mast, and let the XO sort it out." The indiscriminate use of non-judicial punishment against Sailors on charges that subsequently are found to be largely unfounded is a direct reflection on the Chief Petty Officer involved. Many things can be settled in the work center or in a forceful conversation on the fantail. Carefully investigate all angles of the case before placing a Sailor on report, and then do so only if convinced of the guilt of the person or when there is such grave doubt of the person's innocence that further investigation and more mature judgment by the commanding officer is necessary to exercise justice.

Reprimand privately, praise publicly. It is a cardinal rule to reprimand only in private, but to praise publicly. This concept is at the heart of positive discipline. We'll repeat this point time and again in this handbook.

The Chief Petty Officer and Unit Morale

An important role of Chief Petty Officers is developing and nurturing high morale among Sailors. High morale is an index of effective leadership. No control of human behavior is possible without it, and no failure is final unless the failure destroys morale. Morale is based on a Sailor's belief in himself or herself and in the cause for which we labor. High morale usually results when:

- Personal convictions and standards provide a positive goal and make daily life meaningful and worth living.
- Sailors are aware of specific tasks and problems that must be completed and solved in order to reach personal or unit goals.
- The Sailor's basic convictions and aims are in harmony with those of the other members of the unit. Otherwise, group action will be uncoordinated and the possibility of failure of the unit will be greatly increased.

Experienced Chief Petty Officers can walk aboard a ship or station, and, in a very short time, gauge the level of morale aboard. Ships and units have personalities— you can sense the vibes almost as soon as you cross the quarterdeck. Morale building is not an easy task. Morale is the state of mind of an individual that has been produced by all the circumstances that make his membership in the unit rewarding and satisfying. It is what an individual is getting out of being a member of that group that determines his mental state. Living conditions, food, quarters, discipline, pay, and duties all have a bearing. How important individual members of the group are made to feel will determine how good or how bad group morale is at any given time. Experienced chiefs know that Sailors' attitudes are a dependable measure of morale, and high morale is present only in those groups that have discipline and efficiency. Chief Petty Officers are the critical links.

Morale is generally high in units where Sailors believe:

- The Navy is an honorable and desirable career.
- Policies and practices are reasonable and sound, particularly in their unit.
- Training is thorough and good. If a Sailor is asked to do a job and does it well, the feeling of accomplishment usually improves morale.
- The job is appropriate to the Sailor's abilities and interests.
- All work receives proper recognition and reward.
- The Sailor is receiving consistent and impartial treatment.
- Living conditions are as good as circumstances permit.
- The Sailor's health, family, and personal problems are being cared for.
- As much free time and opportunity for recreation is provided as possible.
- That he or she is accepted and valued as an important member of a first class unit.

Building *Esprit de Corps*

Esprit de corps is the common spirit pervading among members of a unit. It implies enthusiasm, devotion, and zealous regard for the honor of the unit. Although morale usually refers to one person or many, esprit de corps is a unit spirit embodying a definite bond between Sailors in the unit and between Sailors and their leaders. With thoughtful leadership, this bond leads inevitably to a fiercely proud association with the unit. Today's Chief Petty Officer has the challenge of leading and motivating Sailors to the same intense pride in serving in their commands that has been demonstrated throughout the history of the U.S. Navy. Remember, Sailors in years past often manifested that pride by brawling with the crews of other ships in foreign ports! If the mighty battleship USS *New York* was the best fighting unit in the Pacific fleet, then USS *South Dakota* should not make that claim.

We're not suggesting a brawl when the fleet comes ashore—far from it. That's immature behavior and misguided pride. But it was pride nevertheless! Although we can't judge the behavior of the past in the light of today's Navy, we can understand how sailors felt about their commands back then because we feel the same way today. Today's Sailors are not motivated by the same methods as those of years past, but they still have much in common with the work hard, play hard Sailors who won World War II. All of us want to be part of a professional team with high standards, and we look for good reasons to be proud of our units. It is not enough to put up the sign touting the number of unreps conducted this deployment, as is commonly done on the AO, AOE, and other Log ships. Leadership must amplify and detail accomplishments as appropriate. Some Sailors just need one or two more facts to achieve a focused view of the importance of their unit and its mission and their own contributions to that mission. The CPO mess can meet this challenge only when it is part of a full leadership team effort.

Esprit de corps does not automatically appear in units that are efficient and well-disciplined, nor does it depend entirely on the unit being successful in competition with other units. Achieving esprit de corps may not be as difficult as the production of efficiency or discipline, but, in the final analysis, it is the driving force of a unit's success. An efficient, well-disciplined unit with esprit de corps will be hard to beat. Esprit de corps can be indicated or measured by the following:

- The expression of enthusiasm and pride in the unit's command by its members.
- The reputation of the unit among other units.
- The competitive spirit in the unit.
- The unit's staying power under conditions of stress.
- The attitude of the members toward one another and toward their leaders.
- The members' willingness to help one another.

One of the most accurate measures of esprit de corps is the willingness of Sailors to help one another. The Chief Petty Officer who builds esprit de corps in his outfit should point out to his Sailors the value of this spirit of brotherhood and sisterhood. In small, closely-knit units, it is a simple matter to persuade members that helping one another is an investment that always pays dividends.

The achievement and maintenance of esprit de corps requires confidence in leadership, stable leadership, and participation of all the Sailors. True spirit and pride in the outfit can be developed if each member recognizes the group's common interest and will cooperate toward the common goal. This spirit is dependent on the satisfactions that each Sailor gets from being a member of the group, and is aided by:

- The approval each participating member gets from other members.
- The disapproval or punishment received by non-cooperators.
- Competition with standards and other groups.
- The successes of the group and the recognition given to it.
- Ceremonies and the use of symbols of membership.

Points to Ponder

Case Study: Morale and Esprit de Corps

All of us have been at good commands and at not-so-good commands. What factors made your best ship or station best? What factors made your worst ship or station worst? Do you think others felt the same way?

Can one person really make a difference—positive or negative—about morale and esprit de corps? Think of shipmates who were live wires, who brightened a space just by entering it. Think of others who could put a damper on even the best of circumstances. Think about how you've acted at various times. Have you ever had an impact on your unit's morale or esprit de corps?

Author's Note. Not by accident have we highlighted our Seabee brothers and sisters in these chapters on values, discipline, morale, and esprit de corps. You'll find few Navy communities with such intense individual Sailor pride and consistently high unit esprit de corps as the Navy's Seabees. Wherever two or more Seabees are assigned, it's a fair bet they'll organize an annual Seabee ball to formally proclaim their Seabee pride and esprit de corps. This conscious and conscientious effort on the part of Seabee Chief Petty Officers has ensured their success and sacrifice for the past sixty-one years. From Midway to the Middle East, from the Aleutians to Afghanistan, "Can Do" is a motto that embodies esprit de corps. Let the wise chiefs of other communities learn from their success. Can Do—and Done Did!

3

Punishment and Legal Issues

Case Study: Theft of Command Property

"Well, there's not a whole lot of doubt about it, is there?" CMDCM Hebron remarked to MSC Chuckerly. "The police found about a half ton of our food supplies at that black marketer's house, and as they were hauling it out the front door, SA Kettering and CR Belmont were bringing in more stuff though the back door. I don't know how they got it past the gate guards and out the gate, but stick both of 'em in the scullery, with every grimy pot and pan you can find, until I see what we're going to do with them. It might be non-judicial punishment, but we may be getting involved in a special court-martial here, I suppose."

You're no doubt familiar with the fundamentals of military law and naval discipline. You may have been called as a witness at mast or a court-martial. As a Chief Petty Officer, you'll stand beside your Sailors should one be unfortunate enough to rate a mast or court. As sympathetic as you may be to the foibles of young and immature

Sailors, you have a duty to act honorably and fairly, to consider carefully the particulars of the case, and to act with respect for the rights of the Sailor as well as for the good of the unit and the Navy.

Legal Processes

Sources of Military Law

Until relatively recent times, the administration of justice in the Navy was largely the prerogative of the commanding officer, according to the law and customs of the sea. The sea is a cruel place, and ships' captains have traditionally had the power of life or death over the members of their crew. More recently, this power has been tempered by the standardization of laws and regulations designed to prevent the mistreatment and arbitrary punishment of military personnel. This power emanates from:

The Constitution. Article One, Section Eight, states that "Congress shall have the power . . . to make rules for the government and regulation of the land and naval forces."

Uniform Code of Military Justice (UCMJ). The UCMJ is the fundamental military law that applies to all members in every branch of the armed services.

Manual for Courts-Martial (MCM). The MCM explains the UCMJ and prescribes regulations that carry out the basic rules of the code for all branches of the service.

Manual of the Judge Advocate General (JAGMAN). The JAG Manual applies only to the Navy and Marine Corps. It implements the UCMJ and other regulations outlined in the MCM within the Department of the Navy and contains regulations pertaining to administrative law.

Criminal Justice

Articles 78 through 134 of the UCMJ define military crimes. Each crime is defined in terms of a group of facts or elements, each of which must exist for the crime to have taken place. In addition, Part IV of the MCM describes the elements of each article of the UCMJ. Each section provides the text of a UCMJ article, the elements of the crime described in that article, and a short explanation of the elements. Finally, each section identifies the permissible maximum punishment for the crime and provides a sample showing the language that should be used to charge an individual with the crime.

In order for an offense to be disposed of under the military justice system, both the accused and the crime must be under military jurisdiction. In addition, certain other procedural requirements must be met.

Jurisdiction Over the Accused. The accused is subject to military jurisdiction if he or she is an active-duty Sailor or a cadet, midshipman, or reserve member on active duty. Certain categories of reservists not on active duty and certain civilians are also subject to military jurisdiction.

Jurisdiction Over the Offense. An offense is subject to military jurisdiction if it is related in some way to the individual's military service. An offense occurring on board a naval vessel or at a shore installation would always be considered service-connected, although an offense that takes place off base may not be, depending on the circumstances. For example, almost every involvement of military members with the use, possession, and distribution of drugs is considered service-connected.

Statute of Limitations. Article 43 of the UCMJ requires that the trial of most types of offenses begin within five years. Exceptions to this rule are any offense punishable by death, unauthorized absence, or missing a movement of a ship during wartime. For periods of unauthorized absence, the statute-of-limitations clock begins to run when the period of absence ends.

Former Jeopardy. This concept, often referred to as double jeopardy, means that an accused cannot be tried twice for the same offense. A previous trial that did not result in

an acquittal is not considered a complete trial for purposes of former jeopardy and is not a bar to a second trial.
A trial by a state or foreign country, whatever the outcome, is also not a bar to a trial by court-martial, which is
conducted under federal law.

Former Punishment. An individual who has received non-
judicial punishment for a particular minor offense may
not then be tried at court-martial for the same offense.
The word minor is key. If the offense is not minor, or if
it turns out to be more serious than it appeared at the
time the NJP hearing was held, the imposition of non-
judicial punishment will not serve as a bar to trial by
court-martial.

As the story began to unfold, LN1 Celina met with CMDCM
Hebron. "It looks like we've got a pretty good case here. The MAA
caught both of them with the goods in their hands. Fortunately,
our guys were well enough trained to issue Miranda warnings
right on the spot, as did the department leading chief when he
talked to them, and as everyone else has done every time we've
moved this case forward. We tell everyone that it only takes a
second—and don't feel like you're pretending to be Kojak or Dick
Tracy when you do it—but that's the way the rules are written,
and if we don't follow them, any case can fall apart quickly."

Procedural Rules

As a Chief Petty Officer, you may become involved in specific judicial procedures regarding your Sailors.

Apprehension. Apprehension is the act of taking a person
into custody. Officers, petty officers, masters-at-arms,
and Naval Criminal Investigative Service (NCIS) agents
have the authority to apprehend anyone who is subject to
the UCMJ. Apprehension may entail voluntary submission by the person apprehended, or it may require the use

of physical force. The individual performing the apprehension is required to make the situation clear by first saying, "I am placing you in custody" (or something similar), then identifying himself or herself to the person being apprehended and stating a reason for the apprehension. All apprehensions must be based on probable cause, i.e., facts and circumstances must exist that would lead a reasonable person to conclude that an offense has been or is being committed, and that the person to be apprehended committed or is in the process of committing the offense.

Restraint. Once a suspect is apprehended, the appropriate authority may impose restraint. Restraint may be moral rather than physical, as when a suspect is ordered to remain within the limits of a particular command. Restraint may also, of course, be physical. A suspect may be placed in restraint pending disciplinary action if the appropriate authority, acting in a neutral and detached manner, has a reasonable belief that an offense has been committed, that the person to be restrained committed it, and that restraint is warranted under the circumstances. Restraint is considered to be warranted when the individual is a flight risk or when there are reasonable grounds to believe that he or she will engage in future acts of serious misconduct if not restrained.

Searches and Seizures. The Fourth Amendment, which protects against unreasonable searches and seizures, also applies to military personnel. Evidence obtained by an unlawful search may not be admissible in a court-martial proceeding. Inspections in which the primary purpose is not to seek evidence of a crime (e.g., a health and welfare inspection of a berthing area or an inventory of a supply storeroom) are not considered searches, and evidence that turns up during such inspections is admissible in a trial by court-martial. The products of searches, which are conducted specifically to seek evidence of crimes, are also admissible provided that the searches are legally conducted.

Investigations

If law enforcement professionals such as masters at arms, legalmen, or JAG Corps officers are available, you are not likely to be deeply involved in the investigative phase, but you must be aware of the procedures involved

Initiation of Charges. Any civilian or Sailor may initiate charges against another Sailor, either orally or in writing. Once charges have been initiated and the CO or designated command representative determines that the situation warrants further investigation, the command appoints an investigating officer.

Conduct of the Investigation. If the offense is a minor one, a preliminary inquiry officer (PIO), quite frequently a Chief Petty Officer, normally conducts the investigation. This officer interviews witnesses, examines any physical or documentary evidence, and advises the accused of his or her rights before taking an oral or written statement. After concluding the investigation, the PIO forwards a report up the chain of command that includes a brief summary of the evidence, comments on the performance and prior disciplinary record of the accused, and a recommendation for the disposition of the offense.

Administrative Actions

Appropriate administrative actions might include:

- Performance counseling (oral).
- Performance counseling (written).
- Extra military instruction (EMI).
- Loss of privileges.
- Appropriate comments or downgraded marks in evaluations.
- Adjustment or withdrawal of security clearances.
- Withholding or withdrawal of advancement recommendations.

- Reassignment or delay of reassignment.
- Detachment for cause (DFC).
- Administrative Separation from the Navy.

If privileges are withheld, the individual who has the power to grant the privilege (such as special liberty, the wearing of civilian clothing, or on-base driving) also has the power to revoke that privilege. Although privileges may be withheld, rights such as compensation, medical care, quarters, food, and normal liberty may not be administratively withheld. Normal liberty may be withheld administratively only by the use of extra military instruction (EMI), the extension of working hours as necessary to accomplish mission requirements, limited authorized health and safety reasons, and the overseas liberty risk program. Administra-tive actions are not legally considered punishment and are not intended to serve in lieu of punishment. Punishment may be awarded only at mast or by a court-martial. Administrative actions may be taken in addition to or instead of disciplinary action as circumstances warrant. Such action does not preclude further disciplinary action, and in many cases both disciplinary action and appropriate administrative actions are taken.

Non-Judicial Punishment (NJP)

After completing the investigation, and consulting with the local authorities, the commanding officer decided that non-judicial punishment (captain's mast) was the appropriate course of action for these two Sailors. The skipper considered:

Authority to Impose NJP. The authority to impose NJP rests with the commander, CO, or officer in charge (OIC) of a unit. The CO has NJP authority over all military personnel who are members of the command at the time the punishment is imposed, regardless of whether such authority existed at the time the crime occurred. This authority extends to all personnel temporarily assigned to the command and members of embarked staffs and units.

Types of Offenses. The CO has broad discretion to decide whether to handle an offense administratively, to pursue NJP, or to refer it to a court-martial. In general, NJP is used for minor offenses that could not result in a dishonorable discharge or in confinement for more than one year if tried at a court-martial.

Executive Officer's Inquiry (XOI). Most commands precede NJP with an informal hearing called the executive officer's inquiry. The XO reviews the report of the PIO and may personally examine the evidence and interview witnesses, the chain of command, and the accused before making a determination whether to forward the case to the CO for NJP. Some commands utilize a disciplinary review board (DRB) consisting of the command master chief and other senior enlisted members who review the evidence and make recommendations for disposition of the case prior to, or instead of, XO's mast. Many experienced CPOs consider the DRB to be a developmental as well as disciplinary tool. The DRB will be discussed in detail later in this chapter.

Refusal of NJP. Sailors who are not attached to or embarked in a vessel may refuse NJP and request court-martial. The right to refuse NJP expires when punishment is imposed. The accused has the right to be present at the NJP hearing. Although he or she may request to waive the right to a personal appearance, the CO may require appearance. An NJP hearing may not be held on someone who is an unauthorized absentee or is otherwise in absentia.

Rights at NJP. The accused has the right to remain silent, to have a personal representative (not necessarily an attorney), to examine the evidence against him or her, to present matters in defense or in mitigation and extenuation, and to call any reasonably available witnesses. Civilian witnesses may not be subpoenaed to appear at an NJP hearing. The accused does not have the right to consult with an attorney, and military attorneys are not appointed to represent Sailors at NJP, although those who have the right to refuse NJP must be afforded the opportunity to consult with an attorney specifically about that right. The accused may hire a civilian lawyer at his or her own expense, but this lawyer enjoys no special status at NJP beyond that of any other personal representative. The accused has the right to a public hearing but may request a closed mast. If the CO grants the request for a closed mast, at least one other witness, such as the command master chief, generally remains present.

As the name indicates, NJP is not a judicial proceeding, and imposition of punishment is not considered a finding of guilt or a conviction. Military rules of evidence do not apply at NJP; the commanding officer's standard for imposing punishment is a preponderance of the evidence rather than proof beyond a reasonable doubt. However, commanders generally do not pursue NJP in cases in which the evidence would not be sufficient for a court-martial conviction.

At NJP, the CO may take one of the following actions:

- Dismiss the offense, with or without warning, and/or take administrative measures.
- Impose authorized punishment.
- Refer the matter to a court-martial.
- Postpone the matter, such as when waiting for additional evidence to become available.

The punishments at NJP vary, depending on the pay grade of the CO imposing the punishment. A CO who is a lieutenant commander or above is authorized to impose punishments that include:

- Punitive reprimand or admonition.
- Restriction to the limits of the ship or, for a shore command, to prescribed limits of the command, for up to sixty days; or correctional custody for up to thirty days; or, if attached to or embarked in a vessel, confinement on bread and water for up to three days.
- Extra duties of no more than two hours per day for up to forty-five days.

- Reduction in rate one pay grade.
- Forfeiture of up to one-half of one month's pay for up to two months.

These punishments are more severe than those that may be imposed by COs below pay grade O-4 or by OICs of any rank The entire punishment may be set aside, or the unexecuted portion of it may be remitted by the officer imposing NJP, by his or her successor in command, by the Sailor's next CO if the member is transferred, or by a higher appellate authority. Such actions must normally be taken within four months of the date of the imposition of punishment, and they may be undertaken only to correct a clear injustice. In addition, these same authorities may mitigate the punishment by reducing it in quantity or severity, or suspend the punishment for up to six months. Suspension is normally contingent on another action being performed by the individual, such as completion of a rehabilitation course or restitution to a victim of theft or vandalism. Someone who violates the terms of suspension or UCMJ may have his or her initial sentence vacated by any authority competent to impose punishment.

A Sailor may appeal any punishment awarded at NJP to the area coordinator or flag officer with general court-martial authority. There are only two grounds for appeal: that the punishment was unjust (the evidence did not indicate that the accused committed the offense) or that the punishment was disproportionate (excessively harsh or unfair) in relation to the offense. Appeals must be filed in writing via the officer imposing the punishment within five calendar days, although extensions may be requested and granted. An individual appealing NJP may request a stay of any restriction, extra duty, or confinement on bread and water pending the outcome of the appeal.

Courts-Martial

Courts-martial are used to try more serious offenses than those normally disposed of at non-judicial punishment, although less serious offenses may also be referred to court-martial when a Sailor refuses NJP. The standard of proof for conviction at a court-martial is "beyond a reasonable doubt."

Summary Court-Martial (SCM). The function of a summary court-martial is to exercise justice promptly for relatively minor offenses. Any CO may convene an SCM. Any person subject to the UCMJ, except officers, cadets, and midshipmen, may be tried by summary court-martial. A summary court-martial is composed of one commissioned officer in pay grade O-3 or above in the same armed force as the accused. All personnel have the right to consult with counsel prior to the court-martial, but not to be represented by counsel. Personnel may refuse trial by summary court-martial, in which case the offense will likely be referred to a higher court-martial. The maximum punishment that may be awarded at an SCM is confinement at hard labor for thirty days, for those in pay grade E-4 and below; reduction in rate to pay grade E-1, for those in pay grade E-4 and below, or reduction in rate one pay grade, for those above pay grade E-4; and forfeiture of two-thirds of a month's pay for one month.

Special Court-Martial (SPCM). A special court-martial is convened for non-capital or capital crimes for which the mandatory sentence for the crime does not exceed the maximum punishment that such a court may impose. A CO or anyone senior to the CO in the chain of command may convene an SPCM. The court consists of at least three members; any commissioned or warrant officers are eligible to serve on the court-martial. If the accused so requests, enlisted members, usually Chief Petty Officers, may serve on the court-martial. A two-thirds majority is required to convict. The accused may also request a trial by military judge alone. A Sailor appearing before an SPCM has the right to be represented by counsel, who may be either a military lawyer or a civilian lawyer retained at the expense of the accused. A trial counsel represents the government. The maximum punishment that an SPCM may impose on an enlisted member is either (1) a bad-conduct discharge, confinement at hard labor for six months, forfeiture of two-thirds pay per month for six months, and a reduction in rate to pay grade E-1; or (2) the maximum punishment for that particular offense, whichever is less.

General Court-Martial (GCM). The convening authority for a general court-martial is generally a flag officer or other senior officer serving as an area coordinator. A general court-martial is convened for capital crimes and serious non-capital crimes. The court consists of at least five members; as in the special court-martial, the court may include any commissioned or warrant officers or, if the accused so requests, enlisted members. In most circumstances a two-thirds majority is required to convict; imposition of more than ten years at hard labor requires a three-fourths majority; and imposition of the death penalty must be unanimous. In non-capital cases an accused may request a trial by military judge alone.

A Sailor appearing before a GCM has the right to be represented by counsel, either a military lawyer or a civilian lawyer retained at his or her own expense. A trial counsel represents the government. The maximum punishment that may be imposed on a Sailor by a GCM is the maximum punishment for the particular offense. This may be death, dishonorable discharge, confinement at hard labor for life, total forfeiture of pay, or reduction in rate to pay grade E-1.

Administrative Law

An administrative fact-finding body, which may be as small as one individual, is constituted under the Manual of the Judge Advocate General to collect and record information on a particular incident. Such investigations are commonly referred to as JAG Manual investigations. Common situations in which such an investigation would be initiated are accidents resulting in serious injury, death, or significant damage to or loss of government property. An administrative fact-finding body is not judicial; its findings and opinions do not represent legal judgments. The findings may, however, be used as the basis for a convening authority's decision to pursue a trial by court-martial. JAG Manual investigations may be informal fact-finding bodies, formal fact-finding bodies, or courts of inquiry, depending on the seriousness of the incidents under investigation.

Line of Duty/Misconduct Investigations. Whenever a Sailor is seriously injured or contracts a serious disease, a specific type of JAG Manual investigation, called a line of duty/misconduct investigation, must be conducted. This investigation reviews the circumstances of the injury or illness and makes specific recommendations on whether the injury/illness occurred in the line of duty and whether it was due to the individual's own misconduct.

"Line of duty" is not synonymous with "on duty" or "while performing official duties" but rather indicates the Sailor's good standing at the time of the incident. Injuries or illness that occur while the individual is not an unauthorized absentee, and that do not occur as a result of his or her own misconduct, are presumed to have occurred in the line of duty.

"Misconduct" is wrongful conduct. An illness or injury is considered to be due to the Sailor's own misconduct when it results from gross negligence, reckless disregard of the consequences, or commission of a crime. A finding of misconduct always results in a finding of "not in the line of duty." Although a similar investigation is done when an injury or illness results in death, opinions as to line of duty and misconduct are not expressed in the investigation report. In such cases the Veterans Administration makes this determination.

Disciplinary Review Boards (DRBs)

Disciplinary Review Boards are held by Chief Petty Officers before proceeding to non-judicial punishment at the executive-officer level. The use of DRBs is strictly at the commanding officer's discretion. COs who establish DRBs do so to more formally and consistently utilize the CPO Mess to uphold good order and discipline through additional investigative inquiry, review of case findings, and recommendations for action.

The DRB is not designed to replace or shortcut the chain of command. Rather, it is intended to support the command by providing additional wisdom, experience, and authority in the disciplinary process. Composition of the board may vary, depending on the command, but in general the board consists of at least three Chief Petty Officers, or senior or master chiefs, and is headed by the command master chief. It is essential that newly advanced or newly assigned chiefs observe a few sessions of the command board before participating actively.

The DRB is utilized selectively and may not be convened for every infraction. This is also true for XOI; some particularly egregious infractions go directly to captain's mast with no DRB and no formal XOI. In general, there are some offenses that are likely to be referred directly to the CO for resolution:

- Assault and/or battery.
- Abuse or possession of illegal drugs, and/or illicit use of controlled substances.
- Cases where extensive investigation under UCMJ article 32 are appropriate.
- Cases of a very sensitive nature.

Even in these cases, however, the commanding officer may, in his or her discretion, use the DRB as a fact-finding board after the initial review of the details.

The command master chief will convene the board, establishing time and place of the meeting. Scheduling the DRB is not as flexible as other CPO mess functions such as the professional development board (PDB) but is driven by unpredictable and inflexible factors. The chief master-at-arms will ensure that the necessary paperwork is complete and provided to the board. This includes, but is not limited to, NAVPERS 1626/7 (Enclosure Three)

Report and Disposition of Offenses and NAVPERS 1626/7 (Enclosure Four) Details of Offense Worksheet.

The actual conduct of the DRB is discretionary and varies from a review of the paper work and facts of the case to a full "interview" of selected witnesses as well as the accused offender. In all cases, great care must be taken to ensure the proceedings are dignified and convey the fact-finding and extra attention to detail in meting out justice that the CO intended by chartering and using a DRB.

Recommendations must not be shared with the accused, or for that matter with anyone except the chain of command. The DRB makes thoughtful recommendations and then fully supports the actions taken by the XO and CO, regardless of whether or not their recommendations were acted upon. When the DRB members begin to think they have the final word, the process is out of control, and the CMC must take appropriate action in counseling, training, or reconstituting the board membership.

Legal Protections

To meet our mission requirements, each member of the Navy team must be treated fairly, with dignity and respect, and must be allowed to work in an environment free of discrimination. Additionally, every Sailor is expected to abide by our core values of honor, courage, and commitment. Sailors who believe in and embrace our core values do not engage in negative, destructive behaviors such as sexual harassment and discrimination and will not condone those behaviors in others. Our job, as Chief Petty Officers, is to see to it that the areas we control—our divisions, our work spaces, and, yes, our personal lives—are free from any negative influences which would make any of our shipmates feel uncomfortable or threatened as they serve their nation.

Cultural Diversity

The face of America is changing, and the changing face of our nation means a changing face for our Navy. As recently as World War II, the Navy was overwhelmingly of European descent, and, even then, from a relatively small number of cultures. Today, less than 65 percent of our Navy is Caucasian, and the number of African American, Hispanic, and Asian Sailors continues to outpace the proportional growth in the general population. We're a nation founded on the principles that all men and women are created equal. Equal opportunity simply means the right of all persons to participate in, and benefit from, programs and activities for which they are qualified.

Command Managed Equal Opportunity (CMEO) Program. The Navy has established local CMEO programs to ensure that our practices reflect our principles. Generally under the direction of the command master chief, commands monitor and administer the equal opportunity program and assess the command's equal opportunity climate surrounding morale, teamwork, and communication.

Sexual Harassment

Sexual harassment is not just about sex but about abusing power. In today's Navy, sexual harassment is prohibited. All personnel, either military or civilian, will be provided a work environment free from unlawful discrimination, which includes sexual harassment. Even off-duty or non-duty behaviors that affect the military workplace may also be considered to be sexual harassment.

While at Recruit Training Command and at mandatory general military training sessions every year thereafter, all Sailors receive training in the areas of identification, prevention, resolution, and elimination of sexual harassment. Behavior that is sexual in nature includes, but is not limited to, telling sexually explicit jokes, displaying sexually suggestive pictures, and talking about sex. Some people would consider other behaviors, such as touching, to be sexual in some cases but not in others. Using common sense will normally be enough to determine whether or not a certain behavior is sexual in nature.

For sexual harassment to occur, unwelcome sexual behavior must occur in or impact on the work environment. When recipients are offered or denied something that is work-connected in return for submitting to or rejecting unwelcome sexual behavior, they have been subjected to a type of sexual harassment known as "quid pro quo" or "this for that." Examples include getting or losing a job, a promotion or demotion, a good or bad performance evaluation, etc. Normally, this is from a senior to a junior, because the senior person has something to offer.

When the unwelcome sexual behavior of one or more persons in a workplace interferes with another person's work performance, sexual harassment has occurred. If the behavior produces a work atmosphere that is offensive, intimidating, or abusive to another person, whether or not work performance is affected, a type of sexual harassment called "hostile environment" has occurred. Witnesses of sexual harassment, as well as the recipient of the offending behavior, may experience a hostile work environment.

Following are a few examples of behavior that could create a hostile environment:

- Using sexually explicit or sexually offensive language.
- Displaying sexually oriented posters or calendars.
- Touching someone or self in a suggestive manner.
- Giving someone unwelcome letters, cards, or gifts of a personal nature, particularly when these items have sexual overtones.
- Unwanted or uninvited pressure for dates.

As a Chief Petty Officer, you may be called upon to conduct investigations into alleged incidents of sexual harassment, and, if so, you will receive additional training in current policy on equal opportunity and investigative methods and processes. Some basic principles include:

- Individuals who believe they have been sexually harassed shall be provided the opportunity to seek resolution and redress.

- Commanders and those in supervisory positions shall ensure that notification of sexual harassment can be made in a command climate that does not tolerate acts of reprisal, intimidation, or further acts of harassment.
- All personnel shall be made aware of the avenues of resolution and redress that are available.
- All reported incidents of sexual harassment shall be investigated and resolved at the lowest appropriate level.
- All incidents shall be resolved promptly and with sensitivity.
- Confidentiality will be maintained to the extent possible.
- Counseling support or referral services will be made available for all personnel involved in incidents of sexual harassment.

The penalties for inappropriate conduct are severe. Penalties can range from informal counseling, comments in fitness reports and evaluations, administrative separation, and through punitive measures up to and including court-martial.

All reported incidents of unlawful discrimination or sexual harassment shall be investigated in a fair, impartial, and prompt manner and resolved at the lowest appropriate level. The nature of the investigation will depend upon the particular facts and circumstances and may consist of an informal inquiry where that action is sufficient to resolve factual issues. Administrative investigations will be conducted at the local command as appropriate. Reprisal investigations will normally be handled at the next higher level in the chain of command.

If the subject of the complaint is the commander, and his or her motivation in a particular situation could legitimately be called into question (as in the case of writing the complainant's fitness/evaluation report), the commander shall consider requesting an appropriate reporting senior to fulfill his or her responsibilities.

A sexual harassment complaint should be made within sixty days of the offending incident, or in the case of a series of incidents, within sixty days of the most recent incident.

Commanders may accept complaints beyond this time frame if, in their judgment, circumstances warrant.

Don't Ask—Don't Tell

Much has been written about the Defense Department's position on homosexuality in today's military. Much of what has been written is wrong, and, certainly, most fantail discussions are wrong. In 1994, after extensive study and deliberation that included extensive congressional testimony, the secretary of defense ordered a policy change that was tagged by the media as "Don't ask, don't tell." The actual change involved a deletion of the recruiting questionnaire question on homosexuality and a revised criteria for dealing with homosexual conduct in the armed forces. Homosexual conduct was deemed to be incompatible with naval service. The primary change to procedure stated that a commander may initiate an investigation into alleged homosexual conduct only upon receipt of credible information of such conduct. The fact that a service member reports being threatened or harassed because he or she is said or perceived to be a homosexual shall not, by itself, constitute credible information.

The report of a threat or harassment should result in prompt investigation of the threat or harassment itself. Investigators should not solicit allegations concerning sexual orientation or homosexual conduct of the threatened or harassed person. If, during the course of an investigation, information is received that the service member has engaged in homosexual conduct, commanders should carefully consider the source of that information and the circumstances under which it was provided in assessing its credibility. Such information does not negate the need to investigate the alleged harasser.

Homosexual conduct is grounds for administrative separation only if the service member's commanding officer has received credible evidence of such conduct. Responsibility to determine whether evidence is credible remains exclusively with the commanding officer.

Credible evidence is information that supports a reasonable belief that a service member has made a homosexual statement, engaged, or attempted to engage, in a homosexual act, or entered into, or attempted to enter into, a homosexual marriage. In short, it is reliable evidence from a trustworthy individual who has first-hand knowledge of facts and circumstances surrounding the alleged activity or statement. It may also consist of documents or other evidence that is obtained from a reliable source. Credible evidence is not based on rumor, hearsay, or suspicion.

Investigation is the province of trained personnel who will ensure that individual rights and service policy are respected. Investigations are limited to factual circumstances directly related to specific allegations. In most cases where a service member has stated that he or she is a homosexual or bisexual and does not contest separation, little or no investigation should be necessary. A commander who suspects that a service member has made such a statement for purpose of seeking separation from the naval service in order to avoid a service obligation, such as a deployment, obligated service, or payback of educational benefits, and who believes that the member is not a person who engages in, attempts to engage in, has a propensity to engage in, or intends to engage in homosexual acts, may initiate a more substantial investigation only when authorized.

General Guidelines. The chain of command is the primary and preferred channel for identifying and correcting discriminatory practices. This includes the processing and resolving of complaints of unlawful discrimination and sexual harassment. Commanders have direct responsibility for managing the complaint process. They must ensure that the informal and formal complaint resolution systems are clearly communicated and well understood by all personnel.

Witnesses to unlawful discrimination or sexual harassment are held accountable for reporting offenses through the chain of command promptly, if:

- The situation is not resolved or objectionable behavior does not stop.
- Addressing the objectionable behavior directly with the person concerned is not reasonable under the circumstances.
- Behavior is clearly criminal in nature.

Sometimes the situation is sticky. If the person demonstrating the objectionable behavior is a direct superior in the chain of command or the chain of command condones the conduct or ignores a report, individuals who have been subjected to or who observe objectionable behavior are encouraged to promptly communicate the incident through other available means. That may mean a "workaround" to the next highest level or bringing the matter directly to the attention of the legal department. Never let fear of upsetting the apple cart keep you from bringing a situation to higher authorities. Even uninvolved parties have a clear reporting duty under certain circumstances.

Our Role as Leaders

One of the real challenges that must be met head-on by the chiefs' mess is to ensure that the commitment to our core values is real and true, but not to allow it to be perverted into a pursuit of some hyper-sterile environment. No one, or at least no Sailor I have ever known, is interested in a workplace so politically correct that good-natured fun, whimsy, and creative humor are all out of bounds. You will always be striving to preserve the balance that includes a time and place for good-natured kidding and humor that doesn't threaten or offend anyone. That may sound easy, but it is not. It is a challenge that you are up to, but only with continued vigilance and a full knowledge of what is at stake. Your Navy training and experience, your desire for the command mission to succeed, and your commitment to the core values of the Navy you love all equip and prepare you for the challenge.

Solid, thoughtful leadership is the key to eliminating unlawful discrimination. Sound leadership is the cornerstone of the effort to eliminate sexual harassment. Sound leadership is, among other things, Chief Petty Officers who truly care about the Sailors in their charge. As chiefs we occupy a unique position in the chain of command that gives us constantly recurring opportunity to set the example in treating all people with dignity and respect. These responsibilities regarding sexual harassment are integral parts of the broader responsibility that we as leaders have. We work together to foster a positive climate and swiftly take appropriate corrective action when conduct is disruptive, provoking, discriminatory, or otherwise unprofessional.

Points to Ponder

Case Study: Theft of Command Property

Nothing is quite as destructive to good order and discipline as a thief in our midst. Some might say, "Well, it's not personal property—it's not like they were breaking into lockers or taking shipmates' personal gear." How would you react to that sentiment?

Some Sailors are irritated that the judicial process seems to take forever. They see offenders coming and going as if nothing has happened. "We ought to lock them all up and throw away the key—the heck with all this talk about 'rehabilitation' and giving them another chance." How do you feel about what you've seen and heard on this subject?

Suppose you were at a small or remote command, with little legal support. How would you feel if you were faced with taking action without the close and easy counsel of specialists? Would you know where to turn for support?

4

Leadership in Action

Case Study: A Day in the Life of a CPO Selectee

BM1 McKenzie, a CPO selectee, was late. He checked his watch as he cleared the gate at Naval Station Everett and headed down toward the piers. "Every month the traffic around here gets worse and worse," he thought to himself as he pulled into the parking area near USS *Gerald W. Farrier* (DDG-49). "Wow, I've got ten whole minutes to get on board and get ready for quarters. And after that, we've got to get that radar antenna down to the deck and over the side to the pier. I think I called the yard crew yesterday, or did I? And after that, I've got to be sure that the painting is going OK, and that everything that senior chief told me yesterday gets done. Did he say he wants to meet with me this morning, or is that tomorrow? And, oh, brother! I've got that selectees meeting at 1530, and I've got to look up all that stuff about how to effectively supervise Sailors, monitor their performance, and how best to conduct inspections to make sure everything is up to standard. I'll never get everything done today!"

Leadership in action! The chapter's title conjures up images of the Chief Petty Officer in dynamic situations—combat, fire fighting, damage control—the full range of Navy missions. The real truth of CPO effectiveness is less glamorous, however. The real truth is found in our far less exotic daily routine, in effective planning and training, and in reliable day-to-day direction, supervision, and oversight of the action. These activities require the chief to manage time, to be present on the deckplates, and to constantly anticipate and prepare for the worst-case contingencies.

Most of us feel like BM1 McKenzie sometimes. Operational tempo is higher than ever, manning levels are still not where they need to be, and we're asked to fit ten pounds of (sand) into a five-pound bag. Time is a resource, just like money, parts, tools, or crew. Most of us are cautious with our money, but we know there are always ways to get a little bit more. We're cautious with our tools, too, but in a pinch, good chiefs know how to dig up what's needed when necessary. Time is our one finite and non-renewable resource, and yet we often squander it needlessly.

Time Management

Time management is the skill that balances commitments against the clock and calendar. Just as there are successful strategies to manage your finances, there are strategies to manage your time, too. Try a little experiment for a few days. If time management is a problem for you, draw up a time log detailing where you are and what you're doing at fifteen-minute intervals. The log makes time visible, displays it in black and white, and you can analyze where your time is going. You may find these hints helpful:

Prioritize. Prioritize your commitments. All of us have must-do commitments. Sick call, for instance, doesn't work well if the corpsman isn't there. Other things fall into the nice-to-do category, things like stopping by the mess mid-morning to get the latest gouge. Decide what is really important and be certain it gets done first.

Identify quality time. When you need to accomplish the most, schedule your highest priority assignments for your best time. For some that may be the forenoon, for others, later in the day.

Avoid overscheduling. Try not to over-commit. Sure, we all want to be seen as squared away. But it's better to do a few things well than to do many things poorly. If your plate is full, it may be better to pass on the opportunity to mentor a chief selectee or take an active role in planning the next dining-in.

Develop and use a calendar. You don't need a PDA or a laptop to keep a good schedule. An inexpensive wheel book shoved in your back pocket can help ensure that you are in the right place at the right time.

Control interruptions. Sure, you've got to respond to GQ, Man Overboard, and calls from the executive officer, but does Seaman Henderson really have to see you, right now, about going on leave next month? Unexpected interruptions are the biggest thief of most leaders' time, yet they are the easiest to control. If you have a door, shut it. If you have voice mail, use it. Voice mail and email can store information until you are able to respond.

Complete tasks. Strive to complete tasks adequately before reaching for perfection. Perfection is not worth the extra time that it takes in many routine assignments. Move on to the next task.

Prepare for the unexpected. Build in slack time to handle the unexpected. When unexpected events arise, decide immediately how to make up the planned activities that were missed and adjust your schedule accordingly.

Procrastination

Wise men call procrastination the thief of time. Everyone procrastinates at one time or another—writers of naval manuals are past masters at this. Procrastinators know exactly what we should be doing, even as we develop strategies to avoid unpleasant or difficult tasks. Most procrastinators are optimists, thinking they will be able to complete a task by the deadline. Some procrastinators may be calling attention to how busy they are; some may deliberately delay to irritate others. Whatever the reason, it's often easier and takes less energy to buckle down and do the work required and on time.

Goal Setting

Setting rational goals helps us avoid procrastination and manage our time effectively. Good goals are usually specific. A specific goal has a much greater chance of being accomplished than a general goal. To set a specific goal, answer the six questions reporters ask:

- Who: What Sailors are involved?
- What: What really needs to be done?
- Where: Identify a location.
- When: Establish a schedule, with checkpoints and a firm end date.
- Why: What's the purpose or benefit?
- How: How best can this be accomplished?

Goals are measurable, and measuring progress helps you stay on target. Establish solid criteria for measuring your progress toward the goal. Ask yourself how much, how many, and how will we know when we win?

Goals must be attainable, and you develop the attitudes, abilities, skills, and the capability to reach them. You begin seeing previously overlooked opportunities to bring yourself closer to the achievement of your goals. Ask yourself if the goal is important, meaningful, and within your capability. The answers to all three should be yes.

Develop a time line or schedule and stick to it. There are lots of tools available to assist you in time management, including Gantt charts, Pert charts, and other project-planning systems. They can be invaluable in keeping you on task and on target.

BM1 McKenzie made it aboard in time, and, after quarters, headed for his desk in the bos'n hole. "Man, I know I've got that note from senior chief around here somewhere. Did he want to get together today or tomorrow?" He moved the large fid that kept the eighteen-inch-high stack of folders, papers, memos, and mid-rat boxes together, and the pile tumbled to the deck. He grabbed at the stack at random, looking for the elusive email. "What's today? 29 July? Half this stuff is from last January when we were in the gulf with *Abraham Lincoln.* Darn! Where did I put that note?"

Organization

Some people are organized by nature. For the rest of us, there's still hope. Efficiency experts tell us that more than 90 percent of all paper—memos, emails, letters, and what-have-you—is never consulted after three months. With the exception of those things that are required by law, regulation, or custom (logbooks, classified publications, and the like), almost all informal paper can be deep-sixed as soon as it is no longer relevant. Think of the number of filing cabinets to be freed up. Indeed, as in the case of USS *Pueblo,* which sailed with so much classified material that it filled passageways and could never be destroyed in the time available, keeping paper around may hinder rather than help you complete your mission.

Set aside time to discard or file things lying around. You'll feel better, your workspace will better organized, and you'll save time in the long run.

Paper Shuffling. The oft-quoted secret to office organization is to handle each piece of paper as little as possible. Ideally, you should handle each item only once—when you are taking action. A good system is to classify each item in one of four categories:

- Act: Take action on the issue or delegate it to a Sailor. Make notes to follow up on the appropriate date.
- Hold: Retain the item until all necessary information is in place to help with decisions.

- Stow: Stow the material logically in an orderly and organized system. Your leading yeoman can help you understand the Navy's filing system.
- Deep-six: Shred or otherwise appropriately discard of unwanted material at the earliest opportunity.

To reduce the paper clutter further, file things as you go, use staples rather than paper clips, use colored file folders, and develop a reliable tickler file to let you know what is due and when.

The use of electronic communications like email and electronically transmitted documents does not permit you to save and file everything. Organizations—including the Navy—are increasingly finding that server capacity originally intended to serve their needs for decades is being completely used in eighteen to twenty-four months by those who desire to save every email and electronic artifact just in case. The same decision-making process used to file and discard paper must be applied to the electronic medium. Preserve the audit trail for truly important events and discard the routine on a regular basis.

Case Study: Operational Risk Management

BM1 McKenzie was still searching through the papers on his desk and deck looking for the elusive memo, when he heard a call from Senior Chief Rupertus on his walkie-talkie. "Hey, we're about to begin lowering the SPS-67 antenna from the mast to the deck. The yard crew has shown up with a crane, and your boatswain's mates have been briefed on how to rig this, but we need the paperwork so that they can get started. Bear a hand and lay up here with your ORM plans for this evolution. You DID fill out the safety forms, right?" BM1 McKenzie put his head down on his desk for a moment and sighed.

What is Operational Risk Management? ORM is a decision-making tool used to increase operational effectiveness by anticipating hazards and reducing potential loss. ORM helps conserve assets and protect Sailors so they can complete tasks and missions effectively. ORM is *not* just a function for safety supervisors. Individual sailors take risks daily, and as a Chief Petty Officer, it's your job to understand and manage those risks. You may sometimes hear others criticize the systemization of certain leadership and management responsibilities as unnecessary and an impediment to leadership by presence and common sense. We want to believe that the training we provide and our own close attention to the tasks at hands can somehow prevent accidents, and no complex system of anticipating hazards can improve on a vigilant and professional CPO mess and wardroom. Nothing can be farther from the truth.

Over the past five years, the best practices of the submarine and aviation forces have been adapted and adopted to all segments of the Navy. Well-managed electrical safety programs aboard ship have reduced death by electrocution from an alarmingly high number to nearly zero. Aviation-style safety stand-downs are routinely used to great advantage. The tag-out system has become

Some of the most dangerous conditions under which Sailors labor can be found far from the sea.
U.S. Navy (PHC Johnny R. Wilson)

an entrenched part of the working culture with dramatically positive impacts. Yet even with this tremendous progress, far too many Sailors still lose their lives in preventable accidents. The trauma associated with these incidents is still one of the most awful burdens that any leader must bear. Deckplate leaders need all the help they can get to accurately and efficiently anticipate and mitigate hazards. ORM is an essential leadership tool that changes CPO thinking and planning. Safety, hazard identification, and risk reduction are daunting tasks in all Navy environments, both operational and training. ORM is needed, and it's here to stay.

ORM is a closed-loop process to identify and control hazards. It follows a five-step sequence, is applied on one of three levels depending on the situation, and is guided by four principles. Its purpose is to minimize risks to acceptable levels, proportional to mission accomplishment, and the goal of ORM is to manage risk so the mission can be accomplished safely.

ORM has been proven to reduce mishaps, lower injury and property damage costs, provide for more effective use of resources, improve training realism and effectiveness, and improve readiness. Accidents hurt the Navy and Sailors, and they sometimes even kill. Every petty officer has two goals: accomplish the mission and protect your Sailors. Leadership failures, even among senior enlisted who ought to know better, are often contributing causes of unnecessary mishaps, resulting in one or both of the goals not being accomplished.

BM1 McKenzie hustled to the weather deck. He found Senior Chief Rupertus, a few electronic technicians, and the first lieutenant chatting with the civilian crane operator. As they talked, it became clear that Senior Chief had completed the necessary analysis, and was discussing the best means of rigging the antenna with the crane operator. Nodding in agreement, the operator initialed the form, and Senior Chief handed the completed ORM report to BM1 McKenzie. "See me after noon chow," he said, out of earshot of the others. "We've got a few things to talk about."

Common Causes for Mishaps and Accidents

Senior Chief Rupertus knew that there were five general reasons why accidents "just happen":

Individual Failure. The Sailor knows and is trained to the standard but lacks self-discipline and elects not to follow the standard.

Support Failure. The equipment or material was improperly designed or not provided.

Leader Failure. The leader does not enforce known standards.

Training Failure. Sailors are not trained to known standards—insufficient, incorrect, or no training for the job.

Standards Failure. The standards or procedures were not clear or practical or do not exist.

Although Senior Chief Rupertus may not express it quite so elegantly, there are significant differences between the traditional approach to safety and ORM.

Differences Between the Approaches to Safety	
Traditional	*ORM*
Random, individual-dependent	Systematic
Common sense	Methodical
Uninformed decision	Informed decision
"Can do" regardless of risk	Conscious decision based on risk vs. benefit
Compliance based	Involvement and empowerment
Reactive	Proactive

At lunch, BM1 McKenzie approached his senior chief. "Thanks for covering for me there in front of the first lieutenant," he said. "I'm not all that clear on what this ORM thing is all about. Can you give me some idea of what all goes into an ORM analysis?" Senior Chief Rupertus filled his coffee cup again and began. "It's really not complicated at all, once you learn the specific meaning of the different terms used and the idea behind it all. It's just a simple but very complete way to be sure that we cover all the bases before we plan something dangerous for the ship or the crew. And—trust me on this, McKenzie—as a chief boatswain's mate, almost everything you do will have some danger involved. Think about the terms we use every day, things like *hazard* and *cause* and *risk* and so on."

Chief Petty Officers need to understand the terms, some of which may have somewhat different meanings in the professional context than they do in the everyday world.

Hazard. A hazard is a condition with the potential to cause illness, injury, death, property damage, or mission degradation.

Cause. Causes are things that produce an effect, result, or consequence. A cause can be a person, event, or condition responsible for an action or result. A cause is more specific than a hazard. A method of clarifying whether something is a hazard or a cause is to ask, "Is this specific enough to help identify a corrective control?" If the answer is no, it is a hazard. If the answer is yes, it is a cause. Properly identifying hazards and causes is important because there may be several causes associated with one hazard. If the more specific causes are not identified, necessary controls may be omitted resulting in the hazard not being eliminated or its risk inadequately reduced.

Common Causes of Hazards

Hazards	Causes
Portable crane failure	Operator error, mechanical failure
Weather	Rain-slick deck, high winds
Obstacles	Protrusions to snag antenna
Tangled lines	Improper rigging, crew training

Risk. Risk is a possible loss expressed in terms of severity and probability. You can make better decisions once a hazard is converted to a risk. Risk assessment is the name for the process of detecting hazards and assessing risks.

Severity. Severity is the expected consequence of an event in terms of degree of injury, illness, property damage, or other mission-impairing factor.

Controls. Controls are actions taken to eliminate hazards or reduce their risk. There are three types of controls in use:

- Engineering Controls: Controls that use engineering methods to reduce risk by design, or material selection or substitution. When technically and economically feasible, engineering controls are the best to use because they usually eliminate the hazard. Their drawback is they may not be feasible in many cases.

- Administrative Controls: Administrative controls reduce risk through specific administrative actions that include providing warnings, markings, placards, signs, and notices; written policies, programs, instructions, and SOPs; training Sailors to recognize hazards and take proper action; and limiting the number of personnel, equipment, or time exposed to a hazard.

- Personal Protective Equipment (PPE): This equipment serves as a barrier between a person and a hazard. PPE is the least effective type of control because it does not reduce the probability of a mishap occurring—it only reduces the severity when a mishap does occur. Use PPE when other controls do not reduce the risk to an acceptable level.

"ORM is not all that difficult," Master Chief Rupertus continued. "In fact, I learned an acronym for the process when I was up at the Senior Enlisted Academy recently. Just remember I AM IS, and you'll be OK."

The Risk Management Process: I AM IS

(I) Identify Hazards

Conduct an Operational Analysis, listing the major steps of the operation.

Conduct a Preliminary Hazard Analysis.

List the hazards associated with each step.

List the possible causes of the hazards.

(A) Assess Hazards

Determine degree of risk for each hazard in terms of severity and probability. Use a matrix to provide a consistent framework for evaluation, show the relative perceived risk between hazards and prioritize which hazards to control first.

Risk Assessment Code Matrix

Hazard Severity	Mishap Probability			
	Likely	Probably	May	Unlikely
Critical	1	1	2	3
Serious	1	2	3	4
Moderate	2	3	4	5
Minor	3	4	5	5

Risk Assessment Code (RAC)
1: Critical; 2: Serious; 3: Moderate; 4: Minor; 5: Negligible

Hazard Severity

1. Critical: May cause death, loss of facility/asset, or grave damage to national interests.
2. Serious: May cause severe injury, illness, property damage; or damage to national or service interests.
3. Moderate: May cause minor injury, illness, property damage; or damage to national, service, or command interests.

4. Minor: Minimal threat.

5. Negligible.

Mishap Probability

- Likely: Likely to occur immediately or in a short period of time. Expected to occur several times to an individual item or person, or continuously to a group.

- Probably: Probably will occur in time. Reasonably expected to occur some time to an individual item or person, or continuously to a group.

- May: May occur in time. Reasonably expected to occur some time to an individual item or person, or several times to a group.

- Unlikely: Unlikely to occur.

(M) Make Risk Decisions

Develop controls. Develop controls for each hazard to eliminate the hazard or reduce the risk until the benefit is greater than the risk.

Deploy controls. Deploy controls for the most serious hazards first. You may not have time to control every hazard—control the worst hazards first. Then determine the residual risk.

Assess. Assess each hazard's risk again with the controls in place to determine residual risk.

Make the risk decision. With all controls in place, ask, "Does the benefit outweigh the risks?" If so, accept the risk. If not, discuss the matter with your command, particularly if the risk exceeds permitted levels, or help is needed to implement controls.

(I) Implement Controls

Incorporate selected controls. Incorporate selected controls into all relevant documents, as well as briefings, training, and run-throughs. Don't fall for the line Sailors sometimes use: "We'll do it right when it's the real thing." Nobody does anything the right way in the heat of battle.

Communicate. Communicate selected controls to the lowest level. Who will do what by when? Implementation usually goes wrong because it was the wrong control for the problem, both Sailors and leaders dislike it, cost, and because nobody measures until it is too late.

(S) Supervise

As a Chief Petty Officer, you are responsible for the final and most important element. You must:

- Enforce standards and controls.
- Ensure Sailors are performing tasks to standard.
- Ensure controls are in place and having the desired effect.
- Take corrective action when necessary.

Three Levels of Applying ORM

Our life in the Navy requires the ORM process to be tremendously flexible. You may have to make tough, complex decisions in a matter of minutes or seconds. At other times, many decisions permit weeks or months of staff work. There are three levels of ORM that can be applied in any situation to control risk. As a leader, you must learn to choose which level of ORM to use based on the mission, situation, time available, proficiency level of personnel, and the assets available.

Time-critical ORM. An on-the-run mental or oral review of the situation using the five-step ORM process without recording on paper. Time-critical ORM is the normal level applied in the execution phase of training and operations to control hazards introduced by unexpected events and changes to the plan.

Deliberate ORM. Application of the complete five-step process and recording on paper.

In-Depth ORM. The Deliberate ORM process with a more detailed risk assessment (steps one and two) using advanced tools. Professional expertise will probably be needed when performing in-depth ORM.

"So what does this all mean?" BM1 McKenzie asked. "Well, basically, you can break it all down into four principles," Senior Chief Rupertus replied.

Four Principles of ORM

First Principle of ORM. Accept risk when the benefit is greater than the risk.

- Risk is inherent in the Navy.
- Leaders who are in the risk-taking business must be top-quality risk managers.
- Risk is usually proportional to gain.
- You cannot eliminate all risk.

Second Principle of ORM. Accept no unnecessary risk.

- An unnecessary risk is any risk that, if taken, will not contribute meaningfully to mission accomplishment.

- Leaders who accept unnecessary risks are gambling with the lives of their Sailors—for nothing. The gambler doesn't know what will happen; the risk-managing leader can reasonably predict what the outcome will be.

Third Principle of ORM. Anticipate and manage risks by planning.

- Risks are more easily controlled when identified in planning because more time, assets, and options are available to deal with the risk.
- Planning improves efficiency and saves money if ORM is integrated early in the planning process. If risk controls

are tacked on as an afterthought in training or in combat, they will probably fail.

· Proper prior planning prevents poor performance.

Fourth Principle of ORM. Make risk decisions at the right level.

· The leader directly responsible for the operation makes risk decisions.

· If the risk is greater than the benefit, or goes beyond the command's stated intent, or if help is needed to implement controls, stop the work immediately and contact higher authority for guidance.

"Well, McKenzie, did you get all that?" Senior Chief Rupertus asked. "Just remember that your role as a Chief Petty Officer is vital to safety. Enforce the standards rigorously. When Sailors take shortcuts or do it their way, that's when mishaps occur. Supervise and use ORM in the planning process. Are the right controls actually in place? Are the controls having the desired effect? And keep reminding your Sailors that they are responsible for supervising themselves, too, for exercising self-discipline, and for performing assigned tasks to standard. They must also recognize unsafe acts and conditions, and either take corrective action or report discrepancies up the chain of command. Do that, and you'll have a safe work area, a safe ship, and be the darn good chief that I know you can be!"

Case Study: Training Facilitation

BM1 McKenzie finally got a breather around 1300. "Man, I am in deep trouble now," he thought. "I've got that selectees' meeting in the chiefs' mess at 1530, and Command Master Chief Donovan wants me to lecture on supervision, monitoring, and inspection. I need to be sure that the other selectees learn enough to get by if one of the chiefs asks questions." He thought for a minute. "Well, Master Chief Turner lives right across the street from us, and his wife Joy is a good friend of my wife's. He used to be an instructor at the leadership training unit, I think—maybe he can help me out. He may give me a hard time, but, hey, that's what risk assessment is all about—the benefits are sure going to outweigh the risks if he gives me the straight skinny!" He picked up the phone and called Master Chief Turner, whose shop was just off the pier. "It looks like you've got two problems, McKenzie. The first thing you need to understand is how Sailors learn," he said. "You've got to be sure that your shipmates learn, and not just hear, the material you are going to present. And the second issue is the content itself. But today's your lucky day, Boats. I have good handouts right here on both those topics, and if you hustle over here, you'll have plenty of time to get set up before you've got to face the music at 1530."

Helping Sailors Learn

Some chiefs, unlike Master Chief Turner, have always believed a little too strongly in the throw-them-in-and-they-will-learn-to-swim school of training. This philosophy is unacceptable. It was dangerous and ineffective in years past and is even more offensive today. We cannot depend on the Navy training pipeline and individual Sailor initiative alone to complete the mission. Department, division, and work center CPOs have immensely important training responsibilities. Just as every chief must be an effective counselor, so must each chief be skilled in facilitating learning.

Physical comfort and quiet well-lit classrooms are useful to the training process, but there have been many life lessons taught and learned on the noisy flight deck of a carrier or the engine room of a charging destroyer as well. In many Navy settings, it's simply a matter of doing the best we can to control the environment in which we conduct formal training. But more importantly, you as the instructor, and the sailors under instruction, must share some common goals:

The over-arching goal is knowledge transfer. Training sessions are not intended to show how much you know or how easily you can impress your Sailors. It's what they know and can do at the end of the session that counts.

Don't be tempted to short-cut proper training by emphasizing "tricks of the trade." Sure, you can mention and demonstrate those little techniques that we all pick up from experience. Remember, though, you may not be around on the midwatch when your trainees decide to practice that little trick that Chief taught them. Teach the trade, not the tricks of the trade.

Be sure to set a good example in every training session, even those ad-hoc ones that arise when you are just passing through the work center. Wear all required safety equipment, follow the standards and step-by-step instructions faithfully, and explain each step in words and expressions that the trainees can understand.

Before you walk into the classroom or training area, ask yourself:

What are the terms and concepts I'll be using? Everyone must share the same definitions and agree on what exactly they mean in the context of this training. A wise man once said, "The difference between a scholar and a fool is knowing the right name for things." In our ever-changing and complex Navy, knowing and using the right nomenclature for the system, unit, and components we'll be teaching is critically important.

What are my objectives? Why are we here? What do I want the trainees to learn from this session? One of the best ways to set up the training session is the show-do-explain method. Demonstrate the task or explain the concept to the trainees. Then have them practice the same skill, perhaps several times. Finally, have each trainee explain the concept or procedure to a few of his or her shipmates. Observe closely and intervene as necessary, but real learning comes when the trainee is able to internalize the material.

Integrating knowledge. How will they integrate what is being taught with what they already know? Many of the selectees in BM1 McKenzie's class are already leading petty officers in their divisions. Supervision, monitoring, and inspection are familiar terms and part of their everyday life. Most will have their own opinions on the subject developed from years of experience. As instructors, we must remember that Sailors don't operate in a vacuum—they have previous experiences and life histories that must be considered if training is to be truly effective.

Repeat. Finally, remember the old trainer's adage: tell them what you're going to tell them, tell them, then tell them what you just told them. Don't repeat yourself to the point of boredom, but remember that repetition is the key to successful learning.

"So, if you do all of that," concluded Master Chief Turner, "you won't have any problems with that gang of cutthroats over there on USS *Gerald W. Farrier*. So shake a leg, McKenzie, and hustle over here and make a couple copies of my stuff from the LTU. Command Master Chief Donovan is really going to think that you've got your act together by the time I get done with you, McKenzie!"

Supervision, Monitoring, and Inspection

BM1 McKenzie turned to and quickly retrieved the materials that Master Chief Turner had set aside for him. "This all makes sense," he thought to himself as he read the handouts. "I think I understand the principles of training OK. But let's see . . . that talk I'm supposed to give in the chiefs' mess at 1530 is about supervision, monitoring, and inspecting the work. I've been through a million inspections, but what exactly am I going to tell that class this afternoon?" He continued reading and began to realize some of the reasons for things he had previously taken for granted.

Supervision and monitoring are two of the most important activities for every Chief Petty Officer. Every chief uses these two skills daily; but even more importantly, they work to pass on these time-developed skills to those who relieve them.

Supervision. Supervision is best defined as the careful watching and directing of others to accomplish the mission within the capabilities of the unit. The successful chief is adept at obtaining maximum efficiency from subordinates through effective supervision. Supervision is what an experienced chief does, almost without thinking, to ensure the job is done right. There are, however, five distinct steps that experienced chiefs take when supervising the sailors in their work center or division:

- They set and clearly communicate expectations for level of performance.
- They state consequences of non-performance.
- They hold personnel accountable.
- They match personnel and tasks to achieve best performance, professional growth, and maximum cross training for depth.
- They promote cooperation and teamwork for effective performance.

Supervision applies to all assigned tasks and the typical reason for any failed undertaking is usually a lack of proper supervision. The tie between supervision and assigned tasking is another leadership skill—delegation. Delegation does not mean making assignments and waiting on results while sitting in the CPO mess or some other comfortable spot. You must supervise every delegated task to some degree during task completion. Determining when and how closely to supervise is an art form that grows from experience and is sharpened as we gain a higher level of understanding of the mission The level of supervision must also be considered in degrees of intensity, from no supervision to continuous supervision, with the extreme ends for the most unusual circumstances. Each degree of supervision needs to be defined operationally. The degree to which supervision should take place is dependent upon the mission and circumstances and the proficiency of those involved.

Levels of experience. Why should an inexperienced Chief Petty Officer closely supervise a highly experienced Sailor in the execution of an assigned task? The answer is simple—all of us are life-long learners, and seniors must learn, too. The inexperienced senior is not always going to have the luxury of working with experienced subordinates. The chief who reports from submarine duty to a destroyer has never been involved in many complex special evolutions and must learn them quickly and thoroughly. Some day in the not-too-distant future, he or she will certainly be teaching a division of inexperienced Sailors. This scenario is played out constantly: veteran chief/new division officer, newly assigned chief/highly experienced sailors—the list of variations is endless.

No job is so important, no mission so vital, that we can't take time to do the work as safely as possible.
U.S. Navy (PH2 Andrea Decanini)

Monitoring Performance

Every successful chief knows planning is critical to achieve success. Additionally, common sense tells us it's easier to prevent a possible problem from becoming real than to try to solve the problem after it has happened. Just as in the ORM discussion earlier in this chapter, asking yourself a few simple questions will provide insight into what might later be a problem while now it is out of the norm. Ask yourself:

- What can go wrong?
- What are the real problems?
- What are the risks?
- What are the causes?
- What are the probabilities of a problem occurring?
- How is a possible cause prevented or its effects minimized?

As Chief Petty Officers, we should all realize that plans are really a series of performance points at which certain things are supposed to happen. Looking back at the questions, each CPO must identify the problem issue and must use data to analyze the process. In order to answer these questions, we monitor performance, using yardsticks to assess whether or not a performance point was met.

The most common assessment measures are time, cost, and quality. Frequently these yardsticks are in conflict: not enough time, limited funds, complex quality standards, each requiring the chief to decide which yardstick measure receives the most attention. Effective Chief Petty Officers clearly articulate standards of performance, and, in the execution of responsibilities, put in place the structure to measure time and cost of input, as well as the quality of the output. Three key points to consider regarding monitoring are observing procedures and processes; monitoring records, equipment, and resources; and asking questions to assess personnel readiness.

Despite its routine nature, monitoring serves a critically important function by allowing us to keep track of performance so we can maintain a realistic and timely knowledge of our unit's capabilities. The ideal zero-defect program may be impossible to achieve, but the chief must never believe that is so. Implementing processes designed and intended to produce zero-defect always leads in the right direction. The concept of process improvement requires monitoring. As chiefs, we commonly refer to this as staying in touch or management-by-wandering-around. Why do we wander? To monitor.

Inspectmanship

The word inspection often brings out the worst in a chain of command. Formalities, reports, formations, and interruptions are common elements of any inspection and seem to cause unnecessary anxiety. Why do we worry about inspections? Perhaps it is because we're not always inspection-ready. "Doing it by the book," "ducks in a row," "primed," and "knock their socks off" are the phrases we use when we think we are ready for an inspection, usually after some lengthy period of preparation. Drilling, cleaning, polishing, and paperwork audits are all part of the work-up stage to an inspection.

Working up to an inspection implies an activity that doesn't already work at the anticipated inspection-ready level. Why are there two sets of standards? This question comes about all too frequently. The goal of every organization is to achieve a state of 100 percent readiness and to maintain it, to ensure the unit is capable and prepared to handle any encounter. If we remain in the inspection-ready mode, maintaining a 100 percent mission- and personnel-readiness state, we won't work ourselves into a frenzy preparing for an inspection. We may also begin to see the inspection as a way to improve ourselves rather than a hits-per-minute chore.

What Is an Inspection?

We use the term inspection in many contexts. An inspection is any examination of the personnel, material condition, efficiency, or economy of a unit or activity; any evaluation of the quality, quantity, or management of available resources of a unit or activity; or any determination of the condition or effectiveness in performing assigned missions of a unit or activity.

Higher authority imposes inspections, and the chain of command sanctions them. The results are reported to higher authorities and a follow-up system is involved to ensure problem areas are resolved. Using these definitions, we can now recognize many other events such as area visits, assessments, audits, certifications, checks, evaluations, examinations, reviews, surveys, and tests as inspections. In their simplest form, all of these are merely a look at how we complete our mission day by day.

Naval Command Inspection Program (NCIP)

Keeping in mind the unit's goal of 100 percent readiness, the goal of the NCIP supports our desire to be 100 percent mission-ready. The NCIP provides a realistic evaluation of the operational and material readiness of a unit to perform its assigned mission and to assess its ability to continue to do so in the future. Here's where the chiefs' mess fits in: CPOs represent or accompany commanders/commanding officers on inspections. Likewise, the Chief Petty Officer participates in many boards and programs, all requiring supervision, monitoring, and inspection to ensure they meet command objectives. Having the experience, a keen sense of attention to detail, and the objectivity to identify weaknesses helps the Chief Petty Officer to assess unit readiness, personnel morale, and command climate—key factors in every unit's success.

The successful Chief Petty Officer possesses the competency of inspectmanship, the ability to pinpoint strengths and weaknesses using one's knowledge of standards, regulations, and policies, and to apply this knowledge to perform a comprehensive check or other form of inspection to some aspect of the unit's personnel, material, or operation. CPOs do not need to memorize every rule, regulation, policy, and parameter. The NCIP provides an annual list of special interest items for command inspections. The NCIP list, lessons learned, and type commander and other reports provide assistance in developing the inspectmanship competency. The bottom line is to look at ourselves and our units critically, remain objective, and work toward process improvement.

BM1 McKenzie reviewed Master Chief Turner's handouts thoroughly. "That's pretty heavy stuff," he thought to himself. "But it all makes a lot of sense." He looked around the bos'n hole. "I know that this space isn't ready for inspection right now—not by a long shot—but when it is, it's lots easier to find things quickly, and we seem to get a lot more done when we're squared away." He took the blank transparencies that Master Chief Turner had thoughtfully included in the guard mail envelope and began to jot down bullet points for his upcoming presentation to his fellow selectees. "Old Master Chief Turner sure is a salty old bird," he thought to himself. "But, you know what? Those old chiefs may just know a thing or two about this Navy of ours, don't they?"

Points to Ponder

Case Study: A Day in the Life

Have you ever had days when your schedule contains more work than you know you can complete? How have you handled the situation?

BM1 McKenzie is a good boatswain's mate—the fact that he was competitively selected for chief proves that. But he's got some issues to deal with—time management and organization seem to be two of them. Have you ever worked with a shipmate who was a technical wizard but to whom the term organization was inapplicable? Do you have trouble coming up with required papers and files?

Case Study: Operational Risk Management

How does ORM apply to your rating/work center? How familiar are you with the everyday requirements at your job site?

Gundecking is as old as the Navy. But what can happen when someone pencil-whips the necessary forms or completes them after the fact? Is the five minutes saved worth the serious risk to life, limb, or mission accomplishment? Can you think of an example in your own experience where five minutes more for planning would have saved many hours or days of recovery activity?

What do you think Senior Chief Rupertus said to BM1 McKenzie after noon chow?

Case Study: Training Facilitation

Think about your own work history in the Navy. Where did you learn the real skills you have now? Was it in the schoolhouse or on the deckplates?

Think back to the Sailor or Sailors who taught you best. What characteristics did they exhibit as they taught you your rating? Have you ever learned anything from a junior Sailor? Did you feel at all uneasy in that situation? Remember that part of our role as Chief Petty Officers is to help junior officers grow too. How would you deal with a classroom of, say, midshipmen or newly commissioned ensigns if you were assigned to that task?

Part Two

Communicating

5

Understanding
Communications

During Operation Enduring Freedom, coalition sailors visited USS
Manayunk (LSD-61) in the North Arabian Sea. Chief Cresson was
delighted when the tour reached his communications spaces.
Recently advanced, he had worked on the ship's precommissioning detail and was justly proud of the state-of-the-art equipment
on board, much of which he had helped install. Although he did
not recognize the rating badges on his visitors' tropical uniforms,
he assumed that they were fellow communicators. As Senior
Chief Boone, who had accompanied the visitors, listened, Chief
Cresson provided a thorough and technical explanation of the
equipment and procedures used to maintain communication via
UHF and SHF satellite communications. Hardly stopping to draw
a breath, he explained everything from the power supply to the
antenna connections, and he even offered to accompany the visitors to the weather decks to see the antennas. The coalition Sailors
smiled politely, nodded, but they declined Chief Cresson's offer to
see more.

To borrow from the 1967 movie *Cool Hand Luke*, what we may have here is a failure to communicate. Chief Cresson certainly understands satellite telecommunications, but he may not fully understand interpersonal communications. He has incorrectly assumed that his visitors were fluent in English, that they knew and understood Navy jargon, and even that they were fellow information technicians. Their smiles and nods reassured him that everything he told them was perfectly clear. His message may, indeed, have been clear to Chief Cresson, but his message never made it to the intended receiver.

Communication Theory

Communication is too often seen as a one-way process. "I stand up and explain what to do," say some chiefs, "and my Sailors go do it." Effective communication requires consideration of five elements: the originator, the receiver, the channel, feedback, and noise. If any one of those elements is defective or missing, then effective communication doesn't happen. Let's take a look at those five elements as applied to Chief Cresson.

As the originator of the message, Chief Cresson has three important tasks to perform, even before he opens his mouth.

Think. He must think clearly about what he is trying to communicate. This skill, often called cognition, means that he must first understand what he is trying to say. Does he want to describe what happens in a tactical setting? Is he trying to explain the fundamentals of satellite-based communication? Is he attempting to show the differences between U.S. communications practices and those of our allies? Why exactly have these coalition Sailors been brought to his communications spaces, anyway?

Consider the Audience. No two audiences are identical, and they bring different depths of knowledge and understanding. Perhaps Senior Chief Boone had used exactly the same examples and phrases when describing the sys-

In the modern Navy, our mission often requires us to work closely with Sailors of other nations, whose knowledge and command of our language may make effective communications more challenging. *U.S. Navy (PH2 Erin A. Zocco)*

tem to Chief Cresson, but Senior Chief knew that Chief Cresson has helped install the system in the yards, that he knew and appreciated the difference between an SHF and a UHF signal, and that he'd been in the telecommunications field long enough to understand the jargon and abbreviations used.

Transmit. Lastly, he must transmit in a way that ensures that his listeners fully understand the message. That requires frequent pauses for emphasis and reflection and a chance for his listeners to ask questions or seek additional information. We may think that using slang and jargon makes us appear knowledgeable, but often that's just a tactic that we use when we're unsure of ourselves and don't fully grasp what we're trying to say.

The coalition Sailors were the receivers of Chief Cresson's message. A receiver, the second element in communications, may get the message as you send, or the receiver may distort it to fit his or her own reality.

Sometimes the receiver rejects the message outright if it contradicts beliefs or if decoding takes more effort than the information is worth. Questions from the audience are sometimes an indication of the depth of understanding of the audience. In this case, however, these visitors came from a culture in which authority is highly respected and questions are not encouraged

Chief Cresson understood satellite telecommunications, an important channel that the Navy uses every day. Other communications channels, the third element of effective communications, include face-to-face communications, visual communications like the choreographed signals on a noisy flight deck, and written or print media. Each communications channel has its own rules and procedures, and the chief needs to learn them.

Later that afternoon, Senior Chief Boone joined Chief Cresson in the mess. Over a cup of coffee, she mentioned that the visitors had seemed a bit disappointed after their visit to the comm shack. "They wanted to talk about inter-ship procedures," she remarked, "and they really didn't understand much of what you were telling them about our communications links back to the U.S. They're not quite as sophisticated as we are, I suppose. In fact, I heard their leading radioman remark that they still used Morse code to communicate from time to time. Maybe we ought to think about how we conduct these orientation visits from now on, eh?" Chief Cresson nodded but said nothing.

The feedback provided by Senior Chief Boone is the fourth element of effective communications. Feedback is verbal or non-verbal communication to a person or group that provides information as to how their behavior or message is affecting you. Words, gestures, posture, utterances such as "uh huh," or sometimes the absence of expected reactions are all forms of feedback. Have you ever gone home, walked in the door, and known instinctively that your spouse or roommate was angry with you, even if not a word was said? Some might call that intuition, but most of the time, it's the absence of an expected feedback response, the "Hi, how are you?" that we learn to expect when we turn the key in the door.

Effective feedback is descriptive rather than evaluative. Feedback refers to a person's actions or words rather than translating the behavior into a statement about what he or she is. Descriptive feedback allows someone to have behaviors in need of change, while still being acceptable as a person. Senior Chief Boone practiced good feedback techniques when she explained the visitors' expectations, rather than saying, "You know, Chief, you really blew it when the coalition visitors entered your spaces today."

Effective feedback is specific rather than general. Senior Chief explained that the visitors really wanted to talk about inter-ship communications and not the technical specification of the link back to Norfolk. She was specific, helping Chief Cresson to realize that sometimes our allies' systems are not quite as sophisticated as ours.

Effective feedback takes into account the needs of both the receiver and the giver of feedback. Senior Chief Boone believed it was important that everyone in her division be able to communicate the mission and practices to international visitors. Chief Cresson believed it was important to understand that not every visitor to the communications spaces had quite the technical background that he and his crew possessed.

Feedback is immediately useful if it is directed toward behavior the receiver can control and is delivered at the earliest opportunity. Senior Chief Boone made a mental note to speak to Chief Cresson as soon as she could and did so in a friendly, non-confrontational way.

Guidelines for Giving Feedback

- Speak directly to the person.
- Use "I" statements and eye contact.
- Praise positive performance and point out areas to be improved.
- Consider your non-verbal cues and tone of voice as well as your words.

- Consider the receiver's feelings, readiness to listen, and self-esteem.
- Consider your own attitude, motives, and biases.
- Speak in positive terms as much as possible, using terms like "areas for improvement" rather than "deficiency."

Guidelines for Receiving Feedback

- Listen actively and with an open mind.
- Request specific, descriptive information.
- Ask for clarification without putting the person on the defensive.
- Try to understand the giver's perspective and the impact of your behavior.
- Be willing to receive both positive feedback and points on areas for improvement.
- Acknowledge feedback and avoid being defensive.
- Privately sort out and select what feedback is appropriate for you.
- Seek positive suggestions in areas that appear to need improvement.
- Say, "Thanks, that's enough feedback for now," when it is overwhelming.

Noise is the fifth element in the communications environment. Noise is any factor that interferes with the effective exchange of information.

Ambient or environmental noise, most pronounced on a busy flight deck or in the engine spaces of a charging destroyer, can make a serious conversation or career counseling difficult. Another kind of noise, psychological noise, also can hinder effective communication. Psychological noise may stem from the emotional state of the sender or receiver; fatigue or boredom, attitudes, prejudice, or bias on either part; speech impediments or distracting mannerisms; or differing background, language, or experience.

Effective Listening

Surprisingly, the complex skill of effective listening is something that is rarely taught. After all, we have two ears and only one mouth; surely nature intended us to be effective listeners. One of your most important tasks as a Chief Petty Officer is to listen. You'll be expected to listen attentively when your division officer or department head is passing the word, and you'll be expected to listen with great interest and attention when counseling your Sailors. This special attention is active listening.

Active listening is an expression of our core value of commitment. To know how to listen to someone else, put yourself in the other person's shoes. How would you want others to react when you are relating something important? Experienced Chief Petty Officers know that although the following tips appear to be common sense, all too often they seem to get lost in the heat of battle.

Face the speaker. Sit up straight or lean forward slightly to show your attentiveness through body language.

Maintain eye contact to the degree that you all remain comfortable.

Minimize external distractions. Turn off your walkie-talkie. Close any manuals or folders you have on your desk. Give the matter your undivided attention.

Minimize internal distractions. If your own thoughts keep barging in, pretend the CNO or the MCPON is sitting across from you.

Respond appropriately to show that you understand. Utterances like "yes" and "um-hmm" communicate that "Yes, I'm still here with you." Saying "Really?" or "Is that so?" prompts more discussion as do more direct queries like "What happened then?" and "What did you do then?"

Focus solely on what the speaker is saying. Try not to think about what you are going to say next. The conversation will follow a logical flow after the speaker makes his or her point.

Actively observe the non-verbal postures or gestures.

Keep an open mind. Wait until the speaker is finished before deciding that you disagree. Try not to make assumptions about what the speaker is thinking.

Avoid letting the speaker know how you handled a similar situation. No two situations are ever truly identical, and the differences between your experience and the speaker's may be the critical issue in the entire matter. Try to avoid saying you know how the speaker feels—you don't really know how the other person feels. No one does—our emotions are deep and personal and truly our own.

Don't be defensive. Even if the speaker is launching a complaint against you, wait until he finishes to defend yourself. The speaker will feel as though his point has been made. He won't feel the need to repeat it, and you'll know the whole argument before you respond. Research shows that, on average, we can hear four times faster than we can talk, so we have the ability to sort ideas as they come in and still be ready for more.

As you work on developing your listening skills, you may feel a bit panicky when there is a natural pause in the conversation. What should you say next? Do what the professionals do and learn to settle into the silence and use it to better understand all points of view.

Barriers to Effective Listening

- Listening only for details or facts.
- Distractions from equipment noise, telephones, or other sources.
- Daydreaming.
- Lack of interest in or understanding of the speaker's subject.
- Concentrating on the speaker's mannerisms or delivery rather than on the message.
- Impatience or disagreement with the speaker.
- Jumping to conclusions before the speaker has finished.
- Bias and prejudice.

Communication among all levels is critical if the Navy is to complete its mission effectively.
U.S. Navy (PHC Johnny Bivera)

- Lack of empathy.
- Lack of attention to the speaker's non-verbal cues.

Communications with Seniors

A good rule to follow when giving a presentation to your boss is to remember basic journalistic guidelines for telling a story. Start with the important facts first: who, what, when, where, why, and how of the situation. Most department heads and division officers take a dim view of a chief who begins every report with a lengthy preface, particularly when they recognize a pattern in which this preface takes the form of a series of excuses leading up to the ultimate bad news. Putting the bad news first can prevent the buildup of anxiety in your listeners as they wait to find out what you are trying to say, and it will often make them more willing to hear you out without interruption. When the news is exceedingly bad, however, as in a report of an accident involving members of the

crew, a superior is likely to appreciate hearing early reas-
surances about casualties or damage.

Another good rule is to avoid bringing the boss a problem without also suggesting an appropriate solution you
can implement. The only exception to this rule is when
delaying the report to develop and vet a solution will
make the problem worse. In such cases you must make a
speedy report and commit to returning with an update
and solution set as soon as possible. This kind of interaction with the boss can be a difficult transition for the new
CPO especially, as occasionally happens in some ratings
and career paths, if he or she has not had a demanding
LPO experience. For some, simply reporting the situation
and awaiting instruction is the norm. But remember, now
you are the chief! A report that the starboard anchor has
fouled is not complete without adding what action is
already underway or will be taken ASAP to correct the
situation. Such reports demonstrate your decision-making ability and will enhance your division officer's perception of your competence.

Communications with Juniors

To help juniors develop their own decision-making ability, sometimes it is a good idea to tell them what you want
done without specifying exactly how you want it done.
This is most often true when dealing with your leading
petty officers. At the same time, you should ensure that
you are making clear exactly what results you expect
from their efforts. Once you become familiar with your
subordinates' individual personalities and abilities, and
once they become familiar with your expectations, you
may be able to use a kind of verbal shorthand that elimi-
nates much of the explicit detail in such orders.

Get into the habit of giving frequent feedback to your
subordinates on their day-to-day performance. You can
easily work this kind of communication into your daily
routine, and it will pay big dividends for you and your
organization over the long run. Telling your LPO,
"Overall I was happy with the work you did on the main-

tenance logs, but I noticed some format errors, and I would like you to be careful not to repeat them the next time" is better than saying nothing about the errors and losing your temper the next time she makes the same mistake.

Although you are not required to give justification for your orders, experienced chiefs typically explain their reasons to subordinates when time permits. Sailors who understand the reasons for an order not only appreciate that the chief took the time to explain it but are much more likely to carry it out enthusiastically and thoroughly.

Case Study: Making a Presentation

BUC Rector was at his work center when the telephone rang. It was CMDCM Kashoe. "Say, Chief, weren't you the team leader when MCB-1 rebuilt that school and orphanage after the typhoon on Saipan last year? The XO has gotten a call from the Rotary Club here in town—he's a member, you know—and they want someone to come and talk about how the Navy always pitches in when there's a natural disaster. You're the most senior member of the Public Works Department with a recent tour in a Seabee battalion. Why don't you cruise over and see the XO and see what you can do for him, eh? He needs about a half-hour talk for next Tuesday evening. The XO will introduce you, and I think he said that the skipper will probably come along, too."

Chief Rector was a combat veteran. He'd been in one war, two revolutions, and a couple of good bar fights on liberty. But nothing frightened him quite as much as that phone call.

Presentations

More people report a fear of public speaking than report fears of heights, tight spaces, spiders, or other things that "bug" us. Although it is doubtful that as a Chief Petty Officer you will ever have to become a skilled orator, you may be surprised at the number of activities where the ability to speak clearly and forcefully will be a valued asset. You may be detailed as an instructor or perhaps tapped to be the after-dinner speaker at a dining-in or Khaki Ball. Although not every experienced Chief Petty Officer is capable of rousing and inspiring oratory, virtually all are reasonably adept at speaking to a large group and at presenting a well-organized and informative lecture designed for that particular audience. For some the ability to speak comfortably in public may be a gift requiring little practice to master, but for most of us it is a skill that demands many years of practice and experience. Your earliest opportunities to speak will be at morning quarters with your own division.

The human voice has several distinguishing qualities, among them pitch, resonance, projection, and a less definable attribute that we will call tension. You are born with physical vocal traits, but to some extent you can improve upon or control them.

Pitch is the average frequency of tones produced by the vocal cords. A low-pitched voice is more pleasing to the ear than a high-pitched voice, even though the latter carries farther. Nervousness or stress tends to increase the pitch of your voice, but you can counteract this by mastering proper breathing techniques. The female voice is naturally pitched higher than the male's, but pitch can be affected using the techniques of an opera singer. A singer's chest does not move appreciably because she uses her lower abdomen for breathing. Both male and female speakers do well to speak using the diaphragm and lower abdomen muscles for breathing. At the same time, consciously relax your chest muscles. You will find that you can learn to speak with a minimum use of the muscles of your upper chest, and that your throat and voice can be made to relax in the process. Lowering the pitch of your voice and increasing resonance and projection will also decrease the discernible tension in your voice.

Resonance is the ability of your voice-producing apparatus to resonate to the vibrations of the vocal cords and produce tones and overtones. Greater resonance makes a voice sound richer and more pleasant in the same way that an orchestra produces richer and more pleasant sounds than does a single violin. Good resonance is a function of the internal cavities and shape of the throat, sinuses, and skull. You can improve your resonance by use of the opera-singer exercise described above.

Projection is the property of a voice that helps it carry over long distances. The ability to project your voice in a noisy situation can be an important skill, particularly on board ships. In addition, the ability to project your voice well will help you be heard by a large group without tiring or straining your vocal cords. The opera-singer exercise will help here, too, as will keeping your mouth pointed in the direction you wish your voice to be projected and opening it as wide as possible to maximize the sound waves you produce.

Tension is a combination of pitch and resonance and is directly affected by stress. The voice of a relaxed speaker is more pleasing to the audience and carries far more authority than the wavering voice of a nervous, tense speaker. In addition to this quality of the voice itself, nervous speakers tend to speak faster, as if to rush through the presentation and get it over with as quickly as possible. This kind of rapid-fire delivery tends to alienate and disengage the audience.

Before making a presentation, you can avoid the jitters that can lead to vocal tension by practicing the breathing exercises described earlier and trying to focus on something else during the hour or so immediately preceding your talk. Some speakers find that it eases their nervousness to pick out one person in the back of the room and talk directly to him or her. Too much caffeine can accentuate your nervousness and should be avoided immediately before your presentation. Although a few stiff drinks before the presentation may make you feel relaxed and witty, rest assured that the audience rarely shares this perception!

The most vibrant, beautiful voice can easily be marred by a delivery that includes faulty grammar, limited vocabulary, poor pronunciation, a regional accent so pronounced as to be unintelligible to the average listener, repeated use of stock phrases ("you know" being one of the worst offenders), or other verbal idiosyncrasies that detract from the speaker's message. The rules of grammar are considerably relaxed in oral communications. You may augment your spoken words with non-verbal gestures and take other liberties to emphasize your ideas or reflect the mood of the conversation. Nevertheless, a speaker's disregard for or utter ignorance of appropriate grammar will become apparent in the course of a conversation or presentation and may have a subtle or overt effect on the listeners' trust. Similarly, verbal eccentricities such as the use of obscure words or reliance on profanity or other offensive language to make a point can interfere with your ability to communicate effectively. Those who have done a tour of duty as recruit division commanders at RTC Great Lakes will recall the signs frequently posted in backstage areas out of view of the recruits: profanity is not quality leadership. Profanity is not presentation-quality speech, either.

The most important rule to remember in oral communications is that your aim is to share your thoughts as clearly and simply as possible with your listeners, to make it easy for them to understand what you want them to know. You should not talk down to your listeners, but you also shouldn't try to impress them with your intellect or your vocabulary; such a goal is almost certain to backfire.

As you become comfortable in your role as a Chief Petty Officer, you may find yourself invited to give talks to groups of people who want to hear about your experiences or who have a particular interest in one of your areas of expertise. For the novice presenter, the best method to ensure that you give a relaxed, professional delivery is to rehearse extensively. After you write your speech, practice into a tape recorder, in front of a mirror, or with a friend. You'll often find messmates dry-running a presentation in front of the other chiefs in the mess. Truth to tell, you'll not find a more effective audience to critique than one comprised of experienced CPOs. This exercise will serve several functions. If you work with your messmates, your rehearsal will give you insight into how your delivery is coming across and will allow you to improve the mechanics of your technique. In addition, the added familiarity you gain with the subject matter of the speech will allow you to be more comfortable, and the partial memorization that results will ensure your ability to make more eye contact with your audience than you do when using notes.

If your speech will be followed by a question-and-answer period, try to anticipate the questions you are likely to be asked, and rough out some notes to use in an answer to each. Even if you are not asked the particular questions you anticipate, you will likely find that the notes you made will come in handy in your answers to other questions. Pick a particularly assertive shipmate and ask him or her to play devil's advocate, dreaming up the most difficult questions possible. You'll be relieved that the live audience wasn't nearly as tough on you as your friends.

Once you have given a few speeches from prepared texts, try to leave the copy of the verbatim text at home and instead rely on a series of file cards with short notes on them. If you can develop the ability to glance briefly at your notes to refresh your memory as to your next point and then look up from your notes while you are speaking, it will prevent those panicked moments when you lose your place in the text. Speaking from note cards also allows you to look directly at your audience, greatly enhancing your credibility as a speaker. Too, your voice will project better because you will be speaking out into the room, rather than down toward the podium.

If you will be using an unfamiliar sound system, you should try to familiarize yourself with its use beforehand. With a stationary microphone, you must adjust it so that you don't have to hunch over to maintain an appropriate distance, normally no more than several inches, and you must take care to maintain a constant distance between your mouth and the microphone to avoid creating distracting fluctuations in the sound level. Lapel microphones are considerably more flexible and easier to use.

Later that afternoon, after calming down just a bit, Chief Rector called his old friend JOC Kingsley at the PAO office. "You know me, Terry," Chief Rector said. "I'm a pretty good carpenter, and I can do plumbing and electrical work, but I'm no public speaker. EO1 Pensdale here in my office said I ought to use a PowerPoint presentation. He just came back from a tour as an instructor at Gulfport, so I suppose he knows what he's talking about. I've got a box full of pictures I took when we rebuilt the orphan's home, and I brought home a couple CDs of local music. You think that will be enough to get me off the hook on this thing I have to do for the XO?"

Almost everyone in the Navy has experienced (or endured!) computer-generated PowerPoint presentations. They've revolutionized briefings, lectures, and training courses. When done well, they add significantly to the transfer of information. When done poorly, though, they can distract from, and even negate, the message the speaker intended to communicate. Chief Kingsley's advice for Chief Rector follows.

Effective PowerPoint Presentations

Don't assume the equipment you need will be available. As far in advance as possible, ask the following technical questions.

- What equipment will be available?
- Will you need to specially request or order anything?
- What is the size of the room and how will it be arranged?
- How large is the screen? Try to avoid presenting against a marker board—reflection makes it extremely uncomfortable for viewers in the hot spot.
- Where will the lectern be placed?
- Does the lectern have a light?
- What type of microphone is available?
- Will an ET or an IC technician be on hand in case of trouble with the equipment?

- Are there extra projector bulbs on hand and where are they stowed?
- Will someone operate the computer or will there be a remote control for your use?
- Who will monitor and adjust the lights?
- What type of pointer will be provided? Laser pointers are inexpensive, and no Chief Petty Officer should be without one.

Most rookies make the mistake of putting too much information into their PowerPoint presentations. Fewer slides is better, and fewer words on each slide even better. Graphic displays like charts and photographs that enhance your audience's understanding are best. Photographs rather than the standard clip art are preferable; some images are available from the World Wide Web. The Naval Historical Center Web site has a rich treasure trove of vintage photos.

- Avoid small type—if your audience can't read the information from the screen, there is no point in projecting it.
- Align words to the left, with a ragged right, for easier reading, in a bold, simple, consistent typeface.
- Use color for emphasis, distinction, and clarity.
- Be careful with dark backgrounds because some colors can make black figures or text less distinct.
- Navy blue and gold are great color combinations, as are Marine Corps scarlet and gold.
- In general, light text on a dark background works best if the room is dimly lit. The reverse is usually true in a brightly lit space.
- Avoid the bells and whistles unless you have the skill of a Hollywood producer.
- Do not read from your slides when presenting.

Make a paper copy for yourself. If you are reading the screen, your back will be to the audience and you lose valuable eye contact. The objectives, venue, and audience reactions will determine the rate your slides should move. The rule of thumb for technical presentations is no more than one slide for every three minutes of time scheduled.

Consider using the PowerPoint slides at key places in the presentation rather than in a linear manner throughout. You need not develop a slide to illustrate every point. Maybe you need to illustrate only your opening and closing points and have the audience focus exclusively on your words for the heart of the presentation or perhaps you need their full attention at the beginning and end. It is up to you. Whatever you do, use your PowerPoint slides when you rehearse your presentation. There is a skill involved in timing slide transitions. Rehearsing with your visual material will help keep you from getting sidetracked and losing your place in your talk. Your audience is there to listen to you, to learn from your expertise. The slides are secondary and should enhance what you have to offer.

Points to Ponder

Case Study: A Failure to Communicate

Think of your own experiences. Have you ever had to present a briefing to visitors, senior officers, or others? How did you feel when you first took the pointer in your hands? After the briefing was over, how did you feel? What response did you get from superiors or shipmates about the quality of your presentation?

Think of the worst briefing you've ever attended. What made it so bad? Do you think the presenter knew that he or she was failing in the task? If you were called upon to give that same presentation today, what would you do differently?

Case Study: Making a Presentation

Have you ever gotten a last-minute call to stand in for a shipmate and were handed a prepared presentation to deliver? How did it make you feel? Do you feel better if you have a chance to develop the presentation yourself before delivering it to an audience?

What happens when your audience is hostile to the message you have to present? What techniques might you consider to be sure that the message was conveyed accurately and effectively, without further irritating the audience or making the situation worse?

6

Group Dynamics and Meeting Management

Case Study: The Task Force Assignment

SHC Roop entered the classroom at Navy Annex. She'd received a week's TAD orders to a task force evaluating various fabrics, designs, and styles for a new working utility uniform. As she entered the room she noticed that she was the only Sailor present. Sitting at various tables in the classroom were DoD civilians, both male and female, as well as representatives from various contractors. Feeling slightly uncomfortable, and not knowing any of the other participants, she sat quietly in the back of the room and updated her PDA. Later, an ensign and a lieutenant commander entered the room and sat together near the front. Chief Roop remained in her seat at the back of the room as the civilian chairman called the meeting to order.

Chief Petty Officers are called on regularly to solve problems well outside their rating and with which they are not equipped to deal through experience or training.

Often the chief is assigned the task of leading or participating in the effort to find a solution. Working with groups can be more art than science, but there are some rules. To be an effective Chief Petty Officer, you must learn them.

Team Development and Maturation

Perhaps you have been the new kid at school, trying to fit into an established crowd. Later you may have arrived at Recruit Training Command as the only person from your hometown. You've reported aboard ship, not knowing a soul, and said to yourself, "How will I ever fit in with these people? Will they like me? Will they respect my opinion? Why is it that they seem to be getting along so well, and I feel so isolated and alone?"

Chief Roop, in her discomfort, was experiencing one of the common characteristics of group interaction: a sense of initial isolation. As she sat, passive and uncomfortable in the back of the room, she looked around and realized that a number of the other participants probably felt the same way. "I guess that's because we've been thrown together here, and we don't know each other," she thought. And, indeed, when the chairman arrived, the first order of business was a round of introductions, as each member stood and spoke for a moment about his or her experience and expectations of the task force.

Groups of individuals can be classified into four categories, depending on the maturity (length of time) and purpose for which they have come together:

Aggregates. Aggregates are simply people who are at the same place at the same time. A classic example might be travelers on an airplane. Unless they are part of a preexisting community like a church group or a ski club traveling together, the only thing they have in common is that they are booked on the same flight. One may be going to a business meeting and will change planes when the flight lands; another may be returning to school in the destination city; others may rent a car and travel several hundred miles to their destination. Chief Roop, as she entered the classroom, was joining an aggregate. The only thing she appeared to have in common with the other members was that all had received orders to be at the same place at the same time for the same purpose.

Cohorts. Members of cohorts have some statistically identifiable characteristic in common. Perhaps you grew up in a small town and attended kindergarten to senior high school with the same kids. That's a classic cohort. By having memory, cohorts are distinguished from aggregates. Watch the crew of any ship as they return from a long or arduous deployment. The crew will make references to or jokes about events that happened during the deployment, comments that, to an outsider, are totally incomprehensible. The mention of a single innocuous word or phrase may send everyone into gales of laughter, as it triggers memories of something that happened weeks or months previously.

Groups. In the technical sense of the word, groups are comprised of individuals who come together often for a common purpose or who share a sense of belonging to a specific entity. The success of the group's mission may not require the same level of commitment or interaction by each member, but, if attacked or threatened from the outside, members will quickly identify with the group. Shipmates on a large-deck warship may never meet, or even have much in common, but let trouble start in a liberty port and an attack on one is seen as an attack on all.

Teams. Teams are comprised of individuals with interdependent responsibilities for the success of the mission. A group of Sailors may be in the ship's library, quietly studying for the upcoming advancement examinations, or a team of Sailors may be taking turns quizzing each other and developing what-if scenarios for various topics that may appear on the examination for their particular rate. The key word is interdependence—the idea that the success of the entire team is influenced by the actions of each member.

As the members of the task force introduced themselves, Chief Roop began to feel more comfortable. Ms. Moyer, a civilian from NEXCOM's Uniform Program Management Office, identified herself as a retired senior Chief Petty Officer, while Mr. Rosedale of Highspire Industries grew up just a few miles from Chief Roop's hometown. Ms. Lusk smiled when Chief Roop mentioned that she had a son and daughter, and mouthed the words "me, too" across the room. "These don't seem to be bad people at all," Chief Roop thought to herself. "Now, if I just knew more about fabric and uniform construction, I'd be all set!"

Chief Roop had spotted the first of two dimensions of team effectiveness, the individuals and the task to be performed. The individuals on the team may be like athletes who "hog the ball" and who seem more interested in personal statistics than the success of the team. The individuals may be passive passengers on the team bus. Either extreme makes it difficult for a team to coalesce and be effective. Friendly, cooperative or cheerful partners can make even the most difficult job worthwhile, however.

The task to be performed can be as simple as conducting a field day or stowing supplies, or as complex as precommissioning a nuclear carrier. Tasks are identifiable units of work with measurable outcomes.

How Successful Teams Evolve

Successful teams learn to balance the needs of the people involved with the real need to complete a certain task in a given amount of time. In 1977, Tuckman and Jensen identified several stages successful teams encounter while trying to balance both the personal needs and the requirements of the task. These stages are:

- Forming: Moving from being an aggregate to a cohort.
- Storming: Moving from being a cohort toward being a group.
- Norming: Moving from being a group toward being a team.

- Performing: Acting like a team.
- Adjourning: Reversion toward individual status and interests.

Because there were so many organizations represented on the task force, the chairperson divided the group into subteams. Chief Roop was assigned to the maintainability subgroup as were representatives of the various manufacturers, and Lieutenant Commander Willow and Ensign Jefferson of Navy Clothing and Textile Research Facility (NCTRF) at Natick, Massachusetts. They moved to an adjoining conference room, but the meeting got off to a rocky start because no one was precisely sure what they were expected to accomplish.

Chief Roop's team was experiencing the first, and predictable, stage of group development. Individuals often focus on themselves as they move toward group effectiveness. Participants often ask, "Who am I and what's my role here?" as they test relationships to determine what attitudes or actions are acceptable to the group. In a newly formed group, there is usually dependence on existing leadership. At first, both Chief Roop and Ensign Jefferson deferred to Lieutenant Commander Willow, even though he made it clear that he had recently been assigned to NCTRF and that most of his experience had been in disbursing. During stage one, many groups:

- Identify the tasks and how the group will accomplish the tasks.
- Exhibit hesitant, insecure participation.
- Define the ground rules.
- Test behavioral expectations and ways to handle violations of them.
- Show suspicion, fear, and anxiety about the new situation.
- Spend time intellectualizing or playing what-if games.
- Complain about the organizational environment.
- Discuss symptoms or peripherals to the task.
- Establish dependency relationship with leaders.

In this forming stage, there is usually low focus on task, high focus on the process, and minimal task accomplishment. The subgroup continued to meet for several days, as they examined the samples provided by various manufacturers. SHC Roop became increasingly concerned that many of the samples would be difficult to clean and maintain under shipboard or field conditions, and she mentioned her concerns several times. Mr. Whiteside of Middletown Mills seemed to treat her objections as trivial, and several times Ms. McKinney of Dauphin Designs rolled her eyes skyward as if to say, "Who cares about what happens in a ship's laundry, anyway?" Chief Roop sensed that the manufacturer's representatives felt that their primary duty was to promote their companies' products, and the representatives from Nadick seemed more interested in keeping costs low than the durability and usability of the fabrics.

The uncomfortable feelings of Chief Roop and the others are characteristic of the second stage of group development. The focus here is on a collection of individuals, each of whom must surrender some autonomy for the team to be successful. At times, members may become resistant or even hostile as they express their individuality and resist giving up some control to others. The conflict and hostility may be overt or covert. Typically, a few members dominate this stage. Eventually, members recognize the urgency of the task and begin to respond to the needs of the team, not just their individual needs. During this predictable stage, members may:

- Resist the group's influence.
- Compete and become defensive or argumentative.
- Exhibit disunity, increased tension, and jealousy.
- Experience polarization of group members.
- Display interpersonal hostility.
- Become concerned over excessive work.
- Participate in inter-group conflict.

In this storming stage, there is usually low focus on task, high focus on the process, and preliminary task accomplishment.

It was late on Wednesday, and the group had been going in circles for some time. Finally, after a particularly biting comment from Ms. McKinney, Ensign Jefferson stood up. "Look, we've been at this for several days now, and we're not getting anywhere. I know each of you wants what's best for your organization, and I do, too. But remember the most important stakeholders aren't at this table. Those are the Sailors who will have to wear and take care of these uniforms. I'm a mustang, and I've been around for years. I know what it's like to try to keep clean and presentable. Why don't we stop the sniping and get down to figuring out what's best for our Sailors?" There was silence around the table. Chief Roop said to herself, "Hmmm, you know, for an ensign, he's a pretty smart fellow!"

At some point for every successful team, the light goes on. Someone will usually stand up and restate the group's aims firmly and clearly. After this moment of catharsis, teams usually exhibit increased tolerance of dissimilar team members. Members accept the group, its norms, and their roles. Resolving the previously conflicting relationships reduces conflict. During this phase:

- Conflicts are avoided or attenuated.
- Cohesion with common goals and spirit is encouraged.
- There is interdependency when performing tasks.
- Trust and communication increase, with increased mutual support.
- There is acceptance of new standards and roles.

During this, the norming stage of team development, there is increasing focus on the task, high focus on the process, and moderate-to-high task accomplishment.

Thursday and Friday morning went much better for the subgroup. The manufacturers listened closely to Chief Roop's concerns about the colorfastness of the fabric and problems that could occur with the large industrial washing machines found on most warships. The NCTRF representatives realized that cost savings on the front end might be negated by additional expense and reduced the pressures on the contractors to provide materials at the lowest possible cost. The manufacturers' representatives even agreed to share coating technologies and to improve the service-ability of the materials, if all three should happen to win the contract. By noon on Friday, the group was ready to report their findings to the main task force team.

After Ensign Jefferson's cathartic moment, the group realized that they must operate both effectively and efficiently. With the report to the main body due on Friday afternoon, there was little time left. Often, time pressures assist a team in cutting through the static and getting to the heart of a problem. Pareto's Principle is often misstated as "Eighty percent of the work gets accomplished in twenty percent of the time." Just imagine how effective teams could be if all the time was dedicated to the task at hand! In this stage, groups usually find:

- Emergence of solutions, insights, and collaboration.
- Constructive self-change.
- Group structure emerges as a task tool, not as an issue for debate.
- Energy channeled into the task.

In this, the performing stage, there is very high focus on task, less focus on the process, and very high focus on task accomplishment.

As the group wound up its deliberations late Friday morning, Ms. McKinney suggested that they have lunch together at the Sheraton's Quarterdeck Lounge. During lunch, she sat next to Chief Roop, and their relationship—strained during the heated discussions earlier in the week—improved markedly. "She's not such a bad person after all," Chief Roop thought. "She's just new at her job and was worried that the other members of the group would override her, making her look bad to her boss when she got home, I suppose." The group promised to stay in touch and exchanged telephone numbers and email addresses.

When a team adjourns, several events may occur:

- Task-maturity level of the group may regress.
- A stated desire to maintain relationships begun, usually followed by diminishing contact with other team members.
- Relinquishment of identity as a team member.

These behaviors are predictable, and they can occur in all settings from a task-force to a service-school classroom or even to a work group on board a ship or at a station. If you understand their predictability and near inevitability, you'll be better positioned to achieve the objectives and handle matters as they arise, and you will be a better Chief Petty Officer for the experience.

Self-Disclosure and Self-Assessment by Team Members

Returning to Norfolk on I-95, Chief Roop rethought the events of the week. She kicked herself as she replayed the meeting again and again in her own mind. She winced as she recalled every time she spoke in the group and subgroup meetings, and every time she remained silent. "They must think I'm a fool," she thought to herself. "All those high-powered civilians seemed to know exactly what they wanted to say and how to say it, and those two officers from Nadick sure had their act together as well. I just sat there like a rock or stuttered and stammered every time I opened my mouth. I wish I hadn't hammered so much about the durability of the fabric. They probably thought that was the only thing I know how to do—to load washing machines on a CVN. I don't know why the skipper wasted the Navy's money sending me up there. There were lots better people to send to that meeting, I bet."

Ensign Jefferson and Lieutenant Commander Willow, too, were discussing the meeting as they sat in the departure lounge of Reagan National Airport. "Those civilian contractors sure were tough," Ensign Jefferson said. "It was hard to get them to budge from defending their own products. I'm sure glad that Chief Roop was there. For a while, I was convinced that she was the only person who really understood what was going on. With all the posturing and politicking among the civilians, she was the only one who was level-headed and focused throughout the meeting."

"You're right," replied Lieutenant Commander Willow. "She kept the thing from being a total disaster. I know her XO. I'm going to drop him an email when we get back and tell him what a real credit she is to his command."

Scottish poet Robert Burns once wrote: "Oh wad [would] some power the giftie gie us/ To see ourselves as others see us." We've all met shipmates whose opinion of themselves didn't really match the way that others perceived them. And, often, like Chief Roop, we really don't perceive clearly what impact we are having on others when we're working in a team environment.

About thirty years ago, Professors Ingram and Luft studied group behaviors. They recognized that our interaction with others is, to a very large extent, driven by how we think of ourselves. They developed a simple model, which they called the Johari Window, from their first names, Joe and Harry. The model portrays graphically the relationships among characteristics we disclose to others and those others see in us:

Johari Window

Things seen by self, and others	Things seen by others, unknown to self
Open area	Blind area
Things seen by self, unknown to others	Things unknown to others, unknown to self
Hidden area	Stealth area

Chief Roop thought she had failed; others thought she had been a great success. Group- or teamwork can be stressful. When stressed, individuals will sometimes try to mask or encrypt their feelings to spare themselves the possibility of rejection, to prevent damage to their egos, or for any number of reasons. No one expects you to be both a team leader and a practicing psychologist. One successful strategy to overcome these natural human tendencies, however, is to identify one or more participants as group facilitators who help the team make informed, intelligent and unemotional decisions. You are likely to be called upon to facilitate team development many times in the course of your career as a Chief Petty Officer.

Case Study: The Base
Parking Problem

CMDCM Keffers had a problem. With the large concentration of ships in port and road and building construction going on everywhere, the number of parking spaces allocated to each ship had been drastically reduced. Moreover, the base bus service was ineffective, and many of the ships' crews faced a very long walk from the front gate to the pier unless the situation could be resolved. Base departments and ships present offered good reasons why they individually deserved more than their fair share of the coveted parking spaces. Keffers called Chief Tremont into his office. "Chief," he began, "I've got a little tasker for you. Put together a quick SWAT team to solve this problem for me. Get a representative from each department and each ship that's here. I want everyone to feel like his or her interests are well represented. You know how many cars we get on station every day, and you know the number of parking spaces we can manage without getting wrapped up with all the construction equipment and contractors. Make this problem go away, will you?"

Facilitation of Groups and Teams

Chief Petty Officers often participate in work groups, task forces, planning teams, or in other settings where an understanding of group dynamics is important. Nowhere is this more important than when you are selected or appointed to facilitate or head a team or group. You will have many things to consider.

Physical Space

One of the first tasks of a meeting facilitator is to find and prepare a space for the team or group to meet. This may not be as easy as it sounds because space, especially on

Particularly in shipboard settings, we may be called upon to communicate complex information under less than ideal conditions. In a
pinch, the ship's messing spaces may be pressed into service as ad
hoc classrooms.
U.S. Navy (PH2 Aaron Ansarov)

board ship, is always at a premium. The physical conditions of a meeting space, however, will have an impact on
the success of the meeting. Although it is difficult to
reconfigure shipboard spaces, facilitators ashore have
more leeway to arrange the meeting space effectively.
You will have a number of options.

Classroom Configuration. Long, narrow tables are positioned before rows of chairs facing a screen or podium.
Tables may be abeam of each other, although to gain maximum use of limited spaces, tables can be angled toward
the speaker in a herringbone pattern to provide better
sight lines. Classroom-style is usually the best setup
when presenters are expected to do most of the talking,
and attendees must take notes, refer to material in
binders, or access laptops or PDAs. It's also the most comfortable design for very long sessions. Ideally, classroom

configuration requires between twenty and twenty-five square feet of space per participant. The classroom configuration tends to increase attention to the speakers but decrease interaction among participants.

Conference Configuration. Participants are seated on all four sides of a table. This works best for smaller groups of no more than sixteen. If a single large table is not available, tables can be combined to form a solid rectangle. For very large groups, choose another configuration, lest the conference table begin to resemble the flight deck of a CVN. Additional chairs are often positioned around the periphery of a conference room. In general, these chairs are occupied by staff or support personnel, usually seated in proximity to their principal. Provide at least two, and preferably three, peripheral chairs for each chair at the conference table. At least twenty-five to thirty square feet

Configuration of meeting spaces can have a large impact on the effectiveness of communication.
U.S. Navy (PHC Johnny Bivera)

of space should be provided for each participant when working in this configuration. The conference-style setup will increase interaction among members, but decrease the impact of a speaker or presenter.

Hollow Rectangle Configuration. Thirty-inch-wide classroom tables are arranged in a square or other multi-sided design in which the center of the design is empty and is used for larger groups to negate the flight-deck effect. This configuration is difficult to use when audiovisual presentations are planned because at least some participants will always face away from the screen. This configuration also requires between twenty-five and thirty square feet of space per participant.

U-Shape Configuration. Rectangular tables are positioned to form a U. Seating is usually on the outside of the U, and it is inadvisable to seat attendees on the inside legs of the U. The U-shape setup is often used for meetings involving audio-visual presentations because all attendees can see the presentation when the screen is placed at the open end of the U. This configuration generally requires between twenty-five and thirty square feet of space per participant. A U-shape configuration provides an ideal mix because it permits a high level of attention on a speaker or presenter and high interaction among participants.

Briefing or Ready-Room Configuration. Chairs are lined up in rows facing the speaker. The rows can be straight, semi-circular, or angled herringbone. If space isn't an issue, it's best to offset each row so that participants are not sitting directly behind one another. When a large number of attendees are listening to a briefer or watching a slide presentation, theater-style is the most efficient setup. This design maximizes the seating capacity of meeting rooms and permits the audience to be as close to the speaker as possible. It is not recommended for taking notes or referring to material in binders unless tablet armchairs are provided. This configuration requires between ten and twelve square feet of space for each participant. Interaction between presenter and attendees can range from low to high, but interaction among participants is generally very low.

Managing the Meeting

You will often be asked to lead formal or informal meetings. A meeting may be as simple as a chance encounter in the passageway or a quick discussion of an issue over lunch in the mess. Experienced leaders use common techniques to make meetings more effective and efficient. Keep in mind that meetings are expensive, especially when you consider the lost time of the participants and what they could be accomplishing if not sitting around a conference table.

Different kinds of meetings demand different kinds of processes. Staff meetings, planning meetings, problem-solving meetings, and other meetings all have certain basics in common.

Selecting Participants. The decision about who is to attend depends on what you want to accomplish. This may seem too obvious to state, but it's surprising how many meetings occur without the right people there. Conversely, excluding the wrong participants can be important. Limiting participants may be necessary because of physical meeting space, subject matter, and objectives.

Inviting Participants. Advise participants in advance of the meeting, its overall purpose, and why they have been selected to attend. "I've got a meeting in the CMC's office at 1330, and I have no idea what it is all about" is a comment heard too often. Unless confidentiality is an issue, giving participants advance notice of the purpose and scope of the meeting allows some thought prior to assembly, and it also permits participants to bring essential materials that otherwise might be left in their work areas.

Follow up your call with a meeting notice by email whenever possible. Again, state the purpose of the meeting, where it will be held and when, and include a list of participants and whom to contact if they have questions. Include a copy of the agenda with the email.

Designating a Recorder. Remember the old adage "It's not what gets said in the meeting that counts, it's what goes into the record." The recorder should log important actions, assignments, and due dates developed during the meeting, and ensure that this information is distributed to the participants as well as to others on the distribution list, as quickly after the meeting as possible. Generally speaking, the XO and relevant department heads should be on distribution for all meeting minutes. This fact alone should sensitize everyone to the need for professionalism, succinctness, and clarity in the record.

Developing an Agenda. Develop the agenda with key participants in the meeting. Consider the desired outcome of the meeting and what activities need to occur to reach those results. The agenda should be organized so that these activities are conducted during the meeting. A good agenda should not be too detailed or inflexible but should consider the following:

- List the time, place, and purpose of the meeting.
- State the expected overall outcome, sometimes called exit criteria.
- Involve the participant in front-end work preparing adequately for the meeting, sometimes called entrance criteria.
- List each major topic, including the type of action needed, the type of output expected, and time estimates for addressing each topic.

Handling the Meeting. Always starting on time shows respect for those who showed up on time and reminds latecomers that the scheduling is serious.

- Welcome attendees and thank them for their time.
- Model the kind of energy needed by meeting participants.

- Clarify your role in the meeting and the importance/ urgency of the issue to the command or other stakeholders.
- Review the agenda quickly.
- Remind participants that a meeting recorder will take notes.
- Appoint a timekeeper to notify you as deadlines you set are approaching, and enlist the participants to keep the meeting on schedule.
- Remind participants of any established ground rules for participation, preparation, focus, and momentum.
- Close on time, summarizing clearly any decisions reached, outcomes anticipated, and communications participants may expect to receive.

Evaluations of Meeting Process. It's amazing how often Sailors will complain about a meeting being a complete waste of time, but they say so only after the meeting. Get their feedback during the meeting, conducting satisfaction checks every five or ten minutes, when you can improve the meeting process right away. Leave time at the end of a meeting to further evaluate the meeting.

The Decision-Making Process

Chief Tremont's team was tasked with making a difficult and probably unpopular decision about rationing the rare parking spaces. Whatever plan they developed, it was a sure bet that someone would be upset. He can limit the discord, however, by using an open and defensible decision-making process. The team will need to identify and analyze alternative solutions, chart a course of action, and then submit their recommendations to the command master chief. Chief Tremont recognizes that parking for POVs is an emotional (and eternal) issue on most stations. However the group acts and whatever decisions it reaches will soon be public knowledge. How the team members feel about the process will determine how vigorously they support the decisions when they return to their own departments or commands. One proven decision-making methodology includes:

Defining the Problem. The problem should be stated clearly so all group members know and understand it. Larger problems should be divided into subproblems. This will allow for better understanding among group members and expedite developing the best possible solution.

Deciding on a Method. There are different ways to arrive at a decision: consensus, voting, or leadership-driven choices. There are advantages and disadvantages to all three methods. Consensus is the synthesis of ideas. When alternatives are discussed, the group hears the views of all the members and discusses the issue until it is felt everyone agrees. A vote is not taken, but the facilitator gives any member the chance to object. Consensus decision making involves all members in the decision and has the potential for win-win. All members must listen carefully, setting the stage for an effective action plan. Consensus decision making can be time-consuming, especially with a large group, and some members may not speak out if the trust level is low. In addition, the leader must be a facilitator, and not all leaders are willing to share the control.

Voting is another method of decision making. After the information has been gathered and alternatives listed, the group decides which will be the best way to solve the problem. Voting requires less time to make a decision. However, members who were on the losing or minority side may not feel committed to the decisions. They may not wholeheartedly support the decision and may attempt to undercut it when they return to their divisions. Generally voting as a resolution method is limited to morale welfare and recreation issues and issues of social and organizational relevance in the CPO mess.

Leadership-driven decisions, although efficient, are often ineffective unless they are preceded by one of the more inclusive methods listed previously as a part of the process. If CMDCM Keffers were looking for a one-man decision, he'd have made it himself. If he considers it important that every stakeholder has a say in the allocation of limited parking spaces, Chief Tremont would do well to consider all the opinions developed, realizing that dictating the decision takes members completely out of the decision-making process and that the group commitment level will be extremely low. Whatever the method, the process should include the following:

Gathering Information. Information on the problem should be shared. The more that is known, the more productive the discussion of alternatives will be. All members should be allowed to add specific information they might have.

Identifying Alternatives and Solutions. Members should list all the possible solutions to the problem. Brainstorming often helps. List responses so none are forgotten.

Identifying Pros and Cons. Listing pros and cons is a useful way of understanding all implications of each alternative. This will provide direction as the group moves closer to deciding on just one solution.

Ranking the Alternatives. Rank the best solutions to move the group ahead. Remember all members need to have a stake in the decision and a part in the plan of action.

Evaluating. Evaluate the outcome of a decision at an appropriate time after the decision has been implemented. If the situation is not better than before, return to the drawing board.

Chief Tremont gathered Chief Petty Officers from each department and ship present, and they met in the administration building. Things went well at first, but after a few hours of discussion, it was clear that many participants were more interested in protecting their own turf than reaching a decision that was fair to everyone. Chief Lorberry complained that his people needed

special parking privileges because they often carried heavy pack-
ages back and forth in their private vehicles. Chief Reinerton felt
that everyone was picking on the medical department, as usual,
and Senior Chief Orwin and Master Chief Muir assumed that,
whatever the group suggested, their XO could fix things with the
base command so that their shipmates would still have the preferred spaces nearest the pier.

Chief Tremont has many options when deciding how to
handle a difficult or less than productive team. He should
observe the group in action, paying close attention to verbal and non-verbal cues of individuals as they interact.
This requires some forbearance on the part of the facilitator—the natural response of most Chief Petty Officers
would be to jump right in and assume control. Ask yourself, "What am I seeing, hearing, and feeling here?" Just
as Chief Roop perceived herself differently than others
perceived her at the CUU meeting, participants at Chief
Tremont's meeting may have subconsciously assumed different roles during the course of the session.

Unfortunately, not everyone approaches every team or
group activity clean of hands and heart. Sometimes, a
group facilitator will have to deal with individuals
exhibiting these or other negative attitudes and postures
as a team develops:

- Aggressor: More than anything else wants to see own
  ideas accepted. Regards any discussion as a fight for
  his/her views.

- Alligator: All mouth and no ears. Always feels that every
  thought, no matter how far off subject, is a valued input to
  group discussion. Clearly feels that he or she has spent
  more time in preparation for the discussion and wants to
  report every detail discovered during preparation.

- Blocker: Believes the team is unable to make an intelligent decision and seeks mainly to keep the group from
  doing anything at all.

- Challenger: Opposes the status quo and existing leadership as a matter of principle. Stirs up disagreements,

may develop a following and attempt to take control of the group.

- Conformist: Agrees with just about everything said. Wants to please everyone, praises every contribution, no matter how far off target it may be.

- Debunker: Has nothing to contribute, and, in his or her opinion, neither does anyone else. Finds fault with anything that is said. Unconsciously, tries to bring the group down to his or her level of ignorance of the problem or solution.

- Detective: Believes firmly that everyone in the group has a hidden agenda. Believe everyone is motivated by selfish interests and will agree only to points through which he or she might profit personally.

- Express Train: Always interested in reaching a quick solution, even if it is the wrong one. Values efficiency and speed. Usually impatient with those who wish to take more time to discuss an issue. Always more interested in keeping things moving rather than the outcome of the deliberation.

- Opera Singer: Everything is an emotional issue. Reacts strongly to the contributions of others. Some of their favorite words are always and never, and they are often illogical. They are the first to let everyone know their opinion, which they are very reluctant to change.

- Recognition Seeker: Ambitious and capable. Likes to have an audience, and remarks are usually not intended to advance the discussion but to draw attention to self.

- Special Pleader: Participate only because he or she has a stake in the outcome of the deliberations. Participates, not to help the group solve a problem, but to protect his or her own interests.

- Strong Silent Type: For many reasons, rarely talks in a group or team setting. Often believes that he or she has nothing to contribute; may be intimidated by rank or stature of other participants.

- Superstar: Intelligent and knows it. As discussions progress, his or her patience may wear thin. If the group doesn't accept the Superstar's opinions, he or she may often feel misunderstood and withdraw from active team participation.

Diagnose the cause of the problem. Ask yourself whether this has happened before, and, if so, how many times? Will it go away on its own? Who or what caused the need to intervene? Is it a problem with the unsolvable, unimportant, or misunderstood task? Or is it a problem with the roles being played by people involved?

What is the overall impact? You may have to devise a corrective action. After you diagnose the situation, the next step is to consciously decide whether or not to act. There are three areas in which situations occur where you may have to make a decision to act. They are:

- Interpersonal and intrapersonal transactions of the group.
- Ideas generated by the group.
- Structure of the product to be developed by the group.

The more conscious the decision you make, the more appropriate your intervention can be to promote good group interaction. You may want to intervene if senior or higher status members are bullying the group to a non-consensus decision. This is a significant issue if there was an expectation of consensus as a process for either decision making or arriving at a recommendation. You may want to intervene if group members do not feel empowered to make a final decision or recommendation.

You will be called on to act on your observations. There are four degrees of responses in using interventions. You could be passive, allowing the situation to continue but monitoring it closely. Particularly in groups operating over a relatively long time line, conflicts will arise and will settle themselves without intervention.

You could be active, stepping in and restating rules and expectations to the group, but not addressing conduct specifically or naming names. Most members of a group will get the hint, and the negative behavior will cease. You could stage a mild confrontation: Like all good correction, it is best done in private. "Say, Chief, Smith, you have already made that point, we need to move on." You may decide you need a more direct confrontation, although this is usually a last resort. You may say, "Look, Chief Smith, we've been at this for four hours now, and your inability to accept the process agreed on earlier is keeping us from making progress. We have a firm deadline to submit a credible solution to this problem. We would like to have consensus but with or without everyone's agreement we are going to implement a plan. We are going to note your objections to the process and move forward."

There are very few jobs in today's Navy for the Lone Ranger. Sailors are called on to work in groups and teams constantly. As a Chief Petty Officer, your effectiveness will be measured by how well you use these tools to manage the group dynamics of the personnel with whom you work.

Points to Ponder

Case Study: The Task Force Assignment

Why did SHC Roop feel uncomfortable when she first entered the meeting room? Have you ever felt the same way in a new situation?

What do you think drove the actions of the other (civilian) members of the task force? Have you ever worked on a joint military/civilian team where similar dynamics were apparent?

Why did it take so long for Ensign Jefferson to step up to the plate and get things under control? Was it a case of perceived status as a newly promoted mustang? How do you think Ensign Jefferson perceived himself in the presence of higher status individuals? Can that happen to a newly advanced Chief Petty Officer, too?

SHC Roop found herself in a situation where people issues overshadowed task issues. Have you ever seen something similar in your work center or berthing spaces? What happens when the task issue is life-or-death? What keeps us from having the same focus on task performance every day?

Case Study: The Base Parking Problem

How many times have you been in the same situation as Chief Tremont? How often has a "little tasker" turned into a potential minefield? Did the CMC know how politically volatile the parking situation would be? Did he adequately telegraph to Chief Tremont all the problems he'd likely face?

The chain-of-command can be a Sailor's best friend. But what happens when problems cross into various commands or organizations? How high do you have to go up the chain of command to find common authority? Is this problem severe enough that the fleet or force master chief should be brought into the fray? And, if not, how can Chief Tremont exert enough moral fiber to steer the participants to an equitable and fair solution?

Lots of folks exhibit one or more of the negative characteristics listed in this section. How do we deal with an Alligator? How do we deal with an Opera Singer? Can you think of times when you've been faced with similar personalities in your work center or organization? How did you deal with the situation then? What would you do differently now?

Chief Lorbery and Chief Reinerton exhibited the characteristics of special pleaders, that is, solving their problems was more important than the good of the whole. We often see this characteristic in special liberty requests, leave chits, and other day-to-day situations. As a Chief Petty Officer, how can you best deal with these situations? If you accede to special pleading, what impact will that have when the next Sailor comes forward with a special request?

7

Written Communications

Civilians think that the Navy floats on water. Sailors
know better. The Navy floats on paper. Tons and tons
of paper. If we don't watch out, we'll drown in all
that paper.

CMC Mike McCalip
USS *George Washington* (CVN-73)

Communications and the Chief Petty Officer

Think back to the day when you got your first orders out
of boot camp. You may have gotten orders to school or
gone directly to the fleet. You no doubt had great expectations, most of them wrong, about what life would be like
in your chosen rating. Perhaps you saw yourself knee-
deep in oil, repairing a main bearing somewhere in the
frozen North Atlantic. Perhaps you saw yourself on the
flight deck, risking life and limb to arm fighter jets for
combat just over the horizon. Or maybe you saw yourself
as an FMF corpsman, saving the lives of your Marine
shipmates. In your dreams, you saw yourself receiving
awards for valor, commendations for courage, advance-

ments for achievement. All of us have done that at one time or another.

Then reality set in. As you advanced, you realized that replacement bearings don't appear magically—someone has to order them. Flight operations don't happen automatically—someone has to schedule them. Commendations don't appear magically at quarters—someone has to write them. Command Master Chief was right. Whatever happens in the Navy usually happens first on paper.

Regardless of your rating, as you advance you have been faced with steadily increasing administrative responsibilities. As a Chief Petty Officer, your ability to quickly read and comprehend complex documents is vital and becomes even more important as you assume greater levels of responsibility and authority. What follow are some techniques that experienced Chief Petty Officers find helpful.

Effective Writing Skills

The Chief Petty Officer's writing ability is often the difference between success and failure. There are performance evaluations, official messages, important emails for reports, and point papers that will influence command decisions. There are formal letters for the captain's signature. "I didn't sign up to be a writer," you may occasionally think. "Why must I worry about verb forms, parallelism, and all this other drivel? Why can't I just get on with the job at hand?" It is likely that you love your work and consider writing a distraction.

The reality is that writing often *is* the job at hand. Fortunately, there are a number of great references that can make the job easier. Start with a good dictionary and a comprehensive thesaurus. No CPO's seabag is complete without three great guides to the written word:

The Naval Institute Guide to Naval Writing, Second Edition (1997). The book's author, Dr. Robert Shenk, is a retired Navy Reserve captain, a former professor at the Naval Academy, and an experienced author and technical writer. He has written a lively, definitive reference for anyone who writes official documents. It is undoubtedly the best single reference on the subject. We've drawn heavily on Dr. Shenk's work in this chapter.

Department of the Navy Correspondence Manual, SEC-NAVINST 5216.5 (as amended). The manual is, arguably, the most readable naval instruction ever written. Much of the information in this chapter is drawn from this instruction as well.

Better Naval Writing, OPNAV 09B-P1-84. This reference work is a workbook and tutorial based on the *Navy Correspondence Manual*.

The Basic Steps to Good Writing

These pointers are adapted from *The Naval Institute's Guide to Naval Writing*.

Check the references. Be sure that you know the basic references controlling the subject about which you write. For example, when doing enlisted evaluations, be sure you consult BUPERSINST 1610.10 so that your format and content meet Navy standards.

Follow the format. Readers have expectations of what goes where. Regardless of how good your content or persuasive your argument, you won't impress if your material just doesn't look right.

Use the gouge. . . . but use it sparingly. Only occasionally will you be required to generate a first-of-its-kind document. Almost always, someone else has gotten there first, and you will have a template of sorts. Consult with a senior yeoman, if one is available, or review examples that you find persuasive. Be cautious, however. Both good and bad examples abound. Ask yourself, "What is it that makes this example sound so good?" Use the good, discard the bad.

Do your homework. Before writing, check other material on the same subject. It's difficult—and unethical—to write a performance evaluation for a Sailor without having a good and defensible idea of his or her performance over the evaluation period. Gather the necessary supporting materials before developing your document.

Develop an outline. It's amazing how often even experienced writers skip this step. "Why go to all the extra work?" writers often think. "Nobody will ever see the outline except me." Someone will see the results of that outline, though, and a well-developed document reflects the strength of the framework that supports it.

Write a first draft. Many of us, including a large number of professional writers, have a terror of the blank page. We'll do everything possible—sharpen pencils, fill the coffee mug, clean out the grease trap in the galley—rather than sit down and write. Get something on paper or on your hard drive. Save it, think about it for a little while, and then come back to polish and revise. That's what experienced writers do.

Edit and revise. Doctor Shenk suggests focusing on content, organization, and language. Ask yourself, "Does this document do what I want it to do?" If you're in doubt, ask someone else. If it doesn't, add information or reword the document until you are certain that your readers will get the key points. Logical order is crucial. Put the important points first. Ask yourself: "If this message were garbled in transmission, would the addressees understand my point if only the top third of the message got across?" Even if your news is unpleasant, put it up front. Let the explanations follow. No one ever ordered that we write in eighteenth century navalese. Sometimes we just do. Perhaps that comes from following the gouge too closely. Ask yourself: "What's the easiest and clearest way to say what I need to say?" Then say it.

Use silver bullets. Nothing has improved readability as much as bullet lists. As a key part of the information mapping initiative developed by technical writers, bullets:

- Help the reader skim.
- Emphasize key points.
- Enliven the text.
- Effectively summarize complex issues.

See, that was easy, wasn't it?

Add subject lines and headings. Make subject lines as descriptive as possible, without trying to squeeze the entire document into the subject field. The subject line reading "Potential Problems" can refer to anything from a zone inspection to repelling boarders. "Potential Problems: Shortage of Cutlasses and Blunderbusses" is more likely to get your reader's attention. Think of headings as if you were developing a table of contents. The reader should be able to see the key points arrayed in the headers and rely on the associated text for background or additional information.

Consider visual impression. Often, a well-crafted chart or table assists the reader in understanding the relationships among data. Realize, too, that the final document represents you: just as you wouldn't appear before your addressees out of uniform, so should your paper appear "in uniform." Check margins, tabs, headers, and footers for consistency and appropriateness before releasing your paper.

Proofread. Check for spelling, punctuation, capitalization, and grammar. Spell-checkers, regardless of the financial strength of the company providing them, are not infallible. Check closely for homonyms: words like *their* and *there.* Check for subject-verb agreement: "They was going down the passageway when the deck gave way" is as jarring to the reader as it was to the Sailors who tumbled into the bilges. Check, recheck, and check again the spelling of any personal name that appears in the document. You can be forgiven for almost any grammatical sin, but allowing your spell checker to change your boss's name from *Conover* to *Conniver* (as this writer once did, to his everlasting chagrin) is not career enhancing.

Writing Well

The following suggestions have been extracted from the *Navy Correspondence Manual.*

Start fast, explain as necessary, then stop. When you write a letter, think about the one sentence you would keep if you could keep only one. Many letters are short and simple enough to have such a key sentence. It should appear by the end of the first paragraph. The strongest letter highlights the main point in a one-sentence paragraph at the very beginning. Put requests before justifications, answers before explanations, conclusions before discussions, summaries before details, and the general before the specific.

There are times when it may be appropriate to delay your main points—to provide enough information to introduce a controversial proposal, for example. But don't delay routinely. Readers, like listeners, are put off by people who take forever to get to the point. In most cases, plunge right in. And to end most letters, just stop. When writing to persuade rather than just to inform, you may want to end strongly with a forecast, appeal, or implication. When feelings are involved, you may want to exit gracefully with an expression of goodwill.

Downplay references. The *Correspondence Manual* makes an apt analogy: reading letters that overuse references is like driving in reverse through alphabet soup. Many letters need no references at all, while others are complete with a reference only to the latest communication in a series. Avoid unnecessary or complicated references. When you respond to an earlier communication, subordinate it to your main point. Don't waste the opening—the strongest place in a letter—by merely summarizing a reference or saying you received or reviewed something.

Avoid mystery stories. Timid writing creeps up on the most important information. First come references, then discussion, and finally the so-what. With luck, the main point follows a sign such as therefore, consequently, or due to the above. Even with such a signal, however, readers must grope for the bottom line. Good writing should follow the newspaper pattern, opening with the most important information and tapering off to the least important.

Use short paragraphs. Paragraphs longer than four or five sentences swamp ideas. Cover one topic completely before starting another, and let a topic take several paragraphs if necessary. Long paragraphs will divide where your thinking takes a turn, and, by adding white space, you make reading easier. Short paragraphs are especially important at the start of letters, as long first paragraphs discourage reading. Call attention to lists of items or instructions by displaying them in subparagraphs. Just don't use so many levels that you lose the reader.

Take advantage of topic sentences. Often, a paragraph needs a topic sentence that will be further developed by the rest of the paragraph. The decision to use a topic sentence is a judgment call. A short paragraph announcing the time, place, and agenda of a meeting does not need an opening like "Here are details about the meeting."

Use more parallelism. Look for opportunities to arrange two or more equally important ideas so they look equal. Parallelism saves words, clarifies ideas, and provides balance.

Parallelism Provides Balance to Your Writing

Unbalanced	Petty Officer Smith qualified in anchoring, launching, and recovering the Captain's gig, and how to rig for towing.
Parallel	Petty Officer Smith qualified in anchoring, boat launch and recovery, and towing.

Natural Writing

When we read, we hear the writer's voice. Make your writing as formal or informal as the situation requires, but do so with words you'd use when speaking. Speak on paper: the most readable writing sounds like a conversation. A spoken style means fewer gears to shift each time we write. It also means less adjustment for new personnel who find the old style increasingly foreign. You probably remember your own difficulty in getting used to round-about writing.

To make your writing more like speaking, begin by imagining your reader is sitting across from you at your desk. If you are writing to a group, picture one typical reader. Then write with personal pronouns, everyday words, and short sentences—just as you would speak.

Though you shouldn't go out of your way to use personal pronouns like we or you, you need not go out of your way to avoid them. Whether you sign "by direction" or with a title, you may want to write for your activity, command, or office as "we," "us," or "our." Use I, me, or my less often in every kind of writing. The exception may be if you are writing for yourself or your commanding officer and want to show special concern or warmth. If we or I opens more than two sentences in a row, the writing becomes monotonous and may suggest self-centeredness. Sometimes a single sentence can call too much attention to the sender: "I would like to extend my congratulations for a job well done." Praise should stress the reader: "Congratulations on the fine job you did."

Don't use big words when little, everyday ones will do. People who speak with small words often let needlessly fancy ones burden their writing. On paper, *help* swells to *assistance*, *pay* to *remuneration*, and *visit* to *visitation*. The list goes on, and so does the damage from word inflation. Try not to use some commonly overdressed and legalistic words.

Downshifting for Comprehension

Every-day Jargon	
Instead of:	Use:
Commence	Start
Facilitate	Help
Optimum	Best
Promulgate	Issue
Utilize	Use

Legalistic Jargon	
Instead of:	Use:
Aforesaid	Them
	That
Heretofore	Until now
Herewith is	Here is
Notwithstanding	In spite of
The undersigned	I
Pursuant	Under

Transition Words	
Instead of:	Use:
Consequently	So
However	But
In addition	Also
Nevertheless	Still

Use some contractions. Contractions link pronouns with verbs (we'd, I'll, you're) and make verbs negative (don't, can't, won't). They are appropriate in less formal writing situations. Yet even when writing formally, you can use contractions in drafts to help you write naturally. Research shows that readers are less likely to skip over *not* when it is contracted. If you are comfortable with contractions, your writing is likely to read easily; you will be speaking on paper. Because the language is clear, you are also more likely to spot holes in your thinking that need to be filled.

Keep sentences short. For variety, mix long sentences and short sentences. No sentence should exceed twenty words. Though short sentences won't guarantee clarity, they are usually less confusing than long ones. You needn't count every word. Try the eye test: no sentence should exceed two typed lines. Or try the ear test: read your writing aloud and break up most of the sentences that don't end in one breath. Break long sentences into manageable units, and then prune needless words and ideas.

Be concrete. Without generalizations and abstractions we would drown in detail. We sum up vast amounts of emotion when we speak of honor, courage, and commitment. But such broad language may not resonate with the reader precisely the same way it does with the writer. Use concrete terms—things you can touch, rather than things you feel—whenever possible. Don't use a general word if the context allows for a specific one. If you are discussing a torpedoman, don't write Sailor; if discussing a plane, don't write aircraft. Be as definite as the situation permits.

Pay particular attention to job descriptions and evaluations. Vague, high-sounding language weakens job descriptions. Someone is said to "assist and advise in the organization management aspects of manpower management." Another "serves as a system proponent to transition from current capabilities to architectural projections." But what do these people really do? After all, a person who "serves as a direct interface with interstate commerce" may be a highway flag holder. Effective evaluations show what a person did and how well he or she did it. They are concrete enough to inspire confidence in the writer's judgment about the Sailor's performance and potential. Performance evaluations suffer when writers make extravagant, unsupported claims.

Listen to your tone. Tone, a writer's attitude toward the subject or readers, causes few problems in routine letters. The roles are straightforward. Subordinates may suggest, request, or recommend, but only superiors may direct. Though pronouns are acceptable, we don't get personal. Courtesy is required, but warmth is not; the tone is neutral. Precisely because much of our writing is routine, tone causes problems when the matter is delicate. The more sensitive the reader or issue, the more careful we must be to promote goodwill. Tactlessness in writing suggests clumsiness in general. When feelings are involved, one misused word can make an enemy.

Tone Sensitivity	
Instead of:	Use:
Opportunity is limited.	Competition is keen.
Stop writing badly.	Start writing well.
Don't use the small hoist.	Use the big hoist.
The cup is half empty.	The cup is half full.

Cut the fat. Give your ideas no more words than they deserve. The longer you take to say things, the weaker you sound, and the more you risk blurring important ideas. Economy requires the right attitude. Write tight. When you revise, tighten paragraphs to sentences, sentences to clauses, clauses to phrases, phrases to words. To be easy on your readers, be hard on yourself.

Tighten Your Writing	
Instead of:	Use:
It is requested	We request or please
It is my intention	I intend
It is necessary that you	You need to, you must
It is apparent that	Clearly
It is the recommendation	We recommend that
For the purpose of	For, to
In accordance with	By, following, per, under
In order to	To
In the event that	If
In the near future	Soon

Naval Communications

The Department of the Navy Correspondence Manual (SECNAVINST 5216.5) and the *Naval Institute Guide to Naval Writing*, from which this section has been adapted, provide much greater depth than is possible here. Consult these excellent references if you have questions on any of the material outlined below.

As a Chief Petty Officer, you'll usually be concerned with seven forms of written communication. Appendix A contains some examples the various kinds of writing. Use the samples as templates for your own writing.

Common Forms of Written Communication

- Standard Navy letters
- Point papers
- Memoranda
- Casualty Reports (CASREPS)
- Enlisted Evaluations
- Citations, Commendations, and Awards
- Messages and email

Letters

A Navy letter is an official communication, usually written by a chief or officer, and signed by the commanding officer. Most often, it is addressed to the commanding officer of another command. The letter is usually signed by the skipper, but may be signed by another member of the command, including Chief Petty Officers, to whom the CO has delegated authority. In most commands, this "by-direction" authority is granted liberally to those with specific responsibilities. With this authority goes the understanding that the chief or officer signing "by direction" speaks directly for the commanding officer—all the more reason to be extremely certain that your letters are perfect in every detail.

Navy letters are usually printed on letterhead and follow a strict format as illustrated in Appendix A. The SSIC, or standard subject identification code, listed in the upper right-hand corner, is a code that permits correspondence to be routed and filed by subject matter. The correspondence manual contains a complete listing of these four- and five-digit codes. Underneath the SSIC is a line with a locally assigned numerical code corresponding to the drafter of the correspondence and a serial number corresponding to the letter itself. Serial numbers are not required on unclassified correspondence but are normally used to assist in correspondence management. If used, serial numbers are assigned sequentially, beginning with the number 001 on the first day of each new year. It's a rare letter indeed that is signed on the same date written, so resist the temptation to type the date when composing the letter. The date can be stamped after the letter has cleared all the hurdles.

To ensure routing to the appropriate individual within the command on the receiving end of a letter, the specific office code may be designated in parentheses in the "To" or address line. A "Via" command is an intermediate level in the chain of command; the format for such a command's endorsement of a letter is discussed below. References, listed in the "Ref" line, are other documents that pertain to the subject matter but are not included with the correspondence; these are designated by letters. Enclosures, listed in the "Encl" line, are supporting documents that are included in the correspondence; these are designated by numbers. All listed references and enclosures are discussed, in order, in the body of the letter.

From time to time, you may send a formal letter dealing with your own or a Sailor's personal or career issues. You may wish to communicate formally with selection boards or detailers, for example. For identification purposes, the "From" line in such a personal letter always lists your rate and enlisted warfare qualification, full name, and social security number, as in the following example: From: BMCM (AW/SW) Thomas J. Carpenter 123-45-6789.

Unless otherwise directed, such letters are normally sent via the drafter's commanding officer and other intermediates in the chain of command. Intermediate activities, designated as "Via" addressees in the letter, endorse correspondence and forward it to the next "Via" addressee or to the ultimate addressee as appropriate. Normally the first word of the first paragraph of an endorsement is "Forwarded." This may be expanded into a phrase such as "Forwarded, recommending approval," or other appropriate remark. If a piece of correspondence disappears into a black hole, the first place to look is to the "Via" signatories and work your way out from there.

Point Papers

The point paper is a useful but often misused document in today's Navy. As originally designed, the point paper is the document by which juniors provide condensed information on key topics to seniors. A point paper should be no more than one page long and should list, preferably in bullet format, the background, discussion, and drafter's recommendation(s) pertaining to the issue identified in the subject line. Sadly, many Chief Petty Officers think that if one page is good, ten pages are better. Nothing could be farther from the truth. Think about the paper's recipient. Extraneous detail just obscures your point. Even when the subject matter is somewhat complex, superiors are not totally clueless. The succinct point paper may not contain all the information needed to fully understand the subject but it can easily contain enough data for interested seniors to ask the right questions. After all, that's the main objective of the point paper—to start a meaningful dialogue on the subject. The ability to write clear, complete, concise point papers is a characteristic of outstanding Chief Petty Officers.

Memoranda

A memorandum is a less formal means of communication used between individuals in the same or different commands. Usually, the signer of a memorandum speaks only for himself or herself and not as a representative of the commanding officer. The format is similar to that of a Navy letter, except that a memorandum is normally written on plain paper or preprinted forms rather than on letterhead, and the word "memorandum" is typed or printed at the top of the page. Memoranda are generally typed, although very informal ones may be handwritten.

The "From" and "To" lines in a memorandum identify the sender and recipient by name and/or position. The signature block of a memorandum does not list the signer's organizational title, although his or her name may be typed underneath for clarity. Even though it is technically incorrect to use a complimentary close in a memorandum, it is still common and, in many commands, expected, for a junior to close a memorandum to a senior with "Very respectfully" and for a senior to close a memorandum to a junior with "Respectfully." In very informal correspondence these complimentary closes may be abbreviated as "V/r" and "R."

Casualty Reports (CASREPS)

One of the most important documents prepared by Chief Petty Officers is the casualty report. You must submit a CASREP when equipment can't be repaired within twenty-four hours, so that the Chief of Naval Operations (CNO) and fleet commanders can manage their forces. The CASREP also alerts the Naval Safety Center of incidents that are crucial to accident prevention. The effective use and support of Navy units and organizations requires an up-to-date, accurate operational status for each unit. When casualties are reported, operational commanders and support personnel are informed of the status of equipment malfunctions that degrade a unit's readiness. The CASREP also reports the unit's need for technical assistance and/or replacement parts to correct the casualty.

General Rules and Procedures. A casualty is defined as an equipment malfunction or deficiency that cannot be corrected within forty-eight hours and that fits any of the following categories:

- Reduces the unit's ability to perform a primary mission.
- Reduces the unit's ability to perform a secondary mission.

- Reduces a training command's ability to perform its mission or a specific segment of its mission and cannot be corrected or adequately accommodated locally by rescheduling or double-shifting lessons or classes.

Forms. There are four forms of CASREP message:

- Initial: The initial CASREP identifies, to an appropriate level of detail, the status of the casualty and parts and/or assistance requirements. This information is needed by operational and staff authorities to set proper priorities for the use of resources.
- Update: The update CASREP contains information similar to that submitted in the initial CASREP and/or submits changes to previously submitted information.
- Correct: A unit submits a correct CASREP when equipment that has been the subject of casualty reporting is repaired and back in operational condition.
- Cancel: A unit submits a cancel CASREP upon commencement of an overhaul or other scheduled availability period when equipment that has been the subject of casualty reporting is scheduled to be repaired. Outstanding casualties that will not be repaired during such availability will not be canceled and will be subject to normal follow-up casualty reporting procedures as specified.

As each type of message is submitted, managers are able to monitor the current status of each outstanding casualty. Through the use of high-speed computers, managers are able to collect data concerning the history of malfunctions and effects on readiness. This data is necessary to maintain and support units dispersed throughout the world.

Message Format. A CASREP message consists of data sets that convey sufficient information to satisfy the requirements of a particular casualty reporting situation. These data sets are preceded by a standard Navy message header consisting of precedence, addressees, and classification.

Text Structure. The text of a CASREP message is composed of data sets as necessary to report a particular situation. Each data set, in turn, is composed of one or more data fields. The fields in each set are grouped according to their relationship. The three types of data sets used in CASREP messages are as follows:

- Linear data set: Consists of a set identifier and one or more data fields present in a horizontal arrangement.
- Columnar data set: Used to display information in tabular form and contains multiple data lines. The first line of the set consists of a set identifier, the second line contains column headers, and subsequent lines contain data fields that are aligned under the appropriate headings.
- Free text set: Consists of a set identifier followed by a single, unformatted, narrative data field. This type of set is used to explain or amplify formatted information contained in one or more of the linear or columnar data sets in a message.

The free text or remarks section is especially critical, because no amount of formatted information can really convey the exact technical information required to fix the casualty. As a Chief Petty Officer you are expected to be both a technical expert and adequate communicator. On most ships, CASREPS are high-priority items. It's important that you consider your audience. Both technical and non-technical personnel will read your CASREP.

To help both audiences find the crucial information, use headings and indentations. In addition, write an executive summary for non-experts. Begin by carefully describing the exact nature and extent of the casualty. Discuss the casualty impact on the ship's operational activities—and the effect on the ship's ability to carry out its mission.

You also will need to write a detailed technical description for the technical staff to be able to set the repair process in motion even before the ship returns to port. Particularly if the message arrives on a holiday or weekend, keep in mind that the technical staff may not have direct expertise in your problem field. Be sure to use correct terminology; when in doubt, look up the correct name in the operations or maintenance manuals.

Enlisted Evaluations

One of the most important duties you'll perform as a Chief Petty Officer is evaluating your Sailors. You remember how you waited, sometimes with bated breath, to find out exactly how your chief viewed your contribution. Although BUPERSINST 1610.10 spells out the way to fill in the blanks for performance evaluations, it tells only half the story. The written comments are the meat of any evaluation, and the system relies on you to faithfully prepare the write-ups as part of the evaluation process. You must always:

Tell the truth every time, with out fear or favor. This is the very heart of being the chief. More complex than simply keeping a record of who has been naughty and nice and transferring that record to the evaluation, evaluating a Sailor requires wisdom and good judgment.

Consider that no one in the chain of command is likely to know your Sailors as well as you. There are, of course, the occasions when a Sailor spends a significant time period assigned to another work center. In those instances, his or her supervisor in that job must provide an assessment to augment your evaluation.

- For this duty, you are the Navy.
- Counsel your Sailors so that they might continue to improve.
- Identify the best possible people for advancement.
- Your time in the Navy is short—your legacy is forever.

The system supports and requires writing in the bullet style shown above and in earlier sections of this chapter, and you'd do well to use bullets whenever you can.

Writing good bullets is an easily learned skill. If writing in this style doesn't come naturally to you, simply write the narrative draft description using as many words as you like and then begin paring it down to the bare essence of what you intend to communicate to the reader. It will not take long to begin writing naturally in this minimalist style. To write a good evaluation:

- Present only the vital facts and key qualities.
- Present facts and qualities succinctly.
- Phrase facts and qualities clearly and in such a way that an evaluator, unfamiliar with the terminology of your rating, can understand them.

BUPERS demands that you avoid wordy preambles and adjective inflation. After reading a dozen or so inflated introductions, fatigue sets in, and everything sounds the same. This is particularly jarring if the reader knows the Sailor being reviewed and has a different perception of his or her performance. Avoid the stock phrases peddled by an evaluator's writing guides. Every advancement board member has seen them all and can usually identify which phrases have been lifted from which guidebooks! Rather than rely on stock phrases, list the best qualities of your Sailors in short, sharp, bullet statements. Combine words like creative, innovative, problem-solver, top-notch, effective, and successful. You should provide a numerical ranking comparison when appropriate.

The system requires that you provide specific details of the actual performance. The specifics should appear first in the evaluation and should comprise the greater part of the written comments. Remember: verifiable performance that can be illustrated by facts, numbers, and specific achievements is the key to effective evaluations. For example: "Petty Officer Farmington refurbished fifteen chairs for the Ready Room, saving the command $5000," or "Seaman Mercer led the entire division in physical readiness, and he leads by example, improving his personal PRT score from 210 (good) to 281 (outstanding) over the past three PRT cycles." Meaningful performances may be described as follows: "Had it not been for Petty Officer Reed's quick action, GTG #2 would have sustained critical damage and may have been destroyed."

In order to end past abuses, typographical tricks such as underlining, highlighting, italics, and script lettering are no longer permitted in enlisted evaluations. The focus now is on the accomplishments of the Sailor, not the evaluator's command of word processing. Nonetheless, remember that the white space in bullet lists, along with the bullets themselves, helps draw the reader's eye to key items and facilitates the reader in the time-consuming but important task of reading a stack of evaluations.

Citations, Commendations, and Awards

Napoleon once said: "A soldier will fight to the death for a piece of ribbon." Things may not be quite that dramatic in the Navy, but there's no denying that public recognition of outstanding contributions greatly improves morale on a ship or station. Whether the award is a Navy Achievement Medal for a Sailor who works long hard hours on an overhaul or a Distinguished Service Medal for a retiring Admiral, we all need to feel that our contributions have been fully appreciated.

As a Chief Petty Officer, you will have many occasions to consider recommending your Sailors for honors or awards. SECNAVINST 1650.1 lists the guidelines and appropriate awards or commendations for various acts. This section is intended to assist you in the preparation of the award after that decision is affirmed. After you've determined which award is most appropriate, you will first need to investigate the facts about the Sailor's performance. Then interview shipmates, superiors, and, if appropriate, subordinates, and verify evaluations, training records, and the Sailor's service record.

Finally, prepare a rough draft, grouping the facts logically to describe the event or characteristics that should be rewarded. Whenever possible, combine similar facts to provide more persuasive evidence that the Sailor deserves the award. For example:

Contributions to the ship or squadron	Superb work on special projects
Contributions to the division	Excellence in training
Accomplishments in primary duty	Excellence in maintenance
Accomplishments in additional duties	Excellence in leading
Accomplishments at sea	Individual/community contributions

Achievement. Refers to measurable results. "Petty Officer Houlton developed new software that reduced the cost of ongoing inventory by $345,000."

Praise—Facts—Results. "Petty Officer Kingfield is a superb leader, whose willingness to devote his off-duty time to training, resulted in fifteen strikers advancing to MM3, the largest number advanced in this command in recent history."

Achievement. "Airman Brunswick was selected as Grape of the Month in the Fuels Division, identified as Sailor of the Year in her department, and was nominated as Sailor of the Quarter for the Atlantic Fleet."

Focus first on requirements of the rating and billet. Then look to the extra duties performed, either by assignment or willingly. Finally, examine contributions to shipmates and others. Position the most important achievement first. Usually this is the one that had the greatest impact on the division, department, or command. Place team and unit results before individual results. Emphasize results and what the Sailor did to cause the results. Some useful words follow.

Words of Praise

Achievements:		
achieved	enforced	rated
attained	ensured	received
carried out	gained	scored
created	made	wrote
developed	mastered	provided

Improvements:		
aided	improved	reorganized
corrected	increased	repaired
enhanced	raised	strengthened
fixed	reduced	upgraded
formed	refined	updated

Leadership:		
coached	headed	managed
commanded	initiated	steered
controlled	influenced	supervised
directed	inspired	tasked
guided	instilled	handled

Training:		
counseled	prepared	taught
drilled	practiced	trained
instructed	presented	tutored
mentored	shaped	planned
molded	sharpened	showed

To describe personal characteristics of the awardee, pull out your trusty thesaurus. Words like able, bold, brave, bright, devoted, dynamic, eager, expert, firm, forceful, helpful, intense, matchless, outstanding, perfect, sharp, skilled, and superb will make your writing glow.

Assert firmly that the Sailor had a positive impact and made contributions. Don't simply praise the Sailor for personal capabilities or potential. Organize the submittal, beginning with an opening statement of praise. Be consistent with the wording of the awards definitions in SECNAVINST 1650.1. For example, you would not write "For exceptionally meritorious service . . ." in the write-up for the Navy and Marine Corps Achievement Medal. In this case it would be more appropriate to write: "For meritorious service . . ." Some examples:

- For professional achievement while serving as Leading Petty Officer in the communications department . . .
- For outstanding performance of duty while assigned as duty driver on 11 November 2001. . . .
- For meritorious service while serving as leading seaman, in the absence of assigned petty officers . . .

Cite a sufficient and specific fact(s) that individualizes the award. Highlight the most outstanding achievement. Remember to outline the impact on the unit's mission and not on the individual Sailor. Set the Sailor's achievement in the context of the unit and the Navy. As examples:

- Your work has been clearly superior. You are a great credit to the USS *Wissahickon* and the U.S. Navy.
- Your achievements have been of lasting benefit. You are a great credit to yourself, VF-104, and the U.S. Navy.
- Your untiring efforts and superior achievements reflect great credit upon you, Mobile Construction Battalion One, and the U.S. Navy.
- Your accomplishments are in the finest traditions of the Seabees and reflect great credit upon you and the U.S. Navy.

Skip abbreviations in the write-up. Spell out unit names, types of equipment, operating areas, etc. You must have your work proofread, always remembering that you cannot effectively proofread your own work. Even using the right-to-left, word-by-word methods of professional proofreaders, you are still too close to the material to improve it or catch every error. Have someone else within the command proofread and sanity check the submission. Finally, submit what you have written via the chain of command.

Nothing has changed the face of communications throughout the
Navy and the world so much as has email.
U.S. Navy (PH2 Kevin Gill)

Messages and Email

Naval Messages

The naval message is the primary means of rapid, official
communications between Navy commands. Messages,
transmitted electronically, permit immediate and highly
secure communications among ships at sea, shore commands, DoD activities, other government agencies, and

even foreign military units. To ensure proper handling and routing to their destinations, Navy messages must be very carefully formatted. Fortunately, Message Text File Editor (MTF) makes proper formatting a relatively simple matter. The information technologists within your command will assist you in drafting specific types of messages, often called pro-forma messages that, for example, report ship movements (MOVREPS).

Electronic Mail

Email may be the greatest communication advance in naval history. It may also be a plague on the Navy—the jury is still out. No element of the information revolution has quite had the impact that email has on the role of the Chief Petty Officer. CMDCM Mike McCalip, speaking as

Your senior information technologists are prepared to assist you in the development and routing of pro-forma messages.
U.S. Air Force (TSGT Cary Humphries)

Command Master Chief, USS *George Washington* (CVN-73), described the personal impact of email as a communications form. "[Each morning] I hit my office and do something I never dreamed would ever happen, and that's check email. I never imagined we'd have the instant connectivity to shore commands, to home, to everybody, that we have today. Just as an example, I just passed a message to the air wing CMC concerning the death of a Sailor's grandmother. We got word to the Sailor within, what, an hour or so of the event? Twenty-four years ago, when I came in—and I was a radioman, so I knew—it would take days, sometimes, for someone to get the word."

Many Sailors now have the ability to send and receive electronic mail messages via the Internet. The format of an email message depends on whether or not it is considered official correspondence. In formal email correspondence, follow the standard format for a naval letter, with the full name of the signer indicated at the close. Less formal correspondence may follow the memorandum format, and no specific format is required for very informal electronic correspondence.

All the writing tips offered earlier in this chapter apply to email. Consider your audience and your purpose and plan accordingly. Email does not disappear into the ether but is a permanent record that sometimes is delivered to places the sender never intended. Your name is perpetually attached to the email, so take some care with it. Never email something you wouldn't say in person.

Reread and spell-check the message before pressing send. Rereading puts you in the recipient's place, and you may detect where you have been overly brief and sound curt. Never forward email to other people without permission—unless it is common practice within your command to copy to other members.

Include your basic contact data in the signature file, but resist the urge to develop overly large signature files for your emails. Adm. William Halsey used to sign messages and letters "Halsey." You may not be as famous as the Bull, but seven-line signature blocks make you look like you think you are. If your mailer allows you to edit your "from" line and return address, make sure yours is correct so that mail does not go astray.

Know the limitations of the email systems you are using. Don't include oversized files unless you coordinate with the recipient. Large files and slow links make information technicians grow old before their time. Save the photo album for your cable modem at home.

Formats. Because not all email systems support formatted text, simplicity is best. You will soon discover what your ship's email can support and how your formatted text may appear as gibberish on the distant screen.

Brevity. Most of us wouldn't send a one-line letter, yet many will send a yes or no email. That's fine, particularly when a reply is attached to the original email, and provided you are certain that the addressees understand to what you refer.

Spelling. Email is often typed in a hurry. Typos and common spelling errors go unnoticed—except by the recipient. Email is still a representation of you and your pride in yourself.

Capitalization. Proper capitalization makes for easier reading, as generations of radiomen reading all caps can attest. Proper names should be capitalized. Other conventions of grammar such as punctuation make email easier to read and therefore more effective as a communication tool. Take pride in whatever you are communicating. Email can be forwarded with ease.

Punctuation. Avoid using special characters in your email. Recipients may not be able to read bullets. If you must use them for emphasis, use asterisks. Avoid dashes to hyphenate. The computer will automatically hyphenate for your reader in places you could not anticipate. Use parentheses, not brackets or braces. Use single quotes or apostrophes rather than double quotation marks.

Communication, as discussed in these chapters, requires an intelligent sender, a receptive audience, a clear channel, a well-crafted message, freedom from noise, and provisions for adequate feedback. All of this requires Chief Petty Officers to continuously improve their reading and writing skills. This is not as hard as some would have you believe. It doesn't necessarily require college courses, although formal courses in English composition or technical writing can be quite helpful. You can help yourself improve by:

- Actively growing your vocabulary with one of the many "word-a-day" primers or other vocabulary self-help courses.

- Using a dictionary when you read. Don't plow through or skip words you don't understand. Look them up and add them to your vocabulary.

- Using a good thesaurus in concert with a good dictionary, intelligently. Just looking up a synonym and plugging it in can lead to rampant confusion and laughable, embarrassing mistakes. The thesaurus should be used only to remind and refresh you of words that you already know.

- Working on recurring, predictable writing projects continuously. Leaving annual performance evaluations or end-of-tour/deployment award writing to the week before it is due adds pressure and guarantees a substandard result. It's much better to work a few minutes at a time on these projects over an extended period. Electronic files and the word processor facilitate this practice. Be sure you back up this work (as well all other files).

As a Chief Petty Officer, many of your seniors will personally observe your performance. But many more will know you by the way you write.

Part Three

Developing

8

Development of Subordinates and Junior Officers

Case Study: What is the Navy coming to?

AZC Dan Bonner walked into the CPO mess aboard USS *James B. Stockdale* (CVN-82). Pouring himself a large cup of coffee, he sat down next to BMCS Mike Judge. "Senior, I don't know where these young Sailors are coming from," he said. "I just came down from forward berthing—we're holding field day to get ready for zone inspection, and you can't hear yourself think up there. One guy has some singer named 50-Cent blaring out hip-hop, another has his boombox cranked up with some heavy metal rocker called Radiohead, and my LPO—you'd think he would know better!—has Marilyn Manson tapes running on the VCR. And on the way back down, Doc Ryan stops me in the p-way and tells me that A. A. Moore, one of my better Sailors, has just been admitted to sick bay. It seems she got a large tattoo of the Ozbourne family on her backside in Hong Kong last week. Doc says it goes from coast to coast, and she now has hepatitis from the dirty needle. Senior, I'm telling ya, I just don't understand Sailors anymore!"

The Culture of Today's Sailors

Somewhere between Fiddler's Green and Davy Jones's locker, seaweed-bearded chiefs smoking clay pipes are chuckling at Chief Bonner's predicament. The conversation that starts with "Today's Sailors ain't what they used to be" has gone on since time immemorial. Every generation has its own culture, and every generation delights in mystifying, irritating, and annoying its elders.

When we see young Sailors on the beach or their civilian counterparts in town, their clothing and behavior may amaze or even offend us. What we are really seeing and hearing are expressions of a generational culture as different from our own as any we might see ashore in a foreign port. Cultural elements or artifacts are in constant flux; indeed, nothing dates us so much as trying to be current when writing about culture. Music, slang, clothing, and electronic games and instruments define a cultural

Today's Sailors represent today's generation of young Americans. Their clothing, speech, and attitudes toward authority may differ from those prevailing when today's chiefs were young Sailors.
U.S. Navy (PH1 Novia E. Harrington)

generation. Although we're all Sailors who have taken an oath to support and defend the Constitution, you'll meet representatives of at least three distinct cultural generations every time you step across the brow.

Baby Boomers

This generation grew up in a stable, usually conservative, environment. Ike was president; television was black and white with three channels, if you were lucky. *Leave It to Beaver* and *Father Knows Best* were perennial 1950s favorites. In the late 1960s, adolescents, with encouragement from social radicals, rebelled and ushered in a counterculture era marked by free love, urban riots, and campus unrest. Nonetheless, this generation knew and understood authority, be it parental, school, or military. A smart mouth or disrespectful attitude usually meant a public trip to the woodshed. Like Chief Bonner, baby boomers are likely to look at today's youth with little comprehension for who they are and how they got that way.

Generation X

As the revolt against authority continued, the next generation, sometimes called Generation X, experienced much less family solidarity thanks to a meteoric rise in single-parent families, unsupervised after-school time, the AIDS epidemic, and skyrocketing youth crime. Many entered the Navy as volunteers, seeking stability, and they are usually economically driven to remain on active duty. They're grateful for the benefits of military life and are quietly patriotic. They like their rock and roll a little harder, their country music a little wilder, and there is a distinct preference for urban music, even among Sailors from a rural background. This generation is proud of its ethnic heritage; it's not unusual to hear Spanish, Tagalog, or other languages whenever they gather. If Mom and Dad were around much, they tried to reason with this generation, as did their teachers. Sadly enough, if Mom and Dad tried to reason too forcefully, the neighbors, far

from applauding as they might have for an earlier generation, were just as likely to call Children's Services to
report the abuse. This was a generation with many privileges but relatively few responsibilities.

Generation Y/Millennials

This generation was born into chaos. School violence is a
fact of life, and drugs continue to plague many of their cities
and neighborhoods. Most of today's young non-rated personnel aboard ship are products of this generation. Their
feelings of helplessness, of being outsiders, have contributed to the anger-filled grunge-and-death metal movements, as well as helped fuel the hip-hop and gangsta-rap
explosion in urban communities. They're technologically
sophisticated; they've grown up surrounded by computers
and technology ranging from ATM machines to laptops,
Gameboys, and MP3 players. They are brand-label conscious, shelling out $150 for a pair of sneakers. Mom and
Dad were probably working two jobs each to make ends
meet, and many of today's Sailors spent a considerable part
of their adolescence in social isolation behind closed doors,
listening to music, surfing the Net, or instant-messaging
friends. If Mom or Dad noticed anything amiss, they were
usually too tired or too frustrated to do much about it, and
this generation sometimes has real difficulties telling right
from wrong. It's not that they're immoral, but the examples
they've seen have been of little help in setting their moral
compass, and no one has helped them along the way.

"I'll tell ya, Senior, if any of my old chiefs ever saw what's going
on these days, they'd roll over in their graves. You remember
when we pulled out of San Diego? I had my division manning the
rail, and do you know I had to grab four or five of my Sailors—and
some of them were petty officers, Senior Chief!—and threaten
them with mast if they didn't put away their cell phones? Imagine
that! We might as well set the uniform of the day as Service Dress
Whites—with telephone!"

For today's young Sailors, email and cell phones are considered a right, and they often feel deprived when these tools are not readily available. Young Sailors even have withdrawal symptoms when they find that Web-surfing is not readily available. They are used to being connected and to having instant access to their friends and to things that interest them. Fortunately, their environment is much more multicultural than that of their seniors. The racial strife that plagued the Navy and the nation a generation ago is pretty well attenuated, although you'll still see voluntary racial segregation (watch who sits where on your messdeck someday). Images of sex and violence have bombarded this generation during their formative years like no other. Cultural icons and common memories of a previous generation like the Vietnam War and the assassinations of John Kennedy and Dr. Martin Luther King, Jr., are ancient history to them. They do know about the attacks at the Oklahoma City Federal Building, the World Trade Center, and the Pentagon, and they were deeply moved by the suicide of Kurt Cobain and the murders at Columbine High. In that context, anxiety, hostility, and non-specific anger associated with many may not be so hard to understand after all.

"They're good Sailors, Senior, don't get me wrong. They'll work for twenty-four hours without a break if we need them to. It's just that, well, I don't really know where they are coming from. I mean, a nice young Sailor like A. A. Moore, polite, hardworking, well-spoken—she's younger than my own daughter, Senior Chief!—with a huge tattoo across her rear end. I'll tell ya, Senior Chief, if my daughter got a tattoo like that, well, that wouldn't be the only thing she'd have to worry about on her backside!"

We tend to forget that we weren't angels growing up, not by a long shot. Our ways of expressing ourselves may have differed, but we were as incomprehensible to our leaders as these Sailors are to us. There are good things about this generation, just as there were about the generations that went before. Take a good look at your young Sailors today, and you'll find:

Optimism. Most young Sailors believe they are special and can accomplish whatever they desire. They're in a bit of a rush, though. Who has not had a young Sailor report on board already dismayed to hear that he or she has got to work his way up and won't be standing OOD or advising the captain within the next two weeks?

Authenticity. As with all of us, honesty is important to today's Sailors. They can spot a phony a mile away. Sometimes they think that the most authentic leaders are those who have been there and done that and whose experiences mirror their own. There is a cautionary tale, here, too. Don't make the mistake of trying to fit in with your younger Sailors. You'll look dumb, and you won't be able to pull it off. Be yourself, and let them be themselves, too. Things work better that way.

Self-Reliance. Because of deterioration in family structure, many of today's young Sailors have been raised to be self-reliant and to believe in their own abilities. That can be a useful characteristic in many situations. Sometimes, however, as any experienced recruit division commander can attest, it can get in the way of teamwork and of looking out for your shipmates and your ship.

These positive youth values are good news for our Navy. But as leaders, we still have to contend with potentially harmful aspects of youth culture. Much of youth culture is based on symbols, the meaning of which can be lost on outsiders. Some symbols are divisive and promote racial or ethnic strife; others, like taking drugs, promote lifestyle choices inimical to Navy life. Most commands have a policy about appropriate civilian clothing on base or on liberty, and strict enforcement often nips problems before they arise.

As Chief Bonner shot the breeze with Senior Chief Judge, the mess quickly filled for noon chow. Chiefs Malvern and Hubert joined the conversation, as did Master Chief Prendergast, the command master chief. "You can always tell one of our new Sailors," Chief Bonner quipped. "But you can't tell him much."

The others seemed to agree that the younger generation had less respect for their elders in generations past, seemed unmotivated, questioned orders, and cared less about fitness and personal appearance. Whatever the reality of the chiefs' perceptions, the training leading and motivating Sailors was their responsibility. Understanding the culture from which their young Sailors have come is a first step.

Voluntary Education Programs

For many years, few subjects have generated as much emotion as the value of off-duty education and how much impact it should have on advancement. At one end of the spectrum are chiefs who believe that all college courses not directly related to the Sailor's rating are a waste of time and, worse, detract from the time and energy available to keep the work center on track. They believe Navy training is enough, that only the U.S. Navy has the laboratories and expertise necessary to grant degrees in naval leadership, seamanship, work center supervisor, or division chief.

At the other end of the spectrum are those who want every Chief Petty Officer to have a bachelor's degree and every senior and master chief to have a master's degree. They believe Sailors who are committed to voluntary education are far less likely to be involved with the disciplinary process. Indeed, a quick survey of Sailors-of-the-Quarter or Sailors-of-the-Year at any command will find a large percentage involved in off-duty education, many to the undergraduate or graduate levels.

Many of the skills required of today's Chief Petty Officer are, in fact, taught in those off-duty college courses and many Chief Petty Officers are better writers and communicators because they honed those skills with off-duty college courses.

One of our Navy's greatest strengths is that a surprisingly large percentage of the officer leadership of our great Navy comes from the enlisted ranks. Most prepare themselves for that transition with off-duty education And, amazingly, they do it in a way that not only doesn't interfere with their job performance, but enhances it.

A CPO is not expected to be a therapist or a chaplain, but on the subject of education, expectations differ. Sailors have a right to expect sound advice on both the full range of opportunities and, more importantly, on when and how best to take advantage of them. There is no one-size-fits-all answer regarding off-duty education, and the discernment of the CPO is needed. The Sailor who writes and spells poorly should be taking a remedial English course, not the more challenging English 101 because he might squeak by and get some free credits. The chief must tell him exactly that. Likewise, it is the chief's responsibility to counsel the Sailor who can't get to quarters on time and has trouble staying awake or concentrating on the job that perhaps he has bitten off too much by signing up for ten hours of classes. The chief must disapprove any TA requests that are clearly inconsistent with the Sailor's demonstrated performance and the command's mission and schedule. These benefits are privileges, not rights.

Some Sailors are not even slightly interested in getting a college degree or further training, and others are highly motivated, deferring all other liberty pursuits for education and training. As a Chief Petty Officer, you should consider a Sailor neither better nor worse solely because of his or her attitude on the subject of off-duty education.

Case Study: Where There's a Will, There's a Way

FCCS Karnataka was in his office when Command Master Chief Prendergast called. "Manus," she said, "I've been looking at our educational records. We've got some fine Sailors on board, folks who have spent a lot of their off-duty time advancing their education. I know that you just earned your master's degree right before we left on this deployment. We're gathering a lot of the undesignated airmen and seamen together in the fo'c'sle tomorrow for school of the ship. Could you come over for about fifteen minutes and describe a few of the programs available for off-duty education?" Senior Chief Karnataka quickly agreed and reached into his desk to pull out some background information so that he'd transmit the straight skinny when he spoke to the GenDets the following day.

The Navy College Program

The Navy College Program (NCP) provides a wide range of educational programs and services for active duty Sailors. There are programs in the NCP portfolio that can assist Sailors in meeting any of their educational needs, from basic academic skills to postgraduate programs. The program's goal is to give every Sailor the opportunity to recognize and achieve his or her personal goals while still maintaining operational readiness.

These programs recognize a number of academic milestones as being particularly significant for Sailors: a high school diploma or equivalent for all personnel, an associate's degree for enlisted personnel, a bachelor's degree for enlisted and officers, and a graduate degree for those who so desire. To further support these goals, all Sailors, active or reserve, who complete an associate, bachelor, or graduate degree will be awarded points toward their promotion multiples when advancing to pay grades E-4 through E-6, in accordance with current Bureau of Naval Personnel (BUPERS) policies.

The Navy College Program, working through local Navy counselors, command master chiefs, and all informed Chief Petty Officers, provides academic and vocational counseling to assist individuals in establishing short- and long-range goals to better plan their educational programs. More in-depth counseling sessions are provided for those who require specific information and guidance. During the course of the session, the counselor may recommend various options and strategies to assist the Sailor. Some of the strategies may include use of the DANTES testing program; information on financial aid such as tuition assistance, Veterans' Benefits, or VEAP; information on career and vocational choices; descriptive materials on college and vocational correspondence courses; information on external degree programs; or enrollment into SOCNAV college degree programs, as described below:

Credit for Military Training. Every two years, the American Council on Education publishes the *ACE Guide*, a guide to the evaluation of educational experiences in the armed forces. The guide recommends college credit for various service schools, ratings, or NECs. Every Navy counselor will have this guide readily available for reference. Fortunately, most colleges and universities will honor these recommendations toward degree requirements.

Additional Counseling Services. Navy counselors use a number of instruments to assist Sailors to further identify their interests and occupational goals. These may be particularly useful for those who are not sure of the direction they would like to take following military service. Some of the instruments available include the Strong Interest Bank (SIB); Kudder Interest Inventory (KII); Career Assessment Inventory (CAI); and the Self Directed Search (SDS). As a Chief Petty Officer, it's your duty to identify those first-term Sailors who have decided not to pursue a career in military service and to assist them in understanding the options available to them.

Defense Activity for Non-Traditional Education Support (DANTES). DANTES supports the voluntary education functions of all military branches. DANTES provides nontraditional education services, including examination programs, independent study, external degree programs, Servicemembers' Opportunity Colleges, and military evaluations. Again, your Sailors can obtain DANTES publications, manuals, handbooks, audiovisual training aids, posters, and brochures through your local command's education officer or through embarked Navy counselors.

Examination Programs. Free testing services are available for all military personnel at most shore facilities and many commands afloat. Some programs available through the Navy College office include:

- General Education Development Examination (GED)
- Scholastic Aptitude Test (SAT)
- American College Test (ACT)
- General and Subject Exams for the College Level Examination Program (CLEP)
- DANTES Subject Standardized Tests (DSST)
- Regents College Examinations (RCE)
- General Examinations for the Graduate Record Examination (GRE)

Certification Programs. Certification examinations allow selected professionals to obtain certification in their particular field. Certification translates military training into civilian terms and provides an opportunity to document skills learned while on active duty. This documentation can then be readily understood and accepted in the civilian, professional, and occupational community. Agreements between DANTES and the various professional organizations have made it possible for these exams to be ordered through Navy counselors. Any fees for the examinations are the responsibility of the Sailor, however.

Independent Study Program. The DANTES Independent Study Program allows Sailors to enroll in more than six thousand courses, covering high school, undergraduate, and graduate studies. Tuition assistance is authorized for eligible personnel. The Sailor is reimbursed at the prevailing authorized rate after completion of the course.

External Degree Programs. External degree programs are offered by regionally accredited colleges and universities. Many Sailors find external degree programs ideal because of flexible schedules, nontraditional delivery, and programs that require little or no on campus residency. *The DANTES Guide to External Degree Programs* identifies those programs that best meet the needs of the military student.

Servicemember's Opportunity Colleges (SOC). SOC is a network of more than 860 colleges and universities whose policies and programs are designed to help meet the higher education needs of service members. SOC schools generally minimize residency requirements for college credits. SOC has developed a degree program known as SOCNAV, which is a group of associate and bachelor degree networks.

National Apprenticeship Program. This program allows active duty personnel to receive recognition for skills learned performing their regular duties. The program requires a participant to maintain a daily log of hours. Upon completion of the required hours, a Certificate of Completion of Apprenticeship is awarded jointly by the Department of the Navy and the Department of Labor. This is the same credential awarded to civilians working in similar fields of work and can assist participants to document their work experiences in the military.

Navy College Program for Afloat College Education (NCPACE). The Navy sponsors tuition-free academic skills and college courses taught on many ships at sea. The consolidated NCPACE program provides for both instructor-taught and technology-based courses with the technology courses being taught via computer-interactive video and CD-ROM. Contact Navy College for details on how you or your Sailors can get involved with this program.

Foreign Credential Evaluation. There are a number of private evaluating organizations that for a fee will review transcripts from foreign institutions and equate that experience to a standard applied to institutions in the United States. Interested students should contact the institution they wish to attend and ask which organization and type of evaluation would be required. Often the college or university has a specific organization they would prefer or may have the ability to assess the transcript internally. The Navy College office will make referrals for your Sailors as appropriate.

Financial Assistance Programs. There are a number of federally funded programs that assist students in pursuing higher education:

- Navy Tuition Assistance Program: Navy Tuition Assistance (TA) is provided to all active-duty personnel. This program pays 100 percent tuition for high school completion courses and up to seventy-five percent for college. Be certain that your Sailors contact their education office or Navy counselors for the most up-to-date information on this program.

- Veteran's Educational Assistance Program (VEAP): Individuals entering the service between 1 January 1977 and 30 June 1985 are eligible to participate in VEAP if they are presently enrolled or have been previously enrolled. VEAP is a contributory program, with personnel depositing between $25 and $100 per month by payroll deduction. Individuals were permitted to deposit up to $2,700 and were matched two to one by the Navy for a total fund of up to $8,100. VEAP may be used after the first period of obligated service has been completed.

- Montgomery GI Bill (MGIB): Those entering active duty after 30 June 1985 will incur a reduction in pay of $100 per month for twelve months, unless they elect not to participate in this program. This is a one-time, irrevocable decision that must be made at the time the individual initially enters active duty. Benefits may be used in service after the completion of two years' active duty. Personnel must have earned a high school diploma or equivalent by the end of their first enlistment and must receive an honorable discharge. Application for benefits may be obtained from the Navy College office or the institution. Personnel have ten years from the last date of discharge to utilize the benefits.

- Other Financial Aid: The federal and state government sponsor several programs. Interested Sailors should work closely with the Education Office or Navy Counselors who will coordinate with the financial aid office at the selected institution. These programs include federal Pell Grants up to $2,200 per year for undergraduates; low-interest federal (Perkins) loans up to $9,000 for eligible undergraduates and $18,000 per year for eligible graduate students; Stafford loans for up to $7,500 for eligible students.

"Well, it's good that we've got fine educational programs for our Sailors," Chief Bonner remarked at chow, "but I came into the Navy during the boom-market times of the 1990s. Our retention rates were terrible, and even senior petty officers were bailing out right and left. It's better now—our retention rates are as high as they've ever been—but I wonder how many Sailors know what incentives we've available to help them when that first decision point comes?"

Retaining Our Sailors

One of the most important tasks facing Chief Petty Officers is the retention of good Sailors, particularly those on their first enlistment, who are making critical decisions about the Navy as a career. Sailors who have completed voluntary education programs are at a distinct advantage when deciding whether to ship over or return to civilian life.

Every Chief Petty Officer must be aware of the various programs that assist our subordinates with furthering their paths of advancement and career opportunities. The Navy Retention Program provides a means of strengthening policy and programs designed to:

- Ensure personnel stability through the retention of top-quality personnel in proper balance and required numbers.
- Provide a means to successfully fulfill the Navy's obligation to keep its personnel and families properly informed.
- Provide continuing career guidance so that individuals might best develop and use their talents while in the Navy.
- Increase goodwill and respect for the Navy in active duty personnel so that, upon leaving the service, they become "Navy ambassadors" to the civilian community.
- Encourage separating members to actively participate in the Naval Reserve.

Career Reenlistment Objectives (CREO) establishes a framework for enlisted career force management and provides guidelines for the operation of current and future Navy programs to meet those objectives. CREO is gender-specific in order to better manage male and female staffing levels and contains three categories of guidance. Category One indicates that there is a shortage of personnel in the rating; Category Two indicates that the balance is about right in a particular rating; and Category Three indicates that a rating is oversubscribed and requires approval from BUPERS for reenlistment.

Rating Entry for General Apprentices (REGA) guides the general apprentice (GENDET) population into ratings where junior level vacancies exist. The *Retention Team Manual*, BuPers 15878H (chapter five) lists specific details of this program.

Enlisted Navy Career Options for Reenlistment (ENCORE) is the Navy's first-term reenlistment and extension management program, designed to balance personnel inventories and requirements and, where appropriate, to convert reenlistees from overmanned ratings to those offering greater opportunities for career advancement. Refer to the *Navy Retention Team Manual* for further details.

The Selective Reenlistment Bonus (SRB) Program encourages reenlistment and provides a means to satisfy the needs of the Navy and the individual. It is our most effective management tool to influence retention in mission-critical skills. Refer to chapter six of the *Navy Retention Team Manual* for further details.

The Selective Conversion and Reenlistment (SCORE) Program offers career incentives for reenlistment and conversion to critically undermanned ratings. Benefits include assignment to a Class A or Class C school or advanced first-term avionics, possible advancement to third class or second class petty officer, and, if eligible, a selective reenlistment bonus (SRB). Chapter seven of the *Navy Retention Team Manual* has more details.

The Selective Training and Reenlistment (STAR) Program offers career designation to first-term enlisted members in programs that provide career incentives similar to those of SCORE. As with SCORE, details are in chapter seven of the *Navy Retention Team Manual.*

The Guaranteed Assignment Retention Detailing Program (GUARD 2000) provides two guaranteed assignments during a career. The member must use the first guaranteed assignment on the first reenlistment. The member must use the second guaranteed assignment before the commencement of the servicemember's twenty-fifth year of active military service. Again, refer to chapter seven of the *Navy Retention Team Manual* for further details.

Assignment to a school or a change in rating are additional reenlistment incentives for those eligible members who reenlist for four or more years. An accompanying change in rating permits members to serve in the rating for which they have the greatest aptitude and interest. Refer to chapter seven of the *Navy Retention Team Manual* for further details covering eligibility requirements concerning incentive programs.

The Navy enlisted-to-officer commissioning programs offer Sailors with exceptional leadership potential an opportunity to pursue commissions as naval officers. These programs include the Naval Academy and Naval Academy Preparatory School (NAPS) Programs; Naval Reserve Officers Training Corps (NROTC) Scholarship Program; Broadened Opportunity for Officer Selection and Training (BOOST) Program; Seaman-to-Admiral (STA) Program; Officer Candidate School (OCS); Enlisted Commissioning Program (ECP); Basic ECP, Aviation AECP, Nuclear NECP, and Civil Engineer Corps ECP-CEC; Medical Enlisted Commissioning Program (MECP); Medical Service Corps In-Service Procurement Program (MSC IPP); and the Limited Duty Officer (LDO) and Chief Warrant Officer (CWO) Programs.

Limited Duty Officer (LDO) and Warrant Officer (CWO) Programs give senior enlisted the opportunity to fleet up to limited duty or warrant officer commissions. LDO commissions require U.S. citizenship, a high school diploma or GED, meeting or exceeding current physical standards, recommendation by the commanding officer, and exemplary disciplinary record, between eight and sixteen years of active naval service, and at least one year of service in current rating. Surprisingly, the requirements for promotion to warrant officer are somewhat more stringent. For example, the CWO grade is open only to Chief Petty Officers; the LDO grade is open to highly qualified or motivated petty officers first class. Pursuit of a CWO commission is generally considered a path for very motivated Chief Petty Officers who, upon promotion, will possess the same authority as any other commissioned officer. Generally, however, they have slightly lower levels of academic achievement than those who strive for LDO commissions. Warrant and chief warrant officers are well qualified by extensive technical training, experience, and leadership in a specific occupational field and are considered a major asset to any command, where they serve primarily as division officers and officers in charge.

For Chief Petty Officers interested in the warrant officer community, the requirements are similar to those required for conversion to limited duty officers, except

Newly commissioned officers can be forgiven if sometimes they appear to "know it all." Wise Chief Petty Officers will mentor and assist young officers as they develop into the leaders of tomorrow's Navy.
U.S. Navy (PHC Terry A. Cosgrove)

that CPOs must have at least twelve but not more than twenty-four years of active service and they must be serving as chiefs, senior chiefs, or master Chief Petty Officers.

A Comparison: Limited Duty Officers and Warrant Officers, FY 2002

	LDO	CWO
Age	33	38
Total years of active service	13 years	17 years
Average rank	E-7	E-7
Average years of total education completed	14–15 years	14–15 years
Warfare qualified	Yes	Yes
Average personal awards (NCM/NAM/FLOC)	4	5
Former unit SOQ/SOY	Yes	Yes
Average total number of duty stations	4	6
Prior recruiting/RTC/ instructor tours	Yes	20%
Average number of sea/ overseas tours completed	2	3
Average total number of correspondence courses not related to advancement	7	7
Average number of training schools completed	7	12
Average sustained performance trait	EP	EP

Developing and Supporting Junior Officers

Many things make Chief Petty Officers unique. We have the absolute obligation to participate in the development of junior officers at the same time as we are being the best, most loyal subordinates possible. Indeed, no role we play is more important or more special than the development of junior officers. It's a role so important that it's listed as a core competency, a key component of that very short statement embodying who we are and what we do.

It's an unusual relationship. Business managers aren't expected to develop their executives; carpenters or plumbers aren't expected to develop their foremen; and ball players aren't responsible for the professional growth of their coaches and managers. Only in the sea services do we readily and willingly take responsibility for the development of our own leaders.

Think for a moment about what Admiral Mike Boorda, the most admired and beloved chief of naval operations, had to say on the subject on the occasion of the commissioning of USS Chief (MCM-14) in November 1995:

> "The title 'chief' raises so many memories for all Sailors," he said. "Every one of us who has served for any length of time can tell you about his or her special chief, indeed, most of us have more than one—a salty individual who took care of them, who taught them all the important things, who set the example, who cared about them and was not afraid to show it in so many ways. We officers have our special chiefs, too: usually somewhat older than we, always wiser in the ways of the Navy than we could possibly be as we started out on our careers, ready with advice, with counsel, and with the know-how to make it happen, to get it done, no matter how difficult. And through it all, those great chiefs were and are also great teachers. They know, as only Chief Petty Officers can know, that getting the job done today is important, but that the task of helping a new officer become a real pro, a true naval officer in the finest sense of the term, is part of the job. It's a key part, a critical role that Chief Petty Officers have been playing for over one hundred years now. Our Navy depends upon them, and the chiefs know that and they thrive on the challenge.
>
> "I am a lucky man for I have served as a new seaman, a petty officer, and an officer. In each phase of my career a great Chief Petty Officer

appeared at just the right time, guiding me, pushing me when necessary, leading me, and, when it was appropriate, letting me think I was leading him. There have been many chiefs in my life, all important, many personal friends, all professionals. And I know, as every Sailor knows, that the word leadership and the title 'Chief Petty Officer' go together. You cannot say one without thinking of the other. In war and in peace, they teach, they provide technical expertise and experience, they know how to get the job done, and they know how to make all the right things happen. They know that combat readiness is based on taking care of people, on keeping their ship requirement-ready at all times. But all of that is just a preamble to leadership in war. No chief, no Sailor, wants to fight in wars. We want to deter them. But when our nation calls, when the fight is no longer optional, no longer avoidable, but now is required, when 'now' is the order of the day, that is when all that Chief Petty Officer leadership—honor, courage, and commitment—really pays off. For deep down, each and every Chief Petty Officer knows that we are warriors and that he or she is a leader of warriors as well. In the smoke and fury and, yes, the confusion of battle at sea, it is then that the Chief Petty Officer proves again and again that everything else was simply preparation for the moment of truth, the moment when all that work pays off. When young Sailors do what is required, they do it almost instinctively, and they look to the chief for the example of all that is great in our Navy."

The Chief Petty Officer who ensured that Petty Officer Boorda became an ensign was a senior chief who ended WWII as an LDO aviator and reverted to Chief Petty Officer to continue to serve in the Navy. He recognized in PN1 Mike Boorda unique qualities and persistently recommended him for a commission in the newest commissioning program. Admiral Boorda was fond of telling the story of how his chief would not let him fail to prepare and submit a package after a first submission was not successful.

Developing junior officers, like developing junior enlisted, is not an easy task. You may face any of the following situations when dealing with junior officers.

The Unheeding Officer

Through immaturity, this junior officer fails to consult with the chief or fails to heed advice freely and prudently given. This is the most common complaint identified by the CPO community. But put yourself in the junior officer's shoes, and you might soon realize that it's an easy mistake to make. The junior officer has been taught to act decisively, to be a leader, and many lack the maturity or wisdom to understand that experience is a harsh mistress—and that lessons learned through experience are much stronger than those learned through books. A wise Chief Petty Officer will note the situation and consider: "Well, what I'm seeing here will delay but not deter me. To make this situation work, I'd do well to appear as nonthreatening and helpful to this junior officer as I can. I'll let him or her know that I'm here to help, not overrule or embarrass, and that listening to the voice of experience can reduce, rather than increase, whatever stressors the young officer may be feeling."

Everybody's Best Friend

This junior officer fraternizes with or allows undue familiarity with junior enlisted. Most junior officers are about the same age as second and third class petty officers. They most likely have more formal education, but the link between education and maturity is not necessarily strong. The junior officer and junior enlisted share a common generational culture: music, electronic games, slang, taste in off-duty clothing. Especially on small ships or at small commands where the wardroom is not large, junior officers might think they can expand their circle of friends through the enlisted community. The junior officer may see the chief as someone roughly the same age as his or her parents and may suffer role confusion in his or her own mind. Your job as chief is to remind your junior enlisted that it is never appropriate to cross the line with their officers, telling them that although it may feel cool for a while to hang out with Ensign Bob or Lieutenant (jg) Suzie, no long-term good is likely to result from flouting the clear and oft-stated rules regarding fraternization.

The Halfback

This young officer performs end-runs around the chain of command. Few situations are more frustrating than finding that your division officer or other officers in your chain of command are passing instructions, orders, or information directly to your subordinates without including you in the information flow. It's a situation fraught with peril because the chain of command is designed to work downward as well as upward. A short, direct conversation with an offending junior officer should help alleviate this situation. If the behavior continues, a discussion with your command master chief, someone who can take the matter directly to the department head, may be in order.

Ensign Two-Hats

This junior officer usurps the role of the Chief Petty Officer. Occasionally, you'll find a junior officer whose energy level, desire to help the chief, or genuine concern for Sailors takes him or her over the line. They'll become involved in things that are traditionally the responsibilities of Chief Petty Officers, things like setting up the watch quarter and station bill or becoming involved in leave and liberty issues. The best way to handle this type of situation is to gently remind the erring junior officer that his or her plate is no doubt full, and taking responsibility for things outside the job description just leaves less time for things that need to be accomplished at his or her own level. Remind the young officer that his or her own watch qualifications and warfare quals are too important to be delayed by admin and technical work that falls within the chief's area of responsibility.

The Circuit Breaker

This junior officer acts as a cut-out, usually inadvertently, failing to pass the word. One exasperating trait of some junior officers is to attend officers' call, show up for morning quarters, and fail to pass the word from one venue to the other. They're seen at officers' call, notebook and pencil in hand—yet important information never seems to make it to the deckplates. The first time this happens it is the division officer's fault, but it is the first signal to the chief to take some firm but respectful action to ensure that the D.O. takes this seemingly routine duty of officers' call seriously.

I'm My Favorite Shipmate

This officer is self-centered and usually overly concerned with obtaining his or her own qualifications and promotion. Being a junior officer in today's Navy is a tough job; everyone from the skipper to the department head is hammering on you to complete your warfare qualifications, Officer of the Deck Underway, or billet requirements. Sometimes junior officers see their division or collateral responsibilities as less important than obtaining their personal qualifications and quickly getting their tickets punched. You will need to remind the junior officer of his or her responsibilities in addition to helping the junior officer meet the required qualifications.

Failed Leaders

The Navy's officer corps, coming from the Naval Academy, NROTC, OCS, or direct commission, is the finest in the world. Regrettably, however, there are officers who fail their moral responsibilities, just as there are Sailors, chiefs, or civilians who fail to meet standards in other parts of the service. If you notice minor failings like uniforms not squared away, inappropriate conduct on the beach, or inattention to detail, a quiet word with the young officer is in order, Let the officer know that you have observed or know of the behavior and that you want to help him or her to excel, and suggest the most appropriate course of action. In more serious circumstances—those involving egregious violation of our core values of honor, courage, or commitment—your duty is clear to report the behavior without fear or favor through the chain of command. The oath that we all took is to protect the Constitution, the nation, and the Navy, and not specific individuals, regardless of rank, rate, or relationship. If you ignore egregious behavior, you've failed too, and your own honor is compromised.

Great officers recognize the contributions Chief Petty Officers have made to their own lives and careers. Journalist John Reese told a story that has often been recounted by his nephew, retired ATCS Jack Reese, at http://www.goatlocker.org, an online meeting place for active, reserve, and retired Chief Petty Officers.

> Admiral William "Bull" Halsey was being honored in Los Angles shortly after the end of World War II. As is naval tradition, a line of side boys, all active duty or retired Chief Petty Officers, lined his path. As Halsey approached one grizzled veteran, the journalist saw them wink at each other. Approached later, Halsey was asked about the wink. Halsey commented: "That man was my chief when I was an ensign, and no one before or after taught me as much about ships or men as he did. You civilians don't understand that. You go down to Long Beach, and you see those battleships sitting there, and you think that they float on the water, don't you?" The journalist nodded. "You are wrong," replied Halsey.

"They are carried to sea on the backs of those Chief Petty Officers!"

Points to Ponder

What's the Navy coming to?

Take a quick walk through the berthing and messing spaces. What cultural indications do you find there (posters, pin-ups, music, off-duty clothes, etc.)? Do they differ from what you'd find in the goatlocker? How do those symbols make you feel?

Think back to your first duty station. How did you feel when you reported to a division consisting of Sailors of varying ages and backgrounds? Were you uncomfortable berthing with a range of Sailors, some of whom might be twenty years your senior? What happened the first time you tried to play your music on a common recreation system? Was your culture accepted by the general community?

9

Advancement and Professional Development

Case Study: Advancement Opportunities

It was one of those days when it's good to be a Sailor. ATC Kristin Logan was gazing out the hangar bay door of USS *Tinian* (LHA-11) when QMCS Dave Girard walked by. "Just look at that water—have you ever seen it so blue?"

"We're deep in the Gulf Stream," Senior Chief Girard replied. "Gentle breezes, warm water—that's one of the things that makes it great to be a Sailor. But you know, it's a shame that more of our young Sailors don't look at their time at sea the way we do. For lots of them, sea time is just a necessary evil that gets in the way of their parties on the beach."

"It's hard to get some of them motivated, that's for sure," Chief Logan replied. "It seems like lots of them aren't interested in learning more about their jobs, or making rate, or any of those things that motivated us back in the day. And it's easier now than ever for a motivated Sailor to move up. Look at all the tools that we provide to Sailors to help them advance. It's a shame, really."

It is a shame when promising young Sailors fail to take advantage of all the opportunities available to them. "It's too complicated," they may say, or, "I don't know where to start." But our job as Chief Petty Officers is to guide them, to help them jump through the right hoops. A solid understanding of the Navy Enlisted Advancement System is a good place to start.

Task Force Excel

Beginning in the late 1990s, the Navy began to study carefully the science of learning and to consider radical changes in Navy training. This led to serious discussions about the relationship of training to advancement, retention, and mission effectiveness and gave birth to the Revolution in Navy Training and Task Force Excel.

Early in his tenure as chief of naval operations, Adm. Vern Clark determined that Navy training had been

Instructing and motivating our Sailors to advance are crucial responsibilities of the Chief Petty Officer.
U.S. Navy (PHAN Mark J. Rebilas)

"good enough for long enough" and set the goal of trans-
forming the Navy into a responsive, agile, and efficient
learning organization with the ability to quickly adapt and
to apply new technologies and new warfighting tactics.
Admiral Clark determined that training philosophy and
practices must change dramatically and quickly because:

- The complexity of both Navy missions and technology
  were growing at an unparalleled rate.
- Experienced Sailors continually leave the Navy through
  retirement and attrition.
- More than ever, Sailors join the Navy with expectations
  of learning and growing throughout their Navy career.
- The extraordinary educational opportunities in the commercial and academic sectors could no longer be ignored.

Additionally, Admiral Clark vigorously promoted
covenant leadership, which demanded aggressive, new
ways of ensuring personal and professional growth and
successes for Sailors.

The result of this effort was Task Force Excel (TFE).
TFE's impact on individual Sailor advancement was
immediate and significant as the new five-vector model
forces a whole-person view of Sailors' development. The
five vectors are:

Professional Development. This vector addresses rating/
community training, including any platform or command-
specific training such as damage control, 3M, and warfare
designators. Wherever possible and as appropriate, this
vector will be closely correlated with civilian and industry
standards.

Personal Development. This vector involves general military training, financial planning, and management and
includes required college-level educational coursework
that allows Sailors to complete degree programs.

Professional Military Education and Leadership. This
vector addresses leadership training, providing Sailors

with the tools and critical-thinking skills needed by effective leaders throughout their careers and replaces the Leadership Continuum.

Certifications and Qualifications. This vector focuses on ensuring that Sailors receive unit-level requirements and related industry certifications directly related to job proficiencies. For example, an IT has the opportunity to earn a Microsoft Network Certification or a construction mechanic may earn an ASE certification. These certification and qualification opportunities are currently being embedded into the relevant training experiences, often in initial skill training.

Performance. This vector assesses Sailors' overall performances, taking into account all of the aforementioned vectors. As these vectors are established for all rates, communities, and proficiency levels associated with pay grade or rank, Sailors will be able to use a grid that will help them determine exactly what is expected of them at any given point in their career.

Under these new training policies, Sailors have more access to education and training opportunities with commercial equivalents, spend less time away from home and their commands, and begin to take more personal control over their careers. Additionally, the pay and benefit increases of the past decade make Navy careers more than competitive with the civilian sector in almost all career fields.

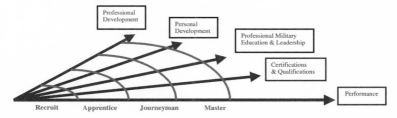

Five-Vector Model for Sailors' Development

The Navy Advancement System and Change

Training and the Navy advancement system are intertwined. Rapid and dramatic changes to Navy training inevitably bring changes in the Navy advancement system. Great care is always taken to ensure that new rules are not applied unfairly to Sailors who had been preparing for advancement under the previous policies and expectations.

Personnel Advancement Requirements (PARs) were ended in 1999, when they were deemed irrelevant to most Sailors' genuine advancement requirements, ineffective, and administratively cumbersome. Only a decade earlier, PARs replaced the rating/paygrade-specific practical factors form that often required Sailors to demonstrate skills in the realm of the ideal. One of the central objectives of the revolution in Navy training is to make all advancement activity meaningful and relevant to the Sailor's career path.

The Navy Enlisted Advancement System or NEAS is the pathway leading to enlisted leadership. NEAS allows qualified enlisted personnel to progress to higher levels of responsibility and authority throughout their careers. We're all products of this system, but a great place to refresh your memory about how it works is a CNET Web site dedicated to advancement, https://www.advancement.cnet.navy.mil. On this site you will find everything from a well-crafted general advancement information section to frequently asked questions (FAQs). You can do everything from contacting your exam writer to downloading Bibliography for Advancements (BIBs) to PowerPoint briefs on the advancement system. CNET also links to other informative sites as of this writing:

http://www.navylearning.com. This is the Navy e-learning site. Three specific courses provide an incredible glimpse into the resources:

- Department of Navy Library (148): Courses range from Academic Basic Skills and Anti-Terrorism Force Protection (ATFP) to Military Leadership and a multitude of shipboard training subjects.

- NETg Library: Information Technology (950). Courses from Microsoft, Oracle, Novell, Lotus, Cisco, and many more.
- SkillSoft Library: Leadership, Management, and Personal Development (768). Courses range from Administration Support and Business Law to Team Building and Safety and Health.

https://www.courses.cnet.navy.mil. Naval Education and Training Professional Development and Technology Center (NETPDTC) Web site with course list and catalog sections.

https://www.navycollege.navy.mil/index.cfm. Although predominantly related to off-duty college courses, this site contains a wealth of advancement-related information including: Academic Skills, U.S. Military Apprenticeship Program (USMAP), Rating Roadmaps, Degree Roadmaps, and more.

The Navy's steadily increasing use of the Internet ensures you'll always find up-to-date information about advancement opportunities, not only for your Sailors, but also for yourself. Under NEAS, occupational and naval standards comprise the minimum performance requirements for any rate or rating. Occupational standards define the minimum occupational or trade skills. Naval standards indicate the military requirements for Sailors throughout the fleet. Advancement examinations, rate training manuals, training courses, and other supporting materials are derived from these standards, which are listed in *Manual of Navy Enlisted Manpower and Personnel Classifications and Occupational Standards*, Volume I, NAVPERS 18068.

The path of advancement defines the roadmap a Sailor uses to move from recruit to master chief, and in some cases, to warrant or limited duty officer status. In most ratings, a Sailor progresses from PO3 through MCPO in the same general rating. There are a few exceptions in which some general ratings do not start at PO3. For example, Navy Counselor (NC) starts at NC1 for qualified PO2s from other ratings. The path of advancement chart for each rating is located in the *Manual of Navy Enlisted Manpower and Personnel Classifications and Occupational Standards*, Volume I, NAVPERS 18068.

Three of the most important aspects of professional development are sustained superior performance, on-the-job experience, and studying for advancement. Always performing at full potential is a lot to ask of anyone but this is the essence of sustained superior performance and is the single most important criterion in every selection board. This represents the single most important routine leadership challenge for the Chief Petty Officer. Sailors will rise to the occasion when special emergency demands are placed on them or their unit, but it takes motivational, even inspirational, leadership to lead Sailors to perform at their best day in and day out.

Every day, Sailors have many opportunities to learn more about their rating and prepare for advancement. Diagnosing and repairing equipment problems, ordering supplies, preparing reports, logging information, making adjustments, attending training, presenting training topics, studying SOPs, reading messages, studying lessons-learned documentation, reviewing safety bulletins, studying technical bulletins, or learning from the chief are all valuable on-the job experiences through which a Sailor learns.

Every rate has bibliographies for advancement (BIBs) prepared, listing important information needed for advancement. A thorough understanding of that material is critical to ensure success on exams. The same references are used by the exam writer for each rating to develop exam questions The references include rate training manuals and nonresident training courses, instructions, technical manuals, guides, and other publications. Encourage your Sailors to check with you or with the education office to be sure they are using the most recent bibliography for the rate to which they aspire.

As part of Task Force Excel, advancement handbooks or rating-specific publications are being phased out and replaced with a variety of online supplements. Additional information on the qualifications and certifications vector is also available at the Navy Knowledge Online (NKO) Web site, https://wwwa.nko.navy.mil/. Through this powerful Web portal, Sailors can access their rating-specific Navy Personnel Development Center as well as an enormous array of other advancement information.

Advancement Eligibility Requirements

Every Sailor must meet the eligibility requirements to participate in the Navy-wide advancement-in-rate exam. At the time of this writing, each Sailor must:

- Be recommended by the commanding officer.
- Meet minimum performance mark average (PMA) of 2.6 for E-4 through E-6 and 3.0 for E-7.
- Be within prescribed physical fitness standards.
- Have minimum time in rate (TIR) or approved waiver.
- Be in proper path of advancement.
- Meet special requirements like citizenship, security, and medical for certain ratings.
- Successfully complete service school, if required.
- Not have a pending request for voluntary transfer to the Fleet Reserve (E-7/8/9 candidates) that is not high-year-tenure (HYT) mandated.
- Complete a performance test, if required by rating. NAVPERS 18068 contains this information (available on BUPERS CD-ROM).
- Complete mandatory rate-training course requirements.
- Attend required Leadership Training Courses (PO1, CPO, and SCPO candidates) within the prescribed time period before administration of the advancement examination.
- For naval reservists, satisfy the required satisfactory drill participation requirements.

Realize that eligibility requirements are dynamic. Check the most recent online notes or consult your personnel organization for the latest requirements. Realize, too, that some ratings have mandatory training requirements, which can be found in NAVEDTRA 12061.

Navy-Wide Examinations

Advancement-in-rate exams are written to rank-order the best-qualified candidates who have met all eligibility requirements and have been recommended for advancement by their commanding officers. The exams objectively test experience and knowledge across a broad range of subjects. The exams are based on the job and are not simply book tests for which a Sailor can read the references and learn the answers to examination questions. Advancement-in-rate exams are norm referenced, which means they measure your performance on a specific examination against only the candidates of the same rating who took the same examination at the same time.

The examination score is combined with the candidate's other factors to establish the final multiple score or FMS. FMS scores for candidates who pass the exam are rank-ordered to determine who will be selected for the limited number of billets available. The examinations, written by experienced Chief Petty Officers, are based on rating experience and knowledge. The exam writer determines the job areas most common to the rating, and then develops examination sections to test across a broad range of the job areas selected. Each section consists of several questions designed to sample the extent of the candidate's knowledge in that job area above the minimum knowledge level required in the rate. The writer validates each job area by personally ensuring that questions are supported by current rating experience, valid references, and Navy standards.

The Selection Process

The Bureau of Naval Personnel determines the number of vacancies available based on current and prospective losses. The CNO then establishes quotas for each rate based on these vacancies. Quotas are used to determine the number of selectees for advancement in each advancement cycle. The selection process is used to rank-order all candidates, to assist the Navy in selecting the top candidates. Rank-ordering is based on the whole-person concept and is accomplished by using the final multiple score (FMS).

The NEAS considers the whole person by calculating performance, experience, and knowledge into the individual's FMS. Performance is shown in the Sailor's day-to-day performance, work ethic, achievements, and so forth, and is documented in performance evaluations. Knowledge and experience are reflected on examination performance; that is, the subject matter tested is based on rating knowledge and experience. FMS results for all candidates are rank-ordered from top to bottom score. The number of quotas available determines the number of selectees.

If a Sailor passes the exam but is not selected, passed-but-not-advanced (PNA) points are awarded toward the next advancement cycle. PNA points are automatically included in the FMS for any E-4 through E-6 candidate who achieves a relatively high exam score. PNA points also are awarded for candidates who achieve a relatively high-performance mark average but were not advanced because of insufficient vacancies. PNA points for performance are awarded for the current exam for the current cycle. A Sailor can receive a maximum of 3 PNA points for any one advancement exam cycle. PNA points are computed in fractions of 0.5 point to a maximum of 1.5 points in the areas of test score and performance mark average. PNA points are cumulative over the last five exam cycles. The maximum cumulative PNA points that may be credited to the FMS for an E-4/5/6 candidate is 30 points.

Profile forms are provided to each candidate during the current examination cycle to assist in understanding their strengths and weaknesses. Understanding the profile will help examination candidates better prepare for future advancement examinations. The profile form reflects only how well candidates performed in relation to their peers on this exam. The next examination will not have the same questions and candidates will not be competing with the same set of peers. There are no shortcuts! For the next exam, candidates should always study the references listed in the bibliography developed for their specific advancement-in-rate exam study.

There is usually a waiting period between passing the examination and advancement. Advancements are subject to a ceiling control on the number of advancements per fiscal year. The Navy "fair-shares" proportionally by rate those advancements to selectees. Selectees are advanced in monthly increments.

Candidates not selected for advancement should begin immediately to become better prepared for the next examination. Identify weaknesses and use the bibliography to identify study materials and study the contents of the listed references. Improve professional performance. Many good performers who are now in senior pay grades were not advanced the first time they were eligible, but they continued to study, to be top performers, and they were eventually advanced. Your opportunity to advance depends equally on current and predicted future vacancies within your rating and on your performance, what you have learned from your rating experiences, and your rating knowledge.

Case Study: Chief Petty Officer Selection Board Process

"You know AT1 Ellsworth, don't you, Senior Chief?" Chief Logan asked. "He lives out there near you in that apartment complex right across from Gate Three at Little Creek. We're trying to get his package together now so that he goes up for chief the next time around. It hasn't been all that long since I made chief, but, you know, I never was really sure what all went on behind the scenes. I sure wish I knew what to tell him about the process and what he can expect this time around."

The Selection Board

Each selection board consists of a post major-command captain, who serves as president, and a junior officer who

Our responsibilities as mentors don't stop at the door of the mess—we also have responsibilities to our newly advanced Chief Petty Officers.
U.S. Navy (PH3 Jason Lee Lagoe)

serves as recorder. In addition, carefully selected officers and master Chief Petty Officers serve as board or panel members. The exact size of a board varies with the availability of temporary additional duty (TAD) funds, the number of records for review, and the time available.

The recorder, assistant recorders, the CNO enlisted advancement planner, and the master Chief Petty Officer of the Navy may provide input to the entire board on any matter concerning selections. With the board president's concurrence, the recorder divides the board members into panels that are responsible for reviewing the records of individuals in one general professional area, such as deck, engineering, and medical or dental. Each panel consists of at least one officer and two master chiefs but normally there are between four and six members.

---

232 *Developing*

Quota Requirements and Restrictions. Enlisted Community Managers (ECMs) establish maximum selectable quotas for each rating. The board cannot exceed quotas, but may leave them unfilled if the panel determines there is an insufficient number of qualified candidates in a rating who meet the board's criteria for advancement. Quotas are vacancy driven. This applies to E-4 through E-9 advancements. Several factors are taken into consideration when establishing quotas:

Current Inventory. The number of personnel on board versus the Navy's requirement for a rating is the current inventory. Only 2 percent of the Navy's total end strength may be senior Chief Petty Officers and only 1 percent may be master Chief Petty Officers. This is established by law (Title 10) and is subject to congressional oversight.

Total Projected Losses and Gains. Losses are the projected number of personnel who will leave a pay grade during the phasing cycle such as fleet reserve, medical discharge, LDO/CWO selectees, demotion, and death. Gains reflect those projected to enter a pay grade during the phasing cycle, such as voluntary recall to active duty, those remaining for advancement from the previous cycle, and so on. Phasing cycles are September through August for E-7 and July through June for E-8 and E-9.

Growth or Downsizing. This number reflects projected growth or decrease of the Navy's authorized allowance during the phasing cycle, if any. A decrease is rare and occurs only when the Navy is changing in accordance with federally legislated force structure changes.

Funding Authorized. This the number of personnel the Navy may pay as authorized by Congress.

Early Selectee Quotas. The Department of Defense has established the Total Active Federal Military Service (TAFMS) requirement that a member must meet prior to advancement to a given pay grade. At this time, TAFMS requirements are eleven years for E-7, sixteen years for E-8, and nineteen years for E-9. The Depart-ment of Defense permits no more than 10 percent of the total number of Sailors in the E-7/8/9 pay grades to have less than the required TAFMS. The limit of early selectee quotas available to the selection board is a percentage of the total selectee quota. BUPERS planners monitor this and inform the board what percentage can be early. This is a source of confusion for some until they learn that the percentage is an overall board figure and not a quota by rate. Because of the retention or attrition characteristics of some ratings, certain panels may receive a larger share of the overall quota while other ratings with higher average TAFMS across their eligible pool receive fewer early selectees.

Board Dynamics. Upon convening, the board establishes internal ground rules and minimum selection criteria that each member uses when screening the records of candidates. The rules for selection criteria apply equally to each candidate within a rating. Application may vary slightly from rating to rating for many reasons, such as sea duty, supervisory opportunities, schooling available, or rotation patterns. Each panel has the freedom to establish its own internal procedures, within the guidelines of the precept, thereby providing for the dynamic nature of the selection process. The board will not divulge the proceedings or recommendations except as authorized and approved by the Chief of Naval Personnel. The board recorders give the records of each rating to the respective panel. For each candidate, there is a folder with their microfiche as well as any correspondence sent by a candidate and the candidate's enlisted summary record (ESR). The ESR contains the candidate's name, Social Security number, exam rate, present rate, exam score, time in rate, and time in service.

The panel reviews and scores five years of evaluations. Depending on the level of competition, panel members may go back even farther to establish performance trends and to break ties. Certain experiences and attributes such as total years of arduous sea duty require the board to audit the entire record, of course. Once they review the entire rating, the process starts again and each candidate gets a second review from a different panel member. If there is a significant difference between the panel members' assessments, either a third member reviews the record or a discussion between the original members will result in a decision.

Before the board convenes, the panel receives all correspondence on a candidate, along with the individual's microfiche record. This ensures that the panel has the most up-to-date information about the candidate.

The board considers several factors:

Professional Performance. Although it is not necessary, of course, that a candidate be currently serving in a sea-duty billet, it is expected that his or her record reflect evidence of professional and managerial excellence at sea or, in some ratings, at isolated sea duty–equivalent assignments. Some ratings do not offer a broad opportunity for sea duty, particularly at the senior levels, and the board factors this in to the process. Additionally, a variety of duty assignments, especially sea duty, give an individual professional breadth. An individual having more demanding but less varied tours may be equally well qualified. Navy members have assurance that their careers will not be unfavorably affected by service over extended periods in important assignments to which they have been ordered.

Out-of-Rating Assignments. Candidates presented to the board compete within their rating. As many candidates frequently perform duties outside their specialties, the board gives due consideration to those candidates who have served particularly demanding tours of duty as instructors, recruiters, career counselors, recruit division commanders, in the Human Goals Program, and in any other tour requiring special qualifications.

Educational Improvement. This includes academic and vocational training, whether the education is a result of the individual's initiative during off-duty hours or as a participant in a Navy-sponsored program.

Evaluation Reports or Fitness Reports. The board closely reviews marks and narratives to identify established trends. Sustained superior performance is the single most important factor influencing selection. The overall promotion recommendation blocks along with the consistency of performance indicated by the performance traits give the board an indication of how the candidate compares against members of the same pay grade at his or her command. Command and community involvement also reflect a well-rounded, career-motivated individual. The whole-person concept is important.

Duty Assignments and History of Duties Performed. This data is determined from the service record transfers and receipts page and from the job description on the evaluations. Using this data, board members can tell whether or not the individual is performing duties commensurate with his or her rate and whether the individual is meeting professional growth expectations.

Navy's Physical-Readiness Test Standards. Failure to meet the Navy's height and weight screening tables and body fat standards will hinder an individual's selection opportunity. Additionally, CNP now requires that advancement be withheld for any individual selected who fails to meet standards. Withholding advancement must continue until the individual meets current height and weight screening and standards for percentage of body fat, or expiration of the limiting date, whichever comes first. The selectee who is unable to meet the standards bears the responsibility to get within standards and deserves the support of shipmates, but must receive no other favor.

Alcohol or Substance Abuse. The board will not deny advancement solely on the basis of prior alcoholism or alcohol abuse provided the member has participated in successful treatment and recovery. However, the board considers any misconduct or reduction in performance resulting from alcoholism or alcohol abuse in determining fitness for advancement.

Disciplinary Problems. Individuals who have had disciplinary problems, received letters of indebtedness, or have other record entries relevant to behavioral difficulties such as drug abuse, demonstrated racial, sexual, or religious discrimination will find the path to promotion more difficult than those with clear records.

Test Scores (E-7 Only). The board takes test scores into account because they give the individual's relative standing on the examination compared to the other candidates.

In summary, the board looks at how the individual performs under various circumstances, duty assignments, and job assignments within his or her commands. Performing well in all assignments, regardless of how arduous or mundane they may be, is extremely important.

The Slating Process

Once the panelists review an entire rating, they arrange all the candidates from top to bottom. At this time, the panel makes a decision where the cut-off will be for non-promotables, promotables, and recommended selectees. Once the board completes the slating, the panel provides a brief for the entire board on the rating's structure, its job peculiarities, number of candidates, and the backgrounds of those people recommended and not recommended for selection. Throughout this briefing, the panel uses no names. The entire board votes on the slate. It is not uncommon for one panel to be calibrated at these sessions and to be required to return to the process with adjusted internal procedures that are more in line with the board precept.

During the course of a board's deliberations, it may see records which clearly indicate substandard performance or, in the board's judgment, questionable advancement recommendations. In these cases, the board lists those candidates by name, activity, and reporting senior, and provides a concise summary of circumstances. Depending on the circumstances, the board will refer such candidates to the Quality Control Review Board or to senior echelon commanders for any action deemed appropriate. At the completion of the process, all members sign the written report of the board's recommendations and submit it to CNP for approval. The report must certify that the board complied with all instructions and directions contained in the precept and that it has carefully considered the case of every candidate submitted for review. The report also defines the demographic breakout of selectees for the record. Once CNP approves the report, he transmits it via NAVOP to the fleet.

Improving Chances for Selection

The Sailor who decides to make the Navy a career and immediately starts preparing for advancement will get a head start with selection boards. You can help subordinates prepare by emphasizing the following.

Roadmap. The Navy has introduced a program called the Navy Goal Card. This program allows a Sailor to chart his progress on a predictable advancement time line.

Sustained Superior Performance. Sustained superior performance is the single most important factor influencing advancement opportunities. Use GUARD 2000 or the current assignment incentive program wisely to ensure obtaining a demanding job instead of just trying to get a geographic location. Advise Sailors to persistently request the duty that will challenge them to demonstrate their leadership and initiative early in their career. Sustained superior performance in a variety of commands and duty types is the goal. Doing their best in each job assigned is paramount.

Record Keeping. Sailors should keep personal records of their accomplishments throughout the evaluation period to assist in summarizing input to their own evaluations. Be sure their specific inputs, presented in a smooth format, address all significant accomplishments like improvements, work achievements, their demonstrated supervisory abilities, and initiatives. The evaluation/fitrep is for individual accomplishments and behaviors and should not be an instrument to list the accomplishments of the organization. Ensure that the evaluation/fitrep is properly formatted and that the detailed information such as Social Security numbers and spelling of names is correct.

Record Update. Encourage or require Sailors to check their official microfiche service records to ensure timeliness and proper order at least six months prior to the board convening and at least once during each enlistment.

Case Study: Personnel Qualification Standards (PQS)

"Well, you know," Chief Girard said, "for a while, the Navy was giving extra credit on rating examinations for folks who had their warfare qualifications all sewn up. We changed that a few years ago because we began to realize that, rather than identify a few selected Sailors as extraordinary because they have their warfare qualifications, it was better to make that the baseline from which everyone is expected to start. As you know, completing your PQS requirements quickly and accurately is a great way for any Sailor—be it AT1 Ellsworth or SR Vine who just came across the brow—to set yourself up to be successful in Navy-wide rating examinations."

Standards

Every Chief Petty Officer is no doubt familiar with the Personal Qualifications Standards, a tool used throughout the fleet to describe the skills and knowledge a Sailor needs to do a particular job. The PQS system is somewhat similar to programmed texts in that each standard provides a detailed, step-by-step breakdown of the learning process. *The Standard Answer Books* (SABs) are available for only a limited number of PQSs. The SABs should be controlled by the PQS Unit Coordinators and made available only to PQS Qualifiers.

The standards tell what must be known, studied, and demonstrated. They are a natural evolution of the Practical Factors requirements used in the fleet for much of the last century. As the need to provide detailed training guidance became apparent, the Navy, with the urging and input of the Chief Petty Officer community, developed standardized checklists for various billets on similar platforms. Prior to the development of PQS, local qualification standards were usually developed by the Chief Petty Officers at each command, with significant redundancy but only uneven accuracy. As the Navy's ships and aircraft became more sophisticated and the operating schedules remained rigorous, it became increasingly difficult for the division and department Chief Petty Officers to provide detailed direction. Standardization was the answer.

The PQS development Web site, https://wwwcfs.cnet. Navy.mil/pqs/, provides connectivity to the current guiding instruction, OPNAVINST 3500.34E, an entry to the full catalog, links to communicate with PQS managers, and a downloadable version of the Unit PWS Coordinators Guide.

The PQS program is only one element of the command's training program. As a division Chief Petty Officer you are still responsible for the training of Sailors under your care, and the PQS complements, but does not supersede, normal division training. It will, however, act as a core curriculum and guide for much of the maintenance and watch-station training. The standards are broken down into several sections:

- Introduction
- Glossary of Qualification Standard Terms
- Table of Contents
- 100-Series Fundamentals
- 200-Series Systems

- 300-Series Watch Stations/Final Qualification
- Bibliography and Feedback Forms

The format and organization of the PQS are explained in the introduction. Throughout the PQS system, the terminology has been standardized, and the key terms and phrases are defined in the glossary.

PQS Record Keeping

Under the PQS system, the qualification entry in the individual's service record and the Qualification Progress Record Chart are required. The Shipboard Non-Tactical ADP Program (SNAP II/III) enables you to make PQS assignments and to review and update them quickly and easily. All applicable PQS standards are maintained within the computer's database and may be located quickly to make PQS assignments to members of your division. Many units are now maintaining PQS records (other than the service-record entries) in the SNAP II/III system, while others use personal computers. Both methods work well. As each person completes the entire qualification package and is certified by the commanding officer, an entry is made on page four of the service record. To avoid duplication in record keeping, the completion of training that is covered by PQS need not be recorded elsewhere. The following records are eliminated: Division Drill Schedule, Group Record of Practical Factors, Supplementary Record of Equipment Qualification, and Individual Drill Record. When a formal PQS program is in place, you need only maintain two sets of records: one for the PQS-covered areas (the Qualification Progress Record Chart) and the other, standard records, for any additional shipboard training.

Case Study: The Enlisted Warfare Qualification Program

"I know how hard EWQS can be," responded Chief Logan. "It took me a long time to get my EAWS, back when I was at Moffett

Field. And when I came aboard *Tinian*, well, it seemed to take me forever to get around to all the spaces and get qualified on damage control, communications, safety, and all the other elements I needed to get my ESWS, too. But it was worth it—I'm a lot better Sailor for the effort, and I know I make a better contribution to the command because of all the time I spent learning about how the other half lives!"

No innovation over the past twenty-five years has increased the operational effectiveness of Sailors in all mission areas so much as the enlisted warfare qualification programs.

History of Community-Specific Qualifications

The spiritual antecedents of these programs can be traced to the period just after World War I, when Capt. (then Comm.) Ernest King, Submarine Division Three (and later fleet admiral and commander in chief, U.S. Fleet), suggested to the secretary of the Navy that a distinguishing device for qualified submariners be adopted. He submitted a pen-and-ink sketch showing a shield mounted on the beam-ends of a submarine, with dolphins forward of, and abaft, the conning tower. The suggestion was strongly endorsed by the commander of Submarine Division Atlantic. Over the next several months, the Bureau of Navigation solicited additional designs from several sources. One striking design consisted of a bow view of a submarine, proceeding on the surface, with bow planes rigged for diving, flanked by dolphins in a horizontal position with their heads resting on the upper edge of the bow planes. In March 1924, the Navy accepted the design, and, with only slight modifications, that emblem has pride of place as the first of the enlisted warfare qualification insignia.

Originally, the submarine insignia was to be worn at all times by Sailors qualified in submarine duty while attached to submarine units or organizations, ashore and afloat, but was not to be worn while not attached. In 1941 the uniform regulations were modified to permit Sailors who were eligible to wear the submarine insignia to do so after they had been assigned to other duties in the naval service, unless such right had been revoked. Officers wore metal insignia, and enlisted men wore an embroidered silk insignia on the outside of the right sleeve, midway between the wrist and elbow. The device was two and three-quarter inches long.

In 1943, the uniform regulations were again modified to permit an enlisted man who was qualified and then promoted to commissioned or warrant rank to wear enlisted submarine insignia on the left breast. After promotion, he would replace the insignia with the officer's submarine pin. In mid-1947, the embroidered device shifted from the sleeve of the enlisted man's jumper to above the left breast pocket. A change to the uniform regulations dated 21 September 1950 authorized the embroidered insignia for officers, in addition to the pin-on insignia, and for enlisted men, a bronze, silver plated, pin-on insignia in addition to the embroidered device.

The operative word in this short history lesson, of course, is qualified. The Submarine Service has long required that every Sailor must be familiar with and capable of operating the various systems aboard each boat. Submarines operate in a hostile environment, and in the event of casualty, rate or rating matters not if the lives of the submarine and crew are at stake. The PQS process, albeit under different names and with different requirements, has always been strictly enforced in the submarine community. In the mid-1970s, the Navy, with the enthusiastic support of then-MCPON Bob Walker, expanded the concept first to enlisted surface warfare qualification, and, soon after, to enlisted air warfare, FMF corpsman, Seabees, and other special communities. Today there are multiple enlisted warfare qualification programs within the Navy.

Like many programs, stabilization took some time; there were periods of neglect and even outright abuse in the administration of the warfare qualification programs.

By the time I became MCPON in 1992, administration was poor and inconsistent. New and meaningful guidelines, with teeth, were developed, and the program was restricted to Sailors serving full tours of sea duty in the warfare communities. I'm very proud of what we accomplished to make warfare qualifications the meaningful program that it is today.

Then-chief of naval operations, Adm. Jay Johnson shared in my concern. In a message transmitted to the fleet in August 1997, he directed that an enlisted warfare qualification requirement for advancement to E-6 and above would be phased in during the next three years "in a move designed to focus qualifications on mission effectiveness. Three changes will be phased in during the next three years," he wrote.

After a shake-out period, the program called for the following:

- All E-5 and above serving at sea must be warfare qualified to advance in pay grade.

- Requalification of a condensed, command-specific PQS in subsequent sea tours. A core PQS and ship/unit-specific PQS will be established, which, in combination, will constitute initial qualification criteria. Thereafter, only the condensed, command-specific PQS will be required to maintain the currency of the requirement.

- Sailors must know the warfighting capability of their ship, squadron, or unit and be totally and intimately familiar with the mission of their command to achieve this objective.

- The professional achievement of warfare qualification is key to the development of leadership skills carried through all ranks.

- Achievement of warfare qualification by all hands is both the mark of, and the foundation for, teamwork. Long-term, effective command programs are never the product of one or two leaders.

- Warfare qualification is a symbol of the professional pride of every Sailor who earns a warfare insignia.

Pride in advancement
is shared by family
members, too!
*U.S. Navy (PH1 Paul J.
Phelps)*

The Programs Today

Today, enlisted warfare qualification programs are locally administered through the Chief Petty Officer community, under the direction of the command master chief. Although there are specific rules for each of the major enlisted warfare qualifications (submarine, air, surface, special warfare combat crew, FMF Corpsman, Seabee, etc.) the overall structure and process for qualification is similar.

Enlisted Surface Warfare

ESWS qualification recognizes the efforts of enlisted individuals trained in surface ship operations. Attainment of ESWS designation signifies that a Sailor has achieved a level of excellence and proficiency in surface ships. The ESWS insignia signifies that the Sailor is competent in his or her rate and has acquired additional general knowledge that enhances understanding of warfighting, mission effectiveness, and command survivability. Sailors who wear the ESWS insignia stand out as significant contributors to the surface force.

Qualification is mandatory for all active-duty E-5 and senior enlisted personnel who meet the eligibility requirements. Active-duty E-4 and junior personnel and enlisted selected reservists may qualify for ESWS qualification if they are permanently assigned to a commissioned U.S. Navy or Military Sealift Command (MSC) surface ship and meet the eligibility requirements:

- They must be enlisted personnel serving on sea duty or non-rotational sea duty, who are assigned to U.S. Navy or MSC afloat staffs or to commands that deploy aboard commissioned U.S. Navy or MSC surface ships as members of a detachment. These detachments must have the support of these ships and/or the ships' embarked staffs as their primary mission.

- Staff or detachment personnel billeted to sea duty or non-rotational sea duty (example: HSL or HC detachments) must make a deployment of at least ninety consecutive days while embarked in a commissioned U.S. Navy or MSC ship. Staff or detachment personnel shall use the ESWS Program of the ship in which they are embarked.

- All personnel assigned to precommissioning units (PCUs) may complete those portions of the ESWS qualification program that do not require the ship to be under way. Prospective commanding officers of these PCUs may not, however, award final ESWS qualification to PCU crew members until after commissioning.

- Personnel assigned to a surface ship or afloat staff are expected to qualify in the primary warfare mission of the unit embarked, with one exception: aviation rating personnel assigned to a surface ship with a shipboard Enlisted Aviation Warfare Specialist (EAWS) Program are required to qualify in the EAWS Program.

Enlisted Selected Reservists. Reservists who desire to qualify as ESWS must be assigned for a minimum of twelve months prior to final qualification to a naval reserve unit that is, or whose gaining command is, a commissioned U.S. Navy or MSC surface ship, U.S. Navy or MSC afloat staff, or a command that deploys aboard commissioned U.S. Navy or MSC surface ships as members of a detachment. In addition, selected reservists must be in a satisfactory drill status and complete at least three periods of shipboard annual training or an equivalent active duty special work of which a minimum of two periods of annual training or special work period is on the same class of ship in which the member is qualifying.

Enlisted Surface Warfare Standards include:

- Complete at least twelve months accumulated Type Two or Four duty prior to final qualification.
- Demonstrate effective leadership and directing ability, receive at least one observed evaluation, have an overall trait average of not less then 3.0, and be promotable during the most recent reporting period.
- Complete the following PQS for initial qualifications:

    Damage Control (NAVEDTRA 43119 SERIES). Complete Watch stations 301 through 308.

    Ship's Maintenance and Material Management (3M) Systems (NAVEDTRA 43241 SERIES). Qualification commensurate with pay grade.

    Complete all PQS for those watch stations, both in port and under way, to which the rating and pay grade would normally be assigned at that point in overhaul, predeployment phase.

    Enlisted Surface Warfare Specialist (NAVEDTRA 43901 SERIES). Both core PQS and platform-specific PQS shall be completed for ESWS qualification.

    Be recommended for ESWS qualification by their chain of command.

    Display general knowledge of the ship's overall mission, engineering plant capabilities, combat systems, other mission-essential systems, and basic deck equipment through written examination, hands-on demonstration of knowledge, and an oral examination by a multi-member board.

The membership of this board shall include, at a minimum, one senior ESWS qualified member from each of the following areas: engineering, deck, combat systems, operations, and supply. On Navy ships, the board will be chaired by the ship's command master chief. On MSC ships, the ESWS program manager (Military Sealift Command Force Master Chief, Atlantic or Pacific) will designate a senior ESWS-qualified chairperson. Detachments, afloat staffs, and SELRES personnel must use the qualifying board of the ship in which they are embarked. ESWS PQS (core- and platform-specific) and the ability to demonstrate shipboard knowledge should be used as the foundation for the examination. The oral board will make a recommendation of qualification to the qualifying officer, in most cases the commanding officer. The qualifying officer will review the results and recommendations of the board and make the final determination for qualification.

Enlisted Air Warfare

Attainment of the EAWS designation signifies that enlisted members achieved a level of significant professional skills, knowledge, and experience in the direct support of the naval air warfare mission and the specific unit they are currently serving. Wearers of the air warfare pin stand out as significant contributors to the aviation force.

Sailors eligible to participate in EAWS programs must be assigned to deployable aviation squadrons and their detachments; aviation-capable ships (limited to CV, CVN, LPH, LHA, LHD, and MCS); and aviation staffs afloat (CVW). Staffs other than CVW, or detachment personnel, such as CCG, EOD, and SEAL Teams, who have completed all other eligibility requirements, may participate if they are making a deployment of at least 180 continuous days embarked in an aviation-capable ship (CV, CVN, LPH, LHA, LHD, and MCS). Additionally, staff or detachment personnel shall use only the EAWS program of the ship in which they are embarked. SEAOPDETS personnel may participate in the program of the ship in which they are embarked but may not establish a program of their own.

Enlisted air warfare standards include:

- Promotable status on the most recent evaluation/fitness report.
- Attainment of the grade of E-3 or above.
- Be recommended for EAWS qualification by the chain of command.
- Completion of the Aviation Maintenance Requirements Fundamental Course and the Aviation Maintenance Requirements Supervisor Course.
- Completion of all PQS and qualification for those watch stations to which the member's particular rating, Navy Enlisted Classification, and/or pay grade would normally be assigned.
- Completion of all requirements for advancement to the next higher pay grade (with the exception of time in rate and time in service).
- Where applicable, qualified in basic damage control prior to final qualification.
- Where applicable, completion of aircraft/shipboard fire fighting prior to final qualification.
- Completion of the common core (NAVEDTRA 43902) and unit-specific PQS with eighteen months of entry into the program.

Special Warfare Combat Crew. Attainment of SWCC qualification signifies that a volunteer for naval special warfare duty has achieved a level of excellence and proficiency in the operation of special warfare combatant-craft. The SWCC qualification signifies that a Sailor is operationally competent and has acquired additional knowledge that enhances the understanding of warfighting, mission effectiveness, and unit survivability as demonstrated by knowledge of navigation, communications, engineering, weapons, deck systems, and tactical operations of special warfare combatant-craft.

Special warfare combat craft crewman must have graduated from the SWCC basic training course, CIN k060-0030, and have completed following core personnel qualification standards (PQS):

- Naval Special Warfare Combatant-Craft Crewman (NAVEDTRA 43403-B), watch stations 301 through 312.
- Basic Damage Control (NAVEDTRA 43119-2 SERIES), watch stations 301 through 306 and 310.
- Ship's Maintenance and Material Management (3M) Systems (NAVEDTRA 43241 SERIES), qualifications commensurate with pay grade.
- Communications Security Material System (CMS) (NAVEDTRA 43462-B), achieving qualifications commensurate with level of access requirements (minimum qualification is CMS USER).

Complete NSW command-specific qualification requirements will include:

- Special Warfare Combatant-Craft Crewman individual (SWCCI) Skills Tactical Training Program. (COM-NAVSPECWARCOMINST C3503.1 (NOTAL).
- Combatant-Craft specific Job Qualification Requirements (JQR).
- Recommended for SWCC qualification by Sailor's chain of command.
- Successful demonstration of specific combatant-craft knowledge pertaining to combatant-craft navigation, communication, engineering, weapons, and deck subsystem capabilities; emergency procedures and immediate action; and other mission-essential tasks through written examination, practical demonstration of knowledge, and an oral examination by a multi-member board.

Board membership shall include, at a minimum, the command master chief or senior enlisted advisor and at least two SWCC qualified members and one SEAL qualified E-7 or higher. Under normal circumstances, the command master chief is the SWCC coordinator. SWCC PQS (core- and combatant-craft specific) and the ability to demonstrate command knowledge should be used as the foundation for the examination. The board will make a recommendation of qualification to the commanding officer. The commanding officer will review the results and recommendations of the board and make the final determination for qualification.

For each type of qualification, final qualification must be documented on page four in the candidate's service record. Subsequent requalifications will also be documented. Documentation will include the appropriate warfare specialist PQS completed. Personnel will have twelve months to complete initial appropriate warfare specialist qualification upon reporting or must demonstrate significant progress toward qualification.

If qualification has not been achieved upon transfer to another command, the new command shall recognize recorded PQS attainment to date, but may require a redemonstration of knowledge in any area deemed appropriate.

Approval of Qualification. After satisfactory completion of the requirements of this instruction, approval of appropriate warfare specialist will be as follows:

- Commanding officer's approval/written designation.
- When members have been qualified or requalified for appropriate warfare specialist designation, an entry shall be made in their service records on page four (PQS qualification) as well as page thirteen.
- The appropriate designator (SW/AW, etc.) is placed in parentheses immediately after the member rate abbreviation, such as BM2 (SW).

To ensure consistency on the standards of qualification, commands, and the Chief Petty Officer community specifically, are urged to ensure the spirit and intent of the program are followed by closely monitoring and evaluating qualifiers and qualification programs.

Continuing Qualification. For active duty personnel, once qualification has been achieved, transfer to another command will require renewal of qualification. A warfare pin is not a decoration. It is not the equivalent of a warfare-specific Navy Achievement Medal that, once presented, may be worn from that day on without additional work. Warfare qualification requires continuous maintenance, maintenance that is the essence of professionalism on sea duty.

Transfers Between Same Types of Platforms. When an individual transfers between commands of the same type, the individual must redemonstrate core fundamentals and specific knowledge of the command's overall mission and mission-essential tasks through an oral demonstration of knowledge. An individual renewing qualification on the same type of unit shall not be required to recomplete the platform-specific PQS if previously completed. Specific PQS, however, may be used to facilitate requalification. The individual renewing qualification must update or requalify as required to meet the program. Specifically, personnel will have twelve months to complete requalification upon reporting.

Transfers Between Different Combatant-Craft Type Commands. When an individual transfers between different platforms, the individual must demonstrate core fundamentals and specific knowledge of the command's overall mission through written examination, practical demonstration of knowledge, and an oral examination by a multi-member board. The board will be conducted as outlined previously. An individual renewing qualification on a different type of platform will be required to complete the platform-specific PQS as required to meet requirements.

Disqualification. Warfare-qualified personnel shall be disqualified by their commanding officers if any of the following conditions exist:

- Failure to maintain overall performance trait average of 3.0 and overall performance recommendation of Promote (or above).
- Failure to requalify upon transfer to another NSW command within a maximum of twelve months.
- Refusal to accept or perform professional duties.

- Culpable negligence and lack of moral integrity.
- Commanding officer's loss of confidence in member's ability to perform the duties required of the specific program.

Disqualification shall not be in lieu of disciplinary action but should be considered coincidentally.

"I guess the point of all of this," Chief Logan concluded, "is that the avenues for advancement are available to all Sailors, no matter what their rating, whether they are on shore duty or at sea. And, as chiefs, our job is to inform them about the available choices."

"More than that," Senior Chief Girard rejoined, "much more than that. Our job is to motivate them so that the next generation of Sailors has the great leaders that we had when we were young and impressionable. And you know what? That's probably the most important thing that we as chiefs can do."

10

Counseling and Mentoring Sailors

Case Study: Problems Ashore

PC1 Quinn stopped by Chief Terry's office. "You know, I just can't seem to get through to PCSN Dennis these days. Normally, she's been a great worker, but ever since we've deployed, she just sits around and stares off into space. One of the Sailors who berths with her, YN3 Hall, came up to me in the p-way and told me that she's been crying herself to sleep ever since we left San Diego. You might want to have a talk with her, Chief."

Advising and Counseling

One of the most important responsibilities of every Chief Petty Officer is counseling Sailors. You have the opportunity to leave a personal mark on the Sailors in your charge—it's a key element of Chief Petty Officership. Sailors are, on average, young men and women just starting out in life. Mom and Dad are far away. Who else can they turn to? You may be called upon to hold formal, structured, prescheduled counseling sessions that you will document in writing and forward for the record. You may provide on-the-spot guidance from the pitching weather deck during underway replenishment or from the quiet bridge of the routine midwatch. You'll find an entire range of counseling situations and protocols between these two extremes. You'll even find yourself providing guidance while on liberty, when you would prefer to be somewhere else. Don't grumble and think to yourself how much other important stuff you have to get done. There's nothing more important than counseling your Sailors, and the rewards for doing it well and faithfully will outweigh the sacrifice a thousandfold.

Effective counseling need not always be time consuming. Two or three minutes of thoughtful reinforcement for a job well done can be meaningful. Often, a good chief will initiate counseling to discuss a Sailor's effectiveness, discipline, appearance, or other issue; at other times, the Sailor will approach the chief. Problems range from job performance to emotional or financial trouble. Whatever the situation, you must always take time to assist to the best of your ability. As chiefs, we both advise and counsel. Advising means helping Sailors initiate action to correct a problem by providing information about functions, procedures, rationales, opportunities, or alternatives for action with, for example, legal, financial, or personal problems.

When we counsel Sailors, we explore, better understand, and determine a solution or range of possible solutions to a problem. The counselor's role is to encourage the Sailor to create alternatives and to initiate problem-solving action on his or her own. There are four types of counseling:

Performance Counseling. Performance counseling focuses on growth and learning, evaluation of actions, and improvement of performance. Although exceedingly important and demanding, performance counseling is really the most routine and easiest of all the counseling you will do. You will occasionally convey unpleasant facts—you can tell only 5 percent of your Sailors that they are in the top 5 percent—but this counseling will recur routinely and you will get good at it if you take it seriously.

Personal Counseling. Personal counseling focuses on the Sailor's personal problems. You will be called upon without notice to address the problems of a distraught Sailor. Don't get in over your head. Knowing when to get the chaplain involved is one of the most important skills you must develop.

Disciplinary Counseling. Disciplinary counseling, focusing on the Sailor's actions in relation to regulations and standards, might well be the most difficult sort of counseling. You are dealing with a full range of Sailor attitudes from contrition and responsiveness to distrust and animosity. No matter what the Sailor's attitude, you are responsible for providing sound, thoughtful counseling.

Professional Growth and Guidance Counseling. Professional growth and guidance counseling focuses on career

Counseling our Sailors is a critical responsibility of Chief Petty Officers.
U.S. Air Force (TSGT Janice H. Cannon)

guidance and professional development. Navy counselors are the experts but many Sailors strongly desire to have this professional advice corroborated by their chief.

The Role of Senior Enlisted

Although we are not psychologists, psychiatrists, or chaplains, chiefs who knows their Sailors and truly care about their welfare may be better positioned to have an immediate positive impact on their lives than any of the professionals who may later become involved. We know where they live and a lot about what makes them tick. Very often we have lived through similar situations and can provide an immediate firsthand report that "this too shall pass."

As chiefs we must prepare, conduct, and follow up counseling sessions. We must:

- Praise, coach, and constructively critique Sailors during everyday contacts. Praise our junior leaders, too.
- Identify Sailors who need personal or performance counseling.
- Know our own capabilities and limitations. Get chaplains, medical officers, and other professionals involved as soon as the need is determined.
- Be fully knowledgeable of the different referral agencies and follow command policy for using them.
- Maintain accurate counseling records. Certain disciplinary and performance counseling requires detailed formal records, but it is a good practice to maintain detailed records of all counseling sessions no matter what the subject or requirement.
- Keep the chain of command informed.
- Ensure our junior leaders are preparing for and handling their own counseling responsibilities.

Characteristics of Good Counseling

Chief Petty Officers who are effective counselors share several characteristics. They are excellent role models, they have a strong desire to help Sailors and their families, and they know what method of counseling is best for the person and the situation. They have current knowledge of regulations, policies, and resources available to Sailors, and they understand their Sailors' job requirements, capabilities and limitations.

Work to fit your counseling style to the particular Sailor and circumstances while respecting each Sailor as a unique, complex person with a set of values, beliefs, and attitudes. Establish open, two-way communication with Sailors, using verbal and non-verbal actions, gestures, and body language. Effective counselors listen more than they speak. Motivate Sailors to actively participate in counseling and appreciate the value of counseling.

Remember that all of the information a Sailor reveals during counseling sessions is highly personal and confidential. As a rule, only information relevant to command and mission effectiveness should be passed to others in the chain of command. Involvement in criminal acts or any indication that the Sailor may harm him- or herself or act irrationally must be passed quickly to the appropriate authority. When necessary, the Chief Petty Officer should inform the Sailor of the limitations on confidentiality.

Counseling Opportunities

Personal counseling opportunities might include financial, legal, interpersonal, educational, moral, or religious issues. Experienced Chief Petty Officers know that the overwhelming majority of issues are related to financial difficulties and family problems. Respond quickly to schedule a session and ensure complete privacy and unhurried time for discussion. If the situation is beyond your resources or capability, refer the Sailor to the appropriate counselor.

Work with the Sailor to generate and evaluate alternatives to the problem. The next step is a plan of action that leads to a solution to the problem. You cannot solve the problem; only the Sailor can do that, but the Sailor should leave with a renewed sense of trust in you and the Navy.

In career counseling, the Sailor is usually looking for one of three things: options or ideas to plan a career path, advice on making a significant change, or information on further education or training. Informally analyze the Sailor's skills, experience, and training. You may also wish to refer the Sailor to a Navy counselor or trained career counselor. Ideally, the Sailor will leave the counseling session with the information necessary for making an informed choice, an action plan for change, and more alternatives to consider.

Disciplinary counseling sessions occur when the Sailor has violated a specific rule or regulation. In this case, you inform the Sailor of the action the chain of command is taking. You must determine if the behavior is indicative of related personal problems with which you must deal separately. The encounter may be purely for information gather-

Not every counseling session need be formal. Leading by example and reminding Sailors that we're not "above the work" are sometimes the best forms of performance counseling.
U.S. Navy (PH2 Alicia Tasz)

ing, or it may be a formal legal notification to the Sailor that he or she has violated a regulation and what action you will take. In either case, you must ensure that the Sailor fully understands the situation, including the violation, why it occurred, and the range of potential command actions.

Performance counseling is called for to recognize effective and ineffective performance. When we counsel effective performers, our goal is to motivate the Sailor to continue as before and even raise the level of performance. In stressing the Sailor's strong points, you also should suggest areas for improvement that will make him or her more competitive for advancement. Ideally, the Sailor leaves the encounter feeling greater loyalty to the Navy and the command, more confident, and with a strong desire to do even better.

In counseling ineffective performers, you need to provide specifics about the performance and explore, with the Sailor, the factors behind the performance. During the session, you and the Sailor must set mutual standards and expectations for behavior. The Sailor should leave the encounter motivated to improve.

Counseling Techniques

Chief Terry met with PNSN Dennis as scheduled. At first, she seemed quite anxious—it's not every day that you're called into the chief's office for a chat. But Chief Terry made it very clear that, although her performance had slipped a bit, this wasn't a disciplinary session. He was truly interested in what was going on in her life. Seaman Dennis began to relax a bit, and it became clear as the interview went on that she was concerned about some serious problems that she'd left behind on the beach. "You guys on the ship have been great," she confided. "But I'm really wondering whether I can go through this six-month deployment with everything that's happening back home."

All Sailors are different, and no single counseling technique will work in all situations. There are two basic approaches and a third approach that combines the two basic approaches:

Directive. The counselor-centered directive approach provides short-term solutions. The Chief Petty Officer needs the skills and knowledge to assess the situation and to offer courses of action leading to specific outcomes. The chief talks, the Sailor listens. You state the problem, identify the causes, offer explanations, and tell the Sailor what to do.

Non-Directive. The non-directive technique is Sailor-centered. The counselor's role results in the Sailor taking responsibility for solving the problem. More relaxed and focused on self-discovery, this approach takes more time than the directive approach. As you help the Sailor become more self-reliant, the Sailor has the opportunity to work out solutions to the problem through personal insight, judgment, and acceptance of the facts. If this approach is to succeed, Sailors must understand that defensive attitudes will get in the way of open and honest discussion and that they alone will be responsible for the problem-solving process and the decisions that come from it.

Combined Approach. In the combined approach to counseling, the Chief Petty Officer uses parts of the directive and non-directive approaches, or whatever works best for the Sailor. The combined approach assumes that the Sailor must eventually be responsible for planning and decision making. The Sailor will take charge of solving the problem, but may need some help along the way. This approach allows both you and the Sailor to participate in defining, analyzing, and solving the problem. Although the purpose is to develop self-reliant Sailors who can solve their own problems, you can be directive when the Sailor seems unable to make decisions or to solve a particular problem. In counseling a Sailor for poor performance, for example, you might wish to begin with a directive approach. When further discussion shows that a personal problem is causing poor performance, it may be necessary to switch to the non-directive approach and change the tenor of the session or to quickly wrap up the performance counseling and schedule a follow-on session in a different setting in order to effectively address the personal issues.

There are six counseling techniques that are useful methods to help communicate your understanding of a problem to another person:

Repeating. In repeating, you specifically restate what the person just said. This is not paraphrasing or interpreting. It can be as simple as changing the pronoun from "I" to "you."

PCSN Dennis: "I'm really worried about what's happening back home."

Chief Terry: "You're really worried about what's happening back home?"

Active Listening. Active listening goes beyond simple repeating. You accomplish it through the use of two techniques. The first is paraphrasing. Paraphrasing puts what the Sailor said into your own words without changing the basic meaning.

PCSN Dennis: "My husband is drinking again, and my mom is looking after our baby."

Chief Terry: "You're worried about what's happening to your little girl, then?"

Restatement. Restatement goes a little further than previous techniques because it includes some simple and preliminary interpretation of the situation. The purpose of restatement is to check what you believe might be occurring for the Sailor.

PCSN Dennis: "My mom is good with kids, but I hate having to load this on her."
Chief Terry: "What is your mother's situation? Does she welcome the opportunity? Or is it a burden to her?"

Open-Ended Questions. Open-ended questions are questions you ask the Sailor that cannot be answered with yes, no, or any one-word response. Encourage or leave room for the respondent to elaborate on the situation.

Chief Terry: "Your mother appears happy to have your daughter, so it is good that you don't have to worry as much about her welfare. What is your most urgent concern?"

Summarizing. Summarizing is the restatement of the key aspects of the problem and discussion. You bring the discussion to an end by focusing on the next step of planning for the future.

Chief Terry: "You're losing a lot of sleep. That doesn't help your daily routine, does it?"

Suggesting. By suggesting, you draw from the Sailor's own description of options. You are offering ideas without forcing your personal opinion.

Chief Terry: "Why don't we try to get you a priority call through tonight to ease your worries about your daughter, and then reassess your situation after that?"

Mistakes Made in Counseling

Experienced Chief Petty Officers know that our likes, dislikes, biases, and prejudices are potential pitfalls that can interfere with the counseling relationship. Some of the most common follow.

Playing "Shrink." We must recognize and accept our limitations in counseling. Simple problem solving, providing facts, and evaluation of duty performance and conduct are within the range of most Chief Petty Officers. We must avoid the temptation to become amateur psychologists or psychiatrists. Do not try to change deep-seated personality traits. Most important is being able to identify those situations that are clearly beyond our capabilities and to refer the Sailor to the appropriate professionals.

Reluctance to Counsel. Young, inexperienced Chief Petty Officers often hesitate to counsel Sailors on areas for improvement. Some may want to avoid the unpleasant duty of discussing shortcomings for fear of becoming unpopular. Others may fear Sailors who have been in the unit or service longer than they have. Problems will get worse without the counseling effort, and fair, objective counseling of Sailors is a responsibility that is an integral part of our "chiefness."

Personal Bias. Values are ideas about the worth or importance of things, concepts, and people that spring from a person's beliefs. Personal values influence personal priorities or desirability of different alternatives. If you ignore the differences between personal values, facts can become distorted and problems further complicated.

Stereotyping. Judging people on presumed group physical or behavioral characteristics is stereotyping. Make evaluations only on a Sailor's demonstrated behavior or on demonstrated ability.

Rash Judgments. Evaluating Sailors on the basis of appearance or specific behavior traits may lead to positive or negative rash judgments. A favorable first impression or a single significant accomplishment may lend one Sailor a halo, and a bad first impression or association with a troublemaking group may lead to false assumptions about a Sailor. Rash judgments may blind you from seeing significant information that could give you a different, perhaps more accurate, picture of a Sailor. A good chief works hard to base evaluations on more than one factor or observation.

Loss of Emotional Control. If you control your emotions, Sailors will tend to do the same. We can accept differences of opinion but arguments, debates, or heated discussions are not acceptable. Although maintaining a level of military decorum and professionalism is necessary, it is sometimes useful to permit a certain level of "unmilitary" behavior in a private counseling session in order to promote an honest dialogue. If you do so, be sure that you recalibrate the Sailor when the counseling session is over to make sure he or she understands that a line was crossed, but that you felt that making progress and achieving some results were more important at the time.

Inflexibility. Don't try to use the same methods with all Sailors. Sailors vary by personalities, experiences, education, problems, situations, and surroundings. Tailor your approach. Results are important—consistency of approach is not.

Improper Follow-up. Broken promises to a Sailor will cause loss of confidence and loss of respect. Follow-up is particularly important when we refer a Sailor to an agency for assistance. We are not only interested in how much help our Sailor received, but we also need to know if he or she showed up on time, told the same story, and generally played by the rules. Agencies to which we refer Sailors can be confusing and intimidating; we must stay involved at some level to ensure the Sailor doesn't doubt our sincerity or commitment.

Sailors' Reactions

Sailors' reactions to counseling vary depending on the reasons for counseling and how the sessions progress. Most Sailors want their superiors to consider them capable of performing their duties and want their chief's approval. Nevertheless, negative reactions may occur during the counseling session. Negative reactions can block improved performance and development.

Nervousness. Your own nervousness or failure to put the Sailor at ease may cause the Sailor to become nervous. You can eliminate any uncertainty by explaining the purpose of the session and you can ease tension by discussing something the Sailor has done well. Allow the Sailor to respond too.

Cooperation. Guidance and assistance of a competent Chief Petty Officer generally creates a positive reaction from the Sailor. Most Sailors are willing to participate and accept suggestions for improvement. Some may show surprise at parts of the discussion, but they will respond eagerly and may even ask for more constructive guidance in order to gain recognition.

Rational Disagreement. Sailors may not always agree with criticism or evaluation, but disagreement can be rational and emotions can be minimized and controlled. You should expect some disagreement based on differences in information available, personality, and perception of the situation. Disagreement may result from the Sailor not understanding what you have said. Try to clarify misunderstandings, but accept that the Sailor may still disagree even after understanding.

"Too Easy" Agreement. The Sailor may agree completely and almost too easily. This may indicate a lack of understanding or indifference. You must ensure that the Sailor is truly agreeing, rather than avoiding criticism or trying

to avoid confronting a problem. Too, the Sailor may be intimidated by your rate and believe that disagreeing is wrong. The Sailor must feel free to speak honestly and openly.

Determination to Argue. The Sailor may argue or disagree with any evaluations, opinions, or suggestions. This may indicate that the problem is not what it appears to be. The Sailor may be scared or have some disorder that requires professional help. Encourage the Sailor to talk freely, while you listen to determine what the real problem is.

Blame Shifting. The Sailor may seek to avoid blame by shifting criticism to others. Allow the Sailor to explain fully while you listen impartially. You may need to guide the Sailor through the discussion while you organize the information and provide assistance so the Sailor can give specific information to substantiate each claim. The Sailor may retreat from any position that you support with facts. Set up another session, if necessary, so you and the Sailor can provide information not readily at hand. In the end, be sure that the Sailor takes responsibility for personal behavior.

Loss of Temper. Sailors may lose their tempers and become emotional, angry, or abusive. You should listen, not argue, and try to discover what caused the loss of temper. The Sailor may recover, and counseling can continue. If not, you must restore order and explain that such behavior is not tolerable. You may want to postpone the session until the Sailor cools off.

Desire to Quit. As anyone who has served as a recruit division commander or "A" School instructor can readily testify, young Sailors may want to quit and turn away from problems. You must explain ways to overcome the problems and then convince the Sailor to try. You may have to end the counseling session without a resolution and deal with the problem later so that the Sailor does not feel you have forced a solution.

Financial Counseling

In today's economy, many Sailors have difficulty making ends meet. In many cases no one has taught them to be disciplined in budgeting their funds. For others, having a reliable income is a new experience. Unlike their contemporaries in the civilian sector, Sailors enjoy job security and great benefits. Perhaps because of this, businesses may subject them to a constant barrage of high-pressure advertising and offers of easy credit. Sailors are often targets of high-pressure advertising and easy credit offers to buy, buy, and buy some more. Supervisors view Sailors as irresponsible when they're not paying their debts. Their bad debts become the subjects of official correspondence, or preoccupation with financial difficulties results in decreased job productivity. Financial problems can have a detrimental impact on military careers, resulting in disciplinary actions, loss of security clearances, negative evaluations, lack of promotions, denial of special assignments, and administrative or dishonorable discharges.

Financial problems are a leading cause of personal stress and family dysfunction in all branches of the military. An estimated 50 percent of all military members experience some level of financial difficulty at one or more times in their careers. We live in a materialistic society that offers a wide variety of goods and services. Sailors must make purchasing choices between wants and needs, one product or another, name brands or generic, and spending or saving hard-earned money. Several factors influence consumer behavior, including the state of the economy, expectations, attitudes about money, and the psychological makeup of the customer. Advertising targets one or more of these factors to influence consumers to buy their products.

Young servicemembers are especially vulnerable to salesmen and advertisers because of their inexperience and because they are on their own for the first time. Because they generally have money and a willingness to spend it, they become easy targets for both honest and dishonest merchants. According to a presidential crime commission study, more than 90 percent of victims of consumer fraud never do anything about it. The majority of people either do not know businesses have cheated them, or they will not report it because they are embarrassed or feel that the police are not going to do anything about it.

As a result, far too many of our people unintentionally get in over their heads. Adults have a basic responsibility for keeping personal affairs in order, and that certainly includes the management of money. Chief Petty Officers—older, and we hope, wiser—can help with financial counseling. By helping a Sailor with a financial concern early, not only do we assist him or her, but also the division and command avoid letters of indebtedness, bad checks, and The Man from MasterCard.

Large commands often have trained financial counselors to assist Sailors in difficulty. If financial counselors are not readily available, however, you may need to provide assistance yourself. If you get involved in financial counseling, you should make at least two appointments with the Sailor. In the initial meeting, you should advise the Sailor of what you expect the counseling session to accomplish and how to prepare for it. There are certain facts and figures that only he or she can supply for the counseling interview. The Sailor should bring:

- Current leave and earning statement.
- Record of take-home pay from any moonlighting jobs, spousal income, and any extra income from other sources.
- Record of expenditures made by the Sailor and spouse during the two weeks from initial contact to the interview.
- Amounts or average amounts for basic living expenses: rent/mortgage, utilities, food, transportation, telephone, clothing, etc.
- List of any installment debts and outstanding bills, with details on amount per month, total debt remaining, and who creditor is.
- The Sailor's spouse or prospective spouse.
- List of Sailor's goals or expected changes in his or her situation such as advancement, purchase of a car, and move to housing.

The second contact is the actual counseling session. You can understand the apprehension a Sailor might experience when discussing personal finances with a senior. Be alert to the behavior and non-verbal messages sent by the Sailor or the couple. The Sailor may be defensive or may want to rationalize or to talk about subjects other than the one at hand. If there is a financial problem, feelings of guilt may surface. Many times alcohol, drug, or marital problems tie into a financial problem. Unless you have special training in these complex psychological areas, you should limit the session to financial matters or refer the Sailor to the appropriate professional.

While preparing for the sessions, the Sailor has probably begun to recognize some errors in spending habits. You gain little by dwelling on such errors, other than to reassure the Sailor that he or she isn't the only one to make mistakes. As the interview progresses, the Chief Petty Officer should phrase questions to draw out the what, where, when, and how of significant expenditures. Sometimes a "why" question may be in order to clarify a trouble area. If a Sailor is contributing substantial sums to assist at home, support a charity, make an investment, or pay off an expensive purchase, the "why" is important. Often Sailors will question their commitment when they consider the reason for their expenditures. The answers to these questions may be the foundation for the control process the session is to accomplish.

During the interview, the Chief Petty Officer must keep his or her own role in mind. Maintain control of the session while encouraging the Sailor to exercise thought and judgment. If the session begins to derail, the CPO should firmly but courteously bring the discussion back to the subject at hand: what is the income and where should it go?

Some important sources of information you should be aware of include SECNAVINST 7220.38, the Fair Debt Collection Practices Act (P.L. 95-109), MILPERSMAN 6210140, NAVPERS 15608A9 (the *Command Financial Specialist Training Manual*), and, most especially, your command financial specialist.

In general, a budget work-up should take forty-five minutes to one hour. Controlling the budget will take much longer. If you feel this Sailor needs more than you can offer, it might be time to call in the command financial specialist, whose mission is to assist in training all assigned personnel in the basics of personal financial management (PFM) and to provide counseling and referral service to those experiencing problems in this area. Retention of quality personnel is directly related to the Sailor's perception and satisfaction with the quality of life in the military. The military lifestyle can create special and unique financial concerns such as frequent moves, family separations for extended periods of time, deployments, and fluctuations in pay, to mention only a few. With this comes increased financial responsibility.

Getting into Debt. There are many ways to incur indebtedness. The following are only a few:

- Lack of budgetary discipline and instant gratification as a prime motivator.
- Spouse who lacks budgetary discipline.
- The member fails to notify disbursing when a change affecting pay status occurs.
- Allotment changes, starts, or stops.
- Tax changes including changes in exemptions, state of legal residence, or additional withholding.
- Assignment of government quarters for members with family members, marriage, divorce, or other change in dependency status.
- Changes in rent or mortgage payment.
- Sharing of household with other military members.

Legal Financial Issues

Sailors are not only bound by military law but also by civilian law. It is important to understand the nature of legal processes affecting the Sailor and what means are available to alleviate the Sailor's legal difficulties. Some common legal issues with a major financial impact include domestic relations, spousal and child support, and non-support of family members, The Soldiers' and Sailors' Civil Relief Act, and credit laws.

Spousal and Child Support. All states have laws governing this type of support. Generally, a Sailor can end up in court at any time during the marriage if the spouse with the greater income fails to adequately support the other spouse. Most states provide for specific dollar amounts of child support, based on the number of children and gross income of both parents. If parties cannot agree, the court will impose the statutory amount.

Non-Support of Family Members. The military recognizes a Sailor's moral and legal obligation to support dependents and uses its resources to ensure that we meet this obligation. The Navy does not possess the direct authority to force the Sailor to provide support by allotment or other means. Under Federal law, it is now possible to garnish the earnings of any Sailor who fails to abide by a court decree ordering the payment of child or spousal support. Your command should first determine if the complaint is from a family member and review a copy of the court order or mutual agreement if one exists. If one does not exist, the command should recommend the Sailor follow the support guidelines set forth in MILPERSMAN Article 6210120.

Garnishment and Involuntary Allotment. When support payments are in arrears, the Sailor may find that the court order for support payments is now a judgment. Once there is such a judgment, the Sailor's pay and/or federal tax return is subject to garnishment. An involuntary allotment may occur where the Sailor has failed to support payments as ordered by a court for two months or more.

Consequences of Non-Support. In intolerable cases, disciplinary action by the Navy, ranging from non-judicial punishment to a court-martial proceeding and possible separation from the Navy, may be appropriate. Administrative separation, reduction, or termination of BAQ-Family Member or ineligibility to reenlist or extend could result.

The Soldiers' and Sailors' Civil Relief Act of 1940. The act contains provisions designed to relieve Sailors from worry over their inability to meet their civil obligations by temporarily suspending enforcement of certain civil liabilities if their ability to meet their obligation is impaired by reason of their military service. This act has a very narrow focus and applies to a very small percentage of Sailors. It does not provide any relief to the overwhelming majority of Sailors experiencing financial difficulties. Provisions apply only to those Sailors with financial obligations that exist prior to enlistment or recall to activity duty and include:

- Non-garnishment of military paychecks, for indebtedness to a creditor
- Right to request a stay of default judgment when military service hinders appearance in court to properly represent oneself
- Exemption from paying state income taxes on military pay earned in states that are not the legal residences of Sailors
- Exemption from paying personal property taxes in any state except state of legal residence. This does not relieve the Sailor's spouse from paying the tax.
- A reduction, under certain circumstances, of interest rates in excess of 6 percent on installment contracts entered into prior to joining the armed forces
- The requirement that creditors obtain a court order prior to repossessing real or personal property purchased prior to entering the military.

The act does not help the Sailor rescind a rental or purchase agreement entered into after entry onto active duty, nor does it confer exemption from local real estate taxes. The act also does not assist in avoiding or postponing court action resulting from civilian criminal charges.

Credit Laws. Sailors, as citizens, share the protection of a number of laws designed to curb the excesses of some businesses.

- Truth In Lending Act requires lenders to provide a complete disclosure statement of all credit terms before making a loan or extending credit, helping consumers better understand their options.
- Fair Credit Reporting Act requires consumer credit reporting agencies to furnish correct and complete information to businesses evaluating applications for credit, insurance, or employment.
- Fair/Credit Billing Act helps consumers resolve disputes with creditors over billing errors and ensures fair handling of credit accounts.
- Fair Debt Collection Practices Act helps protect debtors by prohibiting creditors, or debt collectors acting on their behalf, from using certain methods of debt collection like harassment, making false statements, or engaging in unfair practices.
- Equal Credit Opportunity Act ensures credit is granted to all consumers in a fair manner.

Credit Reporting Agencies (CRA) and Credit History. CRAs are commercial firms that distribute credit information to requesting department stores, banks, or other financial institutions. The Fair Credit Reporting Act (FCRA) requires creditors tell you the name and address of the CRA that supplied the credit report if it was used to deny your credit application. That CRA must then allow you to review your credit file, free of charge, if you request it within thirty days of being denied credit. The FCRA limits the length of time that negative information stays on your report and sets up a process for correcting errors in your report.

Letters of Indebtedness. Navy policy is that Sailors pay their just debts in a timely and proper fashion. The Navy doesn't adjudicate claims or arbitrate controversies concerning asserted default in fulfillment of private obligations, nor will it act as an agent or collector for the creditor. You should inform the Sailor of the letter, recommend that he or she make contact with the creditor to work out a debt repayment plan, and explain the available financial counseling services. Disciplinary action is rarely appropriate, unless there is evidence of intentional deceit or non-payment.

Advance Pay. The purpose of advance pay is to provide a Sailor with funds to meet the extraordinary expenses of a government-ordered move. Appropriate uses of these funds do not include such items as vacations or investments in or purchase of consumer goods not related to a permanent change of station (PCS) move. You may be required to review a request with concern for the Sailor's general financial well-being. Justification is necessary when the Sailor requests an advance outside of the normal parameters of one month's basic pay less deductions, a twelve-month repayment schedule, and eligibility in the window of thirty days in advance of travel until sixty days after reporting into the new duty station. Justification must be in writing and illustrate extenuating circumstances, severe hardship, or unusually large expenses requiring an extension of the normal parameters. A Sailor may request no more than three months' basic pay, less deductions, and/or repayment schedule more than twenty-four months. The command can authorize an advance up to ninety days before departure or 180 days after arrival. You should counsel members eligible for advance pay to avoid the pitfalls of long-term debt and reserve such advances for their intended purpose.

Rehabilitation Plan. You can encourage and guide Sailors in developing a plan for earnings, spending, and achieving goals. The CFS will assist your Sailors in their efforts to help themselves with creating a "life after debt." Encourage your Sailors to keep track of expenses, plan a household budget, shop and spend carefully, and save and invest for the future. Rehabilitation has the negative connotation that a problem existed at one time. Helping Sailors understand the importance of a savings plan, strategies for the purchase of necessities, preparation for family and debt care during deployments, and securing the family's future with a good life insurance plan are in fact preventative measures that can keep any financial problems from arising.

The Chief Petty Officer as a Mentor

It's a pretty good bet that most long-retired chiefs will look back on their career and recall those times where they helped a shipmate succeed as one of the most important and meaningful moments of their service. Names for those conversations range from career counseling to being a "sea daddy," but the formal name is mentoring. Mentoring is at the heart of how a good Chief Petty Officer interacts with Sailors and junior officers. In the broadest sense of the word, every chief is a mentor, and all the Sailors protégés. Mentoring is an extended interaction between a teacher and student for purposes of professional and personal growth.

Mentoring provides a powerful form of professional development for Sailors. In addition to dramatic impact on Sailor professionalism and personal development, mentoring improves morale and quality of life for Sailors. Chiefs have been mentors since the introduction of our rate in 1893, and it's a fair bet that old salts mentored their shipmates in the days of wooden ships and iron men. The Chief Petty Officer is unique among Navy mentors in that the protégé can be a senior from the wardroom or a junior from the crew.

Mentoring links our Sailors with experienced petty officers or chiefs so that they might intelligently discuss and understand the options that are available for them through the Navy. Mentors facilitate personal and professional growth for Sailors by sharing the knowledge and insights they've learned through the years. Mentoring may be a very easy, natural process, or you may feel uncomfortable at first, but you'll soon get the hang of it. You have probably had a mentor or two of your own, even though your mentors might cringe at the sound of the social science term. It's a fair chance too that you've acted as a mentor for someone, perhaps when you were an LPO or a work center supervisor. Start off easy and natural!

A mentoring relationship outside the chain of command is most frequently triggered by regular contact on duty between a CPO and a Sailor who desires a mentor. Perhaps the quartermaster of the watch has regular contact with a chief standing junior officer of the deck watch in his or her section. Perhaps a messenger of the watch stands duty with an OOD in the same in-port watch section, spending many long slow midwatches together. When junior Sailors and junior officers are exposed to professional chiefs who share the same vigilance and attention to detail on a slow midwatch as during the busiest evolutions, mentoring is occurring. Long midwatches can evolve into the formal, structured, focused mentoring that produces spectacular results and great satisfaction for all concerned.

The purpose of the mentoring relationship is to:

- Give information.
- Explore opportunities for change, promotion, and /or training.
- Informally analyze skills, experience, and training.
- Analyze problems and develop solutions.

Successful mentoring will result in more informed choices, an action plan, and increased alternatives. A good mentor is respected, people-oriented, a good listener, supportive, approachable, fair and honest, a motivator, a teacher, and an achiever. Although the mentoring relationship is special, it is important to remember that certain behaviors and relationships are inappropriate at any time, and the guiding rules cannot be suspended to facilitate a mentor-protégé relationship. In addition, all members of the chain of command should be aware and approving of any formal relationship that does not fall in the chain of command.

There are also may be times to discourage, modify, or disapprove a formal mentoring arrangement, including:

- The potential mentor is not yet ready for that responsibility. A chief struggling with his or own professional assignment should not be taking on additional responsibilities.
- The Chief simply has too many other high-priority tasks to take on additional responsibilities. We must avoid creating expectations that cannot be met.
- In some instances it may not be advisable for a chief from one department to mentor someone from another department.
- Gender should not normally be a consideration but there are instances in which gender, the maturity of the participants, the situation, and other factors make some matches inappropriate or impractical. Senior leadership must not shy away from pointing out the potential for problems in mixed-gender mentoring and perception issues.

Responsibilities as a Mentor. The first responsibility of an effective mentor is to enjoy mentoring. A lukewarm attitude, a shrug of "Well, it comes with the job," will not do. Mentoring is voluntary, but enjoying mentoring is mandatory! If you don't find it satisfying, you probably won't be good at it. Once you have good lines of communication, then:

- Set realistic expectations.
- Maintain contact.
- Listen with empathy and provide feedback.
- Be open-minded.
- Provide support and encouragement.
- Foster the relationship.
- Follow through on commitments.
- Keep alert for development opportunities.
- Share successes and failures.

If you find yourself in a position where you've been asked to provide guidance and mentoring to an up-and-coming individual, be it a Sailor or a junior officer, evaluate yourself to be sure you can commit. You don't have to mentor every person who asks; time constraints, among other things, make that impossible. The match should be a comfortable one for both of you. Establish guidelines, making sure the Sailor knows the relationship brings no special privileges and will end immediately if any trade-off is attempted. Develop the relationship so the Sailor understands that you may be the coach, but the Sailor must be a player with goals to accomplish.

Four Stages of Mentoring

Prescriptive Stage. These steps are usually necessary when the Sailor has little or no experience at the job or in the activity. In this stage, the mentor:

- Directs and advises Sailor who depends heavily on this support and instruction.
- Gives a lot of praise and attention to build Sailor's self-confidence while providing detailed information on many issues and procedures.
- Gives examples of how to handle situations with consequences.
- Assumes role of coach, teacher, and motivator.

Persuasive Stage. During this stage the mentor, acting as a counselor and guide, may need to persuade the Sailor to:

- Find answers.
- Seek challenges with direction.
- Take risks.
- Make new discoveries by suggesting new strategies, questions, and challenges.

Collaborative Stage. The Sailor and mentor work together to jointly solve problems. The Sailor actively cooperatives in his or her professional development plan, while the mentor acts as career advisor and role model.

Validating Stage. The Sailor requires the mentor's wisdom and professional insight into policies and people. The mentor is a sounding board, empathetic listener, and a supporter. As a sponsor, the mentor watches for, creates, or negotiates opportunities for the Sailor that may not be known by the Sailor.

Advantages of Mentoring Relationships

To the Mentor	To the Sailor	To the Navy
Learn about your Sailors	Build confidence	Better Sailors
Pride in another's achievement	Career satisfaction	Supports diversity
Opportunity to practice leadership and interpersonal skills	Increased opportunity for advancement	More qualified and motivated senior enlisted

Counseling and mentoring are part of who we are and who we want to be. In your own career, some chief some time took you aside and set you on the right path. Remember what you owe him or her and "pay it forward." Do unto others what that Chief did for you. That's what chiefness is all about.

Points to Ponder

Case Study: Problems Ashore

Have you ever had to deploy during times of family difficulty or crisis? How did it make you feel? How did you work through your concerns while away from home?

Some commands give Sailors the option of not hearing about family difficulties when on arduous or remote deployments. How do you feel about that policy? If you were deploying to an area where recovery was not likely, and personal communication was extremely limited, what level of knowledge would you like about what's happening back on the beach?

Suppose you were PNSN Dennis's shipmate. How would you feel if she's not carrying her load? Would you sympathize with her—"The same thing happened to me last year"—or would you resent her personal problems interfering with getting the job done. What does your response tell you about yourself?

11

Caring for Sailors and Families

Case Study: A Simple Transfer

MMCM (SS) John Duffy was sitting at the chief's table aboard USS *Pottsville* (SSN-791) when the chief of the boat came down the passageway. "Hey, Bull Nuke, today's your lucky day. The XO just approved my leave, and for the next ten days, you get to play COB. Not much going on—we're going to be here on the river for at least three months, and most of the crew are parceled out to other boats working on their qualifications. You've got some personnel movements scheduled: IT2 McCann finally got those orders he's been wanting to the USS *Adak Island* at La Maddelena, but that's about it. I'm going fishing up by the SERE camp at Rangeley, Maine, but you shouldn't have any trouble. Everything you want to know is contained in the ring binder on my desk."

Relocation and Sponsor Training

No one understands the hassles—and the excitement—of moving, be it across base or across the world, quite like a military family. IT2 McCann and family are going to have the experience of a lifetime, their very first move overseas, to the sunny isle of Sardinia. To make things easier for Sailors like Petty Officer McCann, the Navy implemented the Relocation Sponsorship Program in 1970. Designed to ease the difficulties and reduce the apprehension normally associated with a permanent change of station (PCS), the sponsorship program assists Sailors who are expecting PCS orders by requiring that receiving commands at the new duty station assign a seasoned Sailor as sponsor for the incoming shipmate and family. Commands are required to provide sponsors for all personnel going overseas, as well as for personnel returning to CONUS or relocating within CONUS when requested.

The success of the Navy Sponsorship Program depends heavily on the qualifications and attitude of the individual sponsor. The best command instruction and strongest commanding officer support for the sponsor program are completely ineffective if the sponsor is not qualified and motivated. Sponsors must be assigned early enough to have time to execute the program requirements. The act of assigning and training sponsors is a command responsibility of the highest order. Sponsors for enlisted Sailors are normally assigned at the CMC or department LCPO level, but because the LCPO of the gaining division has the most at stake, he or she is normally heavily involved in the process. To be effective, the sponsor must:

- Have a positive attitude toward the program and toward being a sponsor.
- Communicate promptly with the incoming personnel and family prior to, during, and after their arrival.
- Render necessary assistance. Get answers to all questions the newcomer might have.
- Help arrange necessary appointments with the housing office, PSD, and the personnel property office.
- Assist in the relocation of the member and the family upon arrival by arranging their temporary lodging facilities and transportation. The sponsor should check and

double-check to be sure that any temporary housing is clean and ready for move-in.

- Personally assist the new member with check-in procedures.
- Provide the new member with close personal contact throughout indoctrination period within the command.

Relocation is stressful and demanding mentally, physically, and emotionally. A sponsor's assistance can make all the difference by providing realistic expectations, basic guidance, local newspapers, and suggestions to new arrivals. Sponsors ease the adjustment of the new shipmate and family by providing individual assistance throughout the moving process. They help the newcomer and family gain a positive first impression about their new location and make them feel properly appreciated and welcome to the team. Sponsorship is crucial to the retention and readiness of a quality force. The Relocation Sponsor Program supports the Navy's mission in a variety of ways.

Improves Operation Readiness. Assisting Sailors and their families through the "relocation maze" and speeding the Sailor's transition to Navy duties. A positive attitude and early satisfaction with the new location also means less disruption in the work schedule.

Enhances Quality of Life. Alleviating a Sailor's concerns about family stability during PCS moves permits a Sailor to focus attention on Navy duties. Sponsors help support the mission by ensuring Sailors and their families are taken care of upon arrival at the new duty station. Both accompanied and unaccompanied Sailors will want to know about recreational facilities, opportunities for volunteering, PCS process workshops, athletic development programs, educational programs, and social activities.

Improves Recruiting and Retention. Spousal satisfaction can influence the decision to stay Navy or separate. One bad PCS move can have such a negative impact on family attitudes toward Navy life that recovery is a long time coming. The sponsor's duty is to minimize surprises and take every reasonable step to make the Sailor and his or her family feel welcome.

Special-Needs Groups. Experienced sponsors recognize that some Sailors and their families are more intensely impacted by the mobile Navy lifestyle. They might be single parents, dual-career military, foreign-born spouses, or families with an exceptional family member. Some require specific information and assistance to meet their special needs. All of the groups may be interested in military and civilian childcare facilities both before and after school hours, certified family home child care, and twenty-four hour child care. Families with exceptional family members will need additional information on special medical facilities, TRICARE, and support groups.

IT2 McCann caught up with MMCM Duffy later that day. "Hey, Master Chief! The COB said you'd be covering his watch for a while. Man, my wife and daughter are really excited about going overseas. That's what we wanted when we joined the Navy, and Captain Golden tells me that you've been stationed in Guam, Japan, and Naples, too. What's it going to be like when we move? Can you tell me?"

Understanding the Relocation Cycle

PO2 McCann will soon find that there are several phases of a relocation, and we seem to be always on the move. We are most clearly aware of these recurring events or cycles when it comes time for orders and realize we've been through all of this before. Be it a local move along one coast or an overseas assignment twelve thousand miles away, relocation is always a challenge and an opportunity, a potentially hazardous undertaking, and a certain adventure.

The Predeparture Phase. The predeparture phase is usually one of frantic activities accompanied by positive and negative feelings of anticipation and apprehension. Accurate, current information is critical in this stage. Research has shown that the better prepared the Sailor and family are before the move, the more rapid the adjustment and reconnect in the new community.

The Transition Phase. The transition phase is a short, energy-intensive period that includes the actual departure, travel, and arrival at the new installation (often with some time lapse for a visit home, TAD, etc.). It is a time of disconnecting from the old location and continued enthusiasm about the new location. It also can be a very demanding time, which drains mental and physical energy reserves.

The Arrival and Orientation Phase. The arrival and orientation phase is the time when the need for information is ever greater than in the predeparture phase. In this phase, the Sailor and family have a better frame of reference of the information they received. Expectations and reality are reconciled, for better or worse, in this phase. Energetic, effective welcomes and orientation programs have a major impact. Sponsorship is particularly effective at this point.

The Reconnect Phase. The reconnect phase occurs between two and six months after arrival and may, at first, be marked by bewilderment and disillusionment. These negative reactions, if they occur, usually disappear as newcomers learn their way around, make friends, and become involved in the life of the community. How quickly people reconnect can influence their attitude and performance throughout the entire tour. Indoctrination division, newcomer information, orientations, and welcome programs play a major role in this phase. The longer the adjustment for the service member and family, the less productive the Sailor is likely to be on the job. Although sponsorship obligations to the new Sailor are being ratcheted down during this period, it is important that the sponsor continue to follow the new Sailor's

The feelings of sadness and separation engendered by long deployments can be offset by the sure and certain knowledge that our loved ones will be looked after while we are away.
U.S. Navy (PH2 Michael Sandberg)

progress in integrating into the command and inquire about the family's well-being.

The Stabilization or Mid-Tour Slump Phase. The mid-tour slump lasts from about six months after the move until about six months before the next anticipated move. Even though this is the most productive phase for those who have made a good adjustment, a mid-tour slump is not unusual. Separations and deployments may be part of the cause of this phenomenon, because they can constitute ongoing mobility between PCS moves. Some Sailors find it difficult to adjust because knowing that the next move is inevitable often makes them less willing to form strong shipmate and friendship bonds or to invest time and effort into the community.

The Re-entry Phase. The re-entry phase is associated mostly with returns to CONUS from overseas. The need for assistance for those going overseas is usually recognized, but coming back from overseas also can be a real jolt—in part because most people simply do not anticipate any problems coming home. Returnees do find, however, that their overseas experience has changed them in ways of which they were unaware until they try to connect with old friends and familiar places. Sometimes they feel guilty for not wanting to be back stateside, and they miss the security and financial benefits associated with some overseas duty. This phase is more compressed than the overseas culture shock adjustment, but it is no less intense and demanding.

The Overseas Screening Process

Sailors who receive orders for overseas shore duty must undergo an extensive overseas screening process to ensure they and their family members, if accompanied, are suited or eligible for the overseas environment. Issues include:

- Mandatory completion of level-one anti-terrorism training for all adult family members.
- Mandatory completion of financial counseling for all adult family members.
- Mandatory compliance with the Navy family care policy covering obligations to provide care for children during and after normal duty hours at the overseas location.
- Obligation of command and member to report any disqualifying medical or dental conditions before or after initial screening.
- Obligation of command and member to report any family members who are enrolled in the Exceptional Family Member Program (EFMP).

When the overseas screening process fails, it affects the service member, family members, shipmates, and the command mission-readiness. The sponsor is a vital link and the most important communication channel between the gaining command. Through mail, phone, or email, the sponsor should ask all the right questions and report any possible disqualifying factors immediately to the personnel officer or through the chain of command. If problems cannot be solved, orders must be canceled in sufficient time to allow identification of a replacement, or the tour changed to unaccompanied with appropriate adjustment of the tour length.

Case Study: Sailors with Exceptional Family Members

"You know, Master Chief, there's only one thing worrying me. My daughter was just diagnosed with Type I diabetes, and, although my wife is doing a great job working with her and her medications, I'm worried that if something happens to us in Italy, we might not have the support that we need for her. I love the Navy, don't get me wrong, but my little girl comes first in everything I do, you know?"

The Exceptional Family Member Program

The Navy takes care of its own, and that includes family members. Occasionally, circumstances such as having a family member with special medical or education needs makes it difficult for some Sailors to fulfill their military obligations as readily as others. The Navy's Exceptional Family Members (EFM) Program was established in September 1987 to meet federal mandates that all Sailors with exceptional family members be assigned only to overseas areas where their specialized needs can be met. The EFM Program has evolved to include the identification of all family members with special needs, regardless of where the sponsor is assigned. Unfortunately, some Navy members have been reluctant to pursue identification of their Exceptional Family Member's status, resulting in unnecessary family hardship and turbulent personnel practices, such as early reassignment of the sponsor due to inadequate educational and/or medical support.

Enrollment in the program is now required when special needs of family members are first identified or at least nine months prior to the Projected Rotation Date (PRD). At this time, detailers can consider the family's needs as well as the Navy's needs when selecting the Sailor's next duty station. Once special needs are identified, the Sailor must submit the Exceptional Family Member Medical and Educational Summary form (DD 2792) on behalf of their special-needs family member. To be eligible, the family member must be the Sailor's dependent, enrolled in DEERS (with I.D. privileges), and reside with the service member. Enrolling in the EFM Program ensures that the family member gets the special help he or she needs, the service member knows that the family's needs are being met, and the Navy has a satisfied Sailor working to meet our mission.

As a Chief Petty Officer, you may be called upon by a Sailor to assist in identification of one of his or her dependents as a person who is eligible for the Exceptional Family Member Program. If the answer to any of these general questions is yes, have the Sailor contact the medical department for further assistance:

- Is there a family member who has a disability?
- Is there a child receiving special education services and/or a child receiving medically related services?
- Is there a spouse or child receiving treatment for cancer, lupus, heart disease, leukemia, diabetes, mental health, or long-term illness?
- Is there a family member in a residential treatment facility?
- Has the Sailor ever applied for a humanitarian reassignment for an immediate family member's medical condition?
- Has the Sailor considered a hardship discharge because of special family medical or educational needs?
- Has the Sailor recently been returned from overseas because medical or special educational services were not available?

- Has the Sailor recently had to take an unaccompanied tour because a family member failed overseas/isolated area screening?
- Is the Sailor enrolled in the TRICARE program for people with disabilities?
- Does the Sailor have a child receiving medical care through a state medical program?
- Does the Sailor have a family member receiving Social Security Supplemental Income (SSI) benefits?
- Is the Sailor a geographical bachelor because of a family member's special medical or educational needs?

Enrollment in the Exceptional Family Member Program does not mean the end of the Sailor's career progression or that the Sailor cannot be stationed overseas. Detailers will continue negotiating with the Sailors about how best to handle sea/shore rotations and rating requirements. Family members in the program will continue to be overseas-screened, and the Navy will make every effort to assign Sailors with EFM family members within the Navy's geographical area of medical responsibility. Currently, the Navy is responsible for Japan, Australia, the Caribbean region, Bermuda, Newfoundland, and New Zealand. Navy dependent children with educational disabilities will not be sent to another military department's designated area of responsibility without prior approval from that service. To further protect the interests of the dependent, a Sailor may be denied command-sponsored travel of dependents to an overseas location when it is determined by the gaining medical treatment facility that the general medical services required by a family member, including exceptional members, are not available.

Finally, to maintain a Sailor's obligation to remain worldwide-assignable, EFM sponsors may be required to serve unaccompanied tours as necessary to fulfill sea/shore obligations of their rate and rating. EFM sponsors may also voluntarily elect to serve these unaccompanied tours. In those cases, the transferring commanding officer must review the decision with the sponsor to ensure that the separation will not create an undue hardship on the family that could result in an early return of the sponsor. The go/no-go decision is irrevocable—EFM sponsors electing to serve an unaccompanied tour will not be eligible for command sponsorship of their dependents at a later date. In rare instances, EFM sponsors may be assigned to involuntary unaccompanied tours, but these tours must have the active approval of a flag-level office within the Bureau of Personnel. In the event that a condition is first identified or significantly worsens while the family is overseas, requests for early return of sponsors and their families must be initiated if medical needs exceed the capability of medical services available. The family member will promptly be enrolled in the EFM Program at that time.

Being sure that our Sailors know the resources available to support their families is an important task for today's Chief Petty Officer. *U.S. Navy (Tom Watanabe)*

Family Support Services

"Well, McCann, I can tell you that the Navy will do everything in its power to be sure that you have a successful tour over at La Mad. But you know what? You can help yourself, and your wife, too, if you take a run over to the Family Services Center and have a quick talk with the folks over there. When my youngest son was diagnosed with a learning disability a few years ago, they were great in helping me understand what was going on and what resources were available to Navy families. Why not give them a call?"

We all know that family satisfaction is a key issue in retaining good Sailors. The Navy provides extensive resources to support Sailors' families. Surprisingly, many first-enlistment Sailors don't know much about what's available, and it's our responsibility as Chief Petty Officers to be sure that they have complete access to all the services provided through the fleet and family support centers (FFSCs) worldwide. Located in every fleet concentration and on many smaller bases both at home and overseas, the FFSCs link Sailors' families with the resources needed to handle almost any situation. At one time or another, most Sailors and Navy families can benefit from one or more of these services.

Counseling Services. One of the basic functions of an FFSC is to provide counseling for Sailors and families. Counseling provided at FFSCs assists in achieving operational readiness, superior performance, member retention, and improved quality of life for service members and families. At most centers are clinical counselors who meet strict licensing and accreditation standards. Confidentiality is assured. The short-term counseling provided is solution focused, and referrals are offered for longer-term counseling. Families dealing with abuse issues are offered treatment until family safety and stability return. Most clients at FFSCs are self-referred, but you should refer a Sailor when he or she is experiencing family or personal problems. Sailors should not feel embarrassed or ashamed. Remind them that, at times, everyone needs an objective way to look at things. If one of your Sailors or someone in your family is looking for ways to prevent personal and family problems and learn effective ways to deal with them, counseling often helps.

Counseling is most frequently requested for marital problems, particularly those associated with geographic moves, lack of support systems, or the absence of a spouse, but counselors also can help with family and job stresses, bereavement, life transitions, sadness, or other adjustment problems. Counselors work closely with the medical and mental health staff, chaplains, and other providers to assure that counseling clients are offered the help they need to alleviate their problems. Some FFSCs offer workshops on topics like anger management, career exploration, forgiveness and personal growth, relationships, and managing stress.

Family Advocacy Program (FAP). FAP is a military-wide program that assists with problems resulting from spousal abuse, child abuse, child neglect, and child sexual molestation. FAP offers prevention, intervention, and treatment resources at no cost to military family members. The Family Advocacy Program is a comprehensive response to families and is designed to prevent or stop the violence, and includes:

Spouse Employment Assistance Program (SEAP). SEAP is a program designed to assist in overcoming the difficulties associated with finding employment, especially during relocations. Comprehensive and standardized employment information services are available at the Fleet and Family Support Centers worldwide. Family members of active duty personnel can take advantage of SEAP services, which include job and employment agency listings, a reference library, resume preparation assistance, federal job information, career counseling, and skill-building advice.

Employment/Transition Assistance. The Transition Assistance and Spouse Employment Assistance Programs offer a variety of services similar to those of SEAP. Individual employment counseling covers topics such as interviewing, career changing, and job-fair preparation.

Personal Financial Management. The Personal Financial Management Program provides one-on-one assistance, financial education, and consumer awareness classes and workshops. Special interest topics can be designed to meet the needs of the command, spouse group, or community. Typical programs include:

- Communicating About Money
- Home Buying
- Investing in Your Future
- Reading Your Credit Report
- Saving to Invest
- Thrift Savings Plan (TSP) for Military Members

Transition Assistance Management Program (TAMP). At your chief's initiation, someone no doubt said to you, "Remember, once a chief, always a chief." You may be a chief forever, but the day is going to come sooner than you expect when you'll cross the brow for the last time, and you will head off to civilian life again. The Transition Assistance Management Program (TAMP) ensures that all transitioning military personnel—including you and your Sailors and families—have access to quality transition assistance services. Services include preseparation counseling, employment assistance, and an individual transition plan to aid in making an effective transition from military to civilian life. Delivery of these congressionally mandated services is achieved through a cooperative effort involving the Departments of Defense, Labor, and Veterans Affairs, as well as community and nonprofit service organizations. It's never too soon to consider what comes next. As soon as you've made your retirement decision, see the Fleet and Family Support Center or your command contact for handling retirement issues, and sign up for your TAMP sessions.

Command Ombudsman

A few days later, Master Chief Duffy ran into IT2 McCann as they crossed the brow at the end of the day. "Hey, I just got an email from the command master chief over on the USS *Adak Island*. He says they have a great ombudsman program running there at La Maddelena, and if your wife drops a quick email to Piney Duppa—her husband is an MR1, I think—she'll forward all kinds of information that will be helpful when you first get over there. You know, McCann, Navy wives do a bang-up job helping each other, especially when there's a relocation or big deployment in the offing. Have your wife contact her."

At one time or another, every chief in the mess is likely to need the services of the command ombudsman, especially on sea duty where the services an ombudsman provides are more critical. Chiefs must fully understand the role and limitations of the ombudsman and provide him or her all possible support.

One major quality-of-life development over the past quarter century has been the establishment of the Navy Family Ombudsman Program. The Swedish term *ombudsman* means a person who oversees relationships between citizens and their officials and is empowered to cut through the red tape and get things done. No title can better describe those generous Navy spouses who volunteer their time and energy to be the official—and critical—communication link between families and commands afloat and ashore. Once appointed, the volunteer receives standardized ombudsman basic training.

Ombudsmen are primarily information and referral specialists who help command family members gain the assistance they need to succeed as part of the extended Navy family, an especially critical task for deploying commands. Although ombudsmen are not paid for their services, authorized expenses, such as mileage, child care, and office supplies are reimbursed when approved by the command. Ombudsmen most enjoy the satisfaction of helping other command family members and gaining new skills and experience through the assignment.

As the primary link between families and the command, ombudsmen communicate with families through newsletters, a telephone service or phone tree, or email. They cooperate with the Fleet and Family Service Centers, chaplains' offices, medical treatment facilities, Navy-Marine Corps Relief Society, American Red Cross, Navy Wifeline Association, and the legal assistance offices. Although they don't counsel, they may need to refer family members to the right professionals.

Sometimes ombudsmen assist in organizing and implementing welcome programs that are part of the command sponsor programs. Ombudsmen also represent the command on committees, boards, and working groups in the military or civilian communities concerned with services and support to command families. They maintain a close working relationship with the command family support team that includes the commanding officer, executive officer, command master chief, and others designated by the commanding officer.

Ombudsmen candidates should have maturity, judgment, discretion, reliability, and a positive attitude. They should understand and support the Navy and command programs and policies, and must have the time, dedication, and commitment to be a command family ombudsman. As a Chief Petty Officer, you should always be on the lookout for Sailors whose spouses exhibit these qualities and encourage them to be open to serving as command ombudsmen at some time in the future. Stress to them that, before submitting a resume, they must carefully consider the effect of the position on their own family. The time commitment can be extensive.

The Navy Family Ombudsman Program and Family Service Centers are complementary programs. Ombudsmen reach out to individual command family members. Family Service Centers are a resource for ombudsmen in carrying out their responsibilities and offer support to ombudsmen in such areas as coordination of ombudsman training, establishment of ombudsman support groups, provision of resources and information when individual family problems are presented to the ombudsman, assistance to commands in the effective use and recognition of ombudsmen, and maintenance of area ombudsmen rosters.

Navy Wifeline Association volunteers perform many of the same functions as command family ombudsmen in that they provide a vital communication link between the Navy institution and service members and their families while serving in this capacity.

The Navy's programs signal the Navy's commitment to taking care of Sailors and their families. It's up to Chief Petty Officers to make sure that Sailors know the breadth of resources available to them.

Part Four

Supporting

12

Tradition, Custom, Courtesy, and Protocol

Case Study: Lessons Learned in the Ceremonial Guard

BMC Reid was crossing the quarterdeck at MCPON Hall—the visitor's center at Recruit Training Command—when GMC Cushing and SM1 Perkins hailed him. "Hey, Boats, I was just telling Perkins here that you were once in the Navy's Ceremonial Guard Unit in Washington, and that's why you've got such a good handle on marching and facing movements." "Darn right, I do," replied BMC Reid. "Why, do you know that we had to 'drill out' of the fourth platoon—the training unit—before we were able to go on the street in front of the public? And I betcha we did at least fifteen, maybe twenty, funerals and other ceremonies each week. It was great duty, representing the Navy in our nation's capital. And I've never lost that awe about who we are and what we represent, even though it's been nearly twenty years since I left there and went back to sea. Maybe I can get some of these young Sailors to understand a little bit about that before they leave here, huh?"

You, too, are a Navy Chief Petty Officer. As such, you share with every chief—those who have gone before us, those who serve now, and those yet to come—in the sacred trust of guarding and cherishing our customs and traditions. Shortly before I left office as the eighth MCPON, I addressed the Brigade of Midshipmen in these words:

> Our Navy life is immersed in tradition. Tradition dictates the way we greet one another and cross the brow. It prescribes the way we relieve the watch, begin and end the day, and it guides much of the routine in between. Naval traditions are the best parts of our past that we preserve in ceremonial and many other ways, from the routine to the spectacular. I was once asked "How do we tell the difference between a good tradition and a bad tradition?" "There are no bad traditions," I replied. By their very nature, naval traditions can only be good—that is why they are preserved and ultimately classified as traditions—for their goodness.

Tradition

Tradition consists of transmitting information, beliefs, and customs by word of mouth or by example. Our traditions evolved from the day-to-day activities of our Sailor "ancestors." Sailors who know something of our history recognize the value of traditions in the Navy. But tradition does not mean shackling yourself to the ironclad concepts of the past. Far from it—real Navy traditions are ones that recognize and enshrine those immutable elements that are of lasting importance, whether the war being fought is against the Barbary pirates or modern terrorists.

Custom

Tradition is made up of customs and military courtesies. A custom is a way of acting consistently over such a long period of time that it has become like a law. A courtesy is a form of polite behavior and excellence of manners. Customs and courtesies help make life orderly and are a way of showing respect. There's usually a good reason why we practice a particular custom or courtesy aboard ship, and it's not just to please a hard-headed skipper or command master chief. Almost every rule and regulation aboard ship has evolved for our safety and efficiency. Sailors who live in ships and others exposed to shipboard life have come to understand and respect those rules and the standard of discipline as part of who we are as Sailors in the world's greatest Navy. A custom:

- Requires continuous usage for a long enough period of time that no one can remember when it was different. Not even veteran chiefs, wise in the way of the Navy, can remember when it wasn't so.
- Must be enforced, if by no other means than peer pressure.
- Must be certain and uniform, known widely, and consistently applied.
- Must be harmonious with other customs and regulations. For example, the custom of wearing the cover square is consistent with the customary procedure of rendering the hand salute. The fingertips touch the lower edge of the cover, just above the eye. Wearing the cover on the back of the head makes it difficult, if not impossible, to properly execute our customary greeting.

Military Courtesy

Courtesy is behavior marked by polished manners, gallantry, or social usage. Being courteous to others—both seniors and juniors—shows respect and consideration. Navy personnel usually live and work in close quarters; and we must practice courtesy in all that we do. Courtesy drives us to dress by the dim red glow of a maglight because others are sleeping, and it's discourteous to turn on overhead lights when a tiny flashlight will do. We greet others differently than civilians do, and, as a matter of courtesy, the junior member takes the initiative, and the senior member reciprocates the behavior.

Honors and Ceremonies

Honor, in this context, is simply a showing of merited respect. We may proffer honors to people, places, or things. Military personnel render honors in a variety of ways, including gun salutes, passing honors, and international honors modified by agreement. Ceremonies are formalities observed on some solemn or important occasion in order to render it even more imposing or impressive. They are valuable because they bind us to the past and fill a persistent need for connectedness. We value our ceremonies because they are a function of discipline, and they have definite regulations for important occasions.

Protocol is a code of established guidelines on proper etiquette and precedence, which, when followed, lays the foundation for a successful event. Protocol is an integral part of Navy ceremonies, customs, and traditions. As Chief Petty Officers, we're expected to be familiar with the protocols surrounding many events, including presenting of colors, honors to flag officers, quarterdeck arrangements, and dining-in or dining-out functions. To do things correctly, we need a sense of etiquette and precedence on ceremonial occasions. Etiquette is the behavior of forms and manners prescribed by authority in social and official life. Precedence is the right to superior honor on a ceremonial or formal occasion. In the military, we usually establish this by seniority based on grade.

"You know," Chief Reid reminisced, "I learned a heck of a lot about the Navy and about who we are and what we do when I was in the Ceremonial Guard. We had an old chief—he'd worked with Del Black there before Master Chief Black became our first MCPON—and there wasn't a thing about protocol or ceremonial acts that he didn't know. More than that, he loved what he was doing. I was a raw seaman back then, and he taught me a lot about who we are and what we do."

Our Role as Chief Petty Officers. With those definitions and thoughts in mind, we can look at specific examples and understand the "why" as well as the "what" of the various steps required. Navy ceremonies have individual specific purposes that are usually obvious to most who attend (retirement, change of command, Navy birthday, etc.), but all ceremonies serve critically important common functions that we as Chief Petty Officers must always remember. Ceremonies represent a break in the action and give a time to pause and reflect. As chiefs we must not forget these important objectives of Navy ceremonies, including:

- Creating an awareness of our heritage
- Binding Sailors to history and tradition
- Instilling a sense of personal pride in naval service

As many of us have found out the hard way, ceremonies don't just happen. They require leadership, supervision, and guidance to succeed. Your personal involvement in the actual ceremony may vary, but your oversight and quality assurance in the planning and execution of ceremonies must be constantly high. The overall responsibility of sustaining our naval heritage lies directly on the shoulders of the CPO mess. We'll talk more about that heritage in the following chapters on the CPO mess and our history.

Basic Guidelines for Planning a Ceremonial Occasion

Research the Appropriate Ceremony. There are multiple sources to draw from when planning an important ceremony. One of the best sources may be the command history file or the audit trail of the last such ceremony conducted. If available, use caution. Use such a template only as a guide to get started planning unless you are sure that circumstances are essentially the same as those prevailing the last time.

Develop a Basic Plan. A plan must be completed months in advance of any important ceremony in order to ensure there is time to order materials, reserve banquet halls, mail invitations, print programs, and complete other tasks.

Publish a Schedule of Events. This step involves scheduling the dry runs and rehearsals, designating key participants (side boys, emcees, ushers, etc.), documenting that materials are ordered and sites reserved, and gaining command approval of the guest list and overall plan.

- Diagram the ceremonial site: This begins the detailed planning phase and marks the time when all parts of the plan gain final commanding officer approval.
- Publish an order of ceremony: This must be complete in advance of the first rehearsal and requires absolute attention to detail prior to going to print.

Ceremonial Music. The right music played correctly at the right time in the ceremony is extremely important. Surprisingly, planning for this key element to a successful ceremony is often overlooked. The command master chief should have access to a high-quality sound system and maintain a full set of traditional martial and Navy music. Key Navy songs, with and without lyrics and in several lengths, on compact discs are essential.

- "Anchors Aweigh": This song embodies all that is unique and valuable about our great Navy. It is appropriate to almost every ceremony and indispensable to many. A discussion of the power and value of this Navy treasure along with the full history and all known lyrics are found in Appendix C.
- The Navy Hymn: This song, known to Sailors and citizens around the world, is officially titled "Eternal Father, Strong to Save." It is a musical benediction that has a powerful special appeal to Sailors. A history of the music along with all known verses is also contained in Appendix B.

Our Nation's Emblem

One of our most important and sacred duties is protecting and honoring our national emblem. She has many formal names, and, under varying circumstances, she's been called the national flag, national ensign, national color, or national standard. The term *national flag* is applicable regardless of size or manner of display, but the other terms have certain well-defined usages within the armed services. We use the term *national ensign* in a general manner, although it actually indicates the national flag flown by airships, ships, and boats. The term *national color* pertains to flags carried by dismounted units of the landing force and is stubbier than the national ensign. *National standard* pertains to flags carried by mounted, mechanized, and motorized units. The Navy provides detailed regulations for the display of the national ensign and the flags of our government officials, but every Chief Petty Officer should know the basics of flag decorum under common circumstances.

National Flag. There are long-standing customs regarding the display of the national flag ashore:

- When displaying against a wall with another flag, the U.S. flag will be on the right with its staff crossing over the staff of the other flag.
- When flown from a staff in a church or speaker's platform, the flag should be on the speaker's right. If placed elsewhere than on the platform, it should be on the right of the audience as they face the platform.
- If the flag is not flown during the playing of the national anthem, all present stand and face the music. If covered, Sailors in uniform salute at the first note, holding it until the last note. Others stand at attention, men removing their hats. If the flag is on display, all present should salute (hand salute for those in uniform, hand over heart in civilian clothes, uncovered Sailors stand to attention, facing the flag but do not salute or place hand to heart).
- When flying a state, local, or organizational flag from the same halyard, the U.S. flag must always be at the peak. When flying flags from separate staffs, we must always hoist the U.S. flag first and lower it last. The national flag should always be larger then the adjacent flags.

- In displaying the flag from a staff projecting from a building, the union should be at the peak, unless flown at half-mast. When flown from a halyard over a sidewalk from a building pole, we should hoist the flag union-first from the building.

- Although the flag should be a distinctive feature at an unveiling of a statue or monument, you should never use it as the covering or veil.

- When displaying flags of two or more nations, they should be the same size and flown from separate staffs. Custom forbids the flag of one nation to fly over another in peacetime.

- Unless flown from a staff, the flag should lie flat or in such a manner that its folds fall free. When suspended over a street, the union should point either north or east.

- When carried in a procession with other flags, the national flag should be on the marching right. If there is a line of flags, it should be front center of that line. Always use a staff when carrying the flag on a float.

- Always center the national flag with the union pointed upward when displaying the flag among a group of three or more flags. When shown in a row of flags, the national flag will be at the right of the line (i.e., the viewer's left).

- Never fly any flag or pennant above or to the right of the U.S. flag at the same level, except the church pennant. You may fly the church pennant above the flag during religious services at sea.

National Ensign. In addition to displaying the flag on ships and stations between 0800 and sunset, we also fly the U.S. flag outside those periods on special occasions. A ship entering port at night should hoist the ensign at daylight for a short period to enable port authorities and other vessels to determine her nationality. It is customary for other ships to show their colors in return. Display the national ensign at the gaff upon anchoring or getting under way in sufficient light to be seen. Chapter five of the 1920 *Navy Regulations* directs that "Under no circumstances shall an action be commenced or battle fought without display of the National Ensign."

We also display the national ensign on shore from 0800 to sunset, and the national ensign may fly at Marine barracks, naval hospitals, and outlying reservations within station limits, at the discretion of the base commander. Boats belonging to naval vessels should display the national ensign as follows:

- When away from the ship between 0800 and sunset in a foreign port.
- In a homeport when boarding a foreign vessel.
- When waterborne while the parent vessel is dressed or full dressed.
- In a homeport when a vessel has any officer or official embarked officially; or when any flag officer, unit commander, commanding officer, or chief of staff in uniform on a ship belonging within his command or a boat assigned for his personal use or a junior officer who is temporarily in command is embarked, and at other times prescribed by the senior officer present.

Custom dictates that when under way, the normal point of display is at the gaff, while the flagstaff is the point of display at anchor. Prior to 0800 or after sunset, the unit will hoist the flag at the gaff.

Returning Salutes. Upon receiving a salute by dipping of the flag from a vessel registered by a nation formally recognized by the United States, the Navy ship must return the compliment dip-to-dip. The unit will dip the national ensign in the following manner:

- Hauled down slowly to about halfway between the top of the hoist and deck or other structure and held at the dip for a short interval.
- Two-blocked smartly without waiting for the other vessel to two-block. No Navy vessel dips her ensign unless returning the compliment.
- For all occasions of hoisting, lowering or half-masting the colors on ship or station, follow the motions of the senior officer present, except when answering dips.

Union Jack. The union jack, that part of the national ensign signifying union of the states, traditionally flies from the jack staff from 0800 to sunset when the ship is at anchor. Recently, however, to show our commitment to the union and the Constitution in the face of domestic terror, we're reverted to the first known naval jack, the red-and-white striped flag with the rattlesnake and "Don't Tread on Me" superimposed. Formally authorized by NavAdmin 305-02, it represents our steadfast intent to maintain our liberties in the face of cowardly terrorists.

President's Flag. In 1882, the Navy authorized the president's flag for use on Navy ships. The presidential flag changed twice: in 1916 by President Woodrow Wilson and in 1945 by President Harry Truman. Naval vessels hoist the president's flag at the main the moment the president reaches the deck and remains flying until his departure. They haul it down with the last gun of the salute. A Navy boat with the president embarked flies the flag at the bow.

Navy Department Flag. The Navy officially adopted the newest flag, the Navy Department flag, in 1959. On a field of deep blue, the official seal, in gold, of the department is centered; the flag's border is trimmed in gold.

Personal Flags. Except for the fleet admiral's flag, which originated with the rank in 1944, the Navy formulated personal flags for admirals and the broad pennant for commodore in 1866. We hoist the personal flag of a flag officer when he assumes command and until he relinquishes command. Only one ship can display the flag at any one time.

Broad Command. The broad command pennant flies at the starboard yardarm of a naval vessel at anchor to represent an officer below flag rank who is temporarily exercising the command of a force, squadron, flotilla, or cruiser division during the absence of the regularly assigned commander. We fly it at the after truck of a naval vessel, replacing the commission pennant, or at the bow of a naval boat on an official occasion to represent the presence of an officer of the rank of captain or commander who the Navy regularly assigned to command a force, squadron, flotilla, or cruiser division.

Burgee Command. Hoisted at the starboard-after yardarm of a naval vessel at anchor, the burgee command pennant represents an officer below flag rank who is temporarily exercising the command of a division (except cruiser division) during the absence of the regularly assigned division commander. Replacing the commission pennant at the after truck of a naval vessel or in the bow of a naval boat on an official occasion, the burgee command pennant denotes the regularly assigned division commander. The Navy classifies the broad and burgee command pennants as personal command pennants, denoting the presence of an officer of less than flag rank in command of ships or aircraft.

Unit Citation. Unit citations are awarded for outstanding performance in action on or after 16 October 1941. After the first Presidential Unit Citation, a blue star is added to the gold part of the pennant each time another citation is received. It flies from the fore truck of a vessel at anchor from sunrise to sunset.

Battle Efficiency. One of the most coveted awards of the peacetime Navy, the Battle Efficiency pennant is awarded only to the highest 10 percent of competing units in each administrative command. At anchor, the winning vessels display the pennant at the fore.

Church Pennant. The church pennant signifies that a naval chaplain is conducting divine services for naval personnel at sea. This is the only flag flown over the national ensign. Like many other naval customs, the church pennant came down from the British Navy, which used it also as a signal for man overboard if displayed from the ensign staff. American vessels began use of the church pennant at a very early date.

Commissioning Pennant. In the earliest days of the U.S. Navy, the commissioning pennant came in various sizes, ranging from four feet in length with seven stars to seventy feet in length with thirteen stars. In modern times, the increasing number of guns and other equipment topside made the longer lengths undesirable. In 1933, the Navy approved two smaller sizes. Those selected have only seven stars and can be either four feet or six feet in length. All commissioned ships in the Navy fly the commission pennant night and day at the masthead, unless replaced by the flag or pennant of an officer in command. The commanding officer of a ship or station not entitled to fly a personal flag or a command pennant may fly it in the bow of a boat when on board officially. In this case, fly the ensign on the staff at the stern.

Homeward-Bound Pennant. Traditional usage of this pennant calls for its display by a vessel that has been on foreign duty continuously for one year or more. Hoisted upon getting under way for the United States, the pennant remains on display until sunset of the day of arrival. The first white star represents the first year of continuous duty in foreign waters outside continental limits of the United States, and additional stars are added for each six months following. Overall length is normally one foot for each person on board in excess of one year. When this results in an exceedingly long pennant, practical limits determine its length. Upon arrival in a U.S. port, the command presents the blue portion containing the stars to the commanding officer and divides the remainder equally among the officers and enlisted crew members.

The National Anthem

The "Star Spangled Banner," the national anthem of the United States, must be played by a naval band in its entirety as written. Playing the national anthem of the United States, or of any other country, as part of a medley is prohibited. The recent and despicable practice of "artistic interpretation" of the national anthem by singers, celebrities, or others who know no better can never be acceptable at any Navy function. If there's any doubt, a quick call to your nearest bandmaster can get you an official score of the music, which you might tactfully, but forcefully, pass on to the civilian "celebrity." Remember, too, when a foreign national anthem is prescribed in connection with honors, it is played first, and our national anthem is performed last.

Whenever the national anthem is played, all Sailors not in formation stand at attention and face the national ensign. In the event that the national ensign is not visible, they face the source of the music. When covered, they should salute at the first note of the anthem and remain saluting until the last note is played. Persons in formation are brought to order arms or called to attention as

Morning colors, 11 September 2003, aboard USS *Chicago* (SSN-721).

Knowledge of proper ceremonial procedures under changing circumstances is part of our responsibility as Chief Petty Officers.

U.S. Navy (JOC David Rush)

appropriate. The formation commander faces in the direction of the ensign or, in the absence of the ensign, faces in the direction of the music and renders the appropriate salute for the unit. The same marks of respect prescribed during the playing of the national anthem are shown during the playing of a foreign national anthem.

Morning and Evening Colors

In the twenty-fourth edition of *The Bluejacket's Manual*, editor Tom Cutler wrote: "[At first call to colors] . . . you will be able to tell youth from experience at this point because veterans of battle with the enemy and the elements will often come out to take part in the ceremony while the young and inexperienced will hurry inside to avoid participation because they have not yet come to appreciate what it symbolizes." Well said, Tom.

Here's how to conduct the ceremonial hoisting and lowering of the national ensign at 0800 and sunset at a naval command ashore or aboard a ship, should you, as a Chief Petty Officer, be called upon to conduct the ceremony:

- The duty section or others designated parade at the point of hoist of the ensign.
- "Attention" is sounded, followed by the playing of the "Star Spangled Banner."
- At morning colors, the ensign is started up at the beginning of the music and hoisted smartly to the peak or truck.
- At evening colors, the ensign is started from the peak or truck at the beginning of the music and the lowering timed to be completed at the last note.
- At the completion of the music, "Carry On" is sounded.
- In the absence of a band or appropriate recorded music, "To the Colors" shall be played by the bugle at morning colors and "Retreat" at evening colors. If there's no music at all, "Attention" and "Carry On" are the signals for beginning and ending the salute.
- During colors, a boat under way within sight or hearing of the ceremony lies to or proceeds at the slowest safe

speed. The boat officer or the coxswain stands and salutes except when dangerous to do so. Other persons in the boat remain seated or standing and do not salute. Motor vehicles within sight or hearing of the ceremony stop, and passengers remain seated at attention.

- After morning colors, if foreign warships are present, each ship's national anthem is played. These national anthems are played in the same order that gun salutes would be fired—usually alphabetical order. When in a foreign port, that nation's national anthem is played first, followed by the national anthems of any other ships present.

"You know, though, I used to envy the Marines," Chief Reid continued. "They got to fire the howitzers for most of our ceremonies, and, I tell ya, you ought to see the look on little kids' faces when those field pieces go off. The Marines used to time the five-second interval by singing to themselves 'If I wasn't a gunner, I wouldn't be here.' I guess if it was one of us, we'd be saying, 'If I wasn't a gunner's mate second class, I wouldn't be here,' and we'd screw up the rhythm, eh?"

Gun Salutes

In days of yore, it took as long as twenty minutes to load and fire a gun, so that when a ship fired her guns in salute, thereby rendering herself temporarily powerless, it was a friendly gesture. That practice has come down through the ages as a form of honoring an individual or a nation. The issue of gun salutes is complex, and, if you find yourself responsible for arranging or returning such salutes, arm yourself first with a current copy of OPNAVINST 1710.7, which treats the matter in exhaustive detail. Generally, no ship fires a salute unless directed by SOPA, and the matter is well thought out and planned in advance. It is possible, however, that unexpected circumstances will dictate use of the saluting batteries. Let common sense and a keen appreciation of military tradition be your guide. But keep 1710.7 handy, just in case!

Saluting Various Personages

- The president rates a twenty-one-gun salute.
- Foreign heads of state rate twenty-one-gun salutes.
- Cabinet members rate nineteen-gun salutes.
- Secretaries of the various services rate nineteen-gun salutes.
- Admirals rate nineteen-gun salutes.
- Assistant, deputy, and undersecretaries rate seventeen-gun salutes.
- Vice admirals rate fifteen-gun salutes.
- Rear admirals, upper half, rate thirteen-gun salutes.
- Rear admirals, lower half, rate eleven-gun salutes.
- Consuls general rate eleven-gun salutes.

Returning a Salute

- A salute fired to the nation by a foreign ship arriving in port is not returned gun for gun.
- A salute fired to a flag or general officer by a foreign ship is not returned gun for gun.
- A salute fired in honor of the president of the United States, or of the secretary of state when acting as special representative of the president, is not returned.
- A salute fired in honor of any official or officer on the occasion of an official visit or inspection is not returned.
- A salute fired in honor of an anniversary, celebration, or solemnity is not returned.
- A salute fired in honor of a foreign nation, or of a foreign official or officer, may be expected to be returned gun for gun, except on the occasion of a foreign anniversary, celebration, or solemnity, or an official visit.

Restrictions on Gun Salutes

- Salutes shall not be fired in ports or locations where they are forbidden by local regulations.
- No official or officer, U.S. or foreign, except those entitled to seventeen or more guns, shall be saluted by the same ship or station more than once in twelve months

unless he or she has been advanced in grade, makes an official visit or inspection, or is on special duty in which international courtesy is involved or exceptional circumstances exist.

- No officer of the armed services, while in civilian clothes, shall be saluted with guns, unless he or she is at the time acting in an official civil capacity.

- No salute shall be fired between sunset and sunrise, or before 0800 or on Sunday, except where international courtesy so dictates, or when related to death ceremonies. If the dignitary arrives early in the morning, fire the salute at 0800.

Passing Honors

Passing honors are those honors other than gun salutes that are rendered on occasions when ships or embarked officials or officers pass, or are passed, close aboard. Close aboard means passing within six hundred yards for ships and four hundred yards for boats. When in doubt, render the honors. When passing honors, sound "Attention," and all persons in view on deck and not in ranks render the hand salute. Passing honors are exchanged between ships of the Navy passing each other and between ships of the Navy and the Coast Guard passing close aboard. Honors are acknowledged by rendering the same honors in return.

- Persons on the quarterdeck salute when a boat passes close aboard in which a flag officer, a unit commander, or a commanding officer is embarked as indicated by a display of a personal flag, command pennant, commission pennant, or miniature thereof.

- The honors prescribed for the president of the United States are rendered by a ship of the Navy being passed close aboard by a ship or boat displaying the flag or standard of a foreign president, sovereign, or member of a reigning royal family, except that the foreign national anthem shall be played in lieu of the national anthem of the United States.

- Passing honors are exchanged with foreign warships passed close aboard and consist of parading the guard of the day, sounding "Attention," rendering the salute by all persons in view on deck, and playing the foreign national anthem.
- "Attention" is sounded by the junior when the bow of one ship passes the bow or stern of the other, or, if the senior is embarked in a boat, before the boat is abreast, or nearest to abreast, the quarterdeck.
- The guard, if required, presents arms, and all persons in view on deck salute. The music, if required, sounds off. "Carry on" is sounded when the prescribed honors have been rendered and acknowledged.
- Dispensing with passing honors: Passing honors are not rendered after sunset or before 0800 except when international courtesy requires.
- Passing honors are not exchanged between ships of the Navy engaged in tactical evolutions outside port.
- The senior officer present may direct that passing honors be dispensed with in whole or in part.
- Passing honors are not rendered by nor required of ships with small bridge areas, such as submarines, particularly when in restricted waters.

On entering or leaving port, the crew is paraded at quarters during daylight on occasions of ceremony except when weather or other circumstances make it impracticable or undesirable to do so. In lieu of parading the entire crew at quarters, an honor guard may be paraded in a conspicuous place on weather decks. Occasions of ceremony include:

- Visits that are not operational.
- In the homeport, when departing for a lengthy deployment or returning from a lengthy deployment.
- Visits to foreign ports not visited recently and other special occasions so determined by a superior.

When a ship of the Navy is passing Washington's tomb at Mount Vernon, Virginia, between sunrise and sunset, the following ceremonies shall be observed as much as is practicable. The full guard and band is paraded, the bell tolled, and the national ensign half-masted at the beginning of the tolling of the bell. When opposite Washington's tomb, the guard presents arms, persons on deck salute facing in the direction of the tomb, and "Taps" is sounded. The national ensign is hoisted to the truck or peak, and the tolling ceases at the last note of "Taps," after which the national anthem is played. "Carry on" is then sounded. When a ship of the Navy is passing the USS *Arizona* Memorial in Pearl Harbor between sunrise and sunset, the ship passes honors by sounding "Attention," and all persons in view on deck and not in ranks render hand salutes.

Ceremonies for National Holidays

- On President's Day and on Independence Day, every ship of the Navy in commission and not under way will full dress the ship. At noon each saluting ship, and each

No ceremony has more solemnity and seriousness of purpose than those conducted for our fallen shipmates.
U.S. Navy (PHAN Kristi Earl)

naval station equipped with a saluting battery, fires a national salute of twenty-one guns.

- On Memorial Day, each saluting ship and each naval station having a saluting battery fires at noon a salute of twenty-one minute guns. All ships and naval stations will display the national ensign at half-mast from 0800 until the completion of the salute or until 1220 if no salute is fired or to be fired.

Case Study: Deaths and Funerals

"Gee, Chief, it must have been tough attending that many funerals every week. How did you deal with all that grief and sadness?" Petty Officer Perkins asked. "It wasn't easy," Chief Reid replied. "We realized that our conduct there had to be letter-perfect. After all, this was usually the funeral of a Sailor who had served long and honorably or who had been lost in combat or in an accident, and we were representing both the Navy and the nation at his or her final ceremony. It was something we never took lightly, that's for sure."

From time to time, you may be called upon to lead a detachment honoring a Sailor who has passed on. No other ceremony carries the emotional content of a funeral, and no funeral is as solemn and dignified as one in which the military has been invited to participate. The level of participation depends upon the expressed wishes of the family. When requested, the military aspect of a funeral usually begins at the home of the deceased, at the funeral home, church or chapel, cemetery gates, or the grave. The funeral director will provide guidance, but remember that depending on the family's preference, the Navy will assist in any way requested. In addition, Navy ships and stations commemorate the passing of dignitaries and senior officers with special ceremonial acts.

When a senior U.S. civil official dies and official or authoritative notification is received, the national ensign is half-masted. When the day after receipt of the notice of death falls on a Sunday or national holiday, gun salutes will be fired on the day following.

On the death of a person in the military service, the senior officer may direct that the prescribed ceremonies be observed during the transfer of the body of the deceased from the ship or naval station, rather than during the funeral. At joint installations or commands, the procedures prescribed by the responsible military commanders will be executed uniformly by all the U.S. military units.present. In the event of a military funeral for a person in the naval service on the retired list, prescribed ceremonies shall be rendered insofar as may be practicable.

If there is no chaplain or clergyman available, the commanding officer or a designated representative conducts the funeral service. There are six pallbearers and six bodybearers, and, if practicable, they are the same grade or rating as the deceased. The mourning badge is to be worn by the escort for a military funeral as prescribed in the appropriate uniform regulations but is discretionary for those in attendance at a funeral. Boats taking part in a funeral procession display the national ensign at half-mast. If the deceased was a flag or general officer, or at the time of death a unit commander or a commanding officer of a ship, his or her flag or command pennant, or a commission pennant, is draped in mourning and displayed at half-mast from a staff in the bow of the boat carrying the body. The casket is covered with the national ensign, placed so that the union is at the head and over the left shoulder of the deceased. The ensign is removed from the casket before it is lowered into the grave or committed to the deep.

Persons in the naval service salute when the body has been carried past them, while the body is being lowered into the grave or committed to the deep, and during the firing of volleys and the sounding of "Taps." Three rifle volleys are fired after the body has been lowered into the grave or committed to the deep, after which "Taps" is sounded by the bugle. In a foreign port, however, when permission has not been obtained to land an armed escort, the volleys shall be fired over the body after it has been lowered into the boat alongside. During burial at sea, the ship is stopped, if practicable, and the ensign is displayed at half-mast from the beginning of the funeral service until the body has been committed to the deep. Further display of the ensign at half-mast may be prescribed according to circumstances by the senior officer present.

The most frequent burial-at-sea ceremony is the scattering of ashes of the cremated body of the deceased. Most often, there is no relative or friend of the deceased present, and the ceremony is carried out by ship's company. The next of kin must be given photos, a written summary, and a marked chart of the location of the ceremony. As with all other ceremonies, it is exceedingly important that all participants are fully briefed as to the solemn and dignified nature of the ceremony. OPNAVINST 5360.1 provides detailed guidance.

Funeral honors are not rendered between sunset and sunrise. When it is necessary to bury the dead at night, such funeral services as are practicable shall take place.

Before a person in the naval service is buried in a foreign place, the senior officer present arranges with the local authorities for the interment of the body and also requests permission to parade an escort under arms. The senior officer present informs the senior foreign officers present and the appropriate local officials of the time and place of the funeral and of the funeral honors to be rendered by U.S. forces present.

On the death in a foreign place of a diplomatic or consular representative of the United States, the senior officer present arranges, as circumstances permit, for appropriate participation in the funeral ceremonies by persons in the naval service. When a ship of the Navy is transporting the body of a deceased official, the honors and ceremonies prescribed for an official visit are rendered, if directed by the senior officer present or higher authority, when the body is received aboard or leaves the ship.

Pallbearers or bodybearers are very visible elements of a military funeral. As a Chief Petty Officer, you may be in charge of this honor guard. Generally, when the remains are received at the chapel before the services, bearers form in two ranks facing inboard at the entrance with the juniors nearest the door. They must allow room between ranks for the casket to pass between them. As the casket is removed from the hearse, they execute the first movement of the hand salute. The second movement is executed as the casket passes, after which they face toward the door and follow the casket into the chapel. Seats are usually reserved for them among the left front pews.

Each time the bodybearers remove the remains, remember that:

- The escort is brought to present arms.
- The pallbearers salute.
- All observers in uniform, except the bodybearers, salute.
- All civilian-dressed naval personnel, except women, uncover and hold their covers over their hearts with the right hand.
- Women place the right hand over the heart without uncovering.

When the national ensign is draped on the casket, it is placed so the stars are at the head of the casket over the left shoulder of the deceased. Nothing rests on top of the national ensign. The ensign will be removed as the casket is being lowered into the grave and in time to keep the ensign from touching the ground. The casket is always carried foot first, except in the case of a chaplain whose casket is carried into and out of the church or chapel head first. This curious exception honors the clergy, who, it is said, never turn their backs on their flocks.

The senior pallbearer will give necessary commands to the others in a low voice. All salute on command. The personal flag of a deceased flag officer will be carried immediately in front of the hearse or caisson. If he was a unit commander or ship's captain, the command or commission pennant will also be carried. Often, organizations such as the VFW, Fleet Reserve Association, or American Legion will be invited to participate in the ceremony. In that case their rites will begin immediately after the military ceremony. If it includes the firing of three volleys and "Taps," these features of the military ceremony may be postponed until their appropriate places in the ritual, at which times the military firing party and bugler may render the honors.

When the remains arrive at the cemetery, the pallbearers form in a single rank on the flank of the escort, opposite the hearse and in such order of rank that moving to position alongside is facilitated. They execute and terminate the hand salute on the commands of the escort commander or chief. When all units are in position, and on the signal of the Chief Petty Officer or officer in charge, the bodybearers remove the casket from the hearse and carry it between the pallbearers and in front or the escort, then place it on the lowering device over the grave. They raise the national ensign by the corners and sides and hold it waist or shoulder high until the end of the services. As the bodybearers remove the casket from the caisson or hearse:

- The band renders prescribed honors, if rated, after which they play appropriate music. The music stops when the casket is placed on the lowering device. When a bugler is not available, a high-quality portable sound system is used to sound "Taps." One member of the funeral detail is assigned to a discreet location (preferably not easily visible, but within clear audible range) to play the bugle call when directed.

- The escort presents arms until the casket is placed on the lowering device.

- The clergy precedes the personal flag and the casket to the grave.

- The flag-bearer follows the clergy, preceding the casket, and takes position at the head of the grave. He remains there during the service.

- The pallbearers salute as the casket passes between them. When the casket has passed, they terminate the salute, face the grave, close interval, and follow the casket. On arrival at the grave, they form in two ranks facing the grave, usually just in rear and to one side of the clergy.

- The family of the deceased follows the pallbearers and takes the position provided.

When the funeral party has arrived at the gravesite, care should be taken that the firing party be located at least fifty feet from the grave so that the mourners will not be disturbed by the volleys. After the commitment services, the escort commander orders "Escort, Attention." He then commands "Escort, present arms." The petty officer in charge of the firing party then gives the command for the firing of volleys. The firing party executes present arms after completion of the three volleys.

The pallbearers come to attention on the command of the escort commander and salute on his command for present arms. "Taps" is sounded immediately after the last volley, and the firing party executes present arms. He salutes again, faces about, and rejoins his unit. After the last note of taps has sounded, the escort commander brings the entire escort to order arms and, after the ensign has been folded by the bodybearers and presented to the next of kin by the Chief Petty Officer or officer in charge, marches the escort and band to a suitable place for dismissal.

"On behalf of the president of the United States and the chief of naval operations, please accept this flag as a symbol of our appreciation for your loved one's service to this country and a grateful Navy."
U.S. Navy (JOC Alan J. Baribeau)

When personnel are limited, such as for a funeral not in close proximity to a major ship or station, military honors for funerals may be efficiently rendered by a detail of eight Sailors and one bugler. The firing squad will stack arms at the place from which volleys will be fired, which should be approximately fifty feet from the head of the grave. They then return to the hearse and convey the body to the grave. After placing the casket over the grave, six members of the party will take position as the firing squad while the remaining two will remain at the grave and hold the flag over the casket during the service and rendition of military honors. The bugler should take position approximately fifty feet from the head of the grave until the volleys have been fired, at the conclusion of which he shall sound "Taps." Then the two men holding the flag fold it. The flag will be handed either to the chief in charge of the detail or to the military escort commander. He will present it to the next of kin in a dignified manner with a short statement such as, "This flag is offered by a grateful nation in memory of the faithful service performed by your (relationship)."

A Personal Note. Traditions and customs, once absorbed, are powerful things. One author of this guidebook last served on active duty nearly forty years ago. Yet one morning not long ago, he accompanied business associates on a fishing trip to Lake Erie. Boarding the charter boat, he stopped—unconsciously, imperceptibly, and just for an instant—and faced aft. Catching himself, and realizing what he had just done, he chuckled and continued on board. The charter captain, standing at the head of the brow, smiled. "Permission granted, shipmate," he said softly, "permission granted." And at that moment, we two old men shared a bond that the others did not, or *could not*, ever share. We were Navymen, linked by traditions that stretch back to time immemorial, traditions that had become part of us. We were Sailors, once and forevermore.

13

The Chief Petty
Officer's Uniform

MS1 Romero ran into YNCS Perez as he was coming out of the Navy Exchange. "Betcha you were in the uniform shop, getting ready for the big day, eh, Romero?"

"I sure was, Senior Chief. Man, I didn't know how many variations there were of the chief's uniform. I count nineteen in the uniform regulations—and that doesn't count the BDUs that chiefs still wear, along with everyone else. How do you guys keep 'em all straight?"

"Oh, it's not hard—you get used to it, fast. But, if I were you, next trip I'd go with my sponsor, and I wouldn't go shopping without a current copy of NavPers 15665 close at hand!"

Petty Officer Romero was right. There are nineteen variants on the male Chief Petty Officer's uniform, and a further nineteen on the female version. Knowing what elements go with which uniform combinations and the proper way to wear these uniforms is an important part of the journey into the mess we all make as we prepare to advance to Chief Petty Officer. As Senior Chief Perez pointed out, you can't go far wrong if you consult NavPers 15665 whenever you are in doubt. It's always current—it updates much more frequently than this handbook and can often be accessed on CD-ROM or on the Internet. So, when in doubt, check it out! You'll feel more confident and look better, too.

We've tried to organize this chapter so that the most frequent uniform combinations are highlighted. Most chiefs, on most days, will wear one of the more common combinations of uniform elements. Indeed, there are authorized variants that are rarely worn, although you'd do well to know what they are and under what conditions to break them out. That way, in the unlikely event that the chief of staff of the Elbonian Navy invites you yachting some afternoon (service-dress blue, Yankee!), or you're scheduled to be the guest of honor at the Elbonian Ball (full-dress white), you'll represent the world's best Navy—in style!

Commonly Worn Male Uniforms

Service Dress Blue

May be prescribed for wear year-round to all official functions when dinner dress or full dress uniforms are not prescribed and civilian equivalent dress is coat and tie.

Service Dress Blue

Coat, Service Dress Blue	Note 16
Shirt, White, Dress	Note 49
Trousers, Blue, Dress	Note 90
Cap, Combination, White	Note 9
Shoes, Dress, Black	Note 54
Socks, Black	Note 78
Undershirt, White	Note 101
Undershorts	Note 102
Belt, Black, w/Gold Clip	Note 2
Necktie, Black Four-In-Hand	Note 37
Buckle, Gold	Note 7
Rating Badge/Service Stripes	Section II
Ribbons	As Authorized

Prescribable Items

All-Weather Coat, Blue	Note 1
Gloves, White/Black	Note 24
Reefer	Note 42

Optional Items

Cap, Garrison, Blue	Note 10
Cuff Links, Gold	Note 19
Earmuffs (w/outergarment only)	Note 22
Jacket, Black	Note 30
Overcoat, Blue	Note 39
Overshoes	Note 40
Scarf (w/outergarment only)	Note 43
Sweater, Cardigan, Blue	Note 81
Sweater, V-Neck Black	Note 83
Tie Clasp/Tack	Note 87
Umbrella, Black	Note 99
Name/Identification Tag	

Service Dress White

May be prescribed for summer wear when dinner dress or full dress uniforms are not prescribed and civilian equivalent dress is coat and tie.

Service Dress White

Coat, Service Dress White	Note 17
Trousers, White	Note 98
Cap, Combination, White	Note 9
Shoes, Dress, White	Note 54
Socks, White	Note 78
Undershirt, White	Note 101
Undershorts	Note 102
Belt, White, w/Gold Clip	Note 2
Buckle, Gold	Note 7
Collar Insignia	Section II
Ribbons	As Authorized

Prescribable Items

All-Weather Coat, Blue	Note 1
Gloves, White	Note 24

Optional Items

Earmuffs (w/outergarment only)	Note 22
Overshoes	Note 40
Scarf (w/outergarment only)	Note 43
Umbrella, Black	Note 99
Name/Identification Tag	

Service Khaki

Worn in summer/winter for office work, watchstanding, liberty, or business ashore when prescribed as uniform of the day.

Service Khaki

Shirt, Khaki, Service	Note 46
Trousers, Khaki, Service	Note 94
Cap, Combination, Khaki	Note 9
Shoes, Dress, Black	Note 54
Socks, Black	Note 78
Undershirt, White	Note 101
Undershorts	Note 102
Belt, Khaki, w/Gold Clip	Note 2
Buckle, Gold	Note 7
Collar Insignia	Section II
Ribbons	As Authorized

Prescribable Items

All-Weather Coat, Blue	Note 1
Cap, Garrison, Khaki	Note 10
Reefer	Note 42

Optional Items

Cap, Ball	Note 8
Earmuffs (w/outergarment only)	Note 22
Jacket, Black	Note 30
Jacket, Khaki Windbreaker	Note 30
Overcoat, Blue	Note 39
Overshoes	Note 40
Scarf (w/outergarment only)	Note 43
Shoes, Brown	Note 54
Socks, Khaki	Note 78
Sweater, Cardigan, Blue	Note 81
Sweater, V-Neck,Black	Note 83
Umbrella, Black	Note 99
Name/Identification Tag	

Summer White

Worn in summer for office work, watch-standing, liberty, or business ashore when prescribed as uniform of the day.

Summer White

Shirt, White, Summer	Note 53
Trousers, White	Note 98
Cap, Combination, White	Note 9
Shoes, Dress, White	Note 54
Socks, White	Note 78
Undershirt, White	Note 101
Undershorts	Note 102
Belt, White, w/Gold Clip	Note 2
Buckle, Gold	Note 7
Collar Insignia	Section II
Ribbons	As Authorized

Prescribable Items

All-Weather Coat, Blue	Note 1
Reefer	Note 42

Optional Items

Cap, Ball	Note 8
Earmuffs (w/outergarment only)	Note 22
Jacket, Black	Note 30
Overshoes	Note 40
Scarf (w/outergarment only)	Note 43
Sweater, Cardigan, Blue	Note 81
Sweater, V-Neck, Black	Note 83
Umbrella, Black	Note 99
Name/Identification Tag	

Tropical White

Worn for office work, watchstanding, liberty, or business ashore in tropical climates when authorized optionally as uniform of the day.

Tropical White

Shirt, White, Summer	Note 53
Shorts, White	Note 59
Cap, Combination, White	Note 9
Shoes, Dress, White	Note 54
Socks, Knee Length, White	Note 78
Undershirt, White	Note 101
Undershorts	Note 102
Belt, White, w/Gold Clip	Note 2
Buckle, Gold	Note 7
Collar Insignia	Section II
Ribbons	As Authorized

Prescribable Items

All-Weather Coat, Blue	Note 1

Optional Items

Helmet	Note 28
Overshoes	Note 40
Umbrella, Black	Note 99
Name/Identification Tag	

Winter Blue

Worn in winter for office work, watch-standing, liberty, or business ashore when prescribed as uniform of the day.

Winter Blue

Shirt, Winter Blue	Note 44
Trousers, Blue, Dress	Note 90
Cap, Combination, White	Note 9
Shoes, Dress, Black	Note 54
Socks, Black	Note 78
Undershirt, White	Note 101
Undershorts	Note 102
Belt, Black, w/Gold Clip	Note 2
Necktie, Black Four-In-Hand	Note 37
Buckle, Gold	Note 7
Collar Insignia	Section II
Ribbons	As Authorized

Prescribable Items

All-Weather Coat, Blue	Note 1
Reefer	Note 42

Optional Items

Cap, Ball	Note 8
Cap, Garrison, Blue	Note 10
Earmuffs (w/outergarment only)	Note 22
Jacket, Black	Note 30
Overcoat, Blue	Note 39
Overshoes	Note 40
Scarf (w/outergarment only)	Note 43
Sweater, Cardigan, Blue	Note 81
Sweater, V-Neck, Black	Note 83
Tie Clasp/Tack	Note 87
Umbrella, Black	Note 99
Name/Identification Tag	

Winter Working Blue

Worn when other uniforms would be unsafe or become unduly soiled.

Winter Working Blue

Shirt, Winter Blue	Note 44
Trousers, Blue, Dress	Note 90
Cap, Combination, White	Note 9
Shoes, Dress, Black	Note 54
Socks, Black	Note 78
Undershirt, White	Note 101
Undershorts	Note 102
Belt, Black, w/Gold Clip	Note 2
Buckle, Gold	Note 7
Collar Insignia	Section II

Prescribable Items

All-Weather Coat, Blue	Note 1
Reefer	Note 42
Shoes, Safety, Black	Note 57

Optional Items

Cap, Ball	Note 8
Cap, Garrison, Blue	Note 10
Earmuffs (w/outergarment only)	Note 22
Jacket, Black	Note 30
Overcoat, Blue	Note 39
Overshoes	Note 40
Scarf (w/outergarment only)	Note 43
Sweater, Cardigan, Blue	Note 81
Sweater, V-Neck, Black	Note 83
Umbrella, Black	Note 99
Name/Identification Tag	

Working Khaki

Worn when other uniforms would be unsafe or become unduly soiled.

Working Khaki

Shirt, Khaki, Working, SS	Note 47
Trousers, Khaki, Working	Note 95
Cap, Combination, Khaki	Note 9
Shoes, Safety, Black	Note 57
Socks, Black	Note 78
Undershirt, White	Note 101
Undershorts	Note 102
Belt, Khaki, w/Gold Clip	Note 2
Buckle, Gold	Note 7
Collar Insignia	Section II

Prescribable Items

All-Weather Coat, Blue	Note 1
Cap, Garrison, Khaki	Note 10
Reefer	Note 42
Shirt, Khaki, Working, LS	Note 47
Shoes, Dress, Black	Note 54

Optional Items

Cap, Ball	Note 8
Earmuffs (w/outergarment only)	Note 22
Jacket, Black	Note 30
Jacket, Khaki Windbreaker	Note 30
Overcoat, Blue	Note 39
Overshoes	Note 40
Scarf (w/outergarment only)	Note 43
Shoes, Brown	Note 54
Socks, Khaki	Note 78
Sweater, Cardigan, Blue	Note 81
Sweater, V-Neck, Black	Note 83
Umbrella, Black	Note 99
Name/Identification Tag	

Tropical Khaki

Worn when tropical white would become unduly soiled and safety is not a factor.

Tropical Khaki

Shirt, Khaki, Working, SS	Note 47
Shorts, Khaki	Note 59
Cap, Combination, Khaki	Note 9
Shoes, Dress, Black	Note 54
Socks, Knee Length, Black	Note 78
Undershirt, White	Note 101
Undershorts	Note 102
Belt, Khaki, w/Gold Clip	Note 2
Buckle, Gold	Note 7
Collar Insignia	Section II

Prescribable Items

All-Weather Coat, Blue	Note 1
Cap, Garrison, Khaki	Note 10
Shoes, Safety, Black	Note 57

Optional Items

Cap, Ball	Note 8
Helmet	Note 28
Overshoes	Note 40
Shoes, Brown	Note 54
Socks, Knee Length, Khaki	Note 78
Umbrella, Black	Note 99
Name/Identification Tag	

Aviation Working Green

When authorized by the prescribing authority, may be worn when engaged in work at aviation activities, flying, or aboard vessels servicing aircraft at advanced bases.

Aviation Working Green

Coat, Aviation Green	Note 13
Shirt, Khaki, Working, LS	Note 47
Trousers, Aviation Green	Note 89
Cap, Combination, Green	Note 9
Shoes, Dress, Black	Note 54
Socks, Black	Note 78
Undershirt, White	Note 101
Undershorts	Note 102
Belt, Khaki, w/Gold Clip	Note 2
Necktie, Black, Four-In-Hand	Note 37
Buckle, Gold	Note 7
Rating Badge/Service Stripes	Section II

Prescribable Items

All-Weather Coat, Blue	Note 1
Cap, Garrison, Green	Note 10
Reefer	Note 42
Shoes, Safety, Black	Note 57

Optional Items

Cap, Ball	Note 8
Earmuffs (w/outergarment only)	Note 22
Overcoat, Blue	Note 39
Overshoes	Note 40
Scarf (w/outergarment only)	Note 43
Shoes, Brown	Note 54
Socks, Khaki	Note 78
Tie Clasp/Tack	Note 87
Umbrella, Black	Note 99
Collar Insignia	Section II
Name/Identification Tag	

Coveralls

Worn when other uniforms would be unsafe or become unduly soiled. The coverall uniform is designed to be the principal underway uniform of the day. When worn in port, it is subject to the following restrictions. When worn aboard ship, coveralls may be worn on the pier in the immediate vicinity of the ship. Ashore (i.e., squadrons and industrial working environments) coveralls may be worn in the immediate work spaces only. Commands may additionally authorize wear of the coverall uniform while transiting to and from and using base galleys or any other eating facility within the fence line of the installation and at personnel support detachments while in a duty status. The navy blue coverall uniform is not authorized for wear other than detailed in this paragraph and under no circumstances may it be worn in either an official or unofficial capacity outside the confines of a military installation.

Coveralls

Coveralls	Note 18
Cap, Garrison, Khaki	Note 10
Shoes, Safety, Black	Note 57
Socks, Black	Note 78
Undershirt, White Crew Neck	Note 101
Undershorts	Note 102
Belt, Khaki w/Gold Clip	Note 2
Buckle, Gold	Note 7
Name/U.S. Navy Tapes	Section II
Collar Insignia	Section II

Prescribable Items

All-Weather Coat, Blue	Note 1
Reefer	Note 42
Shoes, Dress, Black	Note 54

Optional Items

Cap, Ball	Note 8
Jacket, Black	Note 30
Jacket, Khaki Windbreaker	Note 30
Overcoat, Blue	Note 39
Shoes, Dress, Brown	Note 54
Socks, Khaki	Note 78
Sweater, V-Neck, Black	Note 83

Less Commonly Worn Male Uniforms

Service Dress Blue Yankee

When prescribed.

Service Dress Blue Yankee

Coat, Service Dress Blue	Note 16
Shirt, White, Dress	Note 49
Trousers, White	Note 98
Cap, Combination, White	Note 9
Shoes, Dress, White	Note 54
Socks, White	Note 78
Undershirt, White	Note 101
Undershorts	Note 102
Belt, White, w/Gold Clip	Note 2
Necktie, Black Four-In-Hand	Note 37
Buckle, Gold	Note 7
Rating Badge/Service Stripes	Section II
Ribbons	As Authorized

Prescribable Items

All-Weather Coat, Blue	Note 1

Optional Items

Cuff Links, Gold	Note 19
Earmuffs (w/outergarment only)	Note 22
Overshoes	Note 40
Scarf (w/outergarment only)	Note 43
Tie Clasp/Tack	Note 87
Umbrella, Black	Note 99
Name/Identification Tag	

Dinner Dress Blue Jacket—Basic Uniform Components

Worn to official functions when civilians normally wear black tie. This is an optional winter uniform when dinner dress blue is prescribed.

Dinner Dress Blue Jacket

Coat, Dinner Dress Blue Jacket	Note 14
Shirt, White, Formal	Note 51
Trousers, Blue, Evening	Note 91
Shoes, Dress, Black	Note 54
Socks, Black	Note 78
Undershirt, White	Note 101
Undershorts	Note 102
Cuff Links, Gold	Note 19
Cummerbund, Gold	Note 20
Necktie, Bow, Black	Note 36
Studs, Gold	Note 79
Rating Badge/Service Stripes	Section II
Miniature Medals	As Authorized

Prescribable Items

All-Weather Coat, Blue Note 1	
Gloves, White	Note 24

Optional Items

Boat Cloak	Note 4
Cap, Combination, White (Required w/outergarment)	Note 9
Overcoat, Blue	Note 39
Overshoes	Note 40
Scarf (w/outergarment only)	Note 43
Suspenders, White	Note 80
Umbrella, Black	Note 99

Dinner Dress White Jacket

Worn to official functions when civilians normally wear black tie. This is an optional summer uniform when dinner dress white is prescribed.

Dinner Dress White Jacket

Coat, Dinner Dress White Jacket	Note 15
Shirt, White, Formal	Note 51
Trousers, Blue, Evening	Note 91
Shoes, Dress, Black	Note 54
Socks, Black	Note 78
Cuff Links, Gold	Note 19
Cummerbund, Gold	Note 20
Necktie, Bow, Black	Note 36
Studs, Gold	Note 79
Undershirt, White	Note 101
Undershorts	Note 102
Rating Badge/Service Stripes	Section II
Miniature Medals	As Authorized

Prescribable Items

All-Weather Coat, Blue	Note 1
Gloves, White	Note 24

Optional Items

Cap, Combination, White (Required w/outergarment)	Note 9
Overshoes	Note 40
Scarf (w/outergarment only)	Note 43
Suspenders, White	Note 80
Umbrella, Black	Note 99

Dinner Dress Blue

Worn to official functions when civilians normally wear black tie. When dinner dress blue jacket is prescribed, Master, Senior, and Chief Petty Officers may wear dinner dress blue in winter.

Dinner Dress Blue

Coat, Service Dress Blue	Note 16
Shirt, White, Dress	Note 49
Trousers, Blue, Dress	Note 90
Cap, Combination, White	Note 9
Shoes, Dress, Black	Note 54
Socks, Black	Note 78
Undershirt, White	Note 101
Undershorts	Note 102
Belt, Black, w/Gold Clip	Note 2
Necktie, Bow, Black	Note 36
Buckle, Gold	Note 7
Rating Badge/Service Stripes	Section II
Miniature Medals	As Authorized

Prescribable Items

All-Weather Coat, Blue	Note 1
Gloves, White	Note 24

Optional Items

Cuff Links, Gold	Note 19
Overcoat, Blue	Note 39
Overshoes	Note 40
Scarf (w/outergarment only)	Note 43
Shirt, White, Formal	Note 51
Studs, Gold	Note 79
Suspenders, White	Note 80
Umbrella, Black	Note 99

Dinner Dress White

Worn to official functions when civilians normally wear black tie. When dinner dress white jacket or tropical dinner dress blue is prescribed, Master, Senior, and Chief Petty Officers may wear dinner dress white in summer.

Dinner Dress White

Coat, Service Dress White	Note 17
Trousers, White	Note 98
Cap, Combination, White	Note 9
Shoes, Dress, White	Note 54
Socks, White	Note 78
Undershirt, White	Note 101
Undershorts	Note 102
Belt White, w/Gold Clip	Note 2
Buckle, Gold	Note 7
Collar Insignia	Section II
Miniature Medals	As Authorized

Prescribable Items

All-Weather Coat, Blue	Note 1
Gloves, White	Note 24

Optional Items

Overshoes	Note 40
Scarf (w/outergarment only)	Note 43
Umbrella, Black	Note 99

Tropical Dinner Dress Blue

An optional uniform worn in tropical climates when other dinner dress uniforms would be uncomfortable.

Tropical Dinner Dress Blue

Shirt, White, Summer	Note 53
Trousers, Blue, Dress	Note 90
Cap, Combination, White	Note 9
Shoes, Dress, Black	Note 54
Socks, Black	Note 78
Undershirt, White	Note 101
Undershorts	Note 102
Cummerbund, Gold Wraparound	Note 20
Collar Insignia	Section II
Miniature Medals	As Authorized

Prescribable Items

All-Weather Coat, Blue	Note 1
Belt, Black, w/Gold Clip	Note 2
Buckle, Gold	Note 7

Optional Items

Overshoes	Note 40
Scarf (w/outergarment only)	Note 43
Umbrella, Black	Note 99

Full Dress Blue

Worn on the following formal occasions: a. Participating in Change of Command Ceremonies; b. Official Visits with Honors as prescribed in Navy Regulations; c. Visits of Ceremony to Foreign Men-of-War and Foreign Officials; d. Occasions of State, Ceremonies, and Solemnities.

Full Dress Blue

Coat, Service Dress Blue	Note 16
Shirt, White, Dress	Note 49
Trousers, Blue Dress	Note 90
Cap, Combination, White	Note 9
Shoes, Dress, Black	Note 54
Socks, Black	Note 78
Undershirt, White	Note 101
Undershorts	Note 102
Belt, Black, w/Gold Clip	Note 2
Gloves, White	Note 24
Necktie, Black Four-In-Hand	Note 37
Buckle, Gold	Note 7
Rating Badge/Service Stripes	Note a
Large Medals/Ribbons	As Authorized

Prescribable Items

All-Weather Coat, Blue	Note 1

Optional Items

Cuff Links, Gold	Note 19
Overcoat, Blue	Note 39
Overshoes	Note 40
Scarf (w/outergarment only)	Note 43
Tie Clasp, Tack	Note 87
Umbrella, Black	Note 99

Full Dress White

Worn on the following formal occasions: a. Participating in Change of Command Ceremonies; b. Official Visits with Honors as Prescribed in Navy Regulations; c. Visits of Ceremony to Foreign Men-of-War and Foreign Officials; d. Occasions of State, Ceremonies, and Solemnities.

Full Dress White

Coat, Service Dress White	Note 17
Trousers, White	Note 98
Cap, Combination, White	Note 9
Shoes, Dress, White	Note 54
Socks, White	Note 78
Undershirt, White	Note 101
Undershorts	Note 102
Belt, White, w/Gold Clip	Note 2
Gloves, White	Note 24
Buckle, Gold	Note 7
Collar Insignia	Section II
Large Medals/Ribbons	As Authorized

Prescribable Items

All-Weather Coat, Blue	Note 1

Optional Items

Overshoes	Note 40
Scarf (w/outergarment only)	Note 43
Umbrella, Black	Note 99

Commonly Worn Female Uniforms

Service Dress Blue

May be prescribed for wear year-round to all official functions when dinner dress or full dress uniforms are not prescribed and civilian equivalent dress is coat and tie.

Service Dress Blue

Coat, Service Dress Blue	Note 16
Shirt, White, Dress	Note 49
Skirt, Blue, Unbelted	Note 62
Cap, Combination, White	Note 9
Shoes, Dress, Black	Note 54
Hosiery, Flesh Tone	Note 29
Brassiere	Note 6
Underpants	Note 100
Slip	Note 77
Necktie, Black	Note 34
Rating Badge/Service Stripes	Section II
Ribbons	As Authorized

Prescribable Items

All-Weather Coat, Blue	Note 1
Gloves, Black/White	Note 24
Handbag, Black	Note 25
Reefer	Note 42
Shoes, Service, Black	Note 58
Slacks, Blue, Unbelted	Note 69
Socks, Black	Note 78
Undershirt, White	Note 101

Optional Items

Beret	Note 3
Cap, Garrison, Blue	Note 10
Earmuffs (w/outergarment only)	Note 22
Earrings, Gold Ball	Note 23
Handbag, Black Dress	Note 26
Jacket, Black	Note 30
Overcoat, Blue	Note 39
Overshoes	Note 40
Scarf (w/outergarment only)	Note 43
Sweater, Cardigan, Blue	Note 81
Sweater, V-Neck, Black	Note 83
Umbrella, Black	Note 99
Name/Identification Tag	

Service Dress White

May be prescribed for summer wear when dinner dress or full dress uniforms are not prescribed and civilian equivalent dress is coat and tie.

Service Dress White

Coat, Service Dress White	Note 17
Shirt, White, Dress	Note 49
Skirt, White, Unbelted	Note 66
Cap, Combination, White	Note 9
Shoes, Dress, White	Note 54
Hosiery, Flesh Tone	Note 29
Brassiere	Note 6
Underpants	Note 100
Slip	Note 77
Necktie, Black	Note 34
Collar Insignia	Section II
Ribbons	As Authorized

Prescribable Items

All-Weather Coat, Blue	Note 1
Gloves, White	Note 24
Handbag, White	Note 25
Shoes, Service, White	Note 58
Slacks, White, Unbelted	Note 74
Socks, White	Note 78
Undershirt, White	Note 101

Optional Items

Beret	Note 3
Earmuffs (w/outergarment only)	Note 22
Earrings, Gold Ball	Note 23
Handbag, White Dress	Note 26
Overshoes	Note 40
Scarf (w/outergarment only)	Note 43
Umbrella, Black	Note 99
Name/Identification Tag	

Service Khaki

Worn in summer/winter for office work, watchstanding, liberty, or business ashore when prescribed as uniform of the day.

Service Khaki

Shirt, Khaki, Service	Note 46
Skirt, Khaki, Service	Note 63
Cap, Combination, Khaki	Note 9
Shoes, Dress, Black	Note 54
Hosiery, Flesh Tone	Note 29
Brassiere	Note 6
Underpants	Note 100
Slip	Note 77
Belt, Khaki, w/Gold Clip	Note 2
Buckle, Gold	Note 7
Collar Insignia	Section II
Ribbons	As Authorized

Prescribable Items

All-Weather Coat, Blue	Note 1
Cap, Garrison, Khaki	Note 10
Handbag, Black	Note 25
Reefer1	Note 42
Shoes, Service, Black	Note 58
Slacks, Khaki, Service	Note 72
Socks, Black	Note 78
Undershirt, White	Note 101

Optional Items

Beret	Note 3
Cap, Ball	Note 8
Earmuffs (w/outergarment only)	Note 22
Earrings, Gold Ball	Note 23
Handbag, Brown	Note 25
Handbag, Black Dress	Note 26
Jacket, Black	Note 30
Jacket, Khaki Windbreaker	Note 30
Overcoat, Blue	Note 39
Overshoes	Note 40
Scarf (w/outergarment only)	Note 43
Shoes, Dress, Brown	Note 54
Shoes, Service, Brown	Note 58
Socks, Khaki	Note 78
Sweater, Cardigan, Blue	Note 81
Sweater, V-Neck, Black	Note 83
Umbrella, Black	Note 99
Name/Identification Tag	

Summer White

Worn in summer for office work, watch-standing, liberty, or business ashore when prescribed as uniform of the day.

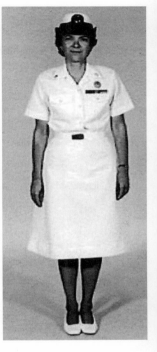

Summer White

Shirt, White, Summer	Note 53
Skirt, White, Belted	Note 65
Cap, Combination, White	Note 9
Shoes, Dress, White	Note 54
Hosiery, Flesh Tone	Note 29
Brassiere	Note 6
Underpants	Note 100
Slip	Note 77
Belt, White, w/Gold Clip	Note 2
Buckle, Gold	Note 7
Collar Insignia	Section II
Ribbons	As Authorized

Prescribable Items

All-Weather Coat, Blue	Note 1
Handbag, White	Note 25
Reefer	Note 42
Shoes, Service, White	Note 58
Slacks, White, Belted	Note 76
Socks, White	Note 58
Undershirt, White	Note 101

Optional Items

Cap, Ball	Note 8
Beret	Note 3
Earmuffs (w/outergarment only)	Note 22
Earrings, Gold Ball	Note 23
Handbag, White Dress	Note 26
Jacket, Black	Note 30
Overshoes	Note 40
Scarf (w/outergarment only)	Note 43
Sweater, Cardigan, Blue	Note 81
Sweater, V-Neck, Black	Note 83
Umbrella, Black	Note 99
Name/Identification Tag	

Tropical White

Worn for office work, watchstanding, liberty, or business ashore in tropical climates when authorized optionally as uniform of the day.

Tropical White

Shirt, White, Summer	Note 53
Shorts, White	Note 59
Cap, Combination, White	Note 9
Shoes, Service, White	Note 58
Socks, Knee Length, White	Note 78
Brassiere	Note 6
Underpants	Note 100
Belt, White, w/Gold Clip	Note 2
Buckle, Gold	Note 7
Collar Insignia	Section II
Ribbons	As Authorized

Prescribable Items

All-Weather Coat, Blue	Note 1
Handbag, White	Note 25
Undershirt, White	Note 101

Optional Items

Beret	Note 3
Earrings, Gold Ball	Note 23
Handbag, White Dress	Note 26
Helmet	Note 28
Overshoes	Note 40
Umbrella, Black	Note 99
Name/Identification Tag	

Winter Blue

Worn in winter for office work, watch-standing, liberty, or business ashore when prescribed as uniform of the day.

Winter Blue

Shirt, Winter Blue	Note 44
Skirt, Blue, Belted	Note 60
Cap, Combination, White	Note 9
Shoes, Dress, Black	Note 54
Hosiery, Flesh Tone	Note 29
Brassiere	Note 6
Underpants	Note 100
Slip	Note 77
Belt, Black, w/Gold Clip	Note 2
Necktie, Black	Note 34
Buckle, Gold	Note 7
Collar Insignia	Section II
Ribbons	As Authorized

Prescribable Items

All-Weather Coat, Blue	Note 1
Handbag, Black	Note 24
Reefer	Note 42
Shoes, Black Service	Note 58
Slacks, Blue, Belted	Note 68
Socks, Black	Note 78
Undershirt, White	Note 101

Optional Items

Cap, Ball	Note 8
Beret	Note 3
Cap, Garrison, Blue	Note 10
Earmuffs (w/outergarment only)	Note 22
Earrings, Gold Ball	Note 23
Handbag, Black Dress	Note 26
Jacket, Black	Note 30
Overcoat, Blue	Note 39
Overshoes	Note 40
Scarf (w/outergarment only)	Note 43
Sweater, Cardigan, Blue	Note 81
Sweater, V-Neck, Black	Note 83
Umbrella, Black	Note 99
Name/Identification Tag	

Winter Working Blue

Worn when other uniforms would be unsafe or become unduly soiled.

Winter Working Blue

Shirt, Winter Blue	Note 44
Slacks, Blue, Belted	Note 68
Cap, Combination, White	Note 9
Shoes, Service, Black	Note 58
Socks, Black	Note 78
Brassiere	Note 6
Underpants	Note 100
Belt, Black, w/Gold Clip	Note 2
Buckle, Gold	Note 7
Collar Insignia	Section II

Prescribable Items

All-Weather Coat, Blue	Note 1
Handbag, Black	Note 25
Hosiery, Flesh Tone	Note 29
Reefer	Note 42
Shoes, Dress, Black	Note 54
Shoes, Safety, Black	Note 57
Skirt, Blue, Belted	Note 60
Undershirt, White	Note 101

Optional Items

Beret	Note 3
Cap, Ball	Note 8
Cap, Garrison, Blue	Note 10
Earmuffs (w/outergarment only)	Note 22
Earrings, Gold Ball	Note 23
Jacket, Black	Note 30
Overcoat	Note 39
Overshoes	Note 40
Scarf (w/outergarment only)	Note 43
Sweater, Cardigan, Blue	Note 81
Sweater, V-Neck, Black	Note 83
Umbrella, Black	Note 99
Name/Identification Tag	

Working Khaki

Worn when other uniforms would be unsafe or would become unduly soiled.

Working Khaki

Shirt, Khaki, Working, SS	Note 47
Slacks, Khaki, Working	Note 73
Cap, Combination, Khaki	Note 9
Shoes, Safety, Black	Note 57
Socks, Black	Note 78
Brassiere	Note 6
Underpants	Note 100
Belt, Khaki, w/Gold Clip	Note 2
Buckle, Gold	Note 7
Collar Insignia	Section II

Prescribable Items

All-Weather Coat, Blue	Note 1
Cap, Garrison, Khaki	Note 10
Handbag, Black	Note 25
Reefer	Note 42
Shirt, Khaki, Working, LS	Note 47
Shoes, Service, Black	Note 58
Undershirt, White	Note 101

Optional Items

Beret	Note 3
Cap, Ball	Note 8
Earmuffs (w/outergarment only)	Note 22
Earrings, Gold Ball	Note 22
Handbag, Brown	Note 25
Jacket, Black	Note 30
Jacket, Khaki Windbreaker	Note 30
Overcoat, Blue	Note 39
Overshoes	Note 40
Scarf (w/outergarment only)	Note 43
Shoes, Service, Brown	Note 58
Socks, Khaki	Note 78
Sweater, Cardigan, Blue	Note 81
Sweater, V-Neck, Black	Note 83
Umbrella, Black	Note 99
Name/Identification Tag	

Tropical Khaki

Worn when tropical white would become unduly soiled and safety is not a factor.

Tropical Khaki

Shirt, Khaki, Working, SS	Note 47
Shorts, Khaki	Note 59
Cap, Combination, Khaki	Note 9
Shoes, Service, Black	Note 58
Socks, Knee Length, Black	Note 78
Brassiere	Note 6
Underpants	Note 100
Belt, Khaki, w/Gold Clip	Note 2
Buckle, Gold	Note 7
Collar Insignia	Section II

Prescribable Items

All-Weather Coat, Blue	Note 1
Cap, Garrison, Khaki	Note 10
Handbag, Black	Note 25
Shoes, Safety, Black	Note 57
Undershirt	Note 101

Optional Items

Beret	Note 3
Cap, Ball	Note 8
Earrings, Gold Ball	Note 23
Handbag, Brown	Note 25
Helmet	Note 28
Overshoes	Note 40
Shoes, Service, Brown	Note 58
Socks, Knee Length, Khaki	Note 78
Umbrella, Black	Note 99
Name/Identification Tag	

Aviation Working Green

When authorized by the prescribing authority, may be worn when engaged in work at aviation activities, flying, or aboard vessels servicing aircraft at advanced bases.

Aviation Working Green

Coat, Aviation Green	Note 13
Shirt, Khaki, Working, LS	Note 47
Slacks, Aviation Green	Note 67
Cap, Garrison, Green	Note 10
Shoes, Service, Black	Note 58
Socks, Black	Note 78
Brassiere	Note 6
Underpants	Note 100
Belt, Khaki, w/Gold Clip	Note 2
Necktie, Black	Note 34
Buckle, Gold	Note 7
Rating Badge/Service Stripes	Section II

Prescribable Items

All-Weather Coat, Blue	Note 1
Handbag, Black	Note 25
Hosiery, Flesh Tone	Note 29
Reefer	Note 42
Undershirt, White	Note 101

Optional Items

Cap, Ball	Note 8
Earmuffs (w/outergarment only)	Note 22
Earrings, Gold Ball	Note 23
Handbag, Brown	Note 25
Overcoat, Blue	Note 39
Overshoes	Note 40
Scarf (w/outergarment only)	Note 43
Shoes, Service, Brown	Note 58
Umbrella, Black	Note 99
Collar Insignia	Section II
Name/Identification Tag	

Coveralls

Worn when other uniforms would be unsafe or become unduly soiled. The coverall uniform is designed to be the principal underway uniform of the day. When worn in port, it is subject to the following restrictions. When worn aboard ship, coveralls may be worn on the pier in the immediate vicinity of the ship. Ashore (i.e., Simas, squadrons, and industrial working environments) coveralls may be worn in the immediate work spaces only. Commands may additionally authorize wear of the coverall uniform while transiting to and from and using base galleys or any other eating facility within the fence line of the installation and at personnel support detachments while in a duty status. The navy blue coverall uniform is not authorized for wear other than detailed in this paragraph and under no circumstances may it be worn in either an official or unofficial capacity outside the confines of a military installation.

Coveralls

Coveralls	Note 18
Cap, Garrison, Khaki	Note 10
Shoes, Safety, Black	Note 57
Socks, Black	Note 78
Brassiere	Note 6
Underpants	Note 100
Undershirt, White Crew Neck	Note 101
Belt, Khaki w/Gold Clip	Note 2
Buckle, Gold	Note 7
Name/U.S. Navy Tapes	Section II
Collar Insignia	Section II

Prescribable Items

All-Weather Coat, Blue	Note 1
Reefer	Note 42
Shoes, Service, Black	Note 58
Optional Items	
Cap, Ball	Note 8
Earrings, Gold Ball	Note 23
Jacket, Black	Note 30
Jacket, Khaki Windbreaker	Note 30
Overcoat, Blue	Note 39
Shoes, Service, Brown	Note 58
Socks, Khaki	Note 78
Sweater, V-Neck, Black	Note 83

Less Commonly Worn Female Uniforms

Service Dress Blue Yankee

When prescribed.

Service Dress Blue Yankee

Coat, Service Dress Blue	Note 16
Shirt, White, Dress	Note 49
Skirt, White, Unbelted	Note 66
Cap, Combination, White	Note 9
Shoes, Dress, White	Note 54
Hosiery, Flesh Tone	Note 29
Brassiere	Note 6
Underpants	Note 100
Slip	Note 77
Necktie, Black	Note 34
Rating Badge/Service Stripes	Section II
Ribbons	As Authorized

Prescribable Items

All-Weather Coat, Blue	Note 1
Handbag, White	Note 25
Shoes, Service, White	Note 58
Slacks, White, Unbelted	Note 74
Socks, White	Note 78
Undershirt, White	Note 101

Optional Items

Earmuffs (w/outergarment only)	Note 22
Earrings, Gold Ball	Note 23
Handbag, White Dress	Note 26
Overshoes	Note 40
Scarf (w/outergarment only)	Note 43
Umbrella, Black	Note 99
Name/Identification Tag	

Dinner Dress Blue Jacket—Basic Uniform Components

Worn to official functions when civilians normally wear black tie. This is an optional winter uniform when dinner dress blue is prescribed.

Dinner Dress Blue Jacket

Coat, Dinner Dress Blue Jacket	Note 14
Shirt, White, Formal	Note 50
Skirt, Blue, Unbelted	Note 62
Shoes, Formal, Black	Note 55
Hosiery, Flesh Tone	Note 29
Brassiere	Note 6
Cuff Links, Gold	Note 19
Underpants	Note 100
Slip	Note 77
Studs,	Note 79
Cummerbund, Gold	Note 20
Handbag, Black Dress	Note 26
Necktie, Dress, Black	Note 35
Rating Badge/Service Stripes	Section II
Miniature Medals	As Authorized

Prescribable Items

All-Weather Coat, Blue	Note 1
Gloves, White	Note 24

Optional Items

Cap, Combination, White (Required w/outergarment)	Note 9
Cape Gold Lining	Note 12
Earrings, Pearl	Note 23
Overcoat, Blue	Note 39
Overshoes	Note 40
Scarf w/outergarment only	Note 43
Shoes, Formal, Black, Flat	Note 56
Skirt, Blue, Formal	Note 61
Slacks, Blue, Formal	Note 70
Tiara	Note 86
Umbrella, Black	Note 99

Dinner Dress White Jacket

Worn to official functions when civilians normally wear black tie. This is an optional summer uniform when dinner dress white is prescribed.

Dinner Dress White Jacket

Coat, Dinner Dress White Jacket	Note 15
Shirt, White, Formal	Note 50
Skirt, Blue, Unbelted	Note 62
Shoes, Formal, Black	Note 55
Hosiery, Flesh Tone	Note 29
Brassiere	Note 6
Cuff Links, Gold	Note 19
Underpants	Note 100
Slip	Note 77
Studs, Gold	Note 79
Cummerbund, Gold	Note 20
Handbag, Black Dress	Note 26
Necktie, Dress, Black	Note 35
Rating Badge/Service Stripes	Section II
Miniature Medals	As Authorized

Prescribable Items

All-Weather Coat, Blue	Note 1
Gloves, White	Note 24

Optional Items

Cap, Combination, White (Required w/outergarment)	Note 9
Earrings, Pearl	Note 23
Overshoes	Note 40
Scarf (w/outergarment only)	Note 43
Shoes, Formal, Black, Flat	Note 56
Skirt, Blue, Formal	Note 61
Slacks, Blue, Formal	Note 70
Tiara	Note 86
Umbrella, Black	Note 99

Dinner Dress Blue

Worn to official functions when civilians wear black tie. When dinner dress blue jacket is prescribed, Master, Senior, and Chief Petty Officers may wear dinner dress blue in winter.

Dinner Dress Blue

Coat, Service Dress Blue	Note 16
Shirt, White, Dress	Note 49
Skirt, Blue, Unbelted	Note 62
Cap, Combination, White	Note 9
Shoes, Dress, Black	Note 54
Hosiery, Flesh Tone	Note 29
Brassiere	Note 6
Underpants	Note 100
Slip	Note 77
Handbag, Black Dress	Note 26
Necktie, Black	Note 34
Rating Badge/Service Stripes	Section II
Miniature Medals	As Authorized

Prescribable Items

All-Weather Coat, Blue	Note 1
Gloves, White	Note 24
Slacks, Blue, Unbelted	Note 69

Optional Items

Cuff Links, Gold	Note 19
Earrings, Pearl	Note 23
Overcoat, Blue	Note 39
Overshoes	Note 40
Scarf (w/outergarment only)	Note 43
Shirt, White, Formal	Note 50
Shoes, Formal, Black	Note 55
Shoes, Formal, Black, Flat	Note 56
Skirt, Blue, Formal	Note 61
Studs, Gold	Note 79
Umbrella, Black	Note 99

Dinner Dress White

Worn to official functions when civilians normally wear black tie. When dinner dress white jacket or tropical dinner dress blue is prescribed, Master, Senior, and Chief Petty Officers may wear dinner dress white in summer.

Dinner Dress White

Coat, Service Dress White	Note 17
Shirt, White, Dress	Note 49
Skirt, White, Unbelted	Note 66
Cap, Combination, White	Note 9
Shoes, Dress, White	Note 54
Hosiery, Flesh Tone	Note 29
Brassiere	Note 6
Underpants	Note 100
Slip	Note 77
Handbag, White Dress	Note 26
Necktie, Black	Note 34
Collar Insignia	Section II
Miniature Medals	As Authorized

Prescribable Items

All-Weather Coat, Blue	Note 1
Gloves, White	Note 24
Slacks, White, Unbelted	Note 74

Optional Items

Cuff Links, Gold	Note 19
Earrings, Pearl	Note 23
Overshoes	Note 40
Scarf (w/outergarment only)	Note 43
Shirt, White, Formal	Note 50
Studs, Gold	Note 79
Umbrella, Black	Note 99

Tropical Dinner Dress Blue

An optional uniform in tropical climates where other dinner dress uniforms would be uncomfortable.

Tropical Dinner Dress Blue

Shirt, White, Summer	Note 53
Skirt, Blue, Unbelted	Note 62
Cap, Combination, White	Note 9
Shoes, Dress, Black	Note 54
Hosiery, Flesh Tone	Note 29
Brassiere	Note 6
Underpants	Note 100
Slip	Note 77
Cummerbund, Gold Wraparound	Note 20
Handbag, Black Dress	Note 26
Collar Insignia	Section II
Miniature Medals	As Authorized

Prescribable Items

All-Weather Coat, Blue	Note 1

Optional Items

Earrings, Pearl	Note 23
Overshoes	Note 40
Scarf (w/outergarment only)	Note 43
Shoes, Formal, Black	Note 55
Shoes, Formal, Black, Flat	Note 56
Skirt, Blue, Formal	Note 61
Slacks, Blue, Formal	Note 70
Umbrella, Black	Note 99

Full Dress Blue

Worn on the following formal occasions: a. Participating in Change of Command Ceremonies; b. Official Visits with Honors as Prescribed in Navy Regulations; c. Visits of Ceremony to Foreign Men-of-War and Foreign Officials; d. Occasions of State, Ceremonies, and Solemnities.

Full Dress Blue

Coat, Service Dress Blue	Note 16
Shirt, White, Dress	Note 49
Skirt, Blue, Unbelted	Note 62
Cap, Combination, White	Note 9
Shoes, Dress, Black	Note 54
Hosiery, Flesh Tone	Note 29
Brassiere	Note 6
Underpants	Note 100
Slip	Note 77
Gloves, White	Note 24
Necktie, Black	Note 34
Rating Badge/Service Stripes	Section II
Large Medals/Ribbons	As Authorized

Prescribable Items

All-Weather Coat, Blue	Note 1
Handbag, Black	Note 25
Shoes, Service, Black	Note 58
Slacks, Blue, Unbelted	Note 69
Socks, Black	Note 78
Undershirt, White	Note 101

Optional Items

Earrings, Gold Ball	Note 23
Overcoat, Blue	Note 39
Overshoes	Note 40
Scarf (w/outergarment only)	Note 43
Umbrella, Black	Note 99

Full Dress White

Worn on the following formal occasions: a. Participating in Change of Command Ceremonies; b. Official Visits with Honors as Prescribed in Navy Regulations; c. Visits of Ceremony to Foreign Men-of-War and Foreign Officials; d. Occasions of State, Ceremonies, and Solemnities.

Full Dress White

Coat, Service Dress White	Note 17
Shirt, White, Dress	Note 49
Skirt, White, Unbelted	Note 66
Cap, Combination, White	Note 9
Shoes, Dress, White	Note 54
Hosiery, Flesh Tone	Note 29
Brassiere	Note 6
Underpants	Note 100
Slip	Note 77
Gloves, White	Note 24
Necktie, Black	Note 34
Collar Insignia	Section II
Large Medals/Ribbons	As Authorized

Prescribable Items

All-Weather Coat, Blue	Note 1
Handbag, White	Note 24
Shoes, Service, White	Note 58
Slacks, White, Unbelted	Note 74
Socks, White	Note 78
Undershirt, White	Note 101

Optional Items

Earrings, Gold Ball	Note 23
Overshoes	Note 40
Scarf (w/outergarment only)	Note 43
Umbrella, Black	Note 99

Chief Petty Officer Insignia

The chevrons on CPO rating badges measure 3-¼ inches wide for male CPOs and rating badges measure 2-½ inches wide for female CPOs. Just as with your rating badges from E-4 to E-6, rating insignia, chevrons, and rockers for women are three-quarters the size of the men's rating badges.

Background material for rating badges and service stripes match the color of the uniform coat or jacket. Colors of the eagles, specialty mark, stars, chevrons, and service stripes for prescribed uniforms are as indicated below:

Uniform	Background	Eagle/ Rate/Stars	Badge
Service Dress Blue	Navy Blue	Silver	Gold/Scarlet
Dinner Dress Blue Jacket	Navy Blue	Silver	Gold/Scarlet
Dinner Dress White Jacket	White	Silver	Gold/Blue
Aviation Green Working	Forestry Green	Blue	Blue

Position. Rating badges are sewn on the left sleeve of service dress blue jacket, dinner dress blue jacket, and dinner dress white jacket centered on the sleeve midway between the shoulder seam and the elbow, thus:

Collar Insignia. Wear metal collar devices (approximately one inch) on the collar points of khaki and blue shirts. Wear miniature-sized (approximately 1-¼ inch) embroidered grade insignia tapes on Navy coveralls. Note that the embroidered collar devices may be slightly larger than metal collar devices.

Collar grade insignia are worn on both collar points thus:

Long Sleeve Khaki and Blue Shirt. Center the insignia 1 inch from the front and upper edges of the collar. This procedure applies whether the collar is worn open or closed:

Open Collar Short Sleeve Shirt and Navy Coveralls. Center the insignia at a point one inch from the front and lower edges of the collar and position the vertical axis of the insignia along an imaginary line (A) bisecting the angle of the collar point.

Service Dress White. Men wear collar insignia on the standing collar of the service dress white coat. The anchor shank will be parallel to the vertical edge of the collar, with the center of the insignia on the midline of the standing collar, one inch from the vertical edge of the collar.

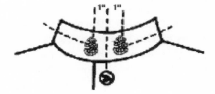

Women wear collar insignia on the ends of the collar of the service dress white coat. The anchor shank will be in the vertical (upright) position, with the center of the insignia approximately one inch from the bottom edge of the collar and midway between the edges (seam and outer edge) of the collar.

OLD STYLE   NEW STYLE

Metal Rank Insignia on Outer Garments. Chief Petty Officers wear metal devices on khaki windbreakers, black jackets (relaxed fit with knit collar), and all-weather coats. We wear no insignia on reefers and overcoats.

The same device as worn on garrison cap (approximate size: 1-¼ inch). Wear metal rank insignia on each epaulet centered from side to side with the bottom edge of the device approximately ¾ inch from the squared end of the epaulet.

Soft Shoulder Boards. Chief Petty Officers wear soft shoulder boards on the service dress blue white shirt and black V-neck sweater. The soft shoulder board is black cloth with anchor and stars as appropriate, indicating rank. The bottom of the anchor is approximately ¾ inch from the end of the board. The same size soft shoulder boards are worn by men and women. Place soft shoulder board on each epaulet with insignia resting on the squared end of the epaulet.

Cap Insignia. The cap device consists of a gold fouled anchor with silver block letters "USN" superimposed on the anchor's shank. There is also a black patent leather or vinyl chin strap, adjusted to fit snugly against the cap. Wear the chin strap with the grommet to your left.

Combination Cap. Wear the cap insignia on your combination cap. Gold Navy eagle buttons attach the black chin strap to the cap frame through a black mounting band. The cap device is attached to the mounting band with the stock's unfouled arm to the wearer's right.

Helmet, Tropical. Center a miniature cap device on the front as shown below.

Garrison Cap. Center a miniature CPO cap device on the left side of the garrison cap in the manner shown below.

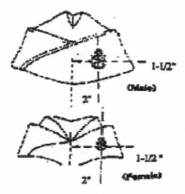

Beret (Female). Wear the miniature CPO cap device on the beret as pictured below and aligned above the left eye.

Dimensions of CPO Devices. It's important to remember that there are three metal devices, all slightly different in size. Check to be sure that you have the right device in the right place!

Cap Device

1-3/4 inch

Miniature Cap

Device
1-1/4 inch

Collar Device

1 inch

Notes on the Proper Wear of Various CPO Uniform Elements

1. *All-Weather Coat, Blue.* Button all buttons except the collar button. Collar button may be buttoned in inclement weather. Insignia placement per Section II.

2. *Belt with Clip.* Gold clip for all CPO uniforms, Fabric should match uniform. Wear the belt through all loops. Men wear the belt with clip to the LEFT of the buckle and women wear the belt with clip to the RIGHT of the buckle.

3. *Beret (Women).* Wear the beret toward the front of the head, approximately ¾ of an inch from the forehead hairline, and tilted slightly to the right. Align insignia above the left eye.

4. *Boat Cloak.* Cloak is closed at the neck with hooks and eyes and on the chest by one set of silk or mohair fasteners. Wear with all fasteners closed.

6. *Brassiere (Women).* Shall be white or wearer's skin tone when worn with white shirts; otherwise, color is optional.

7. *Buckle.* A plain anodized Navy belt buckle is authorized for inspections and ceremonial functions. A plain or decorated gold buckle with appropriate naval insignia, designs, or devices to which the wearer is entitled, representing the individual's present command, or if stationed ashore a previous sea command/ squadron may be authorized for optional wear. Men wear the buckle so that the belt clip end touches the LEFT side of the buckle. Align the right side of the buckle with the opening of the shirt and opening of the fly, forming a straight line. When authorized to wear a decorated buckle that is larger than the standard Navy buckle, it shall be worn centered with the clip end concealed. Women wear the buckle so that the belt clip end touches the RIGHT side of the buckle. Align the left side of the buckle with the opening of the shirt forming a straight line. When authorized to wear a decorated buckle that is larger than the standard Navy buckle, it shall be worn centered with the clip end concealed.

8. *Cap, Ball.* The cap shall be a conventional baseball cap style with "Navy" embroidered or sewn in approximately 1-¼ inch gold block letters centered on the front and may have

adjustable hat band and mesh back section. "Navy" logo may be substituted with the command name, designation, and/or command logos in good taste. If the individual's name is affixed, it is centered on the back of the cap in sewn or embroidered letters. The lettering may be in traditional command colors. The cap may be worn with civilian attire on or off base, without insignia. Authorized position held or rank (LCPO, etc.) or rank/rate with surname that are professional and in good taste may be centered on the back of the cap in sewn or embroidered letters and the lettering may be in traditional command colors. (No nicknames.) Ball caps with titles are not authorized for wear with civilian attire. Garrison cap insignia may be worn. Wear squarely on the head, with bottom edge parallel to and 1-½ inch above the eyebrows.

9. *Cap, Combination.* For Men: A military style cap with black visor, rigid standing front, flaring circular rim and black cap band worn with detachable khaki, green, or white cap cover, as required. Fabric match of cap cover and uniform is not required. When wearing an all-weather coat, a clear or blue plastic combination cap rain cover may be worn. See insignia in Section II. For Women: A military style cap with black visor, circular brim with rigid upsweep sides, and black cap band worn with detachable white or khaki cap cover, as required. When wearing an all-weather coat, a clear plastic combination cap rain cover may be worn. See insignia in Section II. Wear squarely on the head, with bottom edge parallel to and 1-½ inch above the eyebrows.

10. *Cap, Garrison, Blue (All), Khaki, Green.* Fore and aft cap made of same fabric and color as uniform with which worn. Optional wear of men's style garrison cap is authorized for women with corresponding uniforms. See insignia in Section II. Wear squarely on the head, with fore and aft crease centered vertically between the eyebrows and the lowest point approximately one inch above the eyebrows.

12. *Cape (Women).* Wear closed at the neck with hooks and eyes, and at the breast with fasteners.

13. *Coat, Aviation Green.* Button all buttons. Coat may be removed in immediate office/work spaces. If coat is removed, shirt collar insignia are required.

14. *Coat, Dinner Dress Blue Jacket.* Men wear with gold elastic or link chain closure. Women wear jacket open. See insignia in Section II.

15. *Coat, Dinner Dress White Jacket.* Men wear held together using two 28-line Navy eagle buttons with a link approximately ¾-inch-long fastener. Women wear jacket open. See insignia in Section II.

16. *Coat, Service Dress Blue.* Button all buttons. Coat may be removed in immediate office space. Commanders specify the areas within the command where coats are required. See insignia in Section II.

17. *Coat, Service Dress White.* Men: Wear with all buttons and fasten the collar. Women: Button all buttons. Coat may be removed in immediate office space. Commanding officers specify the areas within the command where coats are required.

18. *Coveralls (Navy).* Close zipper at least three-quarters of the way, button sleeves, and wear a belt through all loops. Coveralls shall hang approximately two inches from the floor at the back of the shoe. Coveralls should be tailored to include a two-inch hem to provide material for adjustments. Embroidered tapes (i.e., name, U.S. NAVY, breast insignia [if worn], collar devices) are required. Present command crest/logo patch may be worn op-tionally, centered on the right breast pocket. Sleeves may be rolled up at the option of local commanders. When authorized, sleeves will be rolled with the inside out, forming a roll approximately three inches wide, and terminating at a point approximately two inches above the elbow. Men wear the belt with clip to the left of the buckle and women wear the belt with clip to the right of the buckle. The buckle is centered on the zipper flap. When authorized to wear a decorated buckle that is larger than the standard Navy buckle, it shall be worn centered with the clip end concealed.

19. *Cuff Links.* Gold link or stud pattern of conservative design; mother-of-pearl cuff links are worn with formal dress (white tie). Wear with the face of the cuff link directed outboard from the wearer.

20. *Cummerbund.* Gold, plain, pleated, to fasten in the back. Wear a wraparound style with tropical dinner dress blue uniform. An adjustable cummerbund is authorized with formal dress and

dinner dress jacket uniforms. Wear with pleats up, around the waist overlapping the skirt/trouser top at least one inch.

22. *Earmuffs.* Plain, Navy blue cloth earmuffs with black elastic retainer. Wear earmuff retainer underneath the cap/hat.

23. *Earrings, Ball, Pearl (Women).* All earrings (ball or pearl) must be 4 mm–6 mm (approximately ⅛ inch–¼ inch). Yellow gold ball earrings may be plain with shiny or brushed matte finish, screw-on or post type. Pearl earrings have one small single white pearl. Pearl earrings may be worn with dinner dress or formal uniforms; ball earrings may be worn with all other uniforms. Only one earring may be worn per ear, centered on the ear lobe.

24. *Gloves, Black, White.* Black gloves are made of smooth leather or smooth synthetic leather; white gloves are made of authorized fabric. Glove stitching is the same color as the basic glove material. Black leather gloves are worn, never carried. White gloves (when required) may be worn or carried with uniforms. Gloves are removed to shake hands.

25. *Handbags, Black, Brown, White (Women).* A plain black, brown, white leather, or synthetic material envelope-style handbag of semi-rigid construction approximately 10-¼ inches wide, 7-¼ inches high, 3-½ inches deep, with three separate inside compartments and one inch adjustable shoulder strap. The bag has an outside lined pocket and is closed by means of a gold twist lock and flap plate. Color of handbag will match color of shoes worn. Carry over the left shoulder or forearm, placing the top of the handbag at waist level.

26. *Handbags, Black, White Dress (Women).* A small clutch type black or white handbag. A collapsible inside handle is optional with dinner dress uniforms. May be carried with service uniforms.

28. *Helmet.* A conventional style tropical helmet, the same color as the uniform (khaki or white), with a chin strap. See Section II for insignia. Wear squarely on the head.

29. *Hosiery (Women).* Made of nylon, wearer's skin tone, undecorated and seamless. They may be panty/hose combination.

30. *Jacket, Black / Jacket, Khaki Windbreaker.* A black jacket, 55/45% poly/wool with a stand-up knit collar and knit cuffs and bottom. Jacket is single-breasted with a zipper front

closer, two inverted slant pockets, and shoulder epaulets. Close zipper at least three-quarters of the way. Button collar button back when not in use. May be worn with liner. Patches and name tags are not authorized for wear on jackets.

34. *Necktie (Necktab), Black (Women).* Navy blue necktie (necktab) made of authorized fabric. The necktab's outer edges should be parallel to the outer edges of the collar. An equal amount of necktab should show on each side of the collar.

35. *Necktie, Black Dress (Women).* A small, crescent-shaped, black, velvet ribbon tapering to each edge from one inch width at center. Wear under the collar with the front slightly above the top of the shirt.

37. *Necktie, Black Four-In-Hand (Men).* Made of authorized fabric measuring no more than 3-¼ inches wide. May be clip-on or hand tied. Wear hand tied knotted with a four-in-hand, half Windsor, or Windsor knot. Wear the top of the knot parallel to and slightly above the top of the shirt collar closure, hiding the shirt button. The bottom hangs within one inch of the top of the belt buckle. The tie does not cover the belt buckle.

39. *Overcoat, Blue.* Men: A double-breasted coat made of blue woolen fabric. May be water repellent treated and fitted with removable sleeveless liner. Extends one-third the distance from kneecap to ground, shaped at waist, held by a two section half-belt at back with the end of the belt overlapped and fastened with two 40-line Navy eagle, gilt buttons. There is a sword slit over left hip, a vertical slash side pocket on each front, and a single row of five 40-line Navy eagle, gilt buttons down each forefront. The collar is made so that the coat may be buttoned to the neck. There are two loops on each shoulder for hard shoulder boards. Women: A double-breasted, water repellent coat made of dark blue napped woolen or worsted fabric, and may be fitted with a removable sleeveless liner. The overcoat has a single row of four 40-line Navy eagle, gilt buttons on each forefront. A strap on each shoulder is fastened at inner end by a 24-line black plastic button.

40. *Overshoes/Rain Or Snow Boots.* Overshoes are black rubber, conventional, low-cut style. Rain or snow boots are made of plain black vinyl or leather and may be from mid-calf to

knee high. Close all fasteners. Wear only during inclement weather with an outer garment and remove indoors.

42. *Reefer.* Men: A double-breasted, hip-length coat made of dark blue authorized fabric with a convertible collar, a set-in pocket in each forefront, and a single row of four 35-line or 40-line buttons on right front and three on left. Men's reefer buttons to the right. Women: A double-breasted, hip-length coat made of dark blue authorized fabric with a convertible collar, shoulder epaulets, a set-in pocket in each forefront, and a single row of four 35-line or 40-line buttons on left front, and three on right. Women's reefer buttons to the left. Women may wear either the men's reefer (with two loops) or the women's reefer (with epaulets) as long as serviceable. Button all buttons except collar button. Collar button may be buttoned in inclement weather. Sleeves are to reach about three-quarters of distance from the wrist to the knuckles when arms hang naturally at side. CPOs wear no insignia on outer garments.

43. *Scarf, White.* Plain white scarf made of knitted or woven silk or synthetic fabric. May be worn under reefers/peacoats, all-weather coats, overcoats, or jackets.

44. *Shirt, Blue, Winter.* Button all buttons, tie/ribbons required. Winter working blue unbutton top collar button, tie/ribbons not worn.

46. *Shirt, Khaki, Service.* Made of authorized fabric, with short sleeves, two breast pockets with button flaps, and an open collar forming a V-neck. Women's shirts button to the left and men's shirts button to the right. The shirt and trousers/slacks/skirt fabric must match (i.e., poly/cotton with poly/cotton, CNT with CNT and poly/wool with poly/ wool). Button all buttons.

47. *Shirt, Khaki, Working.* Made of authorized fabric, with two breast pockets with button flaps. The short sleeve shirt will have an open collar forming a V-neck. The long sleeve will have a button closure at the neck. May be either long or short sleeve as prescribed. Women's shirts button to the left and men's shirts button to the right. Button all buttons except the collar button on the long sleeve shirt when worn with working khaki uniform.

49. *Shirt, White, Dress.* Button all buttons. Wear appropriate soft shoulder boards on the epaulets.

50. *Shirt, White, Formal (Women).* A plain white formal dress shirt with tuxedo pleats and french cuffs. Plain gold shirt studs and cuff links are required for dinner dress jacket uniforms. Wear with all studs, buttons, and cuff links fastened.

51. *Shirt, White, Formal (Men).* A plain white formal dress shirt with a turndown collar and a plain stiff or wide pleated soft front. Plain gold shirt studs and cuff links are required with dinner dress jacket uniforms. Wear with all studs, buttons, and cuff links fastened.

53. *Shirt, White, Summer.* Men: Made of plain white authorized fabric, with short sleeves, two breast pockets with button flaps, and an open collar forming a V-neck. Collar points measure no longer than 3-¼ inch with a medium spread. The shirt and trouser fabric must match (i.e., poly/cotton with poly/cotton, CNT with CNT). Women: Made of plain, white authorized fabric, with short sleeves, two breast pockets with button flaps, epaulets, and a convertible collar. Collar points measure no more than 3-¼ inches with a medium spread. The shirt and skirt/slacks fabric must match (i.e., poly/cotton with poly/cotton, CNT with CNT). Men button all buttons; women button all buttons except the top collar button.

54. *Shoes, Dress (Black / Brown / White).* Men: Plain toed, oxford style black, brown, or white, low-quarter, lace shoe, made of smooth leather or synthetic leather. The heel shall be an outside heel ¾ inch–⅞ inch high with a flat sole. Women: Plain black, brown or white dress pumps made of smooth leather or synthetic leather, with closed heels and toes. Heels shall be no higher than approximately 2-⅝ inches nor less than approximately ⅝ inch measured from the forward edge, and no wider than approximately 1-¾ inches at the base. Sole shall be no thicker than approximately ¼ inch. Wedge heels are not authorized. Keep well shined and in good repair. Men lace shoes from inside out through all eyelets and tie. Navy certified brown leather shoes and khaki socks are optional for Chiefs with khaki and aviation working green uniforms.

55. *Shoes, Formal, Black (Women).* Plain black pumps with closed heels and toes, of suede, silk, or peau de soie meeting the same heel requirements as the black dress pumps. Keep clean and in good repair.

56. *Shoes, Formal, Black, Flat (Women)*. Plain black formal dress flat shoes with closed heels and toes, made of suede, silk, or peau de soie. Keep clean and in good repair.

57. *Shoes, Safety, Black*. Plain-toed, laced-safety shoes, made of water resistant leather. Outsoles constructed from nitrile rubber, which is inherently heat and flame resistant. Keep clean, well blackened, and in good repair. Lace shoes from inside out through all eyelets and tie.

58. *Shoes, Service (Black/Brown/White) (Women)*. Plain or moccasin-stitched toed, oxford-style black, brown, or white, low-quarter, lace shoe, made of smooth leather or synthetic leather. The heel shall be an outside heel ⅝ inch–1 inch high, and the sole shall be ³⁄₁₆ inch–⅜ inch thick. Wedge heels are not authorized. Keep well shined and in good repair. Lace shoes from inside out through all eyelets and tie. Navy-certified brown leather shoes and khaki socks are optional for Chiefs with khaki and aviation working green uniforms.

59. *Shorts*. Same correct wear as slacks/trousers except hem two inches above the crease behind the knee.

60. *Skirt, Blue, Belted (Women)*. Length may range from 1-½ inches above to 1-½ inches below the crease behind the knee. Wear belted skirts with the zipper centered in back and a belt through all loops.

61. *Skirt, Blue, Formal (Women)*. Wear zipper on the left side.

62. *Skirt, Blue, Unbelted (Women)*. Length may range from 1-½ inches above to 1-½ inches below the crease behind the knee. Wear the zipper on the left side.

63. *Skirt, Khaki, Service*. A plain, khaki, belted skirt made of authorized fabric, with two welt pockets in upper front and a zipper in back. The shirt and skirt fabric must match (i.e., poly/cotton with poly/cotton, CNT with CNT, and poly/wool with poly/wool). Length may range from 1-½ inches above to 1-½ inches below the crease behind the knee. Wear the zipper centered in the back and a belt through all loops.

64. *Skirt, Khaki, Working*. Made of khaki poly/cotton fabric in the same style as the Skirt, Khaki, Service. Length may range from 1-½ inches above to 1-½ inches below the crease

behind the knee. Wear the zipper centered in the back and a belt through all loops.

65. *Skirt, White, Belted.* A plain, white, belted skirt made of authorized fabric, with a full lining, two welt pockets in upper front and a zipper in the back. The shirt and skirt fabric must match (i.e., poly/cotton with poly/-cotton, CNT with CNT). Length may range from 1-½ inches above to 1-½ inches below the crease behind the knee. Wear the zipper centered in the back and a belt through all loops.

66. *Skirt, White, Unbelted.* A plain, white, six-gored skirt made of authorized fabric, with a waistband pocket in the upper right front. The welt pocket style may be worn as long as serviceable. Skirt matches the coat in color and fabric. Length may range from 1-½ inches above to 1-½ inches below the crease behind the knee. Wear the zipper on the left side.

67. *Slacks, Aviation Green.* Made of the same fabric as the aviation green coat with fore and aft creases, belt loops, zippered fly front closure, and two side and back pockets. May be either straight legged or slightly flared. Button all buttons, close fasteners, and wear with a belt through all loops. Slacks shall hang approximately two inches from the floor at the back of the shoe. Slacks should be tailored to include a two-inch hem to provide material for adjustments.

68. *Slacks, Blue, Belted.* Made of plain, authorized blue fabric, with fore and aft creases, belt loops, zippered fly front closure, two side pockets, and two back pockets. The welt pocket style and slacks with no back pockets may be worn as long as serviceable. Button all buttons, close all fasteners, and wear a belt through all loops. Slacks shall hang approximately two inches from the floor at the back of the shoe. Slacks should be tailored to include a two-inch hem to provide material for adjustments.

70. *Slacks, Blue, Formal.* Made of plain, authorized blue fabric, with high waist, straight legs, fore and aft creases, and left side zipper. Button all buttons and close all fasteners. Slacks shall hang approximately two inches from the floor at the back of the shoe. Slacks should be tailored to include a two-inch hem to provide material for adjustments.

72. *Slacks, Khaki, Service.* Made of authorized fabric with fore and aft creases, belt loops, zippered fly front closure, and

two side pockets. Poly/cotton slacks have two back pockets. May be straight legged or slightly flared. The shirt and slacks fabric must match (i.e., poly/cotton with poly/cotton, CNT with CNT, and poly/wool with poly/wool). Button all buttons, close all fasteners, and wear a belt through all loops. Slacks shall hang approximately two inches from the floor at the back of the shoe. Slacks should be tailored to include a two-inch hem to provide material for adjustments.

73. *Slacks, Khaki, Working.* Made of poly/cotton in same style as slacks, khaki, service, except slacks have two back pockets. Button all buttons, close all fasteners, and wear a belt through all loops. Slacks shall hang approximately two inches from the floor at the back of the shoe. Slacks should be tailored to include a two-inch hem to provide material for adjustments.

74. *Slacks, White, Dress, Unbelted.* Made of plain, authorized white fabric with fore and aft creases, left side zipper, and a waistband pocket in the upper right front. Fabric of slacks must match the service dress white coat. A full free-hanging liner is required in slacks. Modification of liner is prohibited. Button all buttons, close all fasteners. Slacks shall hang approximately two inches from the floor at the back of the shoe. Slacks should be tailored to include a two-inch hem to provide material for adjustments.

76. *Slacks, White, Summer, Belted (Women).* Made of authorized white fabric with fore and aft creases, belt loops, zippered fly front closure, and two side pockets. The shirt and slacks fabric must match (i.e., poly/cotton with poly/cotton, CNT with CNT). The welt pocket style may be worn as long as serviceable. A modesty liner, which extends to the bottom of the pockets, is required in certified Navy twill (CNT, 100% polyester) slacks. Button all buttons, close all fasteners, and wear a belt through all loops. Trousers shall hang approximately two inches from the floor at the back of the shoe. Trousers should be tailored to include a two-inch hem to provide material for adjustments.

77. *Slips (Women).* May be full or half slip. Shall be white or wearer's skin tone when wearing white uniform components. A slip is optional with lined skirts.

78. *Socks (Black/Khaki/White).* Made of undecorated, plain, or ribbed knitted material. Knee length or mid-calf socks are authorized.

79. *Studs.* Plain gold without design or ornamentation; mother-of-pearl studs are worn with formal dress (white tie). Wear fastened on the formal wing collar and the formal turn-down collar shirts.

80. *Suspenders, White (Men).* Shall be plain white without design or ornamentation. Wear fastened to the top of the trousers. They may be crossed in the back.

81. *Sweater, Cardigan.* A plain single-breasted cardigan style sweater made of authorized navy blue woolen or synthetic yarn, with a button front closure, long sleeves, wristlets, and V-neck. A pocket in the lower part of one or both foreparts is optional. Women's sweaters button to the left and men's sweaters button to the right. Button all buttons. Wear only within the immediate office space. Shirt collar is worn inside the sweater when a tie is worn and outside the sweater when no tie is worn.

83. *Sweater, V-Neck.* Black V-neck style pullover sweater, in both light (acrylic) and heavy (wool) weaves, with fabric epaulets, and shoulder and elbow patches. A Velcro-backed, black leather name tag (2" x 4") is required. Identification badges are not authorized to be worn on the sweater. The sweater is authorized for daily wear to and from work, in public places, on board ship, on base and station, and for attending working level meetings/briefings. Wear soft shoulder boards on the epaulets. Shirt collar is worn inside the sweater when a tie is worn and outside the sweater when no tie is worn

86. *Tiara (Women).* Small and crescent shaped, to fit over crown of the head. It is made of black velvet with appropriate cap device embroidered at the center. Wear over the crown of the head. The tiara need not be removed indoors.

87. *Tie Clasp/Tack (Men).* Gold, decorated or plain with appropriate insignia to which the wearer is entitled. Tie clasp shall be not more than ⁹⁄₁₆ inch wide. Tie tack shall be no more than ⅝ inch in diameter. May be worn on the four-in-hand tie, one inch below the center of the tie in a horizontal position. The uniform coat should cover it.

89. *Trousers, Aviation Green.* Made of same fabric as the aviation green coat with fore and aft creases, belt loops, zippered fly front closure, and two side and back pockets. May be either straight legged or slightly flared. Button all buttons, close

fasteners, and wear with a belt through all loops. Trousers shall hang approximately two inches from the floor at the back of the shoe. Trousers should be tailored to include a two-inch hem to provide material for adjustments.

90. *Trousers, Blue, Dress.* Made of plain, authorized blue fabric with fore and aft creases, belt loops, zippered fly front closure, and two side and back pockets. May be either straight legged or slightly flared. Fabric of trousers must match the uniform coat/shirt worn (i.e., service dress blue trousers must match the service dress blue coat, and winter blue trousers [75/25% poly/wool] must match the winter blue shirt.) Button all buttons, close all fasteners, and wear a belt through all loops. Trousers shall hang approximately two inches from the floor at the back of the shoe. Trousers should be tailored to include a two-inch hem to provide material for adjustments.

91. *Trousers, Blue, Evening.* Made high waisted with two front pockets and fore and aft creases of same fabric as blue dinner dress jacket. Button all buttons and close all fasteners. Trousers shall hang approximately two inches from the floor at the back of the shoe. Trousers should be tailored to include a two-inch hem to provide material for adjustments.

94. *Trousers, Khaki, Service.* Made of authorized fabric with fore and aft creases, belt loops, zippered fly front closure, and two side and back pockets. May be straight legged or slightly flared. The shirt and trousers fabric must match (i.e., poly/cotton with poly/cotton, CNT with CNT, and poly/wool with poly/wool). Button all buttons, close all fasteners, and wear a belt through all loops. Trousers shall hang approximately two inches from the floor at the back of the shoe. Trousers should be tailored to include a two-inch hem to provide material for adjustments.

95. *Trousers, Khaki, Working.* Made of poly/cotton fabric in same style as trousers, khaki, service. Button all buttons, close all fasteners, and wear a belt through all loops. Trousers shall hang approximately two inches from the floor at the back of the shoe. Trousers should be tailored to include a two-inch hem to provide material for adjustments.

98. *Trousers, White, Summer (Men).* Made of authorized white fabric with fore and aft creases, belt loops, zippered fly

front closure, and two side and back pockets. May be straight legged or slightly flared. The trousers and shirt or service dress white coat fabric must match (i.e., poly/ cotton with poly/cotton, CNT with CNT). Button all buttons, close all fasteners, and wear a belt through all loops. Trousers shall hang approximately two inches from the floor at the back of the shoe. Trousers should be tailored to include a two-inch hem to provide material for adjustments.

99. *Umbrella.* Plain, solid black, collapsible (in length) umbrella. May be carried when weather conditions warrant, provided safety regulations or practices are not violated (for example, FOD hazard). The umbrella should be carried in the left hand to permit saluting. The umbrella shall not be carried during military formations.

100. *Underpants (Women).* White or wearer's skin tone when worn with white uniforms. Color is optional with other uniforms.

101. *Undershirt, White.* Made of white cotton or poly/cotton. May be sleeveless, V-neck, or crew neck. Wear right side out, front of shirt to front of body. Crew neck shirts must be worn with dungaree/utility uniforms, jumper style uniforms, coveralls, and with all uniforms aboard ship and in areas where an industrial fire hazard exists. Other than as required above, women may wear undershirts optionally at shore commands, except with dungarees and jumper style uniforms crew neck shirts are required.

102. *Undershorts (Men).* White boxer shorts or knitted brief style when worn with white uniforms. Color is optional with other uniforms.

A Complete Sea Bag for Chief Petty Officers

Male

Belts

Black, w/brass buckle	One Each
Khaki, CNT w/brass buckle	One Each
Khaki, Work w/brass buckle	One Each
White, CNT w/brass buckle	One Each
White, Ctn w/brass buckle	One Each
Buttons, Gold (Reefer), set	One Set

Cap Covers

Khaki, CNT	One Each
White, CNT	One Each
Cap, Gar, Kh, Poly/Ctn	One Each

Combination Hat

Chin Strap, Vyl, Blk	One Each
Cap Cover, Poly/Ctn, Wh	Two Each
Cap Frame, Black	One Each
Coveralls, Utility	Two Pair
Gloves, White	One Pair

Insignia

Cap Device w/band	One Each
Cap Device (garrison)	One Each
Collar Devices, set	One Set
Coverall Embroidery Pkg	One Each
Rating Badge, Black	One Each
Shoulder Boards, Soft, set	One Set
Shoulder Devices, set	One Set

Shirts

Khaki, CNT	Two Each
Khaki, Work, Poly/Ctn	Two Each
White, CNT	One Each
White, Poly/Ctn, LS	Two Each

Shoes/Socks

Shoes, White	One Pair
Socks, White	Two Pair

Trousers

Khaki, CNT	One pair
Khaki, Poly/Ctn	Two Pair
White, CNT	One pair

Uniform

Service Dress Blue	One Each
Service Dress White	One Each
w/collar devices	

Plus these items from your E-6 seabag:

Coat

All-Weather	One Each

Drawers

Ctn, White	Eight Pair

Gloves

Black Leather	One Pair

Necktie

Black	One Each

Overcoat

Melton Wool, Black	One Each

Shirts

Blue, Poly/Wool, LS (wash)	Two Each
White, Ctn/Poly	Two Each

Shoes

Black, Dress	One Pair
Safety, Man's	One Pair
Socks, Ctn/Nyl, Black	Six Pair

Trousers

Blue, Poly/Wool (wash)	Two Pair
White, Ctn/Poly	Two Pair

Undershirt

Ctn, Wh	Eight Each

Female

Belts

Black, w/brass buckle	One Each
Khaki, CNT, w/brass buckle	One Each
Khaki, Work, w/brass buckle	One Each
White, CNT, w/brass buckle	One Each
White, Ctn, w/brass buckle	One Each

Buttons

Gold (SDB)	One Set
Gold (Reefer)	One Set

Cap Covers

Khaki, CNT	One Each
Cap, Gar, Khaki, Poly/Ctn	One Each

Combination Hat

Complete	One Each

Coveralls

Utility	Two Pairs

Gloves

White	One Pair

Handbag

White	One Each

Insignia

Cap Device (combination)	One Each
Cap Device (garrison)	One Each
Collar Devices; set	One Set
Coverall Embroidery Package	One Set
Rating Badge, Blk	One Each
Shoulder Boards, Soft, set	One Set
Shoulder Devices, set	One Set

Shirts

Khaki, CNT	Two Each
Khaki, Work, Poly/Ctn	Two Each

White, Poly/Ctn, LS	Two Each
White, CNT	Two Each

Shoes

White, Dress	One Pair
White, Service	One Pair

Skirt

Khaki, CNT	One Each

Slacks

Khaki, Poly/Ctn	Two Pair
White, CNT	One Pair
Socks, White	Two Pair
Uniform, Service	One Pair
Dress White, w/collar devices	One Pair

Plus these items from your E-6 Seabag:

Coat

All-Weather	One Each
SDB, Gabardine	One Each

Gloves

Leather, Blk	One Pair

Handbag

Vinyl, Black	One Each

Neck Tab

Blk	One Each

Overcoat

Peacoat	One Each

Shirt

Poly/Wl,LS, Bl (wash)	Two Each
Ctn/Poly, SS, Wh	Three Each

Shoes

Oxford, Black	One Pair
Black Dress	One Pair
Safety, Woman	One Pair

Skirt

Poly/Wl, Bl (wash)	One Each
SDB, Gabardine	One Each
Tw, Poly/Ctn, Wh	Two Each
CNT, Poly, White	One Each

Slacks

Poly/Wl, Bl (wash)	Two Pair
SW Poly/Ctn (w/liner)	Two Pair
SDB, Gabardine	One Each

Undershirt

Ctn, Wh	Eight Each

14

The Chief Petty Officers' Mess

Case Study: The Mess Treasurer's Role

It was raining at Roosevelt Roads, as it often does in late September. MRC Tom Coombe was crossing the main deck of USS *Dudley Morton* (AS-38) when he was hailed by DTC Howth. "Hey Tom, the CMC wants to see you in his office. Man, for a guy who just made chief a while back, this is your lucky day!" Chief Coombe went below to CMDCM Rahiny's office. "You know, Chief, that we operate our own CPO mess on board, not only for the chiefs in the ship's company, but also for any of the boats alongside for maintenance. We're looking for a new mess treasurer—it usually goes to a relatively junior chief—and I think you'll be perfect for the job. We thought of Tom Carpenter, too, but he's a storekeeper, and the rules say we can't use anyone who has fiduciary responsibility for supplies or funds. Master Chief Ashtown says he can spare you from the machine shop for a while, and I'm planning to submit your name to the skipper this week."

The Role of the Mess

Aboard ship, the mess is our home. Nothing is more important to a Sailor than a good meal and a warm, dry place to sleep, relax, or just hang out. Indeed, for centuries, groups of Sailors joined together, either voluntarily or by watch assignment, in ad hoc dining clubs. These ship's messes—the word derives from the Latin "mensa" meaning table—long precede the present cafeteria-style food service found on most ships today. Although there is no proven etymological link between the concept of mess as a dining arrangement and today's definition of disorder or disarray, it takes no great leap of imagination to envision what dinnertime must have been like on the lower decks of a pitching, rocking warship, caught in a North Atlantic gale.

In the Royal Navy, Sailors who berth in the same areas customarily join together as messmates. "Messmates before shipmates, shipmates before a landsman, a landsman before a dog" was an old Royal Navy adage. The colonial Navy adopted this custom, like many others, and, because Sailors with similar responsibilities usually berthed together, Sailors eating or messing together further strengthened the bonds between Sailors with common interests. Seamen messed with boatswains and coxswains, stokers with trimmers and firemen, and, indeed, rivalries and tensions were not unknown among the various messes on large warships. These tensions were aggravated by the system of food preparation then in use.

Each mess would nominate one or two members as designated messmen (later messcooks, and even later, food service attendants) who would draw supplies and transport them to the galley, where a full-time cook would supervise meal preparation. Space on the galley range was limited, and, because each mess was responsible for its own cooking gear, "first come, first served" was usually the rule. After the food had been prepared, the messmen would hazard the trip back to the berthing and messing spaces, oftentimes across weather decks awash with rolling waves. Safely back in the mess, the mess cook would turn over responsibility for the equitable distribution of the day's meal to the senior member of the group. This "killick of the mess," so named for the anchor of office worn on the cuff of his sleeve, would ensure that every man received his proper allotment of the day's meal.

Dinner was usually served on a chain-supported table, and the mess members sat on their sea chests, or other convenient articles, as the killick—often with the soup ladle in hand—maintained some semblance of order and discipline. At the end of the meal, the second messman would clear the table, clean the pots and pans, and return them to the galley to be ready for the next meal. The inconvenience of moving steaming hot containers of food from galley to berthing areas, while navigating heaving decks and near vertical ladders, was offset by the camaraderie and fellowship felt among members of a particular mess.

Given the draconian discipline prevalent in those times and the necessity of maintaining stern leadership, it is no surprise that senior members of the ship's company found it desirable and even necessary to berth and dine together. Not only were their facilities less Spartan than the fo'c'sle; dining together gave them the opportunity to relax for a few moments, secure in the knowledge that their tablemates understood and appreciated the stresses of everyday life at sea. The sailmaker might comment to the carpenter about the condition of the spars and masts he noticed in his day-to-day work aboard ship; the master-at-arms and the apothecary might discuss the physical state of particular crewmen and the impact of illness on the ability of ship's company to call away at a moment's notice to board an enemy or to repel boarders on their own ship. The Chief Petty Officers' mess evolved from this early form of messing.

The CPO Mess

At one level, the CPO mess is a physical place. In an SSN it may be as humble as one small table and bench seats in a corner compartment adjacent to CPO berthing, or it may be as impressive as the spacious, well-equipped din-

Our newest messmates sing "Anchors Aweigh" en route to their pinning ceremony in the Pentagon courtyard. Through ritual and long tradition we retain our identity as Chief Petty Officers.
U.S. Navy (PHC Johnny Bivera)

ing area and grandly decorated lounge facilities on a CVN. It may be as unorthodox, humble, and mobile as a tent in a Seabee battalion deployment site or as nondescript as a room in the training command ashore. It's home, nonetheless.

The uninitiated guests enter with the full knowledge that it is a special place and requires special conduct. Young Sailors are warned of the dire consequences of wandering in uninvited. Most messes are located behind closed doors, and it's the rare Sailor who has not stood nervously before the sign "Knock three times, uncover, and do not enter until invited." Newly frocked Chief Petty Officers are reminded that the CPO mess is a tangible symbol of the strong, effective bond among members. During the CPO initiation season special pains are taken to remind initiates that they are about to enjoy special privileges, but that with those privileges comes a unique set of obligations.

The CPO mess is a place where military protocol is relaxed. The unofficial motto is "What's said here, stays here." You can blow off a little steam in the mess, but it is exceedingly important to remember that this motto doesn't translate to "anything goes." It is certainly good to be able to say what's on your mind occasionally, and there is great value in a free and open conversation about all things work and social. It is even more important, however, to ensure that the core values we embrace are not in any way compromised behind the closed doors of the CPO mess by any false perception of personal privilege or some reckless interpretation of the freedom from normal protocol.

The actual decor, style, and layout of the physical CPO mess is exceedingly important. To the extent possible, the CPO mess should reflect the tradition, heritage, and values of the CPO mess.

Most seasoned veterans understand that membership in the chiefs' mess comes with obligations that are not subject to personal interest, but to the CPO community itself. Today's chiefs' mess exists to provide a venue to improve cohesion and to provide training in "chiefness." It provides a visual reminder of the distinct and unique nature of the community, typifies the perks commensurate with newly accepted responsibility, and serves as a place to discuss common problems and seek solutions from the collective wisdom of the entire group.

Messes and Associations

Formal regulations govern a CPO mess, afloat or ashore, and a CPO association. A CPO association is a shore-based private organization supported by the members' personal funds and is described in greater detail below. In general, regulations provide that master chiefs, senior chiefs, and Chief Petty Officers of the Navy and other armed forces enlisted personnel in pay grades E-7, E-8, and E-9 will mess in a separate mess when space and supporting personnel are available. Chief Petty Officer messes are staffed with one mess management specialist for each seventy-five members and one messman for each fifteen members.

Commanding officers are responsible for the proper operation and administration of Chief Petty Officers' messes afloat in their command. The commanding officer exerts positive influence through the mess president and ensures the proper operation of the mess.

The Chief Petty Officer who is senior for purposes of military authority, usually the command master chief, will act as mess president. In the absence of the mess president, the next senior Chief Petty Officer present in the mess will act as president. The mess president exercises a command function and is responsible for mess administration, presiding over and maintaining order in the mess. He or she ensures that all regulations are followed, and preserves the traditions and customs of the mess. Chief Petty Officers not regularly attached to the ship or assigned to an embarked staff are ineligible for mess president.

The command master chief nominates a Chief Petty Officer as mess treasurer, and this appointment is submitted to the commanding officer for approval. This duty is usually, but not always, assigned to a relatively junior member of the mess. However, there is an absolute requirement for a certain minimum exposure to the CPO mess environment, so the CMC will avoid assigning a just-advanced CPO to this duty. In a closed mess, the treasurer acts as mess caterer as well. No Chief Petty Officer having supply, subsistence, retail sales, or disbursing duties will be eligible to serve as mess treasurer. The CMC will determine the length of time an individual will serve as mess treasurer, who will keep an account of receipts and expenditures from which an abstract of the financial condition of the mess may be determined at any time. The mess treasurer is responsible for the efficient management and operation of the mess. He or she must:

- Supervise the overall administration, management, and operation of the mess.
- Maintain accurate accounts and records of the mess.
- Verify receipt of stocks and merchandise.
- Supervise procurement, storage, and issue of all consumable provisions and supplies.

- Prohibit procurement of stores for the mess under an agreement whereby the supplier permits payment upon consumption.

- Assume responsibility for receipt, safekeeping, deposit, disbursement, and accountability of mess funds.

- Prepare monthly financial statements of the mess.

- Incur no indebtedness that has not been approved by the mess and cannot be defrayed with mess funds on hand.

- Authorize in writing those individuals permitted to incur indebtedness in the name of the Chief Petty Officers' mess.

- Post a copy of the monthly financial operating statement in the mess area.

- Ensure that all bills are paid before leaving port. Should circumstances preclude payment, the mess treasurer will notify the commanding officer of the number and amount of unpaid bills on the day the ship leaves port.

- Assume responsibility for government property in the mess.

- Assume responsibility for maintaining and repairing facilities and equipment.

- After obtaining the concurrence of the mess president, approve the menu.

- Supervise preparation and service of food.

- Plan well-balanced and nutritious meals.

- Detail the enlisted personnel assigned to the mess.

- Assume responsibility for training and qualification of assigned enlisted personnel.

- Ensure that enlisted personnel assigned to the mess, whose rations are commuted to the mess, receive the same menu as the members of the mess. This will be accomplished on the basis of providing three meals a day for each day that rations are commuted.

- Assume responsibility for and supervise the cleaning of equipment and spaces assigned to the mess and its members.

- Reimburse the food service officer for provisions purchased from the general mess no later than fifteen days following the end of the month in which the provisions were purchased.

Mess Funding

The closed CPO mess generates funds through commuting the ration allowance for each member, the mess management specialists, and food service attendants assigned to the mess. Members may be assessed a nominal amount monthly if necessary to provide additional food items or other expenses of the mess. Rations commuted to the Chief Petty Officers' mess will be used to purchase food items only. Use of commuted rations for purposes other than subsistence is a violation of Title 31, U.S. Code 628. Occasional nominal assessments may be made against permanent mess members only, and may not be made against temporary mess members, mess management specialists, food service attendants, and other personnel E-6 and below assigned to the mess. Cash rebates of mess funds to mess members or any other party are prohibited, and excess mess funds generated from commuting rations to the Chief Petty Officers' mess will be rebated monthly to the disbursing officer for deposit to the Navy's subsistence appropriation. Chief Petty Officers' messes may retain a percentage of unexpended commuted rations for working capital.

Support Staff. Mess management specialist personnel are responsible for the following:

- Supervising CPO mess personnel and dining facilities.
- Maintaining and operating separate galley facilities, if provided.
- Maintaining CPO living spaces, including routine cleaning and field day.
- Supervising food service assistants and compartment cleaners as assigned.

In most commands, a rotational pool of enlisted personnel in pay grades E-1 through E-3 will be established to provide basic living space maintenance service in CPO quarters aboard ship. All personnel in pay grades E-1 through E-3 will be eligible for assignment to the rotational pool without exception, and they normally will remain in the pool for a period not longer than ninety days. Petty officers will not be detailed to rotational pools except when E-3 and below personnel are not available.

Chief Petty Officers Messes (Ashore)

CPO messes ashore are category V, Morale, Welfare, and Recreation Programs. The messes are designed to promote and maintain the well-being, morale, and efficiency of personnel by providing dining, social, entertainment, and recreational facilities. The CPO messes are non-membership, non-appropriated fund activities, with exception. Commands operate the messes for active-duty military personnel in pay grades E-7, E-8, and E-9, and their families, assigned to a military installation. The messes also serve other armed forces personnel in equivalent pay grades and their families, and the commanding officer may authorize additional patronage if facilities of the mess permit. When approved by the commanding officer, messes may charge membership dues. Membership is voluntary and commands must notify BuPers when establishing dues. When messes charge dues, nonmembers and their families will be denied use of the facilities. Exceptions will be made for essential food service, official functions, and command-recognized group functions as determined by the commanding officer.

Appropriated funds may be used for the construction of facilities; but thereafter, all funding must be from non-appropriated funds. BuPers serves as the designated program manager for both local funds through various activities. They include the resale of food, bar, and sundry items, and the resale of items in other departments. The mess manager may be either a military person or a civilian-salaried employee of the mess, although usually the mess manager is a civilian employee, responsible to the commanding officer for the proper operation of the mess. An advisory board is comprised of personnel from the naval station or base, subordinate activities, tenant commands, and fleet units home-ported or home-based at the station and provides the commanding officer with information about the mess from which to make decisions. Members appointed to the advisory board reflect the messes' command and minority representation. The activity manager attends the meetings of the advisory board in a nonvoting status.

The Chief Petty Officers' Association

Each command usually has a private organization separate and distinct from the CPO mess that provides for the welfare and recreation of its members. The rules and regulations of a closed CPO mess normally do not apply to the CPOA. The CPOA can elect officers, collect initiation fees, assess monthly dues, and spend the money any way members choose. The CPOA is defined as a category VI, Morale, Welfare, and Recreation Program. The commanding officer gives written permission for the CPOA to use base or shipboard facilities to conduct meetings. It's important to note that:

- The CPOA may not operate as a business. The Navy strictly prohibits making loans of money from operating capital.
- The CPOA may raise operating capital from dues or by selling merchandise to members only. Many associations sell t-shirts ("Initiated by Choice" t-shirts always sell well, for example), CPO challenge coins, or similar items.
- CPOA may not receive non-appropriated funding from morale, welfare, and recreation funds.

Chief Petty Officers' associations follow Navy financial accounting procedures. The Morale, Welfare, and Recreation Office is normally assigned to advise and assist the

CPOA in financial procedures, and the CPOA may be subject to an annual informal audit by the commanding officer when operating on a naval base or ship.

As a newly selected Chief Petty Officer, it's sometimes hard to remember the differences between messes afloat, ashore, and CPO associations. The mess, which consists of all personnel E-7 through E-9, provides dining and berthing at sea, and dining facilities ashore. The CPOA, which consists of members who pay dues, supports recreational activities, such as parties, outings, and special events like initiations and khaki balls. Your personal support funds the CPO mess ashore. If you are called on to serve as an officer of the CPO mess, perhaps even as treasurer or caterer, you should consult and become intimately familiar with all the pertinent instructions governing their overall operation.

Case Study: The Dining-in

As the year wore on, Chief Coombe felt better and better about his role as treasurer and caterer of his chiefs' mess. Over dinner one evening, the CMC remarked, "You know, it's been a good long while since we've had a dining-in aboard this ship. Let's get something going right after the new year, Chief, okay? The last couple events we've held have gone really well—why not give the banquet manager over at the El Conquistador Hotel in Fajardo a call and set something up for us? We held a dining-in in their main ballroom a couple years ago, and everyone said it was a real success. You can make this one even better, can't you, Chief?"

One element of life in a Chief Petty Officers' mess that you may find unusual is the custom of dining-in. It's an old tradition, dating back before colonial times. In general, the dining-in is a formal banquet in which members blend a high degree of military atmosphere with an air of tradition and fellowship. It is customary during these functions to pay tribute to those who have made outstanding contributions to the service, to hear an address by a distinguished guest, and to present a series of toasts to dignitaries, heads of state, and to our fallen comrades. The primary elements of a dining-in are a formal setting, a fine meal, the camaraderie of the members of the mess, the toasts, martial music, and the attendance of an honored guest. Frequently, messes will also organize dining-out occasions featuring relaxed formality and to which spouses or significant others are traditionally invited.

Remember that each CPO mess has its own traditions, and that there's no one right way to conduct a dining-in event. Nevertheless, the elements discussed below are typical of what you'll find at most ships, squadrons, or other units.

The Command Master Chief Petty Officer or chief of the boat is the mess president. When an event involves more than one command, the mess president is designated in the planning stages and is normally (but not always) either the CMC of the command planning and executing the dining-in or the CMC of the senior command participating in the joint effort. This individual is responsible for the entire organization and operation of the dining-in. The president:

- Presides over the mess throughout the evening.
- Arranges for a chaplain/mess member to give the grace.
- Greets all guests.
- Appoints the vice president, who is responsible for the logistics of the event.

The vice president, usually called Mister Vice or Madam Vice, is most often the junior member of the mess. The vice president:

- Sounds the dinner chimes or mess call, as appropriate, at the proper time.
- Tests the main course prior to the servers distributing the meal and announces to the members of the mess that the meal is fit for Chief Petty Officer consumption.
- Quiets any disturbance and prepares a list of offenders for the president.
- Seconds toasts as directed by the president.

Planning the Dining-in. As a junior member of the mess, you may be tasked with preparing the dining-in. By all means, start early! At least four weeks, but preferably eight weeks, before the dinner, send out invitations to the guests who are not members of the mess. Use printed or handwritten invitations. Many organizations use the fill-in type. Because this is a formal occasion, use formal wording.

Guests are either official or personal. The mess, as a whole, will host official guests, and everyone shares their expenses. Official guests, who may be a distinguished civilian, a senior official of the government, or a distinguished representative from another armed service, are usually senior in rank to the president. Personal guests invited, with the permission of the president, are usually junior in rank to the president. If you invite a personal guest, you pay all expenses including the bar tab. The wording for official guests should include the phrase "the honor of the presence of . . ." and wording for personal guests should include "the pleasure of the company of . . ." or ". . . your company." The menu usually consists of three courses. Roast prime rib of beef and Yorkshire pudding is traditional but not required. Wine in decanters is served or placed on the table. When seated at a round table, remember to pass the wine counterclockwise.

The president of the mess sits at the center of the head table with the guest of honor to the right and the next ranking guest to the left. Other guests will sit throughout the mess. Normally, members of the mess will sit according to seniority. Date of rate will determine who sits closest when individuals are equal in rate. The vice will sit at a separate table facing the president. No one should sit across from those at the head table. Avoid crowding the tables together. Adjust seating so as many attendees as possible can observe the head table and the vice. Post the seating arrangement for the mess outside the dining area so members will know where to sit prior to mess call. Each place setting in the mess should have a name tag that identifies what the individual is drinking and eating so that the servers can easily accommodate members of the mess. Use colored stars or whatever makes things simplest for you and the hosting facility.

Dining-ins normally follow a specific and generally accepted sequence of events. Most messes try to follow this protocol closely.

Receiving Line/Cocktail Hour. The receiving line forms at the entrance of the cocktail area and consists of the president and the guest of honor. Mess members should arrive a few minutes early to secure head gear, coats, or other items not needed for dinner prior to entering the cocktail area. The president is first in the receiving line, and the guest of honor is to his right. As you come abreast the president, announce your rate and name (Chief Smith, Master Chief Jones, for example) and shake hands. The president will in turn introduce you to the guest of honor, whereby you exchange hand clasps. After greeting the guest of honor, proceed into the cocktail area. The cocktail period is open-bar and lasts approximately thirty minutes. Conversations should be light and of short duration. Attempt to talk with as many messmates and guests as possible, remembering that the cocktail period is for lighthearted conservation and entertainment.

Call to Dinner. The signal for dinner will be the sounding of "mess call" followed by appropriate marching music. As soon as the music starts after mess call, all members not seated at the head table should dispose of their drinks and proceed to the dining area, locate their places, and remain standing behind their chairs. Those individuals seated at the head table will remain in the cocktail area until all others have reached the mess area. The narrator will announce, "Ladies and Gentlemen, the head table." The head table guests will march into the dining room and stand behind their seats. No one may take their places at a table after the head table has entered without the permission of the president. Conversely, no one may leave without the permission of the president. A member desiring to leave for any reason, must stand, ask for recognition, and request the permission of the president or Mister/Madam Vice.

Color Guard. The color guard may contain from one to six color bearers and two color guards. All members of the color guard should be approximately the same height to present the most favorable impression. The color bearer carries the national ensign and commands the color guard. He or she gives the necessary commands for movements and rendering of honors. The organizational colors are always on the left of the national ensign. The layout of the dining area or needs of the organization may dictate the manner in which you post the colors. The president will command "parade the colors" at which time the color guard will march into the dining area. Remember to observe the flag protocol found in chapter twelve.

Grace. The chaplain will say grace. Note that, at Chief Petty Officers' mess functions, this duty is usually performed by a member of the mess and not by a member of the commissioned chaplain corps. Upon its completion, the president will rap once with the gavel, indicating everyone should be seated.

Toasting. After all the members are in place, the colors posted, and the grace offered, the president will open the mess and make welcoming remarks. After the president's remarks, formal toasting will commence. A toast is the traditional and formal way of honoring a country, organization, or institution. It is disrespectful for an individual not to participate in a toast. A non-drinker need only go through the motion of holding the glass to his lips or request the wine substitute when selecting the meal. Never propose formal toasts to individuals. Toasts made to an office such as the CNO or the president are appropriate.

The president will rise and call for a toast to the commander-in-chief. At the sound of the gavel, Mister/Madam Vice rises and seconds the president's toast by saying, "Gentlemen, ladies, to the commander-in-chief of the United States." Each member and guest then stands, repeats in unison the toast (e.g., "the commander-in-chief of the United States"), sips the wine, and remains standing. Do not bottoms-up your drink on each toast. Bottoms-up only on the final toast to the U.S. Navy. Do not get caught in the position of having an empty glass. Immediately after the toast to the commander-in-chief, designated personnel will stand and propose the formal toasts as they appear in the program.

Parading the Beef. When toasting has been completed, members of the dining-in committee will "parade the beef." They will enter the mess and make a formal presentation of the meal to the head table, members of the mess, and finally, to Mister/Madam Vice. Mister/Madam Vice will sample the meal to see if it is fit for Chief Petty Officer consumption. Parading the beef is a traditional and formal part of the dining-in and amounts to a short skit. The variations of this event are endless and should be limited only by good taste. Parading the beef should be one of the most creative and colorful parts of the dining in.

Addressing the Mess. There is a formal way of obtaining permission to address the mess. If you would like to address the mess, stand (when it won't interfere with other proceedings within the mess), then identify yourself by saying, "Mister/Madam Vice, (state your rate and name) requests permission to address the mess" or "Mister/Madam Vice, (state your rate and name) has a point of order." Wait until recognized, and then formally state your issue to the mess.

Limericks, Ditties, and Skits. No toasting is permitted during dinner. A member may stand, however, and address Mister/Madam Vice for the purpose of bringing to the attention of the entire mess topics of timely interest. This is called presenting a limerick or ditty. A word of caution is appropriate here. There are clear lines of decorum, courtesy, and professional respect that may not be breached. That which may appear to be funny to you at the time may not seem so to the other members of the mess. Much good fellowship has been marred by inappropriate remarks. When in doubt, do nothing. Each mess always has chiefs who have that special talent and creative good humor to perform the limericks, ditties, and skits in memorable fashion. Take advantage of their talents, using them as catalysts for others and for helping to set the tone.

By the same token, when any conduct approaches the limit, an appropriate reminder is in order. The form this reminder takes is situational—sometimes a gentle one-on-one between chiefs during a break is in order; occasionally a forceful remark from the mess president is justified. When it is done skillfully and in the right spirit it enhances the evening. That said, limericks and ditties must not be offensive to a member, and a member should present them in good fun and taste. A limerick should be witty to all and solicit a response from the appropriate parties. Remember, before presenting a limerick or ditty, you must receive acknowledgment from the president or Mister/Madam Vice. A BMC with an unfortunate record of manhandling the skipper's gig might be "honored" thus:

> There once was a cox'n named Mike,
> Who would be better off steering a bike,
> The ship's only boat,
> Is now barely afloat,
> Since he ran into the side of the *Ike*.

Skits or other forms of parody are usually enjoyable and often quite clever. Again, without worrying too much about political correctness, be absolutely certain that your planned activity cannot reasonably be interpreted as offensive to others.

After dinner, the president will direct a break to give time for the servers to clear the mess area and to allow for the use of facilities and time to smoke. Although the smoking lamp will remain unlit, some messes will maintain an unlit ceremonial lamp to keep the tradition intact. After returning from the break, the president or another senior member will introduce the guest of honor who will impart wisdom upon the mess.

Informal Toasts and Fines. After the guest speaker's remarks, the president will open the mess for informal toasting. Anyone who wishes to initiate a toast will briefly present justification for desiring such a toast, ending with the words of the proposed toast. Members of the mess greatly appreciate inspired wit and subtle sarcasm. If the president deems the toast justified, he or she will direct Mister/Madam Vice to second the toast in the same manner as in the formal toast. When, in the judgment of the president, the informal toasting has sufficed, he or she will rap the gavel three times and commence the business of the mess by asking Mister/Madam Vice to read the list of offenders who have violated the customs and traditions of the mess. Mister/Madam Vice will assess suitable fines. The fines collected by the mess are normally designated to go for such things as charities or in the case of a school, a class gift. Normally, individuals will not pay more than five dollars in fines. There are always exceptions, however, for those who crave the attention.

The Final Toast. Without rising, the president will call for the final toast, which will be to the U.S. Navy. Mister/Madam Vice will then proceed to the head table and fill each glass starting from the honored guest and ending with the president. The president then fills the glass of Mister/Madam Vice, who then faces the mess and proposes the toast. While Mister/Madam Vice is moving to the head table, all members of the mess rise and ensure their glasses are charged. When Mister/Madam Vice proposes the toast, the mess responds in unison, "To the United States Navy," everyone drains their glass and remains standing for "Anchors Aweigh."

Adjourning the Mess. Following the toast to the U.S. Navy, the president will adjourn the mess and invite those present to join him or her in the lounge. Members and guests should remain in their places until the head table has left the mess. The lounge will open for the purchase of refreshments, and members and their guests will be free to congregate. Attendees should not depart until the president and all official guests have departed.

Despite its formality and ritual, participation in the dining-in should be an enjoyable and enriching experience. To ensure that this cherished tradition continues for future generations of Chief Petty Officers, remember:

- As a member of the mess, you are a host and should act accordingly.
- Do not become intoxicated.
- Do not carry drinks into the dining room.
- Do not delay moving into the dining room.
- No one may take his or her place at the table after the official party has entered the dining area without going up to the president of the mess and requesting permission to enter the mess. No one may leave the dining area without the permission of the president.
- Do not rap on glasses for attention or applause.
- Do not discuss politics or religion in the dining area.
- Do not drink the toasting wine until all members' glasses have been charged and the first toast proposed.
- Toasts are to institutions or communities and never to persons by proper name.
- Do not get caught with an uncharged glass.
- Do not bottoms-up your glass on each toast—only on the final traditional toast.
- Do not stand or drink a toast to your own service, with the exception of the traditional toast.
- Do not depart until all the official guests have departed.

Case Study: Retirement Ceremonies

Chief Coombe was sitting in the mess office one afternoon when Master Chief Pat Stoneybatter stopped by. "You know, Tom, I'm coming up on my thirty-year anniversary this year, and Margaret and I have decided that it's time to unship my oars and head ashore. I haven't told anybody about it yet, but I'll be heading up to Personnel later this week to let 'em know, and I was wondering if you'd do me a favor. I've watched you since you were a third class, back on *Simon Lake,* and Margaret and I consider Erin and you our closest friends on board. I was wondering if you'd do me

We are Chief Petty Officers forever, but the inevitable day comes when we cross the brow as active-duty Sailors for the last time. *U.S. Navy (PHC Eric Benson)*

the honor of being my retirement sponsor and help to organize my retirement ceremony. It looks like I'll go out on 17 March—and I understand that Adm. Anna Liffey will be on board right about then. She and I served together when she was a boot ensign, and I was the LPO of the chain locker on USS *Conshohocken*. Let's see if we can get her to come by and say a few words, okay?"

One of the most important milestones in the life of every career Sailor is that inevitable day when our active service comes to an end. As a Chief Petty Officer, you may be asked to sponsor a retiree from your division, or you may be asked to fill any of several other roles that are part of the tradition of that special day. Retirement ceremonies vary according to command, personal wishes, and circumstances, of course, but all are marked by solemnity and a sense of reverence and gratitude for the sacrifices our shipmate has made over many year's service to the nation.

We're indebted to the Naval Computer and Telecommunications Station (NCTS) Washington for the excellent checklists they've provided to help plan these significant events, but, more importantly, we're all indebted to all those fine Sailors who have "gone ashore" before us.

The Role of the Sponsor

Sponsors should be selected as soon as possible after the command becomes aware of an individual's desire to retire. A sponsor should be identified at least ninety days prior the ceremony. The sponsor's primary responsibility is ensuring that all aspects of the retirement ceremony are addressed. The sponsor takes care that all assigned tasks are on schedule and acts as the primary point of contact for all aspects of the ceremony. Timely submission of requests and continual follow-up are required. The sponsor should:

- Identify himself or herself formally as the retirement sponsor.
- Carefully read through the checklists provided. Pay particular attention to the listed time lines for each task.
- Initiate the checklist and ensure that each task is assigned and that all assignments are fully understood.
- Have the retiree fill out a Retirement Information Sheet and Biography Information Sheet, available from your Navy counselor.
- Be sure that the retiree invites the guest speaker and obtains biographic information for the speaker as soon as possible.

- Ensure that an appropriate article is prepared and submitted for inclusion into the command's Plan of the Week. Inform the retiree of your intentions.
- Begin work on the layout of the retirement program as soon as possible.
- Have the retiree designate side boys as desired. (Six or eight has become the norm.)
- Have the retiree identify guests he or she wishes to invite.
- Ensure that the retiree is fully informed of the sequence of events. If the retiree is a Chief Petty Officer, he or she may have acted as a sponsor for others in the past and has particular wishes as to how his or her own ceremony should be structured.

As soon as possible after the initial notification, the command master chief or department master chief in very large commands should meet with the retiring chief. Sometimes a retiring chief may be reluctant to plan a ceremony—and may even decline or reject a ceremony, expressing a desire to go quietly without fanfare. Although the wishes of the chief are important, this is an emotionally turbulent period of life for Sailors, and it is essential that any initial rejection of a ceremony be properly vetted by the CMC and the outgoing chief's division and department leadership. In no case should a Chief Petty Officer "go quietly." In the rare instance that a formal ceremony is firmly declined, the CMC is obliged to arrange for the proper recognition at the appropriate time, including recognition of the spouse and family. This often requires a certain finesse on the part of the CMC, but it is a professional obligation, and it is worth the effort. Occasionally these "impromptu" ceremonies are as sophisticated and successful as the elaborate and long-planned event. Sometimes they can be even more emotional and memorable.

Summaries of retiree and guest speaker biographies should be completed as early in the planning stage as possible to allow adequate time to print programs and to ensure that all vital items are covered in the initial planning stages. Hold regular meetings to discuss progress of assignments. Don't be afraid to take charge and be aggressive in planning—it only benefits the retiree you are representing. Write down all ideas throughout the planning stages. Your ideas may be beneficial to the next sponsor as lessons are learned with each ceremony.

As with any important ceremony, planning is critical. For a successful retirement ceremony, begin to plan as soon as eighty days before the event. What follows is a suggested timetable for tasks and duties prior to the ceremony:

80 days:	Generate information sheets for retiree
60 days:	Begin luncheon arrangements
	Begin shadow box development
45 days:	Select coordinator and master of ceremony
	Purchase retirement gift
	Complete first draft of program
	Prepare script
30 days:	Select music and prepare tape
	Check all certificates for correct name and date
	Presidential Certificate
	Fleet Reserve Certificate
	Retirement Certificate
	Spouse Certificate of Appreciation
	Flag Certificate(s); Flag flown over desired location
20 days:	Purchase devices for shadow box
	Verify availability of boatswain's mate
	Verify receipt of flown flag
	Verify availability of music
15 days:	Verify official party assignments
	Verify shadow box completion
	Order flowers for spouse/family
	Verify chaplain availability
	Verify availability of photographer

Important Steps and Elements
of the Retirement Ceremony

Information Sheet. The most basic information required for adequate planning will be provided by the retiring chief to the sponsor on an information sheet. A blank sheet needs to be given to the retiree at least eighty days prior to the scheduled ceremony, and the sponsor should ask to have it back within ten days. This information sheet should be completed prior to the first meeting of the retirement committee. It should contain complete biographic information, choices of music, guests, and other data of interest to the retiree. Most CPO messes have sample information sheets readily available in a gouge book or similar file.

The Spouse and Children. We all know that we could not have made it to retirement without the loving support of our families. As a sponsor, be sure that the spouse and children are fully engaged and offered the opportunity to participate in planning the retirement ceremony for their Sailor. There can be no more touching scene than seeing a child—perhaps now grown and a service member— actively participating in this long-awaited and emotional ceremony. Regardless of how non-traditional the request may be, make every effort to support requests that the family might make about this important occasion. It's their day, too. In the event that a family request is inconsistent with inclusion in the formal ceremony, it is almost always possible to include it in the less formal reception.

Shadow Box. Planning should begin sixty days prior to the ceremony. Ask the retiree for any special content requirements. Purchase devices for the box twenty days prior to the ceremony and aim to have the shadow box completed no later than ten days before the ceremony. Consider the American flag, devices, and engraved duty station plates for inclusion. Contact the maker of the shadow box as soon as possible to allow adequate time for construction, and take charge of purchasing all necessary contents. Verify the availability of a suitable flag. The information sheet should list all of the retiree's duty stations.

Normally the CPO Association funds a standard retirement presentation like a shadow box that symbolizes and summarizes the career service of the retiring member. The sponsor should make sure that this standard presentation is what the retiring member wants. Occasionally the retiring chief may prefer a different version of the shadow box or some different presentation. It is perfectly acceptable—and even desirable—for the retiring member to participate in this decision, even to the extent of paying the difference between the standard presentation and that which he or she prefers. Remember to ask the retiree if he or she wishes to contribute any special items for inclusion in the shadow box, or if a shipmate wants to contribute a new device for inclusion, something that offsets some of the expense.

Guest Speaker. The retiree has the option to request a specific person as the guest speaker. If no particular person is requested by the retiree, then an individual should be agreed upon by the sponsor and the retiree. The retiree is responsible for identifying and notifying the guest speaker, and this should be done no later than sixty days before the ceremony. The sponsor may assist in preparing the guest speaker's biography.

Master of Ceremonies. As sponsor, you may be asked to act as master of ceremonies for the event. The choice is always that of the retiree. Selection should be completed within forty-five days of the ceremony date. The sponsor should follow up and verify the availability of the designated master of ceremonies fifteen days prior to the event. The person selected:

- Acts as the emcee for the event.
- Reads all letters, citations, and certificates and is prepared to make presentations as required. All the items to be read must be read before the event so the emcee is

familiar with the wording and any unusual pronunciations.

- Introduces himself or herself to the retiree's family and becomes familiar with their names.
- Must be familiar with the time line and scheduled sequence of events of the ceremony.
- Makes every effort to assist the sponsor with greeting guest speakers and guests of the retiree.
- Attends all practices prior to the scheduled event.
- Knows proper protocol for the purpose of making all presentations.

Chaplain. The chaplain delivers the invocation and benediction at the ceremony. These are not required parts of the program. The retiree may choose any of the following options:

- No benediction and invocation.
- Benediction and invocation delivered by command chaplain.
- Benediction and invocation delivered by Navy chaplain of a specific denomination.
- Benediction and invocation delivered by non-Navy person of the retiree's preference.

Be prepared to provide the chaplain's office some simple biographic information on the retiree. If the retiree desires a personal representative to deliver the invocation and benediction, the personal representative should contact the command chaplain for any information that may be required.

Boatswain's Mate. Obtain the services of a boatswain's mate sufficiently in advance of the ceremony, and recheck availability at the 20-day point. Traditionally, the command master chief boatswain's mate or the leading boatswain's mate in smaller commands will pipe the side for the retiree.

National Ensign. Early in the planning process, check with the retiree to determine his or her wishes regarding the national ensign to be used at the ceremony or included in the shadow box. Many retirees request that the flag be flown over the U.S. Capitol, something that can be obtained through the retiree's congressional representative. Others may desire that the flag be flown over a previous duty station, at the Navy Memorial in Washington D.C., or over USS *Arizona,* or over a location like their home state capital, or simply over their ship or command. Depending on the flag selected, request times will vary—some may take as long as ninety days—so it is important that the location be identified as soon as possible.

Guest List. Obtain the number of guests the retiree wishes to invite to the retirement ceremony. Retiree should provide this list not later than sixty days prior to the ceremony. Ensure that arrangements are made to accommodate the number of guests at the site. Have the retiree ensure that accurate information pertaining to each guest address is complete prior to submitting the request for invitation. The retiree is responsible for making sure that invitations are mailed, but the sponsor should follow up on retirement invitations and offer assistance in mailing. The sponsor should coordinate all matters of security and access of guests to the command.

Official Party. Chief Petty Officers traditionally select eight courtesy side boys for the important final walk ashore. The retiree may ask specific individuals he or she has known throughout his or her career or may choose Sailors of every grade from seaman to MCPO. The retiree chooses, but the sponsor may assist in notifying the selected participants. Be sure that all side boys are informed of the place, time, and uniform and of any rehearsals planned. Have all participants assemble at least thirty minutes prior to the event for a last run-through in the exact location and to ensure that all are aware of the sequence of events and their places for the ceremony. Side boys will sometimes also participate in a flag presentation ceremony, act as ushers, present flowers, or perform other official duties requested by the retiring member. The sponsor should remind any retired members who will participate in uniform that they must meet current grooming requirements to wear the prescribed uniform.

Biographies. Both the retiree and the guest speaker will have brief biographies published in the program, making it important to gather the information early in the process. As sponsor, you may have to communicate with the guest speaker to complete the biographic details.

Ceremony Requirements

Programs. Each guest will be given a printed program. A final formal portrait of the retiree is traditionally included in the program. Many retiring Sailors include a photo from boot camp or their first enlistment with this current portrait. If the guest speaker's biography is included in the program, a current photograph would be appropriate to include. Many retirees also like to add the "Sailor's Creed," a favorite poem, or a ditty. Sponsors may want to speak with spouses about any other additions to personalize the program.

The printing request submitted should include photoready copy, all clip art, and the photographs discussed previously. The printing request should be submitted no earlier than forty-five days and no later than twenty-five days before the ceremony.

Certificates. The sponsor is responsible for ensuring that all appropriate certificates are on hand for the retirement ceremony. Senior Navy counselors can help the sponsor. Extensive lead time is necessary to obtain the required signatures on all certificates. The usual items for presentation include:

- DD 363: Certificate of Retirement
- NAVPERS 1830/3: Certificate—Fleet Reserve
- NAVPERS 1650/59: Performance and Discipline
- Spouse's Certificate of Appreciation

- DD 2542: Certificate of Appreciation for Service in the Armed Forces of the United States (bearing the President's signature)
- Certificate of flag of the United States being flown
- End of tour award
- Letters of appreciation
- CPOA or command plaque
- Shadow box

Music. Generally, taped or recorded music is used for retirement ceremonies. There may be a rare occasion when live music is desired. If live music is to be used, it is important that musicians be requested as soon in the planning stages as possible. Always remember to test the music system before the ceremony starts!

Ceremony Location and Floor Plan. The sponsor should ensure that all involved know the layout of the ceremony location. Consideration for seating, side boys, and procession are of concern. Remember that the location will change from one ceremony to another. Inspect the chosen site well in advance of the ceremony and plan out the area. Things to consider:

- Speaker podium(s)
- Area for presentations
- Side boy location
- Seating (guests and official party)
- Awards table
- Procession routes
- Honor guard and flag placement
- Brow, if piping over the side within a building

Typical Sequence of Events

This sequence of events assumes a published time of 0900 for the retirement ceremony.

0830: Ushers, escorts, and side boys muster at the designated place for briefing. Stand-by to escort visitors into the area. The master-at-arms assists the sponsor or master of ceremonies with last-minute details. Ensure the reception area is readied, awards table is set up, color guard is prebriefed, video is ready, bell is in place, and still and video photographers are in place.

0840: Master of ceremonies takes position. Official party is in position for entrance. Special guests are in position for entrance.

0900: Prelude music begins. All guests are present and seated. All doors are closed. Escorts seat special guests, including spouse, parents, children, special friends, and so on.

0905: Prelude music terminates. Master of ceremonies announces: "Will the guests please rise for the arrival of the official party and remain standing for the parading of the colors and the playing of our national anthem."

0908: Official party arrives, including the retiree, speaker, guests of honor, and chain of command.

0910: After the official party is in place, "Parade the colors." The national anthem is played (all military salute). "Retire the colors."

0915: Master of ceremonies announces: "Would the guests please be seated." Opening remarks by master of ceremonies and introduction of guest speaker. (Sample remarks follow the suggested sequence of events.)

0920: Guest speaker remarks.

0935: Presentations of awards. Master of ceremonies should introduce each presenter by name and title and provide a very brief explanation of the importance of the award. Generally, any personal award is presented by the commanding officer. Other presentations may be made by the guest speaker with the emcee announcing each award separately.

0945: Presentation of shadow box. The retiree may want a personal friend or a mentor, perhaps a retired chief, to present the shadow box and explain the significance of the items.

0950: Presentation of national ensign. A special flag—one flown over the U.S. Capitol, USS *Arizona* memorial, or the like—should be presented with an explanation by either the guest of honor, a member of the chain of command, or a person of the retiree's choosing. Generally, this role is reserved for an active, reserve, or retired military member.

0955: Going ashore. The master of ceremonies asks the boatswain: "Stand by to pipe the side." (Suggested remarks for this poignant moment follow sample opening remarks.)

Sample Opening Remarks

Good morning, I would like welcome all of you to this special occasion marking the retirement of Chief Lastname. I extend an especially warm welcome to Chief Lastname's good [wife or husband], Firstname, parents, and children. I know that you, more than any of us, are vividly aware of the sacrifices that Chief Lastname has made in the service of our country, and I speak for the entire command when I say how pleased we are to have you here today.

The Navy retirement ceremony is a time honored tradition where we pay tribute to a shipmate and recognize years of dedicated service to our nation and to the freedoms we all enjoy. We are proud to share this with Chief Lastname at the end of his distinguished military career and what we all know will be a prosperous and successful new beginning.

[At this point, cover the highlights of the retiree's career. The biography is in the programs, so it is not necessary to repeat details.]

It gives me great pleasure to introduce the guest speaker for today's ceremony. [Read a very short biography at this point; mention only a couple of items and refer to the program if the biography is published there.]

Sample Going Ashore Remarks

[Spoken formally and with great dignity]

Boatswain: Stand by to pipe the side. [Time-keeper rings the ship's bell.]

This order has been passed on naval ships from the 1500s through today. Spanish, French, English, Dutch. Yes, every Navy in the world has used the boatswain's call and side boys to bring aboard or send ashore its officers, visiting officers, and all visiting dignitaries. The side boys would haul on the ropes and raise or lower the boarding platform so officers would not have to climb the rat lines (which were hanging over the side and used by the enlisted crew) when going ashore or aboard. This honor was extended to visiting officers, dignitaries, and port officials. It was not uncommon for the commanding officer of a ship to order up the jolly boat, a crew of eight strong backs, side boys, and boatswain to send an old shipmate to his shore retirement home, never to sail on naval ships again.

"All hands on deck" was passed, and speeches were made about great victories, battles fought upon the open sea, raging storms weathered, and voyages to distant and strange lands with ports-of-call others only dreamed about. Then, a fine sword, a brace of pistols, a rifle or musket, or maybe a sea chest of fine wood and bound in brass was presented to remind him of crews and ships with which he had served. The boatswain would stand tall the side boys, and the retiree would request permission to go ashore; he stepped to the platform and the side boys would lower away. As the jolly boat pulled away, the gunner would fire a salute from the ship's main battery, and the retiree sat in the stern sheets—going ashore.

In the late 1700s, the U.S. Navy set sail with new ideas, new goals, and a desire to build traditions that would stand the test of time. The U.S. Navy led the way in providing honors for crewmen. The 1800s saw enlisted men holding retirements for enlisted men for the first time. The captain would allow the jolly boat to take the enlisted retiree ashore. After the Civil War, commanding officers began to hold enlisted retirement ceremonies to show the crew that they, and the Navy, recognized the contributions of enlisted crewmen.

Today, our Navy has given most of the pomp and circumstance, the honors, traditions, and ceremonies back to history, because time does not give us the freedom to do these things from the past. Nevertheless, we still have time to stop all engines, lay about smartly, and drop anchor to pay honor to one of our shipmates going ashore. We honor the years served, the guidance, the leadership, the friendship, and the expertise that this shipmate has freely given for years.

Chief Petty Officer Firstname Lastname, USN. Aye, mates, for many years, Chief Lastname has stood the watch. While some of us lay in our bunks at night, Chief Lastname stood the watch. While others of us were attending school, Chief Lastname stood the watch. And yes, even before many of us were born, Chief Lastname stood the watch. As our families watched storm clouds of war building on the horizons of history, Chief Lastname stood the watch.

Though he saw his family ashore, often needing his guidance, he still stood the watch. For [number] years he has stood the watch so that we and our fellow countrymen could sleep soundly, in safety, each night. Today, we are here to say, "Shipmate, the watch stands relieved," relieved by those you have led, guided,

and trained. Chief Lastname, you stand relieved—we have the watch!

Boatswain, stand by to pipe the side.
Shipmate, going ashore!

The retiree stands, faces the senior officer present, and
formally requests permission to go ashore. After an
exchange of salutes, permission is granted, and our shipmate departs across the brow to begin a new, and rewarding, part of life's journey.

A final note: it has become very popular to pipe the side
twice, once for the retiring member and a second time for
the member accompanied by his or her spouse (and occasionally children). In the event this variation is chosen, be
sure that the chief returns by walking around the assembled side boys and not back through them. The piping-
over-the-side conclusion to the ceremony provides the
most valuable photo opportunities. Always remind the
official and unofficial photographers that this is one of the
moments that must be captured. The master of ceremonies can help by adjusting the timing slightly as necessary to allow the photographer to get in place or
restaged, if necessary.

15

History, Heroes, and Leaders

Case Study: Honoring History and Heroes

HMCM Dennis Michael picked up the satellite phone and called his good friend, HMCS Terry Patrick, at the Naval Medical Center, San Diego. "Hey, you old skate, sitting out the war again, I see! It's calmed down a little over here with the 1st Marine Division in southern Iraq," he reported. "Although the 3/1 Marines are still having a little trouble out west of here. But that's not why I called. Have you seen the list yet? I've got almost thirty HM1s who have made chief this time. That's almost unheard of, and it presents a little problem for me. With us being forward deployed and all, how about sending me a care package with some material to get these folks ready for their advancement come 16 September? I need a little information on the history of the CPO community. How about sending me a copy of WO4 Lester Tucker's stuff on the evolution of the rate, huh? And maybe that book *Winds of Change* by JO1 Crist, or that book about chiefs that that old radioman wrote on USS *George Washington* a couple years back? I want these guys over here to know that, as much as they're proud of being with the Fleet Marine Force, they're going to be

Navy chiefs, and I want them to know as much about who they are as they can."

A Brief History of the Chief Petty Officer Rate

How did the unique role of Chief Petty Officers evolve? Unlike other armed forces, only the sea services recognize the E-7 through E-9 communities with special uniforms and separate messing when we don "the hat." Some time ago, retired CWO4 Lester B. Tucker traced the history of the CPO rate in which he had served for many years. He discovered that 1 April 1993 marked the one hundredth anniversary of the creation of the grade, although the title "chief"—used as we use "leading" today—was in use as early as 1776. Gunner Tucker believed the earliest use of the term in the Continental Navy occurred when Jacob Wasbie, a cook's mate serving on board *Alfred,* was promoted to chief cook.

Generally speaking, precedence of petty officers was not really introduced until the mid-1850s. Based upon pay tables of the period, though, one can infer the rating structure of the time. By the end of the Civil War, precedence of rates was rather clear. Naval Regulations read: "Precedence among Petty Officers of the same rate shall be established by the Commanding Officer of the vessel in which they serve." Precedence by rating was a fact of Navy life for the next 105 years and was substantiated by rating priority and the date of an individual's promotion. Ratings in the Seaman Branch took precedence over all others, and those with direct responsibility for sailing, navigating, and fighting the ship had higher precedence than those farther removed from the Navy's core mission. Precedence of ratings remained in effect until 1968, when a single system for military and non-military matters based on pay grade and time in grade was established.

On 8 January 8 1885, the Navy classed all enlisted personnel as first, second, or third class for petty officers, and as seaman first, second, or third class for non-petty officers.

Chief boatswain's mates, chief quartermasters, and chief gunner's mates were positioned at the petty officer first class level within the seaman class; masters-at-arms, apothecaries, yeomen (equipment, paymasters, and engineers), ship's writers, schoolmasters, and band masters were also first class petty officers but came under the Special Branch. Finally, machinists were carried at the top grade within the Artificer Branch. Included under the Special Branch at the second class petty officer level was the rate of chief musician who was junior to the band master; that rate was changed to first musician under the 1893 realignment of ratings and carried as a petty officer first class until 1943.

On 1 April 1893, the day the Chief Petty Officer rate was established, the Navy also gave most enlisted men pay raises. Hoary old chiefs often ask new selectees to find the name of the first Chief Petty Officer. Like carrying steam to the engine room, or winding the dog watch, this is a fool's errand. There was no single first Chief Petty Officer: records documenting the promotions are incomplete, and nearly all ratings carried as petty officers first class from 1885 were automatically shifted to the Chief Petty Officer level. Exceptions were schoolmasters (similar to our current recruit division commanders), who stayed at first class; ship's writers, who stayed the same but expanded to include second and third class; and carpenter's mates, who had been carried as second class petty officers but were extended to include chief, first, second, and third classes. The Chief Petty Officer grade on 1 April 1893 encompassed nine rates:

- Chief Master-at-Arms
- Chief Boatswain's Mate
- Chief Gunner's Mate
- Chief Machinist
- Chief Yeoman
- Chief Carpenter's Mate
- Apothecary
- Chief Quartermaster
- Band Master

Prior to the establishment of the Chief Petty Officer grade, and for many years thereafter, commanding officers could promote petty officers to acting appointments in order to fill vacancies in ships' complements. Men served various lengths of time, usually ranging from six months to a year, under acting appointments. If service was satisfactory, the captain recommended to the Bureau of Navigation (called the Bureau of Personnel or BuPers after 1 October 1942) that an individual be given a permanent appointment for the rate in which he served. Otherwise the commanding officer could reduce an individual to the grade or rate held prior to promotion if he served under an acting appointment. The change in status from acting to permanent appointment was always a breathe-easier occurrence that meant the commanding officer could not reduce a Chief Petty Officer without explanation. Only a court-martial and the bureau's approval could reduce a chief serving under a permanent appointment.

The Chief Petty Officer's status was indicated with PA (permanent appointment) or AA (acting appointment) next to his title. After 8 March 1946, the letter A (acting appointment) was integrated with the rate abbreviation. For example, chief boatswain's mate with an acting appointment was abbreviated CBMA. Pay grade 1-A no longer signified acting appointment for Chief Petty Officers after 1 October 1949, thanks to the Career Compensation Act of 1949. From that time, CPOs received the same pay regardless of whether they held permanent or acting appointments. On 1 November 1965, acting appointments were dropped from use.

A pay differential existed between permanent and acting appointments until 1949. In 1902, monthly pay for Chief Petty Officers ranged from fifty to seventy dollars depending upon the specialty held. CPOs holding permanent appointments dated prior to 1 July 1903, the effective date of General Order 134, were required to requalify by standing an examination before a board of three officers. If they passed, they were issued permanent appointments by the Bureau of Navigation. Those who did not requalify remained in their pay and grade level instead of increasing to the seventy-dollar-a-month level.

Pay levels for enlisted men at that time were established by executive order until an act of 13 May 1908 established that the U.S. Congress would set pay for enlisted men. In 1920, Congress standardized pay at all levels from the lowest non-rated grade, apprentice seaman, through Chief Petty Officer. Monthly base pay for permanent appointment chiefs was $126, and for acting appointments, $99. Amazingly, these pay rates remained effective until 1 June 1942 when the act of 16 June 1942 mandated a pay increase to $138 and $126 for CPOs with permanent and acting appointments, respectively.

The pay grades of E-8 and E-9, senior chief and master chief, were created effective 1 June 1958 by an amendment to the Career Compensation Act of 1949. Eligibility for promotion to E-8, the senior chief level, was restricted to permanent-appointment chiefs with a minimum of four years in grade and a total of ten years of service. For elevation from E-7 to master chief, E-9, a minimum of six years' service as a Chief Petty Officer with a total of thirteen years' service was required. Service-wide examinations for outstanding chiefs were held on 5 August 1958, with the first promotions becoming effective 16 November 1958. A few months later, a second group of chiefs from the February 1959 examinations were elevated to E-8 and E-9 on 16 May 1959. The names of the first two groups of selectees are listed in Bureau of Naval Personnel Notices 1430 of 17 October 1958 and 20 May 1959. After the May 1959 elevations, promotions to E-9 were through senior chief only.

On 1 July 1965, several ratings at the two top grades were compressed, and six new rating titles were created: master chief steam propulsionman, master chief aircraft maintenanceman, master chief avionics technician, master chief precision instrumentman, master chief constructionman, and master chief equipmentman. Master chief steam propulsionman was eliminated just four years later when more rates were expanded, including master and senior chief torpedoman's mate, quartermaster, and storekeeper. Seven ratings were reestablished at the E-8 and E-9 grades, presenting the opportunity for chiefs to again advance within their specialty to E-9. The seven affected ratings were signalman, mineman, aircrew survival equipmentman, aviation storekeeper, aviation maintenance administrationman, and boiler technician.

In 1991, three ratings were merged into one: antisubmarine warfare technician, aviation fire control technician, and aviation electronics technician ratings at the E-3 (apprenticeship) and E-4 through the E-8 petty officer grades were merged into the single rating of aviation electronics technician. At the same time, the rating of avionics maintenance technician (E-9 only) remained as the normal path of advancement from the rates of senior chief aviation electronics technician and senior chief aviation electrician's mate. During the Navy's drawdown of the early- to mid-1990s, the Navy recognized the changing nature of propulsion by merging boiler technicians with machinist's mates. In deference to the great "fire-room pride" associated with the BT rating, the rating badge was authorized for wear until the next promotion or retirement.

The rapid technology changes of the past quarter century were behind the creation of the IT rating, which was formed by merging the relatively young rating of data processing technician and the venerable rating of radioman. A period of transition retained both the radioman name as RM21, shorthand for radioman of the 21st century, and the rating badge. In 1999 the rating name was changed to information systems technician (IT) while retaining the historically significant and still relevant lightening bolts of the old RM rating. In 2003 the signalman and quartermaster ratings were merged, and a similar policy was adopted to ensure that the crossed flags of the SM rating will be seen until the merger is complete.

The current number of ratings of Chief Petty Officers falls far short of the 207 listed at the end of World War II. Only two ratings, boatswain's mate and gunner's mate, have remained in continuous use since 1797. Odds are those quintessential sailors will be around as long as the fleet sails the seas!

The one hundredth anniversary of the CPO rating was an occasion for education and celebration that did much to promote Navy-wide CPO pride and awareness of naval heritage. Centennial CPO dinings-in and other special khaki events were conducted around the world. A CPO ship's bell was cast and presented to the Navy Memorial, where it is displayed and loaned out for use in CPO events. The Navy Memorial in Washington was also the site of a ceremony in which area CPOs placed a memento-filled time capsule in the foundation of the great flagpole flying the national ensign. Nearby is the Lone Sailor statue standing watch. From Naples to Yokosuka and in ships deployed worldwide, CPOs stopped what they were doing and paused to reflect on their good fortune, their heritage, and their responsibilities.

Two years later, in November 1995, the third ship bearing the name USS *Chief* was commissioned. Both previous vessels were named for the "head or leader of a group," but not specifically for the Chief Petty Officer rank or grade. Many World War II minesweepers were given the names of positive qualities or words denoting accomplishments, but by 1995 CPO pride was too great to permit any speculation over the namesake of MCM-12. Four thousand people, a majority of them Chief Petty Officers, both active and retired, were on hand to honor the new ship sharing their name and their pride. Active and retired Chiefs dominated the commissioning committee for USS *Chief*, the last of the Avenger class ships, and there was an all-CPO color guard and a fifty-two-member CPO band from all over the world. Chiefs drove all the courtesy vehicles, and Chiefs did all the ushering. Joining other distinguished guests and speakers on the platform were every living previous master Chief Petty Officer of the Navy (MCPON), as well as the incumbent MCPON, Master Chief Electronics Technician (Surface Warfare) John Hagan. USS *Chief* commemorative coins and ball caps and flags flown over USS *Chief* are in great demand.

The Medal of Honor.
U.S. Navy

The Crest of USS *Chief* (MCM-14) reflects our history and heritage. In traditional Navy blue and gold, a mine in the center of the shield represents the *Chief*'s mine countermeasures mission, and the crossed officer's sword and enlisted cutlass symbolize surface warfare excellence. The fouled Navy anchor, insignia of a Chief Petty Officer, is symbolic of the U.S. Navy's leadership. The three silver stars above the fouled anchor honor the ship's sponsor and all MCPONs, past, present, and future.

"Chief. What a great name for a ship," said Adm. Mike Boorda, Chief of Naval Operations and principal speaker at the 1995 ceremony. "The very name says it all. The best, number one, a winner in every way. Everyone knows the word leadership and the title of chief go together."

Chief Petty Officers and the Medal of Honor

Throughout our history, Chief Petty Officers have led from the front, sometimes making the ultimate sacrifice. Four Chief Petty Officers were awarded the Medal of Honor for their extraordinary bravery in saving and leading countless shipmates during World War II.

Chief Radioman Thomas J. Reeves, U.S. Navy

Chief Tom Reeves was the kind of guy who made sure that his crew got off on liberty before he did. They'd been working on the USS *California* transmitters during the midwatch, and his crew had gotten the last TBS up on line. With a little luck, they'd still have time to catch the liberty launch to the fleet pier in Pearl Harbor on this Sunday morning. Chief Reeves had gotten up early, dressed, and headed off to the radio shack to move things along.

Born in Connecticut in 1895, Reeves served as a reservist during World War I, but enthralled with the new marvel called radio, he returned to active duty as a radioman in 1920. During his two decades of service, Reeves rose through the ranks to become chief radioman of a battleship, the pinnacle of service for a prewar "sparks."

Half the Pacific Fleet was there at Pearl Harbor that morning, and USS *California* lay on Battleship Row, on the west side of Ford Island. Alongside were the battleships *Arizona*, *Maryland*, *Nevada*, *Oklahoma*, *Tennessee*, and *West Virginia*. Monday morning would bring a material inspection, and Chief Reeves was determined that his radio shack would be squared away. Many thought *California* (the "Old Prune Barge") was not fully prepared for war, but Reeves and the other chiefs on board were prepared to prove them wrong.

As the chief was making his way to the radio shack at 0753, an initial wave of nearly two hundred enemy aircraft—divebombers, torpedo bombers, horizontal bombers, and strafing planes—descended upon Pearl Harbor. While chaos reigned all around, the guns of *California* kept firing at the Japanese planes targeting her decks. California was struck on her side by a Japanese torpedo, flooding was intense, and still her anti-aircraft guns kept firing at the Japanese planes circling overhead. Chief Reeves was on the second deck at the moment the first torpedo hit. It was clear to him that *California* was badly damaged; she was taking hits from torpedoes and bombs, was on fire, and the mechanized hoists that distribute ammunition to the large antiaircraft guns were quickly out of commission. But still the guns kept firing.

As the passageway filled with smoke and fire, Tom Reeves took charge and began to manhandle ammunition to the guns. Surrounded by death and destruction, Chief Reeves fearlessly kept the supply of ammunition flowing by passing ammunition by hand up to the gunners. Without any concern for himself, he continued to help keep the big guns firing until smoke inhalation and fire overcame him. Chief Thomas James Reeves died in that passageway, just two days before his forty-sixth birthday.

John Finn was awarded the Medal of Honor for his courage under fire as a Chief Petty Officer at Pearl Harbor on 7 December 1941. *U.S. Navy (PH1 R.J. Oriez)*

Due in large part to his work in keeping the ammunition moving and to the heroic actions of the other *California* Sailors, *California* guns kept firing at the Japanese planes until the ship finally sank into the mud of the harbor. For his extraordinary courage and self-sacrifice in sustaining the flow of ammunition that helped USS *California* keep fighting, Chief Reeves was posthumously promoted to warrant radio electrician and awarded the Medal of Honor, the first Chief Petty Officer to be so honored during World War II. The first, but, sadly, not the last.

Chief Aviation Ordnanceman John W. Finn, U.S. Navy

Not only Sailors afloat were heroes that day. John Finn was a redshirt, an aviation ordnanceman. Born in Los Angeles in 1909, he enlisted into the Navy in July 1926. He completed his basic training in San Diego and was transferred to the ceremonial guard company. In December of that year, he completed general aviation utilities training at Great Lakes. By April 1927, he was stationed at the Naval Air Station North Island, where he gained experience in the wing shop and the aircraft repair division. Shortly afterward, Finn was transferred to the ordnance division, where he worked on antiaircraft gun emplacements. Deployments onboard USS *Lexington*, USS *Houston*, USS *Jason*, USS *Saratoga*, and USS *Cincinnati* followed, and in just nine years, he was promoted to chief aviation ordnanceman. Over the next five years, Chief Finn was stationed with patrol squadrons in Panama, San Diego, and Washington.

On 7 December 1941, Chief Finn was at Kaneohe Bay Naval Air Station. He was in charge of thirty ordnancemen, none of whom had ever faced combat before. That morning, Chief Finn was in his quarters, planning a quiet day with his family. In the distance, he heard the sounds of aircraft, and, shortly thereafter, machine-gun fire. Knowing that he had not ordered any firing that day, he sped to the hangars and ordnance shop, where he was shocked to see Japanese planes flying overhead strafing the airfields. Under fire, Finn ran to the armory and broke out machine guns and ammunition, which he passed out to Sailors. He then set up his own .50-caliber machine gun on an instruction stand in a completely open area of the parking ramp. With only the smoke from the fires raging around him to conceal him, Chief Finn returned fire at the Japanese pilots. Later noting that he was too angry to be scared by the destruction surrounding him, Finn stood his ground. Even though painfully wounded numerous times by bomb shrapnel, shot, and bleeding from his many wounds, he continued to return fire. Reports indicate that he shot down a Japanese plane, although Chief Finn admits that it was probably the combined result from all of the Sailors fighting back.

As the Japanese planes began to withdraw from the area, Sailors began to urge Chief Finn to get medical assistance for his many wounds. Knowing, however, that his experience and leadership were desperately needed during this period, he resisted. It was only after he was ordered to seek help that he consented to first aid. He suffered more than twenty wounds, ranging from minor flesh wounds to shrapnel in his arm, elbow, and chest. After brief treatment, he immediately returned to his post where he supervised the re-arming of the planes that had escaped devastation.

On 15 September 1942, Chief John William Finn was awarded the Medal of Honor for his heroism and dedication in performing his duty after being painfully wounded multiple times. In his remaining years of service in the Navy, he was promoted to ensign and then lieutenant in 1944, retiring shortly thereafter. As this is written, Chief Finn is the oldest living Medal of Honor recipient. He lives in Southern California.

Chief Watertender Peter Tomich, U.S. Navy

Peter Tomich, born Petre Herceg-Tonic in Prolog, a town on the Austria-Hungary border, on 3 June 1893, immigrated to this country in 1913. Like many first-generation Americans, even those from enemy nations, he enlisted in the Army in 1917, becoming a naturalized citizen during his enlistment. Immediately after his discharge from the Army, Tomich reenlisted in the U.S. Navy at the age of twenty-six.

Tomich was initially assigned on board the USS *Litchfield*, a destroyer, and served continuously during his career in the Navy, advancing up the enlisted ratings, until he made chief watertender on 4 June 1930. The watertender rating later evolved into boilerman, and today we'd think of them as machinist's mates. By December 1941, he was regarded as one of the most experienced watertenders in the Pacific Fleet, having served eleven years as a chief.

On 7 December 1941 Chief Watertender Tomich was at his post in the fire room of USS *Utah*, not far from USS *California*. At 0801 on that fateful morning, two torpedoes, seconds apart, pierced the side of *Utah*. Water filled the giant chasm in the side of the ship and began to flood the engineering spaces. Chief Tomich, feeling the ship beginning to lean to its side, ordered his Sailors to evacuate. Certain the ship was going to capsize, Chief Tomich thought only of saving his crew. While his Sailors were evacuating, he maintained his post, and, single-handedly, began securing all the boilers to prevent a massive explosion. Shortly thereafter, *Utah* rolled, trapping Chief Tomich and fifty-seven others on board. By preventing the boilers from exploding, he saved the lives of hundreds of men on board and in the water nearby.

Because of his valor and concern for the lives of others, Chief Peter Tomich was posthumously awarded the Medal of Honor. USS *Tomich* (DE-242) was commissioned and named in his honor in 1943. As his next of kin could not be found, his medal was displayed aboard USS *Tomich* until, after decommissioning of the destroyer escort in 1974, it was presented to the Senior Enlisted Academy at Newport, R.I. The medal holds a place of honor at the academy's Tomich Hall, named for Chief Tomich.

Chief Watertender Oscar Peterson, U.S. Navy

Chief Oscar Peterson, from Prentice, Wis., enlisted as a fireman third class in 1920 at the age of twenty-one. In a career quite similar to that of Chief Tomich, Chief Peterson spent three years on active duty and left the Navy. After five years on the beach, he reenlisted as a fireman second class in 1928. During the next four years, he served on board USS *Moody* and USS *Trevor*, leaving *Trevor* as a watertender second class. As his enlistment was coming to a close, Peterson extended for three more years. In October 1934, he transferred to USS *Pruitt*, where he attained the rating of watertender first class. In February 1941 Peterson was appointed acting chief watertender on board USS *Neceies*. In April 1941, he was transferred to the fleet oiler, USS *Neosho*, where he was permanently appointed chief watertender on 28 February 1942.

Chief Peterson was on board USS *Neosho* on 7 May 1942 when it was attacked by Japanese bombers. *Neosho* had been operating in the South Pacific in support of USS *Yorktown* and USS *Lexington*. Escorted by USS *Sims*, Neosho had been detached from the main body of the fleet when, operating independently, both were spotted by a Japanese aircraft. Both ships faced repeated attacks during the day. Around noon, a large force of Japanese dive-bombers appeared and commenced heavy bombing runs on both ships. *Sims* sank within a half hour of its first direct hit, and *Neosho* was heavily damaged. Intense fires raged aboard the oiler, and Chief Peterson took charge of the repair party.

While others were abandoning ship, Chief Peterson remained aboard to close the bulkhead stop valves, preventing explosion of the fuel aboard. With all of the members of the repair party injured and himself gravely wounded, Chief Peterson ignored the extreme danger and succeeded in closing the valves without assistance. In doing so, Chief Peterson was burned badly. USS *Henley* rescued 109 survivors of *Neosho* on 11 May 1942, due to

Chief Peterson's sacrifice in saving his ship. Chief Peterson died two days later from his burns. He was posthumously awarded the Medal of Honor "for extraordinary courage and conspicuous heroism above and beyond the call of duty while in charge of a repair party during an attack on the U.S.S. *Neosho* by enemy Japanese aerial forces on May 7, 1942."

Leadership of the Enlisted Community

Throughout the war years, Chief Petty Officers were the senior enlisted personnel afloat or ashore. Although it was traditional in the submarine service to identify the most senior chief as "Chief of the Boat," all chiefs served in pay grade E-7 throughout World War II and Korea. At the urging of the Army, Congress authorized pay grades E-8 and E-9 for all services in June 1958. Within the Navy, which had not energetically supported the new pay grades, potential nominees were screened by time-in-grade and time-in-service. CPOs with ten years of service and four years in grade were permitted to test for senior chief, and outstanding Chief Petty Officers with at least thirteen years of service and six years as CPOs were permitted to test for promotion to master chief. Two cadres were promoted, the first in November 1958 and a second group in May 1959. Since that time, the current promotion progression from chief to senior chief to master chief has been in place.

One problem immediately facing the Navy was the definition of roles and responsibilities for the new pay grades, then dubbed "super chiefs," a description not always intended as a compliment. Indeed, for a considerable period of time, the major distinction among rates was the pay increment only. Particularly on the khaki working uniform, the different grades were identified only by one or two very small stars above the traditional fouled anchor; a situation which even today causes consternation to recruits when first determining the proper form of address to a newly introduced Chief Petty Officer. Although there are no recorded instances of senior personnel reporting to their juniors, there was little, if any attempt to immediately identify billets requiring or suggesting assignment of senior personnel. It was not until the mid-1960s that the present custom of addressing E-8 and E-9 personnel as "Senior Chief" or "Master Chief" began to be practiced and gradually came into general usage.

Master Chief Del Black, the first Master Chief Petty Officer of the Navy, once noted, "You'd run into some strange situations out in the fleet. There'd be confusion about seniority. In an aviation squadron, for example, you might have a line chief and maintenance chief. Now the maintenance chief was a Master Chief Petty Officer, but the line chief was only a senior chief, yet he was running the squadron." Realizing the problem, Master Chief Black formed a Navy-wide network of senior enlisted advisors. In the beginning these individuals were selected by fleet, type, and district commanders. By 1969, this worldwide network met with Sailors to resolve local and cross-command problems, while referring those that appeared to have broader implications directly to the MCPON's office. While some, including some very senior officers, complained privately that there seemed to be a separate chain of command developing for enlisted issues, this ad hoc process worked well for several years and is credited with attenuating many of the drug, race, and morale issues that plagued the late-Vietnam and post-Vietnam eras. The lessons learned during this time were valuable in shaping future functional and process changes to the senior enlisted leadership organization.

In 1971, Adm. Elmo "Bud" Zumwalt, at the urging of MCPON Jack Whittet, issued a "Z-gram" formalizing the program, which identified the "best and brightest" as Master Chief Petty Officers of the Command (MCPOC). Twenty-three outstanding Master Chief Petty Officers were identified and assigned to major commands ashore and afloat. To further add credibility to these individuals, the Bureau of Personnel changed the specialty mark within their rating badge and permitted the use of a single large gold star in lieu of their identification as radiomen, torpedomen, or the like. The two small silver stars above the eagle on the chevron also were replaced with small gold stars. These command master chiefs met frequently to develop policy recommendations regarding enlisted issues. These concerns and recommendations would be routed to the CNO via the MCPON, making the senior enlisted, in effect, an advisory board to the senior policymakers of the Navy. Later, Admiral Zumwalt extended the practice to include the senior enlisted representatives of smaller commands, allowing all Sailors to be at least one voice away from direct input to their highest superiors.

Fleet and Force Master Chiefs

In order to streamline the process further, Master Chief Petty Officer of the Navy Bob Walker revised the organization to a fleet, force, and command master chief structure in 1977. That structure, which has proven to be effective and efficient, has remained in place to the present time, with only minor revisions to reflect change in mission and doctrine. OPNAVINST 1306.2D states: "Fleet and Force Master Chiefs stimulate better communication at all levels of command throughout the Department of the Navy. They strengthen the chain of command and foster a better understanding of the needs and viewpoints of the enlisted members and their families. Fleet and Force Master Chiefs are principal enlisted advisors to their respective commanders. They formulate and implement policies concerning morale, welfare, job satisfaction, discipline, utilization, and training of Navy personnel in the discharge of these duties. Fleet and Force Master Chiefs report directly to the commander, working with the internal chain of command as directed by the commander. They also maintain liaison with MCPON and are members of the CNO/MCPON Senior Enlisted Leadership Forum."

In addition, even though the basic function description applies to both, fleet or force master chiefs obviously deal with a much larger community of people and as a result each command will likely have some unique duties and responsibilities. The FMC may be a member of or function in close coordination with the:

- Humanitarian reassignment/hardship discharge screening boards.
- Family services programs, such as family service centers and ombudsmen.
- Human resources management programs.
- Habitability afloat programs.

Selection of a fleet, force, or CNO-directed CMC is based on demonstrated superior leadership qualities and broad management skills. The ability to communicate effectively with seniors and juniors is part of the selection criteria. Only individuals with successful tours as command master chiefs or chiefs of the boat are eligible for selection. Selection to these billets will be in accordance with criteria established by the respective commander and will be made without consideration as to rating, type duty, eligibility, or precedence among contemporaries.

MCPON Walker also realized the need for quick and efficient communication among the now growing command master chief community. A series of newsletters, first called "The Word" and later "The Direct Line," addressed issues that concerned the fleet. MCPON Walker and others soon realized that a chain of communication stretching from his office in Washington to and through the fleet, force, and command master chiefs to the CPO on the deckplates was an important step in strengthening the visible links among the evolving "senior management" of the enlisted community.

A most significant revision to policy took place in the summer of 1978. After a great deal of study and debate within the command master chief community, MCPON Tom Crow persuaded the chief of naval operations to formalize the roles and responsibilities of chiefs, senior chiefs, and master chiefs. Chief Petty Officers would be expected to become the top technical authorities and experts within a particular rating, providing the direct supervision, instruction, and training of the lower rated personnel within his or her skill areas. Senior chiefs would be expected to be the senior technical supervisor within a rating and occupational field, and they would provide the total command with technical expertise. Finally, the Master Chief Petty Officer would provide administrative and managerial leadership on issues involving enlisted personnel, and would be expected to contribute in matters of policy formation as well as implementation across the full spectrum of rates. In practical terms, a chief radioman might be responsible for the ship's transmitter room. A senior chief might be responsible for the entire message center, and a master chief might take responsibility for development and implementation of the ship's communication plan, as well as, perhaps, acting as the leading petty officer for the entire operations department.

The Senior Enlisted Academy

MCPON Crow realized the disruptions that these innovations might cause, and he worked to implement the roles carefully. "Changes which impact the chain of command are ones which provide job satisfaction for the affected personnel and strengthen the organization in such a way as to improve the creditability of both the senior and master chiefs, and the junior officers in the Navy," he wrote. To further solidify the credibility of these new incumbents, Crow proposed and championed the development of a senior enlisted academy at Newport, R.I. "We, the senior enlisted personnel, have continuously asked to be given more responsibilities commensurate with our pay grade and expertise and to be held accountable for our actions," he said, "and future expansion of responsibilities for Senior and Master Chief Petty Officers will be determined by how we react and perform to meet these new challenges." Under the leadership of MCPON Crow, the Senior Enlisted Academy opened in September 1981, and, since that date, has provided upper-level leadership for the Navy's top enlisted.

The Command Master Chief Program

The guidelines concerning the command master chief program were further clarified in February 1986, when all E-9 personnel were made eligible for the program. Command master chief billets began to be formally established in commands that met certain standards (afloat commands with more than 250 enlisted Sailors, for example). Sometime earlier, a CMC detailer had been assigned, and a structured but informal selection process was established inside the enlisted distribution branch of the Navy Personnel Command. With the establishment of a detailer and expansion of the shore billet base for CMCs, provisions were devised for follow-on assignments after completion of an afloat CMC tour.

MCPON Placket led the development of a formal course of instruction for command master chiefs, which was implemented during the term of office of his successor, MCPON Duane Bushey. This first formal training, a week in length and covering a number of topics, was coordinated and facilitated on a regional basis. Twice in the 1990s, MCPON Hagan oversaw major revision to the instruction guiding the CMC program. Major changes included:

- Elimination of the "in-house CMC selection process" and establishment of a structured selection board with a process for the command master chief program, and with a selection board with formal precepts and the same rigor as the command selection board.
- Requiring all command master chiefs to be graduates of the Senior Enlisted Academy. Master chiefs and COBs already serving were required to attend before proceeding to another tour as CMC.
- Establishing minimum experience requirements with respect to previous duty assignments and warfare experiences to ensure the CMC was fully equipped to succeed.

Fleet, Force, CNO-Directed Command, and Command Master Chiefs uphold the highest standards of professionalism and stimulate better communication at all levels of command throughout the Department of the Navy. They strengthen the chain of command by working within it to foster a better understanding of the needs and viewpoints of enlisted members and their families. [They] are the senior enlisted leaders who report directly to their respective commanders/commanding officers. They participate in formulating and implementing policies concerning morale, welfare, job satisfaction, discipline, utilization, and training of Navy enlisted personnel. By reporting directly to their commanders, [they] keep their chain of command aware and informed of sensitive and current issues. To qualify for selection as a CMC, the individual must possess and maintain the following qualities:

- Have demonstrated superior leadership abilities and broad management skills.
- Possess effective communication abilities (oral and written) and proven administrative capabilities.
- Have demonstrated effective personnel counseling.
- Have a sharp military appearance, demeanor, and military bearing and meet all health and physical readiness standards.
- Have an outstanding performance record.
- Be a highly motivated role model for all hands to emulate.
- Have demonstrated active involvement in command Quality of Life initiatives and programs.
- Have strong overall potential to be successful as a CMC.
- Have no trait mark below 3.0 in any area on fitness reports for the last five years. Member must maintain this standard while assigned as a CMC.
- Be able to deal effectively with all levels of the chain of command.

Commander/commanding officer recommendations must certify that the candidate is fit to assume duties as a CMC, paying particular attention to the following factors:

- Physical fitness standards: Member must meet Navy standards and have an active, disciplined personal physical fitness program.

- Medical: Any documented condition that could preclude assignment as, or impair performance of, a prospective CMC.

- Alcohol: Personnel with a documented history of alcohol abuse are considered unsuitable for assignment as a CMC. If successfully treated, with no alcohol involvement for three years, member may be considered for a waiver to participate in the CMC Program.

- Human relations/personal behavior: Personnel with a documented history of human relations problems will be considered unsuitable for assignment as a CMC. Similarly, documented (service or medical record, Enlisted Master File, or Navy Central Registry) personal conduct issues (indebtedness, alcohol, substantiated or unresolved family advocacy, etc.) in the past three years will be considered disqualifying.

- SEA: Attendance at the Navy Senior Enlisted Academy (SEA) is required prior to reporting as a Primary Duty CMC or COB. Master chiefs having prior assignments to a Primary Duty CMC or COB billet, but who have not previously attended the SEA, will be assigned to attend the SEA prior to their next assignment in a Primary Duty CMC or COB billet.

(From a December 2000 Navy directive regarding key enlisted leadership roles.)

Master Chief Petty Officer of the Navy

"No matter what we think is the realty of a situation, there is probably another reality on the deck plates, and our people need and deserve leaders who know what that reality is. The Master Chief Petty Officer of the Navy is chartered to observe and act, not to supersede the regular chain of command, but to strengthen it and make it work better. His or hers are the experienced eyes that can see the reality of the deck plates. Indeed, he is the pulse-taker of the command."

Admiral C. A. H. Trost, U.S. Navy
Chief of Naval Operations, 1986–90
On the occasion of the MCPON change of office
9 September 1988

It was inevitable that the office of Master Chief Petty Officer of the Navy—once called, for a very short period, the Senior Enlisted Advisor—would eventually be created. The Marine Corps established a billet for a Sergeant Major of the Marine Corps in 1957, and the Army followed suit in 1966. Congressmen saw value in creating a position for a senior enlisted member who could act as a representative of a large, previously untapped contingency, and, in 1967, reluctantly bowing to both congressional and internal pressure, the Navy established the office as part of the personal staff of the chief of naval operations.

Master Chief Gunner's Mate Delbert D. Black, U.S. Navy

First Master Chief Petty Officer of the Navy, 1967–71

Chief Gunner's Mate Delbert D. Black, a decorated World War II veteran, who had been awarded eight combat ribbons and who survived the attack on USS *Maryland* at Pearl Harbor, was selected to be the first Master Chief Petty Officer of the Navy. When MCPON Black assumed office in January 1967, not every senior officer agreed with the concept of a single spokesman for enlisted concerns. Indeed, during his time in office, MCPON Black met with CNO Adm. David McDonald only once. McDonald's successor, Adm. Tom Moorer, however, quickly realized the value of the office and the particular skill and personality that Del Black brought to the position. They traveled together extensively and addressed the important issues of the day, including very low morale, high attrition rates among first-term enlistees, low retention rates among career personnel, and high absenteeism and desertion rates. MCPON Black was instrumental in implementing changes that helped attenuate these high attrition rates, and, indeed, credits these innovations as being among his most important contributions while holding the highest enlisted office.

After retiring from the Navy, MCPON Black pursued a short but highly successful career in real estate sales and development before fully retiring. He and his wife, Ima, a WWII WAVE, traveled extensively and never passed up an opportunity to participate in Navy events or just to visit with Sailors. At his death in May 2000, MCPON Black was probably better known to Sailors around the Navy than when he served as MCPON. His genuine love for the Navy and unique ability to adapt to the changing times and relate to young Sailors, old salts, and senior officers alike made him a beloved mentor to thousands. MCPON Black was interred in Arlington National Cemetery with full military honors, and a large contingent of Chief Petty Officers marched in his funeral procession.

Master Chief Aircraft Maintenanceman John (Jack) D. Whittet, U.S. Navy

Master Chief Petty Officer of the Navy, 1971–75

MCPON Whittet served in a tumultuous period marked by drastic changes implemented by then-CNO Elmo "Bud" Zumwalt. Just seventeen when he left home, he won his combat aircrewman wings and flew thirty-one missions during World War II from the carriers *Lexington* and *Anzio*. Later, during the Korean War, he sailed aboard *Bon Homme Richard* with Carrier Air Group 102, flying combat air strikes against the North Koreans.

During his term as MCPON, the enlisted "crackerjack" uniform was replaced with a double-breasted suit for all Sailors; a radical innovation not universally appreciated— and one that was reversed a decade later. Operational tempo increased during his time in office, particularly in Southeast Asia and the Seventh Fleet areas of operations, and he is credited with strengthening the concept of fleet, force, and command master chiefs initiated by his predecessor. He successfully managed the transition from a drafted force to a volunteer force, and he walked a fine line between those who advocated and those who resisted change in the Navy's cultural focus. He worked tirelessly to reduce racial strife at sea and ashore, and he helped implement the Navy's zero-tolerance policies toward drug use.

After his retirement in 1975, MCPON Whittet went into business in the San Diego area for several years before losing his life in a recreational diving accident. MCPON Whittet's widow, Helen, often represents him at special events such as the commissioning of USS *Chief* in 1995.

Master Chief Operations Specialist Robert J. Walker, U.S. Navy

Master Chief Petty Officer of the Navy, 1975–79

MCPON Walker's tenure was an echo of an earlier, more disciplined military era. Clean-cut and close-shaven, he soon realized that he could not change the liberal grooming standards of the day. Standards had been generally neglected over a period of several years, and it fell to MCPON Bob Walker to vigorously enforce traditional grooming guidelines for both male and female enlisted personnel. In addition, often-overlooked body fat standards were reconstituted and vigorously enforced. He was relentless in his messages to the chiefs: quit complaining that someone has diminished your authority, stand up and act like Chief Petty Officers.

MCPON Walker energetically supported off-duty educational programs, realizing that in an all-volunteer force the ability to continue one's education was a prime motivator for recruiting and retention. In one small but enormously significant directive, he urged the Navy to drop the traditional forms of reference for enlisted personnel (addressed by last name only) and substituted rating titles such as Seaman Smith or Petty Officer Jones. He was firm in his support of the introduction of surface warfare qualifications for enlisted personnel, which eventually expanded to include aviation, Seabee, and other enlisted warfare qualifications. During his term of office, sea pay imminent danger and other specialty payments were markedly improved, vastly improving morale of Sailors and their families. Since his retirement, MCPON Walker has been involved in a variety of successful business pursuits. He and his wife, Fran, reside in Virginia Beach and participate regularly in Navy events worldwide.

Master Chief Aircraft Maintenanceman
Thomas S. Crow, U.S. Navy

Master Chief Petty Officer of the Navy, 1979–82

"We were having some very serious problems with race relations in the early 1970s," MCPON Crow said. "Equal opportunity was an issue. We were having problems dealing with different races and cultures. I prided myself in being a person who takes people as they are. A good person is a good person, and I really don't care what race or culture they come from. I felt the impact of what I thought were some very racist, sexist kinds of things going on during that time. The Navy was looking for people to work in the area of human resources, so I volunteered. Based on my experiences as force master chief and from watching Bob Walker, I felt that I needed to be out in the fleet. I asked how much access I would have to the CNO, and he answered as much as I needed."

MCPON Crow fought for responsible compensation for enlisted personnel, including increases in allowances for quarters and family support. While he was MCPON, the public became aware that many junior enlisted personnel were eligible for welfare payments, a circumstance Crow and others thought shameful and scandalous. He worked tirelessly on issues concerning habitability of ships and stations and on issues that directly impacted on the quality of life of Sailors at sea and ashore. He had particular interest in seeing that Sailors registered to vote and exercised their franchise, realizing that the voting block of active enlisted personnel would have an impact on those who controlled military budgets. He was interested in continuing the development of senior enlisted personnel, particularly Chief Petty Officers and above, and he was MCPON when the Senior Enlisted Academy opened at Newport, R.I.

Upon his retirement, MCPON Crow pursued a second career in industry as a human resource specialist for McDonnell Douglas in San Diego, retiring as the HR manager in 1995 to work for a time as a lead instructor in Navy senior leadership courses. Fully retired now,

MCPON Crow and his wife, Carol, are frequent participants in Navy events in San Diego.

Master Chief Avionics Technician (Air Crew)
Billy C. Sanders, U.S. Navy

Master Chief Petty Officer of the Navy, 1982–85

MCPON Sanders assumed office on 1 October 1982. During
his tenure as Master Chief Petty Officer of the Navy,
Sanders continued the emphasis on Sailors exercising their
right to vote, and he spoke frequently before congressional
committees alongside his colleagues from the other armed
services. His was generally a time of stability on the human
relations front, although it was during his term that the
Navy reversed its decision regarding the traditional "Sailor
suit," and reintroduced the "crackerjack" uniform for all
personnel E-6 and below. Beards—which had been introduced yet again—were once more banned, and Sanders
urged all senior enlisted personnel to enforce not only the
letter of the law regarding uniform regulations and weight
and grooming standards, but to reflect the spirit of the rules
as well. He continued the emphasis on senior enlisted leadership and championed a return of the Chief Petty Officer
community to its traditional role as the trainers of junior
enlisted personnel and junior officers.

After retiring, MCPON Sanders settled in Pensacola,
Fla., where he still works as the public affairs officer for the
Naval Aviation Museum aboard Naval Air Station,
Pensacola. He was instrumental in a new exhibit that
opened in 1997 showcasing enlisted pilots and naval air-
crewman.

Master Chief Radioman (Surface Warfare)
William H. Plackett, U.S. Navy

Master Chief Petty Officer of the Navy, 1985–88

MCPON Plackett was the first to be groomed for the office
as a fleet master chief. He served first as force master

chief for commander, Training Command, Atlantic, and then as Atlantic Fleet master chief. He helped strengthen the Navy family image through work with family service centers, ombudsmen, and command master chiefs. Educated by the Navy through the Associate Degree Completion Program (ADCOP), he pushed other Sailors to set high educational goals. He was a strong advocate of the Leadership Management Education Training Program and guided it toward the more compressed naval leadership system that he implemented during his term of office. He set and met eight goals during his time in office including enhancement of the "One Navy" concept involving cooperation and communication across warfare lines; maintenance of currency in attitudes and issues in the fleet and the naval shore establishment, and identifi-cation of problem areas affecting welfare and morale of the Navy; improved dissemination of information on per-sonnel-related matters down to the deckplates; placement of the command master chief program on firm footing; and enforcement of the Navy's drug/alcohol program.

During his term of office, he vigorously supported lead-ership training for all levels in the service, and he suc-cessfully navigated the changes involved with women going to sea for the first time in previously closed ratings, steps that led to the highly gender-integrated Navy we know today. Upon retiring from the Navy, MCPON Plackett worked in several businesses for a decade before retiring again in 1999. He and his wife, Karen, live in Virginia Beach and are actively involved in Tidewater Navy activities and their community.

Master Chief Avionics Technician (Air Warfare) Duane R. Bushey, U.S. Navy

Master Chief Petty Officer of the Navy, 1988–92

MCPON Duane Bushey served in a number of aviation-related billets before being named the CINCPACFLT Shore Sailor of the Year for 1973. Leaving the West Coast in 1973 for Norfolk, Va., he was assigned to Aircraft Ferry

Squadron Thirty-one, where he qualified as an overwater navigator in several aircraft, a flight engineer for the P-3 Orion, and a bombardier and navigator for the A-6 Intruder. He accumulated 4,283 flight hours and 844,506 "stork" miles as an enlisted navigator. A strong believer in community involvement, he encouraged his Sailors to volunteer their services during off-duty hours. In 1988, he and his family were recognized as Tidewater's Family of the Year.

On 17 June 1988, CNO Adm. Carlisle A. H. Trost announced that he had selected Bushey to be the seventh Master Chief Petty Officer of the Navy. During his time in office, MCPON Bushey began the process that resulted in the development of the "Journey into the CPO Mess," and he fought successfully to control many of the excesses that had plagued the initiation process. He worked closely with the leaders of the other services to ensure an orderly and humane introduction of the concept of high-year tenure, whereby long service personnel who had been unable to advance in rating were encouraged and assisted in their transition back to civilian life. Bushey participated in the planning for the force structure's downsizing, ensuring that Navy leadership and personnel planners fully anticipated potential negative impacts on the individual Sailor. He urged the development of additional remediation programs for Sailors with basic educational deficiencies, and it was through his efforts and those of others that, at the time of the Persian Gulf War, the Navy was adequately staffed and exceptionally well motivated to carry out the nation's policy under arduous and dangerous conditions.

Upon retirement, MCPON Bushey returned to college to earn a degree in education and is currently achieving great success as a vocational technical teacher in a Norfolk public high school. He holds a national office in a professional organization for vocational technical teachers, and his students consistently achieve superior grades in inter-school competitions.

Master Chief Electronics Technician (SW) John Hagan, U.S. Navy

Master Chief Petty Officer of the Navy, 1992–98

One of the co-authors of this guidebook, John Hagan, was born in Luton, England, on 20 May 1946. He was reared and attended schools in Asheville, N.C. After enlisting in the Navy in December 1964 and attending basic training at Recruit Training Center, San Diego, Hagan's assignments included USS *Lester* (DE-1022), UDT-21 home-ported at Little Creek, Va., USS *Richmond K. Turner* (CG-20), USS *Philippine Sea* (CG-58), and HSL 48, as well as tours at NAS Whidbey Island, Naval Reserve Center Louisville, Ky., and Chief of Naval Technical Training Force Master Chief.

Selected as the eighth MCPON by Adm. Frank Kelso in 1992, Hagan served under three CNOs: Adm. Frank Kelso, Adm. Mike Boorda, and Adm. Jay Johnson. After Admiral Boorda's untimely and tragic death, and at the specific request of the new CNO, Hagan served an extended tour as MCPON and has the distinction of being the longest serving Master Chief Petty Officer of the Navy. His tenure was a turbulent time for the Navy. Downsizing, planned quietly in the years earlier, was executed with a variety of unprecedented personnel actions, some of them harsh. Selective fifteen-year early retirement boards, strict enforcement of newly lowered High Year Tenure (HYT) points, forced rating conversions, and many other similar actions were necessary to reach the smaller Navy size directed by law, while ensuring a minimally acceptable advancement rate and maintaining faith with the force to retain the best Sailors possible for the career force.

Congressional oversight of the drawdown and special interest in several areas gave Hagan more than forty opportunities to testify before congressional committees in his nearly six-year tour as MCPON. He took full advantage of these opportunities to promote resolution of the most pressing inequities in the compensation system including getting single BAQs for single Sailors serving in ships and the expansion of interactive PACE courses to all ships and deploying squadrons.

Hagan put considerable effort into raising the consistency of senior enlisted compliance with all standards, emphasizing that leading from the front required a special personal accountability in the areas of physical fitness, warfare qualifications, and personal conduct. He continued the work of previous MCPONs in improving the viability of the CMC program, and he deleted all references to "senior enlisted advisor" in favor of "senior enlisted leader." He made unprecedented use of "Direct Line," increasing its distribution by mailing it directly to more than five thousand Navy commands worldwide and making it available on line for the first time. He campaigned tirelessly to promote a greater appreciation of naval history, heritage, and tradition and instituted a CPO-required reading list associated with CPO Initiation Season. Defining CPO initiation as a "Season of Pride," MCPON Hagan increased sponsor oversight, instituted mandatory group PT and other team building activities, and instituted naval heritage reading as a requirement for every CPO selectee. MCPON Hagan has been awarded the Distinguished Service Medal, Meritorious Service Medal, Navy Commendation Medal, and various unit and campaign awards.

Since retirement Hagan has worked in Human Systems Integration (HSI) and is currently leading the HSI effort on the DD(X) design program. He and his wife, Cathy, live in Marshall, Va.

Master Chief Machinist's Mate (SS/SW/AW) James Herdt, U.S. Navy

Master Chief Petty Officer of the Navy, 1998–2002

Jim Herdt, a native of Casper Wy., first enlisted in 1966. After attending machinist's mate "A" School in Great

Lakes, Ill., and various nuclear power training schools, he soon served sea tours aboard USS *Independence* (CV-62) and USS *Will Rogers* (SSBN-659G), and shore tours at Nuclear Power Training Unit, Windsor, Conn., and Radiological Repair Facility in New London, Conn. After leaving active duty in 1974, Master Chief Herdt enlisted in the Naval Reserve and served in various selected Naval Reserve units while attending Kansas State University.

In 1976, he served as a Naval Reserve recruiter in Milwaukee, and in 1978 he returned to active duty. Master Chief Herdt served aboard USS *Texas* (CGN-39), USS *Cincinnati* (SSN-693), and on the staff of the Nuclear Power School in Orlando, Fla., prior to his tour as chief of the boat on board USS *Skipjack* (SSN-585). He has served as command master chief at Nuclear Field "A" School, Orlando, Fla., on board USS *Theodore Roosevelt* (CVN-71), and at Naval Training Center, Great Lakes, Ill. He is a graduate of both the U.S. Army Sergeants Major Academy and of the Navy's Senior Enlisted Academy at Newport R.I. He earned a master of business administration degree with a concentration in human resources management from Florida Institute of Technology.

MCPON Herdt qualified as an enlisted aviation and surface warfare specialist, and he qualified to wear the enlisted submarine breast insignia. Master Chief Herdt also certified as a master training specialist. He relieved John Hagan as Master Chief of the Navy in March 1998. Master Chief Herdt served at a time when the nation faced the challenges of asymmetrical threats, greatly increased operational tempo with a down-sized force and aging fleet, and, for at least the first half of his tour of duty, a presidential administration many believed did not understand the military. His personal awards include the Distinguished Service Medal, Meritorious Service Medal with two Gold Stars, the Navy Commendation Medal, the Navy Achievement Medal with Gold Star and various campaign and unit awards.

Upon retirement MCPON Herdt began a career in defense industry consulting work. He and his wife, Sharon, make their home in Pensacola, Fla.

Master Chief Petty Officer of the Navy Terry Scott continues the traditions set by his predecessors and travels throughout the fleet listening to Sailors' concerns.
U.S. Navy (PH1 William R. Goodwin)

Master Chief Missile Technician Terry Scott, U.S. Navy

Master Chief Petty Officer of the Navy, 2002–

Born in Buffalo, Mo., and raised in Louisburg, Kans., Master Chief Scott enlisted under the delayed entry program in December 1976. He completed basic training in October 1977 and went on to attend Basic Submarine School and Missile Technician "A" and "C" schools. In 1983 he completed instructor training in Norfolk, Va. He graduated with academic honors from the U.S. Navy Senior Enlisted Academy in Newport, R.I., in 1990. He has a bachelor of science degree from Southern Illinois University.

Master Chief Scott has served aboard the ballistic missile submarines USS *John Adams* (SSBN-620) and USS *James Madison* (SSBN-627) as missile division Leading Chief Petty Officer. He was chief of the boat aboard the fast-attack submarine, USS *Jacksonville* (SSN-699), and he served as command master chief of Strike Fighter Squadron 192 (VFA-192) based in Atsugi, Japan, and deployed aboard USS *Independence* (CV-62) and USS *Kitty Hawk* (CV-63). During his career he completed a total of fifteen deployments and patrols to the Arabian Gulf, the western Pacific, North Atlantic, and Mediterranean.

Ashore, Master Chief Scott served as an advanced missile flight theory and checkout instructor for the Poseidon and Trident missiles at the Fleet Ballistic Missile Submarine Training Center, Charleston, S.C., where he earned his designation as a master training specialist. He later served at the forward-deployed SSBN base in Holy Loch, Scotland, assigned to commander, Submarine Squadron 14, embarked in USS *Simon Lake* (AS-33) as the squadron missile technician. He also served as the senior enlisted nuclear weapons technical inspector and department Leading Chief Petty Officer, commander, Submarine Force, U.S. Atlantic Fleet.

Master Chief Scott's first ashore command senior enlisted billet was as base command master chief at Naval Security Group Activity, Winter Harbor. In November 2000, he was selected to serve as the CNO-directed CMC for Naval Forces Central Command and Fifth Fleet during Operation Enduring Freedom. He became the tenth Master Chief Petty Officer of the Navy on 22 April 2002.

His personal awards include the Legion of Merit, Meritorious Service Medal, Navy Commendation Medal (five awards), Navy Achievement Medal (four awards), and various service and campaign awards.

Gunner's mates, radiomen, radarmen, electronics technicians. All were newly advanced chiefs once. As they stood to receive their anchors, who among them knew what the future held? Who among us knows what the future holds? Somewhere, a future MCPON is holding this book in his or her hands right now. Is it you?

Appendix A

A Quick
Correspondence "Gouge"

5216
N13
1 Jan 97

From: Author, USNI Textbook
To: Navy and Marine Corps Officers (All Codes)

Subj: HOW TO COMPOSE THE STANDARD NAVAL LETTER

Ref: (a) SECNAVINST 5216.5D, Dept. of the Navy Correspondence
      Manual

1. Follow reference (a)'s superb advice: *Jump right in* with the main point in a *brief* opening paragraph.

2. Putting your chief request or conclusion somewhere in the opening three or four lines helps get the attention of the right people from the very first. As reference (a) puts it,

> When you write a letter, think about the one sentence you would keep if you could keep only one. Many letters are short and simple enough to have such a key sentence. It should appear by the end of the first paragraph. The strongest letter highlights the main point in a one-sentence paragraph at the very beginning. Put requests <u>before</u> justifications, answers <u>before</u> explanations, conclusions <u>before</u> discussions, summaries <u>before</u> details, and the general <u>before</u> the specific.

3. After the opening, spell out the details. Write in relatively brief paragraphs—normally no more than four or five sentences apiece. Writing short paragraphs and punctuating them by white space makes reading easier; long paragraphs can discourage the reader and encourage skimming.

4. Keep most letters down to a single page. Try using enclosures to spell out additional material, if more than a page is necessary. In longer letters use headings to keep the reader oriented and to help in ready reference (see paragraph 6, below).

5. Use the standard naval letter to correspond with DOD activities, primarily, but also with the Coast Guard and some contractors. Send business letters to other external addressees. Of course, before you even write the letter, <u>make sure some other means won't suffice</u>. Telephone calls documented by memos for record or e-mail messages can often take the place of formal correspondence.

6. Follow this additional guidance:

a. <u>Show Codes and Titles in Addresses</u>. Whenever practical, indicate the office that will act on your letter by including a code or person's title in parentheses right after the activity's name.

b. <u>Compose a Good Subject Line</u>. Craft the subject line to make it genuinely informative. Try to limit it to 10 words or less. In a reply, normally make the subject line the same as that of the incoming letter.

c. <u>Make Pen and Ink Changes</u>. Rarely redo correspondence already in final form just for a rare typo, an omitted word, or other minor error. Unless the importance of the subject or addressee justifies the time of retyping, make neat pen and ink changes—up to two per page, and to all copies—and send the correspondence on. This advice holds for word processing as well as typing. Although some features of word processors (like spell-checkers) can help you avoid errors in the first place, making minor changes with word-processing equipment still takes time and can also introduce unnoticed errors in pagination or spacing.

d. <u>Reply Promptly</u>. Answer most received correspondence within 10 days. If you don't anticipate being able to answer within that time, inform your correspondent of the expected delay (by phone, if possible).

e. <u>Get All the Other Details Right</u>. See reference (a) for further details as to standard-letter format, window-envelope format, markings on classified letters, and joint letters.

7. Include your phone and fax numbers and e-mail address when your correspondence might prompt a reply or inquiry, and make sure you include your own office code. Use no complimentary close ("Sincerely," etc.) on a standard naval letter. For rules on signatures (on who signs the letter, on "by direction" authority, on how to put together a signature block, etc.), see reference (a).

R. E. SHENK

Copy to:
USS ALLHANDS (NAV 1)

POINT PAPER

Rank and Name
Staff Code, Phone Number
12 Dec 96

Subj: USE OF POINT PAPERS

BACKGROUND (or PROBLEM)

Point papers are a good means of stating background, ideas, and recommendations in a relatively formal way for the consideration of the command. Use a point paper primarily to direct the attention of seniors to an issue or problem and to seek a solution.

DISCUSSION

• Keep to **one page** in most cases; use tabs for additional material.

• Be factual and objective.

• Keep the language simple. Explain all technical terms or unfamiliar acronyms the first time you use them.

• Don't make the point paper so detailed that significant points are lost in minutiae.

• Indicate who concurs or does not concur.

• For classified papers, follow markings found in Correspondence Manual.

RECOMMENDATION(S)

• State recommended actions. Be brief but specific, outlining who, when, where, how much, etc. List options, if desirable, but always make your choice clear among them.

MEMORANDUM   10 January 1997

From: Writer's name, title or code
To: Reader's name, title or code

Subj: KEY POINTS ABOUT WRITING AN INFORMAL MEMO

1. <u>Plan Ahead</u>. Whether using a preprinted form or this plain-paper memorandum, don't write thoughtlessly. Always plan out a memo; at least jot down a few points and then organize them before writing. On complicated matters, write up a full outline. A few seconds spent in planning will help make the writing go quickly and the correspondence be effective.

2. <u>Get to the Point Quickly</u>. Craft the subject line to state the essential matter briefly, and elaborate on your main point in the first paragraph. Normally, keep your memo to one page.

3. <u>Remember Your Audience; Watch Tone</u>. Figure out, in light of your audience and purpose, what tone to adopt. Tone can be especially important in informal memos because memos are often very personal.

4. <u>Use Formatting as Needed</u>. Formatting helps in memos as in many other kinds of writing. Examples of such formatting include:

   a. Lists (in a, b, c order or in bullets).
   b. Headings (as in this memo).
   c. Occasional <u>underlining</u>, *italics*, **boldface**, or ALL CAPS.

5. <u>Remember These Shortcuts</u>. Very informal memos can be penned, and you need not keep a file copy if the matter is insignificant or short-lived. You can sign a memorandum without an authority line.

T. X. AUTHOR

An Informal Letter of Commendation. An officer in charge commends a sailor freshly and naturally.

DEPARTMENT OF THE NAVY
U. S. NAVY PERSONNEL SUPPORT ACTIVITY DETACHMENT
MISAWA, JAPAN
APO SAN FRANCISCO 96519-0006

1650
Ser 00/841
30 Sep 87

From: Officer in Charge, U.S. Navy Personnel Support Activity Detachment, Misawa
To: PN1 ______ _. _________, USN

Subj: LETTER OF COMMENDATION

1. With great pleasure I commend you on your selection as U.S. Navy Personnel Support Activity Detachment, Misawa's Sailor of the Quarter from 1 July to 30 September 1987.

2. The professional and personal traits that have led to your distinction are numerous. Above all, you have managed busy, pressure-filled days with maturity and grace, and used quieter times to find innovative ways to improve efficiency. As the man "on the front line," you often provide the first impression customers develop about PERSUPPDET Misawa. Customers consistently comment on their appreciation for your outstanding courtesy and patience, and their respect for your professional advice, information, and quick actions on their behalf. Your attention to detail is daily evident in the reports and messages you prepare without discrepancies. You have shown great initiative in designing new ways to improve reporting procedures and keep communication flowing well within the detachment.

3. Your unflagging professionalism has been an inspiration to us all. Well done!

A Letter of Appreciation. This brief letter does well at praising a team of Marines.

DEPARTMENT OF THE NAVY

COMMANDER NAVAL SURFACE FORCE
UNITED STATES ATLANTIC FLEET
NORFOLK, VIRGINIA 23511-6292

1650
Ser 00W/00193
11 Jan 88

From: Commander, Naval Surface Force, U.S. Atlantic Fleet
To: Commanding Officer, Marine Corps Security Force Battalion
Via: Commander, Naval Base Norfolk

Subj: LETTER OF APPRECIATION

1.   The performance of the saluting battery during the
COMNAVSURFLANT Change of Command ceremony on 30 December 1987
was marked by cooperation and professionalism. The battery's
performance and crisp military bearing made this group perfect
representatives of the Marine Corps during this important
ceremony. Many remarks were made on their impressive performance.

2.   Please convey to Corporal _____ and the battery a job
well done.

Message Guidance. This message outlines key guidance for all naval messages.

```
R 151001Z JAN 97

FM   TEXT AUTHOR//N1//
TO       NAVAL PERSONNEL//JJJ//
         MARINE CORPS PERSONNEL//JJJ//

INFO  CIVILIAN DON PERSONNEL//JJJ//

UNCLAS  //N01000//

MSGID/GENADMIN/TEXTAUTHOR  N1//

SUBJ/PREPARATION OF STANDARD NAVAL MESSAGE//
```

RMKS/1.   MSG CIRCUITS ARE OFTEN TIED UP, ESP DURING CRISES.   IN HIGH TEMPO OPS OR DURING COMBAT,.. EVERY PRECEDENCE IS AT LEAST IMMEDIATE, AND FLASH MSGS CAN TAKE OVER AN HOUR TO TRANSMIT.   MSGS ARE ALSO EXPENSIVE. LIMIT NAVAL MSGS TO URGENT COMMS THAT CANNOT REPEAT CANNOT BE HANDLED BY OTHER MEANS.

2.   MAKE USE OF EMAIL, FAX, PHONE, AND MAIL TO EXTENT POSSIBLE, ESP WHEN COORDINATING W/STAFFS.   EVEN AT SEA, EVEN OVERSEAS YOU CAN OFTEN SEND/RCV EMAIL (VIA SALTS, ETC).

3.   ALSO LIMIT MSG SIZE.   CUT OUT UNNEEDED WORDS, AND FREELY USE ABBREVS.   PRETEND EACH WORD COSTS A DOLLAR, AND HONE TEXT.   CUT PAGES, PARAS, SENTENCES, WORDS, EVEN LTRS.

4.   DON'T BURY ACTION.   FIVE PAGE MSGS WITH ACTION AT END, THOUGH COMMON, ARE COUNTERPRODUCTIVE.   PUT ACTION UP FRONT, AND USE SUBJ LINE AS TITLE, NOT JUST ROUTING DEVICE.

5.   PRACTICE ART OF MSG WRITING.   WATCH HOW CO, XO, CSO WRITE MSGS, HOW THEY EDIT YOURS.   NOTICE POLITICS OF MSGS, IMAGE PUT ACROSS, TONE, PROTOCOL, EFFECTIVENESS ABOVE ALL. LEARN TO GET THE MSG THRU.

BT

Appendix B

The Story of the Navy Hymm "Eternal Father"

The song known to U.S. Navy men and women as the "Navy Hymn" is a musical benediction that long has had a special appeal to seafaring men, particularly in the American Navy and the Royal Navies of the British Commonwealth, and which in more recent years has become a part of French naval tradition.

The original words were written as a hymn by a schoolmaster and clergyman of the Church of England, the Rev. William Whiting. Reverend Whiting (1825–78) resided on the English coast and had once survived a furious storm in the Mediterranean. His experiences inspired him to pen the ode, "Eternal Father, Strong to Save." In the following year, 1861, the words were adapted to music by another English clergyman, the Rev. John B. Dykes (1823–76), who had originally written the music as "Melita" (the ancient name for the Mediterranean island of Malta). Reverend Dykes's name may be recognized as that of the composer given credit for the music to many other well-known hymns, including "Holy, Holy, Holy," "Lead, Kindly Light," "Jesus, Lover of My Soul," and "Nearer, My God to Thee."

In the United States in 1879, Rear Adm. Charles Jackson Train, an 1865 graduate of the United States Naval Academy at Annapolis, was a lieutenant commander stationed at the Academy in charge of the Midshipman Choir. In that year, Lieutenant Commander Train inaugurated the present practice of concluding each Sunday's Divine Services at the Academy with the singing of the first verse of this hymn.

The hymn, entitled "Eternal Father, Strong to Save," is found in most Protestant Hymnals. It can be more easily located in these hymnals by consulting the "Index to First Lines" under "Eternal Father, Strong to Save." The words have been changed several times since the original hymn by Reverend Whiting was first published in 1860–61. One will find that the verses as now published differ from the original primarily in the choice of one or two words in several lines of each verse. However, inasmuch as it is not known whether the original words are now available in a hymnal, those original words are given below:

Eternal Father, Strong to save,
Whose arm hath bound the restless wave,
Who bid'st the mighty Ocean deep
Its own appointed limits keep;
hear us when we cry to thee,
for those in peril on the sea.

Christ! Whose voice the waters heard
And hushed their raging at Thy word,
Who walked'st on the foaming deep,
and calm amidst its rage didst sleep;
Oh hear us when we cry to Thee
For those in peril on the sea!

Most Holy spirit! Who didst brood
Upon the chaos dark and rude,
And bid its angry tumult cease,
And give, for wild confusion, peace;
Oh, hear us when we cry to Thee
For those in peril on the sea!

Trinity of love and power!
Our brethren shield in danger's hour;
From rock and tempest, fire and foe,
Protect them wheresoe'er they go;
Thus evermore shall rise to Thee,
Glad hymns of praise from land and sea.

It will be noted that in the hymnal of the Protestant Episcopal Church (1940), the second and third verses of the hymn are different from those second and third verses published elsewhere. These substitutions give recognition to changing aspects of our culture, particularly the advent of additional modes of transportation—the automobile and the airplane. The Episcopal second and third verses are:

Christ, the Lord of hill and plain
O'er which our traffic runs amain,
by mountain pass or valley low,
Wherever Lord thy brethren go;
Protect them by Thy guardian hand
From every peril on the land.

Spirit, Whom the Father send
To spread abroad the Firmament;
wind of heaven, by Thy Might,
Save all who dare the eagle's flight;
And keep them by Thy watchful care
From every peril in the air.

The Presbyterian Church, USA, likewise has added a new verse that recognizes the advent of the field of aviation. The best information available indicates that this new verse to "Eternal Father, Strong to Save" appeared in 1943 in a little booklet then entitled, "A Book of Worship and Devotion for the Armed Forces," published by the Board of Christian Education of the Presbyterian Church, USA. All indications are that this new verse can be traced back to a completely separate hymn, "Lord, Guard and Guide the Men Who Fly," written by Mary C. D. Hamilton in 1915, during World War I. From this hymn, the first verse and the last two lines to the fourth verse were taken to form this new verse to "Eternal Father, Strong to Save." This new verse, as appearing in the little Presbyterian booklet, is as follows:

> Lord, guard and guide the men who fly,
> Through the great spaces of the sky;
> Be with them traversing the air,
> In darkening storms or sunshine fair.
> God, protect the men who fly,
> Through lonely ways beneath the sky.

Apparently, during or shortly after World War II, someone in the Navy familiar with the words above adapted this verse for choral rendition. The adaptation changed a word or two here and there and substituted two new fifth and six lines. What some might call the "Naval Aviation version" is as follows:

> Lord, guard and guide the men who fly
> Through the great spaces in the sky,
> Be with them always in the air,
> In dark'ning storms or sunlight fair.
> O, Hear us when we lift our prayer,
> For those in peril in the air.

This version, together with the original first verse are the verses sung by the men and women of the Navy, particularly those in Naval Aviation.

The tune of "Melita," to which Reverend Dykes adapted the words of "Eternal Father, Strong to Save" in 1861, is, of course, a very moving and inspiring melody. Research indicates that the above additions and alterations to Reverend Whiting's original ode are not the only changes that have been or will be made to the hymn. From time to time, individuals have been and will be inspired to write verses other than those that are indicated in this brief background.

Here are some current alternates:

> Eternal Father, grant, we pray
> To all *Marines,* both night and day,
> The courage, honor, strength, and skill

Their land to serve, thy law fulfill;
Be thou the shield forevermore
From every peril to the Corps.

—J.E. Seim, 1966

Lord, stand beside the men who build
And give them courage, strength, and skill.
grant them peace of heart and mind,
And comfort loved ones left behind.
Lord, hear our prayer for all *Seabees,*
Where'er they be on land or sea.

—R.J. Dietrich, 1960

Lord God, our power evermore,
Who arm doth reach the ocean floor,
Dive with our men *beneath the sea;*
Traverse the depths protectively.
hear us when we pray, and keep
them safe from peril in the deep.

—David B. Miller, 1965

God, protect the *women* who,
in service, faith in thee renew;
guide devoted hands of skill
And bless their work within thy will;
Inspire their lives that they may be
Examples fair on land and sea.

—Lines 1–4, Merle E. Strickland, 1972, and
adapted by James D. Shannon, 1973
—Lines 5–6, Beatrice M. Truitt, 1948

Creator, Father, who dost show
Thy splendor in the ice and snow,
Bless those who toil in summer light
And through the cold *Antarctic* night,
As they thy frozen wonders learn;
Bless those who wait for their return.

—L. E. Vogel, 1965

Eternal Father, Lord of hosts,
Watch o'er the men who guard our *coasts*.
Protect them from the raging seas
And give them light and life and peace.
Grant them from thy great throne above
The shield and shelter of thy love.
                    —Author and date unknown

Eternal Father, King of birth,
Who didst create the heaven and earth,
And bid the planets and the sun
Their own appointed orbits run;
hear us when we seek they grace
For those who soar through *outer space*.
                    —J. E. Volonte, 1961

Creator, Father, who first breathed
In us the life that we received,
By power of they breath restore
The ill, and men with *wounds of war*.
Bless those who give their healing care,
That life and laughter all may share
                    —Galen H. Meyer, 1969;
              Adapted by James D. Shannon, 1970

God, who dost still the restless foam,
Protect the ones we love at home.
Provide that they should always be
By thine own grace both safe and free.
Father, hear us when we pray
For those we love so far away.
                    —Hugh Taylor, date unknown

Lord, guard and guide the men who fly
And those who on the ocean ply;
Be with our troops upon the land,
And all who for their country stand:
Be with these guardians day and night
And may their trust be in they might.
                    —Author unknown, about 1955

Father, King of earth and sea,
We dedicate this *ship* to thee.
In faith we send her on her way;
In faith to thee we humbly pray:
hear from heaven our sailor's cry
And watch and guard her from on high!

—Author and date unknown

And when at length her course is run,
Her work for home and country done,
Of all the souls that in her sailed
Let not one life in thee have failed;
But hear from heaven our sailor's cry,
And grant eternal life on high!

—Author and date unknown

Text extracted from a publication of the Bureau of Naval Personnel and documents archived at the Naval Historical Center (3 November 1997)

Appendix C

The Navy March: "Anchors Aweigh"

"Anchors Aweigh" was written in 1906 as a march for the Naval Academy Class of 1907. The music was composed by Lt. Charles A. Zimmerman, bandmaster of the Naval Academy, and the lyrics were written by Midshipman Alfred H. Miles. It was first performed at the Army-Navy football game in Philadelphia in 1906. (Navy beat Army 10–0!)

Today, the song has become an important part of Chief Petty Officers' training. While there is a proposal to include protocol in the Navy regulations for performing "Anchors Aweigh" and to designate it the official song of the U.S. Navy, it remains an unofficial service song. There are numerous variations to the words of "Anchors Aweigh." This version is considered the original version.

Anchors Aweigh, (1906 version)

Stand Navy out to sea, Fight our Battle Cry;
We'll never change our course, So vicious foe
    steer shy-y-y-y.
Roll out the TNT, Anchors Aweigh. Sail on to
    Victory
And sink their bones to Davy Jones, Hooray!

Anchors Away, my boys, Anchors Aweigh.
Farewell to foreign shores, We sail at break of
 day-ay-ay-ay.
Through our last night on shore, Drink to the
 foam,
Until we meet once more. Here's wishing you a
 happy voyage home.

Blue of the Mighty Deep; Gold of God's Sun
Let these colors be till all of time be done, done,
 done,
On seven seas we learn Navy's stern call:
Faith, Courage, Service true, with Honor, Over
 Honor, Over All.

Appendix D

Cadence Calls
and *Jodies*

Cadence calling has been part of military life since the time of the ancient Romans. A good cadence call can really strip the miles away on a long run. In recent years, cadence calls have also been called *Jodies*, featuring the invidious civilian who lives the good life back on shore, while we military men and women are busy defending the nation. Here are some good Jodies, collected from various nooks and crannies around the fleet. Give them a try as you train together as part of your CPO initiation, or at any CPO event.

The Chief's Mess

Our Chief's Mess is Long and Wide
We're Running now for Navy Pride.

Hoorah, Chief's Mess!
Hoorah, Chief's Mess!

Now, Senior Chief is Fifty-One,
He does PT just for fun.

Hoorah, Chief's Mess!
Hoorah, Chief's Mess!

Master Chief is Fifty-Two,
He runs PT just like you.

CMC is Fifty-Three
He does sit-ups just like me.

Force Master Chief is Fifty-Four
Run Ten Miles, He'll Run Some More.

Fleet Master Chief is Fifty-Five
Fastest Running Chief Alive.

MCPON just turned Fifty-Six
Runs Twelve Miles just for kicks.

Our Chief's Mess is Long and Wide,
We're Running now for Navy Pride.

Navy Chiefs! Navy Pride!
Hoorah—Navy Pride!

We're All Chiefs

Going down the road one day,
When I heard a sailor say:

Airedale Chiefs are mighty fine
Like to hear those turbines wine.

Hoorah, Navy Chiefs!
Hoorah, Navy Chiefs!

Airedale Chiefs are all alive
Dip their Anchors in JP5.

Hoorah, Navy Chiefs!
Hoorah, Navy Chiefs!

Seabee Chiefs are mighty grand
On them 'dozers pushing sand.

Seabee Chiefs are mighty keen
Dip their anchors in gasoline.

Bubbleheads are going deep,
Won't be back for thirty weeks.

Bubbleheads are mighty proud
It's just down there you can't be loud.

See those anchors glowing bright
Stowed on the reactor every night.

Hoorah, Navy Chiefs!
Hoorah, Navy Chiefs!

'Gator Chiefs are tough and mean
Hanging out with those Marines.

'Gator Chiefs say they oughter
Soak those anchors in shallow water.

Hoorah, Navy Chiefs!
Hoorah, Navy Chiefs!

Dental Chiefs are really mean,
Soak their anchors in Listerine.

Gunners mates are also mean,
Stow their anchors in Cosmoline.

[See how many more ratings you can add to this
Jodie.]

Hoorah, Navy Chiefs!
Hoorah, Navy Chiefs!

Ralph Rao's Favorite

Hey Naval Base stop and listen
Hear about 110 years of proud tradition.
I don't know what you been told
CPO anchors are as good as gold.
I don't know what you have seen
Navy Chiefs are lean and mean.
Navy Chief, Navy Pride
Navy Chief, Navy Pride.

Navy Pride, Navy Chief
So Naval Base stop and listen
You don't know what you been missing.

Making Chief

Selectees out in the pouring rain,
Master Chief says it's time for pain.
Grab your gear and follow me
It's time for us to do PT.

We jogged nine miles and we ran three,
Master Chief yelling follow me!

We walked two miles and ran eight!
Making Chief is really great!
Hoorah, Navy Chiefs!
Hoorah, Navy Chiefs!

Appendix E

The Master Chief Petty Officer of the Navy's Heritage and Core Values Reading List

The following books comprise the "Master Chief Petty Officer of the Navy's Naval Heritage/Core Values Reading Guide" as prepared in March 1997 and revised August 2002. This list is updated periodically as part of the Chief Petty Officer Initiation Season. The books are available through the Navy Exchange or the Uniform Center toll-free ordering system.

Required Reading (the "A List")

A Most Fortunate Ship: Narrative History of Old Ironsides by Tyrone Martin

A Sailor's Log: Recollections of Forty Years of Naval Life by Rear Adm. Robley Dungliston Evans with introduction by Benjamin Franklin Cooling

A Voice from the Main Deck by Samuel Leech

Battleship Sailor by Theodore C. Mason

Brave Ship, Brave Men by Arnold S. Lott

Crossing the Line: A Bluejacket's WWII Odyssey by Alvin Kernan

Descent into Darkness by Cmdr. Edward C. Raymer

Devotion to Duty: A Biography of Admiral Clifton A. F. Sprague by John F. Wukovits

Divided Waters: The Naval History of the Civil War by Ivan Musicant

Every Other Day: Letters from the Pacific by George B. Lucas

Good Night Officially by William M. McBride

In Harm's Way by Doug Stanton—new for 2002

In Love and War: Revised and Updated by Jim and Sybil Stockdale

Iwo by Richard Wheeler

Life in Mr. Lincoln's Navy by Dennis J. Ringle

Naked Warriors by Cmdr. Frances Douglas Fane and Don Moore

Nimitz by E. B. Potter

Quiet Heroes by Cmdr. Frances Omori

Raiders from the Sea by John Lodwick

Raiders of the Deep by Lowell Thomas with introduction by Gary E. Weir

Shield and Sword: The U.S. Navy and the Persian Gulf by Marolda and Schneller

Ship's Doctor by Capt. Terrence Riley

Submarine Diary: The Silent Stalking of Japan by Rear Adm. Corwin Mendenhall

The Battle of Cape Esperance: Encounter at Guadalcanal by Capt. Charles Cook, USN (Ret.)

The Fast Carriers: The Forging of an Air Navy by Clark G. Reynolds

The Fighting Liberty Ships: A Memoir by A. A. Hoehling

The Golden Thirteen: Recollections of the First Black Naval Officers by Paul Stillwell with Colin L. Powell

The Last Patrol by Harry Holmes

Thunder Below by Adm. Eugene B. Fluckey, USN (Ret.)

Tin Can Sailor: Life Aboard the USS Sterett, '39–'45 by C. Raymond Calhoun

We Will Stand by You: Serving in the Pawnee, 1942–1945 by Theodore C. Mason

What a Way to Spend a War: Navy Nurse POWs in the Philippines by Dorothy Still Danner

Reference Documents (The "B List")

Admiral John H. Towers: The Struggle for Naval Air Supremacy by William F. Trinmble

Air Raid: Pearl Harbor! Recollections of a Day of Infamy by Paul Stillwell

All at Sea by Louis R. Harlany

American Naval History: An Illustrated Chronology of the U.S. Navy and Marine Corps, 1775–Present by Jack Sweetman

A Quest for Glory: A Biography of Rear Admiral John A Dahlgren by Robert J. Schneller

Assault from the Sea: The Amphibious Landing at Inchon by Curtis Utz

At Dawn We Slept by Gordon W. Prange

Authors at Sea: Modern American Writers Remember Their Naval Service by Robert Shenk

The Book of Navy Songs by The Trident Society

Clash of the Titans by Walter J. Boyne

Cordon of Steel: The U.S. Navy and the Cuban Missile Crisis by Curtis Utz

Crossed Currents: Navy Women from WWI to Tailhook by Jean Ebbert/Marie-Beth Hall

E-Boat Alert: Defending the Normandy Invasion Fleet by James Foster Tent

The First Team and the Guadalcanal Campaign: Naval Fighter Combat from August to November 1942 by John B. Lundstrom

The First Team: Pacific Naval Air Combat from Pearl Harbor to Midway by John B. Lundstrom

Great U.S. Naval Battles by Jack Sweetman

Heroes in Dungarees: The Story of the American Merchant Marines in WWII by John Bunker

History of the U.S. Navy Part II by Robert Love

History of the U. S. Navy, Vol. One, 1775–1941 by Robert W. Love, Jr.

History of U.S. Naval Operations in World War II by Samuel Eliot Morison:

    Vol. I: The Battle of the Atlantic

    Vol. II: Operations in North African Waters

    Vol. III: The Rising Sun in the Pacific

    Vol. IV: Coral Sea, Midway and Submarine Actions

    Vol. V: The Struggle for Guadalcanal

    Vol. VI: Breaching the Bismarcks Barrier

    Vol. IX: Sicily—Salerno—Anzio

    Vol. XI: The Invasion of France and Germany

    Vol. XII: Leyte

    Vol. XIII: The Liberation of the Philippines: Luzon, Mindanao, the Visayas 1944–1945

Honor Bound: The History of American Prisoners of War in Southeast Asia, 1961–1973 by S. I. Rochester and F. Wiley

Kinkaid of the Seventh Fleet: A Biography of Admiral Thomas C. Kinkaid, USN by Gerald E. Wheeler

Longitude by Dava Sobel

The Magnificent Mitscher by Theodore Taylor

Miracle at Midway by Gordon W. Prance

Okinawa: The Last Battle of World War II by Robert Lackie

One Hundred Years of Sea Power: The U.S. Navy, 1890–1990 by George Baer

The People Navy by Kenneth J. Hagan

Prisoners of the Japanese by Gavon Daws

PT 105 by Dick Keresey

Quiet Warrior: A Biography of ADM Raymond A. Spruance by Thomas Buell

Revolt of the Admirals by Jeffrey Barlow

Rocks and Shoals: Naval Discipline in the Age of Fighting Sail by James E. Valle

Run Silent/Run Deep by Capt. Edward L. Beach

Sea Power: A Naval History by E. B. Potter

Submarine Admiral by Adm. J. J. Galantin

Submarine Commander by Paul Schratz

The Two Ocean War by Samuel Eliot Morison

U-Boat Commander by Peter Cremer

The Unsinkable Fleet: The Politics of U.S. Navy Expansion in World War II by Joel R. Davidson

Unsung Sailors: The Naval Armed Guard in WWII by Justin F. Gleichauf

War at Sea by Nathan Miller

War Beneath the Sea by Peter Sudfield

We Pulled Together and Won! Personal Memories of the World War II Era by Reminisce Books

Appendix F

Chief Petty Officers Who Have Been Awarded the Medal of Honor

Do not make the common error of referring to our nation's highest honor as the "Congressional Medal of Honor." The proper title is simply "The Medal of Honor." And the Medal is never "won"; it is *earned* or *awarded* for exceptional bravery.

Spanish American War 1898 and 1899

Bennett, James H.,
Chief Boatswain's Mate
USS *Marblehead,* Cienfuegos, Cuba, 11 May 1898

Brady, George F.,
Chief Gunner's Mate
USS *Winslow,* Cardenas, Cuba, 11 May 1898

Cooney, Thomas C.,
Chief Machinist
USS *Winslow,* Cardenas, Cuba, 11 May 1898

Itrich, Franz A.,
Chief Carpenter's Mate
USS *Petrel,* Manila, P.I., 1 May 1898

Johnsen, Hans,
Chief Machinist
USS *Winslow,* Cardenas, Cuba, 11 May 1898

Montague, Daniel,
Chief Master-at-Arms

USS *Merrimac,*
Santiago de Cuba, 2 Jun 1898

Sunquist, Axel,
Chief Carpenter's Mate

USS *Marblehead,*
Cienfuegos, Cuba, 11 May
1898

Shanahan, Patrick,
Chief Boatswain's Mate

USS *Alliance,* 28 May 1899

Stokes, John,
Chief Master-at-Arms,

USS *New York,* off Jamaica,
31 Mar 1899

Boxer Rebellion 1900

Clancy, Joseph,
Chief Boatswain's Mate

China, 13, 20, 21, and
22 Jun 1900

Hamberger, William F.,
Chief Carpenter's Mate

China, 13, 20, 21, and
22 Jun 1900

Petersen, Carl E.,
Chief Machinist, Peking

China, 28 Jun to
17 Aug 1900

Inter-War Period 1903–10

Bonney, Robert Earl,
Chief Watertender

USS *Hopkins,* 14 Feb 1910

Clausey, John J.,
Chief Gunner's Mate

USS *Bennington,*
21 Jul 1905

Cox, Robert E.,
Chief Gunner's Mate

USS *Missouri,* 13 Apr 1904

Holtz, Aug,
Chief Watertender

USS *North Dakota,*
8 Sep 1910

Johannessen, Johannes J.,
Chief Watertender

USS *Iowa,* 25 Jan 1905

Klein, Robert,
Chief Carpenter's Mate

USS *Raleigh,* 25 Jan 1904

Monssen, Mons,
Chief Gunner's Mate

USS *Missouri,* 13 Apr 1904

Reid, Patrick,
Chief Watertender

USS *North Dakota,*
8 Sep 1910

Shacklette, William S.,   USS *Bennington,*
Hospital Steward   21 Jul 1905

Snyder, William E.,   USS *Birmingham,* 4 Jan 1910
Chief Electrician

Stanton, Thomas,   USS *North Dakota,*
Chief Machinist's Mate   8 Sep 1910

Walsh, Michael,   USS *Leyden,* 21 Jan 1903
Chief Machinist

Westa, Karl,   USS *North Dakota,*
Chief Machinist's Mate   8 Sep 1910

Mexico 1914

Bradley, George,   USS *Utah,*
Chief Gunner's Mate   Vera Cruz, 1914

Inter-War Period 1915–16

Crilley, Frank W.,   Honolulu, T.H.,
Chief Gunner's Mate   17 Apr 1915

Rud, George W.,   USS *Memphis,*
Chief Machinist's Mate   Santo Domingo, 29 Aug 1916

Smith, Eugene P.,   USS *Decatur,* 9 Sep 1915
Chief Watertender

World War I

MacKenzie, John,   USS *Remlik,* 17 Dec 1917
Chief Boatswain's Mate

Ormsbee, Francis E., JR.,   NAS Pensacola, FL,
Chief Machinist's Mate   25 Sep 1918

Schmidt, Oscar, JR.,   USS *Chestnut Hill,*
Chief Gunner's Mate   9 Oct 1918.

Inter-War Period 1927–39

Badders, William,   USS *Squalus,* 13 May 1939
Chief Machinist's Mate

Crandall, Orson L.,   USS *Squalus,* 13 May 1939
Chief Boatswain's Mate

Eadie, Thomas,   off Provincetown, Mass.,
Chief Gunner's Mate   18 Dec 1927

McDonald, James H.,   USS *Squalus,* 23 May 1939
Chief Metalsmith

World War II

Finn, John W.,   NAS Kaneohe Bay, T.H.,
[then a Chief Petty Officer]   7 Dec 1941

Peterson, Oscar V.,   USS *Neosho,* 7 May 1942
Chief Watertender

Reeves, Thomas,   USS *California*
[then Chief Radioman]   7 December 1941

Tomich, Peter,   USS *Utah,* 7 Dec 1941
Chief Watertender

Navy Historical Society and Senate Committee on Veteran's Affairs. Medal of Honor Recipients 1863–1978. Senate Committee Print No. 3. 96th Cong., 1st Sess., 1979.

Appendix G

Resources for Information

Subject	Reference
A	
"A" Schools	Transman 7.07
	Bumedinst 1510.31
Absentees	Milpersman 3430100
	Milpersman 3430300
Collection Unit Staff	Enltransman 9.39
Academy	Navpers 15878
	Cnetinst Is31.3
	Opnavinst 1531.47
	Bumedinst 8120.3
Accelerated Advancement	Bupersman 2230150
Acceptance of Gifts	Secnavinst 4001.2
Accidents	Milpersman 4210100
	Opnavinst 3750.6
	Opnavinst 5100.8
	Opnavinst 5100.12
	Opnavinst 5100.20
	Opnavinst 5100.21

P

Q

R

S

Glossary

A

Abaft—Farther aft, as in "abaft the beam."

Abeam—Abreast; on a relative bearing of 090 or 270 degrees.

Aboard—On or in a ship or naval station.

Accommodation ladder—A ladder resembling stairs that is suspended over the side of a ship to facilitate boarding from boats.

Adrift—Loose from moorings and out of control (applied to anything lost, out of hand, or left lying about).

Aft—Toward the stern.

Aground—That part of a ship resting on the bottom (a ship "runs aground" or "goes aground").

Ahoy—A hail or call for attention, as in "Boat ahoy."

Alee—Downwind.

All hands—The entire ship's company.

Aloft—Generally speaking, any area above the highest deck.

Alongside—By the side of the ship or pier.

Amidships—An indefinite area midway between the bow and the stern; "rudder amidships" means that the rudder is in line with the ship's centerline.

Anchor frogs—Small clasps that secure the fouled anchor device to the collar.

Anchorage—An area designated to be used by ships for anchoring.

Ask the Chief—Household phrase in the Navy, used when all other sources of information have proven futile.

Astern—Behind a ship.

Athwart—Across; at right angles to.

Avast—Stop, as in "avast heaving."

Aweigh—An anchoring term used to describe the anchor clear of the bottom (the weight of the anchor is on the cable).

B

Barge—A blunt-ended craft, usually nonself-propelled, used to haul supplies or garbage; a type of motorboat assigned for the personal use of a flag officer.

Batten down—The closing of any watertight fixture.

Battle E—Annually awarded to the ship or squadron showing the best warfare preparation.

Battle lantern—A battery-powered lantern for emergency use.

Beam—The extreme width (breadth) of a vessel, as in "a CV has a greater beam [is wider] than a destroyer."

Bear a hand—Provide assistance, as in "bear a hand with rigging the brow"; expedite.

Bearing—The direction of an object measured in degrees clockwise from a reference point (true bearings use true north as the reference, relative bearings use the ship's bow as the reference, and magnetic bearings use magnetic north).

Belay—To secure a line to a fixed point; to disregard a previous order or to stop an action, as in "belay the last order" or "belay the small talk."

Below—Beneath, or beyond something, as in "lay below" (go downstairs); or "below the flight deck."

Berth—Bunk; duty assignment; mooring space assigned to a ship.

Bight—A loop in a line.

Bilge—Lowest area of the ship where spills and leaks gather; to fail an examination.

Billet—Place or duty to which one is assigned.

Binnacle—A stand containing a magnetic compass.

Binnacle list—List of persons excused from duty because of illness.

Bitt—Cylindrical upright fixture (usually found in pairs) to which mooring or towing lines are secured aboard ship.

Bitter end—The free end of a line.

Blackshoe—Officer or enlisted in the surface or submarine warfare communities.

Block—Roughly equivalent to a pulley.

Blueshirt—Enlisted Sailor in paygrades E-1 to E-6, from the blue utility shirt worn as part of the working uniform.

Board—To go aboard a vessel; a group of persons meeting for a specific purpose, as in "investigation board."

Boat—A small craft capable of being carried aboard a ship.

Boat boom—A spar rigged out from the side of an anchored or moored ship to which boats are tied when not in use.

Boatswain's chair—A seat attached to a line for hoisting a person aloft or lowering over the side.

Boatswain's locker—A compartment, usually forward, where line and other equipment used by the deck force are stowed.

Bollard—A strong, cylindrical, upright fixture on a pier to which ships' mooring lines are secured.

Boom—A spar, usually movable, used for hoisting loads.

Bow—The forward end of a ship or boat.

Breast line—Mooring line that leads from ship to pier (or another ship, if moored alongside) at right angles to the ship and is used to keep the vessel from moving laterally away from the pier (another ship).

Bridge—Area in the superstructure from which a ship is operated.

Brightwork—Bare (unpainted) metal that is kept polished.

Broach to—To get crosswise (without power) to the direction of the waves (puts the vessel in danger of being rolled over by the waves).

Broad—Wide, as in "broad in the beam."

Broad on the bow or quarter—Halfway between dead ahead and abeam, and halfway between abeam and astern, respectively.

Broadside—Simultaneously and to one side (when firing main battery guns); sidewise, as in "the current carried the ship broadside to the beach."

Brow—Gangplank used for crossing from one ship to another, and from a ship to a pier.

Bulkhead—A vertical partition in a ship (never called a wall).

Buoy—An anchored float used as an aid to navigation or to mark the location of an object.

BUPERS—Bureau of Naval Personnel.

C

Camel—Floating buffer between a ship and a pier (or another ship) to prevent damage by rubbing or banging (similar to a fender except that a camel is in the water whereas a fender is suspended above the water).

Can buoy—A cylindrical navigational buoy, painted green and odd-numbered, which in U.S. waters marks the port side of a channel from seaward.

Can Do—Unofficial motto of the U.S. Navy Seabees (Construction Forces).

Carry away—To break loose, as in "the rough seas carried away the lifelines."

Carry on—An order to resume a previous activity after an interruption.

Chafing gear—Material used to protect lines from excessive wear.

Chain locker—Space where anchor chain is stowed.

Charge book—Book of directions, suggestions and maxims collected by newly selected Chief Petty Officers.

Chock—Deck fitting through which mooring lines are led.

Chow—Food.

CIC—Combat information center, the fighting heart of a warship.

CMC—Command Master Chief Petty Officer (CMDCM).

CNO—Chief of naval operations.

CNOCM—CNO-directed Command Master Chief (Major commands).

COB—Chief of the Boat. In the submarine community, equivalent to Command Master Chief.

Colors—The national ensign; the ceremony of raising and lowering the ensign.

Commission pennant—A long, narrow, starred and striped pennant flown only on board a commissioned ship.

Companionway—Deck opening giving access to a ladder (includes the ladder).

Compartment—Interior space of a ship (similar to a "room" ashore).

Conn—The act of controlling a ship (similar to "driving" ashore); also the station, usually on the bridge, from which a ship is controlled.

Counselor (NC)—Responsible for vocational guidance to Navy personnel and potential recruits.

Course—A ship's desired direction of travel, not to be confused with heading.

Cover—To protect; a shelter; headgear; to don headgear.

Coxswain—Enlisted person in charge of a boat.

CPO—Chief Petty Officer.

Cumshaw—A gift; something procured without payment. Pronounced "comm-shaw."

D

Darken ship—To turn off all external lights and close all openings through which lights can be seen from outside the ship.

Davits—Strong arms by means of which a boat is hoisted in or out.

Davy Jones's locker—The bottom of the sea.

DCC—Damage Control Central.

Dead ahead—Directly ahead; a relative bearing of 000 degrees.

Dead astern—180 degrees relative.

Deck plates—Cognitive with mess decks, form of reference for areas where enlisted Sailors work and live, used by extension to mean enlisted members of the Navy.

Deck seamanship—The upkeep and operation of all deck equipment.

Deck—Horizontal planking or plating that divides a ship into layers (floors).

Decontaminate—To free from harmful residue of nuclear or chemical attack.

Deep six—To throw something overboard (*see also* Jettison).

Dip—To lower a flag partway down the staff as a salute to, or in reply to a salute from, another ship.

Distance line—A line stretched between two ships engaged in replenishment or transfer operations under way (the line is marked at twenty-foot intervals to aid the conning officer in maintaining the proper distance between ships).

Division—A main subdivision of a ship's crew (1st, E, G, etc.); an organization composed of two or more ships of the same type.

Dock—The water-space alongside a pier.

Dog—A lever, or bolt and thumb screws, used for securing a watertight door; to divide a four-hour watch into two two-hour watches.

Dog down—To set the dogs on a watertight door.

Double up—To double mooring lines for extra strength.

Draft—The vertical distance from the keel to the waterline.

Dress ship—To display flags in honor of a person or event.

Drift—The speed at which a ship is pushed off course by wind and current.

Dry dock—A dock, either floating or built into the shore, from which water may be removed for the purpose of inspecting or working on a ship's bottom; to be put in dry dock.

E

Ebb—A falling tide.
Eight o'clock reports—Reports received by the executive officer from department heads shortly before 2000.
Ensign—The national flag; an O-1 paygrade officer.
EOD—Explosive ordinance disposal
Executive officer—Second officer in command (also called XO).
Eyes—The forward most part of the forecastle.

F

Fake—The act of making a line, wire, or chain ready for running by laying it out in long, flat bights, one alongside and partially overlapping the other.
Fantail—The after end of the main deck.
Fathom—Unit of length or depth equal to six feet.
Fender—A cushioning device hung over the side of a ship to prevent contact between the ship and a pier or another ship.
Field day—A day devoted to general cleaning, usually in preparation for an inspection.
Fire main—Shipboard piping system to which fire hydrants are connected.
First and Finest—Motto of USN Mobile Construction Battalion One. Truer words have never been spoken.
First lieutenant—The officer responsible, in general, for a ship's upkeep and cleanliness (except machinery and ordnance gear), boats, ground tackle, and deck seamanship.
Flag officer—Any officer of the rank of rear admiral (lower and upper half), vice admiral, or admiral.
Flagstaff—Vertical staff at the stern to which the ensign is hoisted when moored or at anchor.
Fleet—An organization of ships, aircraft, marine forces, and shore-based fleet activities, all under one commander, for conducting major operations.
Flood—To fill a space with water; a rising tide.
FLTCM—Fleet Command Master Chief.
Fo'c'sle—Forecastle. Cognitive of deckplates; place where enlisted Sailors live and work.

FORCM—Force Command Master Chief.

Forecastle—Forward section of the main deck (pronounced "fohk-sul").

Foremast—First mast aft from the bow.

Forenoon watch—The 0800–1200 watch.

Forward—Toward the bow.

Foul—Entangled, as in "the lines are foul of each other"; stormy.

Fouled anchors—The rating insignia of a Chief Petty Officer. Senior Chief Petty Officer's anchors have a single star above the anchor, Master Chief's have two stars.

G

Gaff—A light spar set at an angle from the upper part of a mast (the national ensign is usually flown from the gaff under way).

Gangway—The opening in a bulwark or lifeline that provides access to a brow or accommodation ladder; an order meaning to clear the way.

General quarters—The condition of full readiness for battle.

Gig—Boat assigned for the commanding officer's personal use.

Goat Locker—Sailor's familiar and usually apt nickname for CPO berthing.

Golden Dragon—Sailor who has crossed the international date line; ceremonies commemorating the event.

Ground tackle—Equipment used in anchoring or mooring with anchors.

Gunny Sergeant—Gunnery Sergeant, USMC. Equivalent in rank and status to a Chief Petty Officer.

Gunwale—Where the sides join the main deck of a ship.

H

Halyard—A light line used to hoist a flag or pennant.

Handsomely—Steadily and carefully, but not necessarily slowly.

Hard over—Condition of a rudder that has been turned to the maximum possible rudder angle.

Hashmark—A red, blue, or gold diagonal stripe across the left sleeve of an enlisted person's jumper indicating four years' service.

Hatch—An opening in a deck used for access.

Haul—To pull in or heave on a line by hand.

Hawser—Any heavy wire or line used for towing or mooring.

Heave—To throw, as in "heave a line to the pier."

Heave around—To haul in a line, usually by means of a capstan or winch.

Heaving line—A line with a weight at one end, heaved across an intervening space for passing over a heavier line.

Helm—Steering wheel of a ship.

Helmsman—Person who steers the ship by turning her helm (also called steersman).

Highline—The line stretched between ships under way on which a trolley block travels back and forth to transfer material and personnel.

Hitch—To bend a line to or around a ring or cylindrical object; an enlistment.

Holiday—Space on a surface that the painter neglected to paint.

Hull—The shell, or plating, of a ship from keel to gunwale.

Hull down—A lookout term meaning that a ship is so far over the horizon that only her superstructure or top hamper is visible.

I

Inboard—Toward the centerline.

Island—Superstructure of an aircraft carrier.

J

Jack—Starred blue flag (representing the union of the ensign) flown at the jackstaff of a commissioned ship not under way.

Jackstaff—Vertical spar at the stem to which the jack is hoisted.

Jacob's ladder—A portable rope or wire ladder.

Jettison—To throw overboard.

Jetty—A structure built out from shore to influence water currents or protect a harbor or pier.

Jury rig—Any makeshift device or apparatus; to fashion such a device.

K

Killick—Anchor. Badge of authority worn by leading seamen in the Royal Navy.

Knock off—Quit, cease, or stop, as in "knock off ship's work."

Knot—Nautical mile per hour.

L

Ladder—A flight of steps aboard ship.

Landing craft—Vessel especially designed for landing troops and equipment directly on a beach.

Landing ship—A large seagoing ship designed for landing personnel and/or heavy equipment directly on a beach.

Lanyard—Any short line used as a handle or as a means for operating some piece of equipment; a line used to attach an article to the person, as a pistol lanyard.

Large deck ships—Generally, aircraft carriers, and large amphibious ships.

Lash—To secure an object by turns of line, wire, or chain.

Launch—To float a vessel off the ways in a building yard; a type of powerboat, usually over 30 feet long.

Lay—Movement of a person, as in "lay aloft"; the direction of twist in the strands of a line or wire.

LDO—Limited duty officer.

Lee—An area sheltered from the wind; downwind.

Leeward—Direction toward which the wind is blowing (pronounced "loo-ard").

LES—Leave and earnings statement.

Liberty—Sanctioned absence from a ship or station for a short time for pleasure rather than business.

Lifelines—In general, the lines erected around the edge of a weather deck to prevent personnel from falling or being washed overboard; more precisely (though not often used), the topmost line. (From top to bottom, these lines are named lifeline, housing line, and foot-rope.)

Line—Any rope that is not wire rope.

List—Transverse inclination of a vessel (when a ship leans to one side).

Lookout—Person stationed topside on a formal watch who reports objects sighted and sounds heard to the officer of the deck.

LPO—Leading petty officer.

Lucky bag—Locker under the charge of the master-at-arms; used to collect and stow deserter's effects and gear found adrift.

M

Magazine—Compartment used for the stowage of ammunition.

Main deck—The uppermost complete deck.

Mainmast—Second mast aft from the bow on a vessel with more than one mast.

Make fast—To secure.

Man-o'-war—A ship designed for combat.

Marlinespike—Tapered steel tool used to open the strands of line or wire rope for splicing.

Marlinespike seamanship—The art of caring for and handling all types of line and wire.

Mate—A shipmate; another Sailor.

MCPO—Master Chief Petty Officer.

MCPON—Master Chief Petty Officer of the Navy

Mess—Meal; place where meals are eaten; a group that takes meals together, as in CPO's mess.

Messenger—A line used to haul a heavier line across an intervening space; one who delivers messages.

Moor—To make fast to a pier, another ship, or a mooring buoy.

Mooring buoy—A large anchored float to which a ship may moor.

Motor whaleboat—A double-ended powerboat.

Mustangs—Officers directly commissioned from the enlisted community.

Muster—A roll call; to assemble for a roll call.

MWR—Morale Welfare and Recreation. Formerly Special Services.

N

Nest—Two or more boats stowed one within the other; two or more ships moored alongside each other.

Nun buoy—A navigational buoy, conical in shape, painted red and even numbered, that marks the starboard side of a channel from seaward.

O

On the beach—Ashore; a seaman assigned to shore duty, unemployed, retired, or otherwise detached from sea duty.

OOD—Officer of the deck.

Outboard—Away from the centerline.

Overboard—Over the side.

Overhaul—To repair or recondition; to overtake another vessel.

Overhead—The underside of a deck that forms the overhead of the compartment next below (never called a ceiling).

P

Party—A group on temporary assignment or engaged in a common activity, as in "line-handling party," or a "liberty party."

Passageway—A corridor used for interior horizontal movement aboard ship (similar to a hallway ashore).

Pay out—To feed out or lengthen a line.

Pier—Structure extending from land into water to provide a mooring for vessels.

Pigstick—Small staff from which a commission pennant is flown.

Pilot house—Enclosure on the bridge housing the main steering controls.

Piloting—Branch of navigation in which positions are determined by visible objects on the surface or by soundings.

Pipe—To sound a particular call on a boatswain's pipe.

Pitch—Vertical rise and fall of a ship's bow and stern caused by head or following seas.

Plan of the Day (POD)—Schedule of a day's routine and events ordered by the executive officer and published daily aboard ship or at a shore activity.

Plane guard—Destroyer or helicopter responsible for rescuing air crews during launch or recovery operations.

Plank owner—A person who has been on board since the ship's commissioning.

POD—Plan of the day.

Pollywog—A person who has never crossed the equator (pejorative).

Port—To the left of the centerline when facing forward.

Q

Quarterdeck—Deck area designated by the commanding officer as the place to carry out official functions; station of the officer of the deck in port.

Quarters—Stations for shipboard evolutions, as in "general quarters," or "fire quarters"; living spaces.

Quay—A solid structure along a bank used for loading and offloading vessels (pronounced "key").

R

Rack—Bunk or bed.

Range—The distance of an object from an observer; an aid to navigation consisting of two objects in line; a water area designated for a particular purpose, as in "gunnery range."

Rat guard—A hinged metal disk secured to a mooring line to prevent rats from traveling over the line into the ship.

Reef—An underwater ledge rising abruptly from the ocean's floor.

Relief—A person assigned to take over the duties of another.

Replenishment—To resupply a ship or station.

Rigging—Line that has been set up to be used for some specific purpose (e.g., lines that support a ship's masts are called standing rigging, and lines that hoist or otherwise move equipment are called running rigging).

Rope—Fiber or wire line (fiber rope is usually referred to as line, while wire rope is called rope, wire rope, or wire).

Ropeyarn Sunday—A workday or part of a workday that has been granted as a holiday for taking care of personal business.

ROTC—Reserve Officer Training Corps, university-based officer training program

Rudder—Device attached to the stern that controls a ship's direction of travel.

Running lights—Navigational lights shown at night by a vessel under way.

S

SCPO—Senior Chief Petty Officer.

Scuttlebutt—A drinking fountain (originally, a ship's water barrel [called a butt] that was tapped [scuttled] by the insertion of a spigot from which the crew drew drinking water); rumor (the scuttlebutt was once a place for personnel to exchange news when the crew gathered to draw water).

SEA—Senior Enlisted Academy, located at Tomich Hall, Newport Naval Station, Rhode Island.

Sea anchor—A device streamed from the bow of a vessel for holding it end-on to the sea.

Seabees—Naval Construction Forces. Their motto, "We Build, We Fight," says it all.

Seamanship—The art of handling a vessel; skill in the use of deck equipment, in boat handling, and in the care and use of line and wire.

Sea state—Condition of waves and the height of their swells.

Seaworthy—A vessel capable of withstanding normal heavy weather.

Second deck—First complete deck below the main deck.

Secure—To make fast, as in "secure a line to a cleat"; to cease, as in "secure from fire drill."

Senior Chief—Senior Chief Petty Officer (E-8)

Service force—Organization providing logistic support to combatant forces.

Shakedown—The training of a new crew in operating a ship.

Shellback—One who has crossed the equator on a warship.

Shift colors—To change the arrangement of colors upon getting under way or coming to moorings.

Ship—Any large seagoing vessel capable of extended independent operation; to take on water unintentionally.

Ship over—To reenlist in the Navy.

Ship's company—All hands permanently attached to a ship or station.

Shipshape—Neat, clean, taut.

Shoal—A structure similar to a reef, but more gradual in its rise from the floor of the ocean.

Shore—Land, usually that part adjacent to the water; a timber used in damage control to brace bulkheads and decks.

Sick bay—Shipboard space that serves as a hospital or medical clinic.

Side boy—One of a group of seamen who form two ranks at the gangway as part of the ceremonies conducted for visiting officials.

Side light—One of a series of running lights (the starboard side light is green and the port side light is red).

Sight—To see for the first time, as to sight a ship on the horizon; a celestial observation.

Skylark—To engage in irresponsible horseplay.

Slack—To allow a line to run out; undisciplined, as in a "slack ship."

Small boys—Naval vessels smaller than cruisers.

Smart—Snappy, seamanlike, shipshape.

Snipes—Members of the engineering ratings (hull technician, machinist's mate, etc).

Spar—The nautical equivalent of a pole.

Special sea detail—Crewmembers assigned special duties when leaving and entering port.

Splice—To join lines or wires together by intertwining strands; the joint so made.

Square away—To put in proper order; to make things shipshape.

Square knot—Simple knot used for bending two lines together or for bending a line to itself.

Stack—Shipboard chimney.

Stanchion—Vertical post for supporting decks; smaller, similar posts for supporting lifelines, awnings, and so on.

Starboard—Direction to the right of the centerline as one faces forward.

Station—An individual's place of duty; position of a ship in formation; location of persons and equipment with a specific purpose, as in "gun-control station"; order to assume stations, as in "station the special sea and anchor detail."

Stay—Any piece of standing rigging providing support only.

Stem—Extreme forward line of bow.

Stern—The aftermost part of a vessel.

Stern light—White navigation light that can be seen only from astern.

Stow—To store or pack articles or cargo in a space.

Structural bulkhead—Transverse strength bulkhead that forms a watertight boundary.

Superstructure—The structure above a ship's main deck.

Swab—A mop; to mop.

T

Tarpaulin—Canvas used as a cover.

Taut—Under tension; highly disciplined and efficient, as in "a taut ship."

Tender—One who serves as a precautionary standby, as in "line tender for a diver"; a support vessel for other ships.

Topside—Weather decks; above (referring to the deck or decks above).

Trice up—To secure (older type) bunks by hauling them up and hanging them off (securing them) on their chains.

Truck—The uppermost tip of a mast.

Turn in—To retire to bed; to return articles to the issue room.

Turn to—To start working.

U

UCMJ—Uniform Code of Military Justice.

UNRWP—Underway Replenishment. An exercise at sea when a fleet supply ship or oiler transfers cargo or fuel to a warship while both are steaming, usually in excess of twenty knots. A very difficult and exciting evolution performed routinely by ships at sea.

Up all hammocks—Admonishment to personnel entitled to sleep after reveille to get up.

V

Void—An empty tank.

W

Waist—The amidships section of the main deck.

Wake—Trail left by a vessel or other object moving through the water.

Wardroom—Officers' messing compartment; collective term used to signify the officers assigned to a ship.

Warrant—Commissioned officer, ranking between Master Chief Petty Officer and ensign. (Technically, warrant officers in grade W-1 are not commissioned but selected).

Watch—One of the periods, usually four hours, into which a day is divided; a particular duty, as in "life buoy watch."

Watertight integrity—The degree or quality of water tightness.

Weather deck—Any deck exposed to the elements.

Weigh anchor—To hoist the anchor clear of the bottom.

Wharf—Structure similar to a quay but constructed like a pier.

Whipping—Binding on the end of a line or wire to prevent unraveling.

Windward—In the direction of the wind.

X

XO—Executive officer; second in command.

Y

Yardarm—The port or starboard half of a spar set athwartships across the upper mast.

Yaw—(Of a vessel) to have its heading thrown wide of its course as the result of a force, such as a heavy following sea.

Useful Sources and References Cited

This appendix lists the major works cited for this handbook. It is not all-inclusive, however, and readers are encouraged to check the latest OPNAV, SECNAV, and other instructions for definitive direction.

Introduction

Chief Petty Officer Indoctrination, Document 38202-B, Part One. Chief of Naval Training and Education, Department of The Navy.

Chief Petty Officer's Core Competencies. Worldwide Command Master Chief Petty Officers Conference. Dallas, Texas. June 25–28, 2001.

Chief Petty Officer's Creed (revised). [Available at Naval Public Affairs Library, U.S. Naval Academy, Annapolis, Md.]

Code of Conduct Training, OPNAVINST 1000.24b. Department of the Navy.

Executive Order 10631. August 17, 1955. *Code of Federal Regulations,* 20CFR6057, 3CFR 1954–58.

"Direct Line," Officer of The Master Chief Petty Officer of The Navy, Department of the Navy. Volume 16, Number 3, May–June, 1996.

Executive Order 12016. November 3, 1966. *Code of Federal Regulations,* 42CFR67941, 3CFR 1966.

Executive Order 12633. March 28, 1988. *Code of Federal Regulations,* 53CFR10355, 3CFR 1988.

Honoring Tradition: Collected Speeches of the Master Chief Petty Officer of the Navy. Office of the Master Chief Petty Officer of the Navy, Department of the Navy. 1997.

Military Requirements For Chief Petty Officers, Document 12047. Chief of Naval Training and Education, Department of the Navy. July 2000.

Chapter One: The Art And Science of Leadership

Mack, William P., and Harry A. Seymour Jr. *The Naval Officer's Guide,* 11th Edition. Annapolis, Md.: Naval Institute Press, 1998.

Montor, Karel, et al. *Fundamentals of Naval Leadership,* Annapolis, Md.: Naval Institute Press, 1984.

Montor, Karel, et al. *Naval Leadership: Voices of Experience,* 2nd Edition. Annapolis, Md.: Naval Institute Press, 1998.

Stavridis, James. *Division Officer's Guide: A Handbook for Junior Officers and Petty Officers,* 10th Edition. Annapolis, Md.: Naval Institute Press, 1995.

———. *Watch Officer's Guide, A Handbook for All Deck Watch Officers,* 14th Edition. Annapolis, Md.: Naval Institute Press, 2000.

Chapter Two: Moral Leadership, Morale, and Esprit de Corps

Acceptance of Gifts, OPNAVINST 4001.1d. Department of the Navy.

Do It Right: An Ethics Handbook for Executive Branch Employees. The U.S. General Accounting Office, January 1995.

Mack, William P., and Harry A. Seymour Jr. *The Naval Officer's Guide,* 11th Edition. Annapolis, Md.: Naval Institute Press, 1998.

Montor, Karel. *Ethics for the Junior Officer: Selected Cases from Current Military Experience,* 2nd Edition. Annapolis, Md.: Naval Institute Press, 2001.

Standards of Ethical Conduct for Government Employees. Human Resources Office, U.S. Navy Pacific Fleet, 2000.

Stavridis, James. *Division Officer's Guide: A Handbook for Junior Officers and Petty Officers,* 10th Edition. Annapolis, Md.: Naval Institute Press, 1995.

Chapter Three: Punishment and Legal Issues

Armed Forces Disciplinary Control Boards and Off-Installation Liaison and Operations, OPNAVINST 1620.2a. Department of the Navy.

Command Managed Equal Opportunity (CMEO), OPNAVINST 5354.5. Department of the Navy.

Disciplinary Review Boards (DRB), COMNAVRESFOR Instruction 1626. Commander, Naval Reserve Force Staff, Department of the Navy.

Navy Affirmative Action Plan, OPNAVINST 5354.3d. Department of the Navy.

Navy Equal Opportunity (EO) Policy, OPNAVINST 5354.1e. Department of the Navy.

Navy Law Enforcement Manual, OPNAVINST 5580.1a. Department of the Navy.

Navy Policy on Sexual Harassment, SECNAVINST 5300.26c. Department of the Navy.

Chapter Four: Leadership in Action

Introduction to Operational Risk Management. Navy Safety Center. Department of the Navy. 2000.

Leadership and Management Manual, CNET P1550/11 (Rev. 08.00). Chief of Naval Education and Training, U.S. Naval Reserve Officer Training Corps. Department of the Navy.

Learning About Operational Risk Management, Speaker's Tips. Office of Naval Research. Department of the Navy. 2001.

Naval Aviation Safety Program, OPNAVINST 3750.6. Department of the Navy.

Navy System Safety Program, OPNAVINST 5100.24G. Department of the Navy.

Navy Traffic Safety Program, OPNAVINST 5100.12. Department of the Navy.

Occupational Safety And Health Program, OPNAVINST 5100.8. Department of the Navy.

Chapter Five: Understanding Communications

Alternate Dispute Resolution, Active Listening (booklet). Department of the Navy, 2001.

Command Leadership School, Executive Officer's Course, Unit Two. Department of the Navy, 2001.

Communicating with Others: Petty Officer Indoctrination Manual, Unit Two, NAVEDTRA 38200-A. Chief of Navy Education and Training, Department of the Navy.

Chapter Six: Group Dynamics and Meeting Management

Educational Theory, Course MN3135. Naval Postgraduate School, Monterey, Department of the Navy.

Facilitator Team Skills, Course OA3. Navy Medicine Center for Organizational Development, NMETC Bethesda, Department of the Navy.

Group Dynamics and Teambuilding, Course MN 3103. Naval Postgraduate School, Monterey, Department of the Navy.

Military Sociology and Psychology: Leadership Dimensions, Course MN4113. Naval Postgraduate School, Monterey, Department of the Navy.

Reimer, Dennis J. *Small Group Instructor Training Course (SGITC): The Johari Window.* Digital Training Library. Department of the Army. 2003.

Tuckman, B. W., and M. A. C. Jensen. Stages of small group development revisited. *Group and Organizational Studies,* 2, 419-427. 1977.

Chapter Seven: Written Communications

Department of the Navy Correspondence Manual, SEC-NAVINST 5216.5D. Department of the Navy.

Executive Writing Course, U.S. Air Force Academy, Colorado Springs, Colo.: Department of the Air Force, 2002.

OPNAV Administrative Manual OPNAVINST 5000.48c. Department of the Navy.

Shenk, Robert. *Naval Institute Guide to Naval Writing,* 2nd edition. Annapolis, Md.: Naval Institute Press, 1997.

Writing Practices, rev. one, NRAD TD-1064. Naval Command, Control and Ocean Surveillance Center, San Diego, Department of the Navy. July 1994.

Chapter Eight: Development of Subordinates and Junior Officers

Boorda, J. M. Remarks at the Commissioning of USS *Chief* (MCM-14), Norfolk, Virginia, 5 November 1994. Department of the Navy. [Available at Navy Public Affairs Library, Annapolis, Md.]

Enlisted Surface Warfare Specialist Qualification, OP-NAVINST 1414.1. Department of the Navy.

Navy College Program Overview (booklet). Naval Air Station Jacksonville Florida, Department of the Navy, 2003.

Personal Qualification System, NAVEDTRA 43100-1. Commander Navy Education and Training, Department of the Navy.

Personnel Qualification Standards (PQS) Program, OP-NAVINST 3500.34e. Department of the Navy.

Seabee Combat Warfare (SCW), NAVEDTRA 43804-1. Commander, Navy Education and Training, Department of the Navy.

Reese, John, quoted by Senior Chief Aviation Electronics Technician (AW) Jack Reese, from www.Goatlocker.org (October 11, 2002).

Chapter Nine: Advancement and Professional Development

Enlisted Navy Leader Development (NAVLEAD), OPNAVINST 5351.2. Department of the Navy.

Enlisted to Officer Commissioning Program Administrative Manual, Enlisted Briefing, OPNAVINST 1420.1, Bureau of Naval Personnel (Pers 211), Department of the Navy, July 2002.

Navy Voluntary Education Programs (Navy Campus), OPNAVINST 1560.9. Department of the Navy.

Physical Readiness Program, DoD Instruction 1308.3. Department of Defense, August 1995.

Physical Readiness Program, OPNAVINST 6110.1f. Department of the Navy.

Suicide Prevention and Intervention. Secretary of the Navy Instruction 6320.24a. Department of the Navy, February 1999.

Chapter Ten: Counseling and Mentoring Sailors

Personal Financial Management (PFM) Education, Training, and Counseling Program, OPNAVINST 1740.5a. Department of the Navy.

Chapter Eleven: Caring for Sailors and Families

Child Development Programs, OPNAVINST 1700.9d. Department of the Navy.

Drug And Alcohol Abuse Prevention And Control, OPNAVINST 5350.4. Department of the Navy.

Exceptional Family Member Program, OPNAVINST 1754.2a. Department of the Navy.

Family Advocacy Program, OPNAVINST 1752.2a. Department of the Navy.

Family Service Center Program, OPNAVINST 1754.1a. Department of the Navy.

Navy Family Ombudsman Program, OPNAVINST 1750.1d. Department of the Navy.

Navy Family Ombudsman Program Manual, NAVPERS 15571 A. Department of the Navy.

Navy Fraternization Policy, OPNAVINST 5370.2b. Department of the Navy.

Navy Housing Referral Service (HRS), OPNAVINST 11101.21d. Department of the Navy.

Navy Voting Assistance Program (NVAP), OPNAVINST. 1742.1. Department of the Navy.

Relocation Guide. Fleet And Family Support Center U.S. Naval Support Activity, La Maddalena, Italy. Department of the Navy.

Suitability Screening for Overseas and Remote Duty Assignment, OPNAVINST 1300.14c. Department of the Navy.

U.S. Navy Family Care Policy, OPNAVINST 1740.4a. Department of the Navy.

Chapter Twelve: Tradition, Custom, Courtesy, and Protocol

Assignment of Funeral Escort Commanders OPNAVINST 5360.3d. Department of the Navy.

Estes, Kenneth W. *Handbook for Marine NCOs,* 4th ed. Annapolis, Md.: Naval Institute Press, 1996.

Hagan, John. "Honoring Tradition," Naval Institute *Proceedings,* December 1997.

Marine Corps Drill and Ceremonies Manual, NAVMC 2691. Department of the Navy.

Mack, William P., and Royal W. Connell. *Naval Ceremonies, Customs, and Traditions,* 5th ed. Annapolis, Md.: Naval Institute Press. [Sixth edition released May 2004]

Saluting Ships And Stations; Designation Of OPNAVINST 5060.5d. Department of the Navy.

Social Usage and Protocol Handbook: A Guide for Personnel of the U.S. Navy, OPNAVINST 1710.7. Department of the Navy, July 1979.

State, Official and Special Military Funerals OPNAVINST 5360.1. Department of the Navy.

Chapter Thirteen: The Chief Petty Officer's Uniform

Uniform Regulations, NAVPERS 15665-I. Navy Personnel Command, Bureau of Personnel, Department of the Navy.

Chapter Fourteen: The Chief Petty Officer's Mess

Administration of Chief Petty Officer's Mess Afloat, Navy Supply Manual Publication 486, Volume II. Department of the Navy.

Chief Petty Officer Indoctrination, Document 38202-B Topic Seven. Chief of Naval Training and Education, Department of the Navy.

Guidance for Utilization of Personal Quarters Mess Management Specialists (PQMS), OPNAVINST 1306.3. Department of the Navy.

Guidelines and Ceremonial Support In Conjunction with Retirements/Transfers to the Fleet Reserve, Naval Support Activity, Norfolk Instruction 1830.1. Department of the Navy.

Social Usage and Protocol Handbook: A Guide for Personnel of the U.S. Navy, OPNAVINST 1710.7. Department of the Navy, July 1979.

Chapter Fifteen: History, Heroes, and Leaders

Biographies of the Master Chief Petty Officers of the Navy. Chief of Naval Information. Department of the Navy. [Available in the Navy Public Affairs Library, Annapolis.]

Congressional Medal of Honor Society, http://www.cmohs.org/recipients/living_cites_eg.htm

Crist, Charlotte D. (Roberts). *Winds of Change: The History of the Office of the Master Chief Petty Officer of the Navy.* The Office of the Master Chief Petty Officer of the Navy and the Naval Historical Center, Washington, D.C.

Fleet, Force, CNO-Directed, and Command Master Chief (CMC) Program Instruction, OPNAVINST 1306.2d. Department of the Navy.

Home of the Heroes: Medal of Honor Citations for America's Heroes. http://www.homeofheroes.com.

Tucker, Lester B. "History of the Chief Petty Officer Grade," *Pull Together: Newsletter of the Naval Historical Foundation and the Naval Historical Center,* Volume 32, Number 1, Spring and Summer, 1993.

USS *Utah* Society, Battle Logs of USS *Utah,* 2003.

Index

About the Authors

Master Chief Petty Officer of the Navy
John Hagan (Retired)

John Hagan was born in Luton, England, and grew up in North Carolina. After enlisting in the Navy in December 1964, he attended basic training at Recruit Training Center, San Diego, Calif. After completing his training as an Electronics Technician, he served in a wide range of billets both at sea and ashore. Selected as the eighth Master Chief Petty Officer of the Navy by Admiral Frank Kelso in 1992, John Hagan served under three CNOs: Adm. Frank Kelso, Adm. Mike Boorda, and Adm. Jay Johnson. After Admiral Boorda's untimely and tragic death, and at the specific request of the new CNO, he served an extended tour as MCPON and has the distinction of being the longest serving Master Chief Petty Officer of the Navy. He has been awarded the Distinguished Service Medal, Meritorious Service Medal, Navy Commendation Medal, and various unit and campaign awards. Since retiring in 1998, John Hagan has worked in Human Systems Integration (HSI) and is currently leading the HSI effort on the DD(X) design program. He and his wife Cathy live in Marshall, Va.

Jack Leahy

Jack Leahy is Executive Director of the Naval Writer's Group and is the author two highly acclaimed books for the Naval Institute Press: *Honor, Courage, Commitment: Navy Boot Camp*, and *Ask the Chief: Backbone of the Navy*.

He is also the co-author of the forthcoming *Navy Petty Officer's Manual*, which will be published by the Naval Institute Press in 2005. Mr. Leahy enlisted in the Navy in 1966, and his service as a Navy radioman includes a combat tour of duty with Mobile Construction Battalion One at Phu Bai and DaNang Vietnam in 1969–70. After leaving active duty in 1970, he completed his graduate and post-graduate education, and embarked upon a long and distinguished career in the intelligence and telecommunications communities, both stateside and abroad. Retiring from a major federal contractor as Senior Manager, International Operations, in 2000, he embarked upon his second career as a university professor and author. He is presently a member of the faculty of the Ross School of Leadership and Management at Franklin University in Columbus, Ohio, where he resides with his wife Margaret.

The Naval Institute Press is the book-publishing arm of the U.S. Naval Institute, a private, nonprofit, membership society for sea service professionals and others who share an interest in naval and maritime affairs. Established in 1873 at the U.S. Naval Academy in Annapolis, Maryland, where its offices remain today, the Naval Institute has members worldwide.

Members of the Naval Institute support the education programs of the society and receive the influential monthly magazine *Proceedings* and discounts on fine nautical prints and on ship and aircraft photos. They also have access to the transcripts of the Institute's Oral History Program and get discounted admission to any of the Institute-sponsored seminars offered around the country. Discounts are also available to the colorful bimonthly magazine *Naval History*.

The Naval Institute's book-publishing program, begun in 1898 with basic guides to naval practices, has broadened its scope to include books of more general interest. Now the Naval Institute Press publishes about one hundred titles each year, ranging from how-to books on boating and navigation to battle histories, biographies, ship and aircraft guides, and novels. Institute members receive significant discounts on the Press's more than eight hundred books in print.

Full-time students are eligible for special half-price membership rates. Life memberships are also available.

For a free catalog describing Naval Institute Press books currently available, and for further information about joining the U.S. Naval Institute, please write to:

Membership Department
U.S. Naval Institute
291 Wood Road
Annapolis, MD 21402-5034
Telephone: (800) 233-8764
Fax: (410) 269-7940
Web address: www.navalinstitute.org